DISCARDED

Cold War Literature

The Cold War was the longest conflict in a century defined by the scale and brutality of its conflicts. In the battle between the democratic West and the communist East there was barely a year in which the West was not organising, fighting or financing some foreign war. It was an engagement that resulted – in Korea, Guatemala, Nicaragua and elsewhere – in some twenty million dead. This collection of essays analyses the literary response to the coups, insurgencies and invasions that took place around the globe, and explores the various thematic and stylistic trends that Cold War hostilities engendered in world writing.

Drawing together scholars of various cultural backgrounds, the volume focuses upon such themes as representation, nationalism, political resistance, globalisation and ideological scepticism. Eschewing the typical focus in Cold War scholarship on Western authors and genres, there is an emphasis on the literary voices that emerged from what are often considered the 'peripheral' regions of Cold War geo-politics. Ranging in focus from American postmodernism to Vietnamese poetry, from Cuban autobiography to Maoist theatre, and from African fiction to Soviet propaganda, this book will be of real interest to all those working in twentieth-century literary studies, cultural studies, history and politics.

Andrew Hammond is a Senior Lecturer in Twentieth-Century Literature at the Swansea Institute, University of Wales.

Routledge studies in twentieth-century literature

1 **Testimony from the Nazi Camps**
   French women's voices
   Margaret-Anne Hutton

2 **Modern Confessional Writing**
   New critical essays
   Edited by Jo Gill

3 **Cold War Literature**
   Writing the global conflict
   Edited by Andrew Hammond

Cold War Literature
Writing the global conflict

Edited by Andrew Hammond

First published 2006
by Routledge
2 Park Square, Milton Park, Abingdon, Oxon OX14 4RN

Simultaneously published in the USA and Canada
by Routledge
270 Madison Ave, New York, NY 10016

Routledge is an imprint of the Taylor & Francis Group

© 2006 Andrew Hammond editorial matter and selection; the contributors their contributions

Typeset in Garamond by Wearset Ltd, Boldon, Tyne and Wear
Printed and bound in Great Britain by MPG Books Ltd, Bodmin

All rights reserved. No part of this book may be reprinted or reproduced or utilized in any form or by any electronic, mechanical, or other means, now known or hereafter invented, including photocopying and recording, or in any information storage or retrieval system, without permission in writing from the publishers.

British Library Cataloguing in Publication Data
A catalogue record for this book is available from the British Library

Library of Congress Cataloging in Publication Data
A catalog record for this book has been requested

ISBN 0-415-34948-6

Contents

Notes on contributors — vii
Acknowledgements — xi

From rhetoric to rollback: introductory thoughts on Cold War writing — 1
ANDREW HAMMOND

1 The Yellow Peril in the Cold War: Fu Manchu and the Manchurian Candidate — 15
DAVID SEED

2 The Cold War representation of the West in Russian literature — 31
ANDREI ROGACHEVSKII

3 'Is it chaos? Or is it a building site?': British theatrical responses to the Cold War and its aftermath — 46
CHRIS MEGSON

4 Beyond the apocalypse of closure: nuclear anxiety in postmodern literature of the United States — 63
DANIEL CORDLE

5 The Reds and the Blacks: the historical novel in the Soviet Union and postcolonial Africa — 78
M. KEITH BOOKER AND DUBRAVKA JURAGA

6 Marxist literary resistance to the Cold War — 100
ALAN WALD

7 Poetry, politics and war: representations of the American war in Vietnamese poetry — 114
DANA HEALY

8 Remembering war and revolution on the Maoist
  stage   131
  XIAOMEI CHEN

9 Revolution and rejuvenation: imagining communist
  Cuba   146
  HAZEL A. PIERRE

10 An anxious triangulation: Cold War, nationalism
   and regional resistance in East-Central European
   literatures   160
   MARCEL CORNIS-POPE

11 'Lifting each other off our knees': South African
   women's poetry of resistance, 1980–1989   176
   MARY K. DESHAZER

12 Outwitting the politburo: politics and poetry
   behind the Iron Curtain   195
   PIOTR KUHIWCZAK

13 The anti-American: Graham Greene and the Cold
   War in the 1950s   212
   BRIAN DIEMERT

14 The excluded middle: intellectuals and the 'Cold
   War' in Latin America   226
   JEAN FRANCO

Bibliography   242
Index   266

Contributors

M. Keith Booker is Professor and Director of Graduate Studies in the Department of English at the University of Arkansas, Fayetteville, USA. He has published numerous articles and more than two dozen books on modern literature, culture and literary theory. These include *The African Novel in English* (1998), *Monsters, Mushroom Clouds and the Cold War: American Science Fiction and the Roots of Postmodernism, 1946–1964* (2001) and *The Post-Utopian Imagination: American Culture in the Long 1950s* (2002).

Xiaomei Chen is Professor of Chinese Literature in the Department of East Asian Languages and Cultures at the University of California at Davis, USA. Her major publications include *Occidentalism: A Theory of Counter-Discourse in Post-Mao China* (1995; revised edition, 2002), *Acting the Right Part: Political Theater and Popular Culture in Contemporary China* (2002) and *Reading the Right Text: An Anthology of Contemporary Chinese Drama* (edited, 2003). She has also published numerous articles on comparative literature, critical theory and modern Chinese literature, drama, theatre, women and culture.

Daniel Cordle is a Lecturer in English and American Literature at the Nottingham Trent University. He is the author of *Postmodern Postures: Literature, Science and the Two Cultures Debate* (1999), and has written on subjects ranging from Milan Kundera's fiction to I.A. Richards's literary criticism. The main foci of his work are contemporary American fiction and the relation between literature and science. He is currently writing a book about the representation of nuclear anxiety in American Cold War fiction.

Marcel Cornis-Pope is Professor of English and Comparative Literature and Chair of the English Department at Virginia Commonwealth University, USA. His publications include *Anatomy of the White Whale: A Poetics of the American Symbolic Romance* (1982), *Hermeneutic Desire and Critical Rewriting: Narrative Interpretation in the Wake of Poststructuralism* (1992) and *Narrative Innovation and Cultural Rewriting in the Cold War Era and After*

(2001). His current project is a multi-volume work (co-edited with John Neubauer) entitled *History of the Literary Cultures of East Central Europe: Junctures and Disjunctures in the 19th and 20th Century* (2004 onwards). His awards include the CELJ Award for Significant Editorial Achievement for his work as editor of *The Comparatist*.

Mary K. DeShazer is Professor of Women's Studies and English at Wake Forest University, North Carolina, USA. She is the author of *Fractured Borders: Theorizing Women's Cancer Literature* (in progress), *A Poetics of Resistance: Women's Writing in El Salvador, South Africa, and the United States* (1994), and *Inspiring Women: Re-Imagining the Muse* (1987), and she edited *The Longman Anthology of Women's Literature* (2001). Her current research focuses on women's poetry in post-apartheid South Africa.

Brian Diemert is an Associate Professor of English at Brescia University College, which is affiliated with the University of Western Ontario, Canada. He is the author of *Graham Greene's Thrillers and the 1930s* (1996) and of several articles on works by authors such as Greene, Philip Kerr, T.S. Eliot, F. Scott Fitzgerald and E.L. Doctorow. A specialist in twentieth-century British and American fiction, Diemert is currently working on a book on detective fiction and occultism.

Jean Franco is Professor Emerita, teaching most recently at the Department of English and Comparative Literature, Columbia University, USA. She has been decorated by the governments of Chile and Venezuela for her work on Latin American literature, and has received a lifetime achievement award from PEN and the Kalman Silvert award from the Latin American Studies Association. She served as President of the Latin American Studies Society of Great Britain and of the Latin American Studies Association in the United States. Her many publications include *An Introduction to Latin American Literature* (1969), *Plotting Women: Gender and Representation in Mexico* (1989) and *The Decline and Fall of the Lettered City: Latin America in the Cold War* (2002).

Andrew Hammond is a Senior Lecturer in Twentieth-Century Literature at the Swansea Institute, University of Wales. In both research and teaching, he has pursued interests in modernism, nationalism, identity and exile, with a particular focus on cross-cultural representation and power within Europe. He has published a number of articles on travel writing, the Balkans and postwar fiction, and has edited *The Balkans and the West: Constructing the European Other, 1945–2003* (2004).

Dana Healy is a Lecturer at the School of Oriental and African Studies, University of London. Her expertise lies in Vietnamese language and literature, particularly in folk narrative and in modern poetry, fiction and theatre. Her publications include *Teach Yourself Vietnamese* (1997) and articles on the writings of Pham Thi Hoai and on Vietnamese literary transitions. She has also contributed to the *Bibliographic Study Guide to the Languages and Literature of South East Asia* (1996).

Dubravka Juraga is currently a research assistant at the Center for Technology in Government, Albany, New York, USA. She has published several articles and co-authored two books on Eastern European and postcolonial literatures. She has also co-edited (with M. Keith Booker) *Socialist Cultures East and West: A Post-Cold War Reassessment* (2002) and *Rereading Global Socialist Cultures after the Cold War: The Reassessment of a Tradition* (2002).

Piotr Kuhiwczak is the Director of the Centre for Translation and Comparative Cultural Studies, University of Warwick. He is currently editing *The Companion to Translation Studies* for Multilingual Matters and researching into the impact of translation on Holocaust memoirs and testimonies. His book *Successful Polish–English Translation: Tricks of the Trade*, published in 1994, is now going into its third edition. Dr Kuhiwczak is on the advisory board of the British Centre for Literary Translation and the Editorial Board of *The Linguist*.

Chris Megson is a Lecturer in Drama and Theatre Studies at Royal Holloway College, University of London, and has worked as an actor and director. He has published on the impact of 1968 on British theatre culture and is currently writing a book on theatrical naturalism. His research interests also include the staging of politics and politicians in theatre practice, twentieth-century American theatre and drama, and performance analysis.

Hazel A. Pierre is a PhD student at the University of Warwick. She is undertaking a comparative cultural study of the notions of nation and identity as manifest in the literary and popular cultural forms of the Caribbean. She has a longstanding interest in the history and literature of the Caribbean, working on such topics during earlier degrees, and has developed a particular research focus on the genre of autobiography.

Andrei Rogachevskii was educated at Moscow State University and the University of Glasgow, and has taught at the Universities of Helsinki, Strathclyde and Glasgow, and at the Royal Scottish Academy of Music and Drama. He has authored monographs on Aleksandr Pushkin (1994) and Eduard Limonov (forthcoming); and co-edited *Central and East European Émigré Literatures: Past, Present – and Future?* (special issue of *Canadian-American Slavic Studies*, 1999), *Bribery and Blat in Russia* (2000), *Russian Jews in Great Britain* (2000) and *Russian Writers on Britain* (2001).

David Seed holds a chair in American Literature in the School of English at Liverpool University. He is a member of the editorial board of the *Journal of American Studies* and a Fellow of the English Association. He has published books on Thomas Pynchon, Joseph Heller, Rudolph Wurlitzer and

James Joyce, as well as *American Science Fiction and the Cold War* (1999). He edits the Science Fiction Texts and Studies series for Liverpool University Press. He is currently completing a study of representations of brainwashing and editing a Companion to Science Fiction for Blackwells.

Alan Wald is Professor of English at the University of Michigan, USA, and was Director of the Program in American Culture from 2000 to 2003. He is the author of six books about the United States cultural Left, most recently *Exiles from a Future Time* (2003). He has served on the editorial board of *American Literature* and has been a fellow of the Guggenheim Foundation.

Acknowledgements

This volume of essays evolved from a conference entitled 'Postcommunism: Theory and Practice', held at the University of Warwick, UK, in June 2002. Thanks are due to all those who assisted in organizing the day, including Piotr Kuhiwczak, Maureen Tustin, Ria Sitompul, Shanshan Zhang, Gillian Bartholomew, Katia Mérine and James Zhan. I would like to express my gratitude to the University of Warwick's Centre for Translation and Comparative Cultural Studies, which hosted and funded the event.

I am indebted to all those who assisted with different aspects of the volume, either in the initial stage of conception or during the editing and revising of the drafts. Here thanks are due to Arthur Hammond, Lynn Guyver, Piotr Kuhiwczak, Susan Bassnett, Jeni Williams and Ashley Morgan for their invaluable comments and corrections. At the same time, I would like to thank Katherine Carpenter, Jo Whiting and Yeliz Ali at Routledge who nurtured the volume over the course of two years.

The permission for reprinting two of the essays is gratefully acknowledged. Alan Wald's 'Marxist Literary Resistance to the Cold War' was originally published in *Prospects: An Annual of American Cultural Studies*, 20 (1995) and is reproduced with the permission of Cambridge University Press (all rights reserved). M. Keith Booker and Dubravka Juraga's 'The Reds and the Blacks: The Historical Novel in the Soviet Union and Postcolonial Africa' was originally published in Dubravka Juraga and M. Keith Booker, eds, *Socialist Cultures East and West: A Post-Cold War Reassessment* (Westport, Conn. and London: Praeger, 2002) and is reproduced with permission of Greenwood Publishing Group, Inc., Westport, USA (all rights reserved).

Andrew Hammond
Swansea, 2005

From rhetoric to rollback
Introductory thoughts on Cold War writing

Andrew Hammond

The 'Cold War' is an erroneous term for a global conflict which, spanning several continents and a multitude of coups, civil wars, insurgencies and interventions, was characterized by ongoing armed aggression. From the crisis in Korea, through Vietnam, Dominica, Afghanistan, Angola to the US invasion of Panama, societies worldwide were torn apart by violent hostility. For a Western population, certainly, the military confrontations may have appeared distant phenomena. The eternal round of diplomacy, arms talks and rhetorical exchanges that marked the more immediate dealings between East and West suggested that the appellation 'cold', and associated terms such as 'freeze', 'thaw' and *'refroidissement'*, had some applicability, capturing the frostiness of superpower relations. Globally, however, the Western experience is a clear exception to the norm. In all, the Soviet sponsoring of left-wing regimes and the US rollback of communism resulted in over a hundred wars through the Third World and a body count of over 20 million.[1] In Asia alone, some 11 million died in the fighting in Korea, Laos, Cambodia and Vietnam, where native communist movements gradually triumphed over US-backed nationalist forces. In Latin America, at least one million died as a result of the right-wing coups that, with US military and financial aid, brought to power 'some of the most barbarous regimes of the modern world'.[2] Through Soviet engagement in Somalia, Ethiopia, Angola, Afghanistan and elsewhere, close to three million lost their lives. Even in Eastern Europe, tens of thousands were killed in border incidents, in prison camps and in the Soviet invasions of Hungary and Czechoslovakia.[3] The itemization of the dead does not even begin to acknowledge the devastating effects in these years of environmental destruction, forced exile, imprisonment, poverty, torture and disease.

To designate the international conflict as 'cold', with its suggestion of inertia and equilibrium, is to do more than falsify the record. The act of understanding a historical period exclusively through the Western experience of that period partakes in the same hegemonic Euro-Americanism that defined the conflict itself, privileging a limited range of subjectivities and relegating all others to insignificance. It is an approach that remains in post-1989 Western historiography, in which the victims of military aggression are still given little coverage or sympathy. When one commentator chooses to emphasize that, for the US population, the Cold War never entailed the 'loss of lives that would accompany a "hot" one', and that the Cold War was never a 'shooting war, except in peripheral regions of the world',[4] the widespread suffering caused by American interventionism is erased, or at least greatly reduced in import. For many historians, it is a short step from downgrading the presence of armed combat (considering them 'peripheral' or 'proxy' wars) to rewriting the superpower stand-off as a feat of triumphant diplomacy. John Mason, for example, asserts that this was 'the longest period of peace in the twentieth century', one in which the Soviet Union and the USA dedicated themselves to the successful 'prevention of a Third World War'[5] (an interpretation that would surprise the many millions caught up in wars in the Third World). This notion that world war should be defined not by the global reach of a conflict but solely by great power participation emerged most famously in the post-revisionist work of John Lewis Gaddis. While accepting that 'limited' wars occurred, Gaddis urges us to believe that 'major war' was absent between 1945 and 1989: this was, he claims, 'the longest period of stability in relations among the great powers' since the days of Metternich and Bismarck, and should be viewed 'not as "the Cold War" at all, but [. . .] as a rare and fondly remembered "Long Peace"'.[6] Although Gaddis has gained some notoriety for his approach, his shift from the accentuating of peace to the eliding of war is a lamentably common strategy.

It is worth recalling, then, that the roots of the Cold War metaphor are actually found in the mid-1940s, before East–West hostilities emerged. Although frequently sourced in a speech given by Bernard Baruch, the US Representative on the Atomic Energy Commission, in 1947, George Orwell had already used it in 'You and the Atom Bomb', an article from 1945. Viewing the possession of atomic weaponry by two or three 'super-states' as conducive to tyranny, Orwell nevertheless foresees a paralysis in international affairs, as each atomic power becomes '*unconquerable* and [enters] a permanent state of "cold war" with its neighbours'.[7] The article's vision of 'an end to large-scale wars'[8] was understandable, given its context in the months following the end of the Second World War. This was prior to Kennan's 'long telegram', to Churchill's 'Iron Curtain' speech, to the Berlin blockade, to the Truman Doctrine and the Marshall Plan, to the growing unrest throughout the Far East, and indeed to all those major indicators that the future was to be far from the broadly peaceable superpower stalemate that Orwell imagined. It is curious, therefore, that a historical epoch should be defined by the inappropriate features of the years that preceded it, though not as curious as all that. The Cold War metaphor had a range of performative functions that proved essential for heads of state, politicians and policy advisors from the 1950s onwards. Most importantly, the term concealed the wide-ranging and violent extension of US global dominion, foregrounding images of tranquil stasis while simultaneously insisting, against all evidence, that stasis was the defining quality of the age.

The privileging of Western experience has not only taken place in the spheres of political rhetoric and Cold War historiography. In that strand of Western scholarship that examines the literary response to the international crisis of 1945 to 1989, there is a similar tendency to define 'Cold War' by the conditions where war was coldest, and to take American and Western European writing as the proper ground of study. As a critical endeavour, it was the 1980s, with the rise of nuclear criticism in American academe, when the analysis of the relation between literary production and the military and ideological stand-off emerged as a field. As détente faltered in the late Carter presidency, and as military spending burgeoned during the Reagan years, there was not only a flourishing of apocalyptic imagery in fiction and poetry but also a developing critical determination to address such themes as nuclear rhetoric, atomic culture, contamination, ecological disaster and nuclear anxiety.[9] There was little attempt, however, in the work of Patrick Mannix, Martha A. Bartter, David Dowling and other nuclear critics, to accommodate writings on conventional warfare. Such exclusivity continued during the late 1980s and 1990s, when Cold War criticism was extended from a predominantly nuclear focus to the rediscovery of the literary left, the deconstruction of East–West representation, the analysis of literary treatments of specific events such as the Rosenbergs' trial, and the reconsideration of postmodernism and critical theory as Cold War discourses. Again, with a few notable exceptions, scholarship remained partial to Western national literatures, concentrating mainly on canonical writers or, as the decade continued, on American populist genres.[10] The failure to contextualize such literature in global cultural trends reproduced the sense that Cold War history was best understood via the Western intelligentsia, whose perspectives, it seemed, could be unproblematically universalised. Such canon formation is remarkable at a time when postcolonial theory was teaching Euro-American scholarship the importance of globally expanding its 'intellectual concerns [...] by the introduction [...] of voices and subjectivities from the margins'.[11]

It is also the case that these margins, or the cultures of the Second and Third Worlds, produced some of the most fascinating viewpoints on late twentieth-century history, and also forged some of the most fertile developments in literature. The point is made in two important collections of essays on socialist culture of the 1945–89 period, edited by Dubravka Juraga and M. Keith Booker, and published in 2002. Although focused specifically on left-wing writing, Juraga's and Booker's arguments that the bourgeois aesthetic values of Western scholarship have worked to peripheralize all other modes of expression bears crucially on its effacement of Eastern bloc literatures. Surveying the culturalist commentaries that have emerged since 1989, Juraga and Booker discover, for example, the persistence not only of a vilification of communism (with ideologues 'feel[ing] it necessary to continue to kick the dead horse of socialism, partly on the off chance that the horse isn't really dead'),[12] but also of the defamation of left-wing cultural production.

In a process that mirrors the Cold War crusade to devalue all literary and artistic works that fail to promote 'free world' ideologies, the post-1989 assumption is 'that political commitment (especially socialist political commitment) is inimical to the production of genuine art'.[13] As they go on to say, however,

> socialist writers have produced some of the most valuable and impressive works of world literature, whether they be Soviets (Gorky, Sholokhov, Alexei Tolstoy), East Europeans (Brecht, Krleža) [or] Third World writers (Ngugi, Sembène, García Márquez) [...]. Western literature was always widely available and highly respected in the Eastern bloc. American writers such as Dreiser and Steinbeck were hugely popular in the Soviet Union, while the socialist realist works of the East were virtually inaccessible to Western readers, who were assured by the [...] literary establishment that those works were such ideological tripe that there was no point in reading them.[14]

The 'literary establishment's' response to socialist authors crystallizes its wider treatment of Second and Third World writing. Most obviously, there is a wide-ranging absence of the rich, multiform literature of communist Eastern Europe from Western university reading lists and scholarly publications on Cold War themes. More surprisingly, the work of African, Asian and Latin American writers, which has gained increasing critical attention since the rise of postcolonial studies, is rarely drawn upon in discussions of the geo-political events of the 1945–89 period. The surprise is compounded when one notes that the Cold War was largely fought in these postcolonial regions, and can even be interpreted as a struggle by the emergent superpowers for control of the wealth, labour and resources of the newly independent nations in a manner akin to nineteenth century colonialism. Unfortunately, as Barbara Harlow points out, neo-imperialism and the accompanying literary resistance to cultural globalization and military interventionism 'has been largely excluded or ignored' in academic study.[15] Aijaz Ahmad deplores the fact that even amongst postcolonial critics 'there appears to be [...] far greater interest in the colonialism of the past than in the imperialism of the present'.[16] The result is that such writings are frequently shorn of their historicity and ideological commitment, with Ngugi being studied solely 'as a representation of exotic African points of view,' for example, or 'García Márquez as a pioneer of magical realism'.[17]

A Cold War criticism is required which can embrace, investigate and theorize the global trends of mid- to late twentieth-century writing. There is a need for a comparative analysis of the thematic and stylistic trends within Cold War literature, a form of literature that one can define, loosely, as a historically focused, international current bearing multiple interactions with the political, military, diplomatic, linguistic and ideological structures of its period. If a specifically Cold War literature can be said to exist, then it lies in exactly these international currents. This collection of essays is an attempt to stimulate debate about worldwide literary responses to the ideological and military conflict, and to assess their value for us today. Drawing on scholars from a wide range of national backgrounds, the volume moves through poetry, theatre, fiction, travel writing and autobiography in order to explore the national literatures of Latin America, Africa, Eastern Europe and Asia, as well as of Western Europe and the USA. The aim is not merely to contextualize Western literature in the wider cultural landscape, and to decentre it within Cold War scholarship, but also to compare literary output in various regions, teasing out an overarching set of concerns and aesthetic values, while at all times remaining aware of local faiths, practices and histories. In doing so, the volume neither claims to be exhaustive nor wishes to conceal its seemingly arbitrary omissions. There is certainly no attempt to incorporate the more prominent treatments of Cold War themes in Western theatre, science fiction or spy novels, or to overemphasize the political despair, the crises of conscience, the existential trials and right-wing hysterias of Western populations. Such experiences have been adequately addressed elsewhere. Rather, Western writing will be invoked merely to trace its commonalities with and divergences from the committed, oppositional literatures of the Second and Third World, whose writers challenged Western political dominance and 'spoke back' to Western cultural hegemony through nativist and oral styles. The volume will attempt to locate within global literature a 'family of resemblances', in the famous phrase: the important attributes, concerns, styles and clusters of socio-historical debates that appeared around the world.

To begin with, one of the most significant attributes of narrative strategy and political rhetoric during the Cold War was their patterns of cultural representation. The Cold War struggle for the control of political belief was grounded in a Manichean opposition between self and other, good and evil, democracy and tyranny, that became 'encrusted, over the years, with successive layers of [. . .] tradition, myth and legend'.[18] This dichotomizing framework was particularly forcible in the United States, where the denigration of the Eastern bloc pervaded all areas of national life, including literature, film, television, sporting events and the space race. Here, the notion of Soviet communism as 'a spreading disease', as a godless, murderous tyranny governed by 'vicious torturers who enjoy inflicting pain and murdering children',[19] worked to vindicate political strategies, from the increase of defence budgets and Third World interventionism, to the intensified regulation of the domestic population. The conjunction of representation and power in anti-Soviet discourse has been increasingly analysed in literary studies. David Seed, whose chapter opens this collection, consequently turns attention from the 'red menace' to the 'yellow peril', and US images of communist East Asia. The Sino-Soviet split in the late 1950s, and the growing ambitions of Maoist China, brought a new superpower on to the scene, and, as Seed details, a burgeoning of orientalist rhetoric was the result.[20] Such rhetoric was epitomized in the cunning, malevolence and global ambition of Sax Rohmer's Doctor Fu Manchu, although it was found most famously in Richard Condon's *The Manchurian Candidate* (1959), a tale of a Korean War veteran brainwashed into assassinating a US presidential nominee that expressed anxieties about both oriental invasion and communist fifth columns. Such rhetorical posturing, of course, was not all conducted by the USA. Interacting with American cultural discourse were complex, shifting patterns of representation that emanated from Russia and China, and that circulated between the superpowers and their dependants. Andrei Rogachevskii's contribution expands upon Seed by analysing the Soviet Union's evolving images of the USA and Western Europe. Surveying a wide range of novels, poems and travel writings, the chapter explores the manner in which the Soviet demonization of the West during the 'first cold war' of the 1950s passed to a more restrained portraiture during détente, although accusations of corruption, injustice and expansionism, that were not dissimilar to the motifs of Western anti-communism, remained. As Philip Taylor has commented, the complementarity of East–West discourse shows how the superpowers, peering at each other through the 'iron curtain', would often discover 'a reflection of themselves, [of] their own hopes and fears'.[21]

The manipulation of language and imagery in the public sphere was a major cause of the scepticism that many view as a defining feature of Cold War culture. With the persistent propagandizing on the part of state systems, and the pervading atmosphere of espionage, counter-intelligence and international plotting, there seemed little truth on which to base one's ideological convictions. Tobin Siebers summarizes Cold War history as 'the story of our skepticism about endings, intentions, interpretations, and calculations concerning numbers, troop movements, weapons, negotiations, and claims to truth and falsehood'.[22] This was an age around which not even historical dates can be allotted or agreed upon. The Cold War had no clear beginnings (1917, 1945 and 1948 being variously cited), no agreed temporal perimeters (with a complex of 'first cold wars' and 'second cold wars') and no tangible ending (whether this be 1989, 1991 or some point in the future). It is little wonder, then, that a dominant literary current was a postmodernism marked by narrative instability, ontological uncertainty, scathing self-reflexivity, and by a suspicion of all forms of metanarrative and historiography. In an era of growing state control, it is also little wonder that this literature became obsessed with the technologies of power. For Mary Kaldor and others, the Cold War brought oppressive 'edifices of power and hierarchy' to Western society, where, subjected to heightened surveillance and indoctrination, populations could no longer 'erect the appropriate borders between their personal lives and their national narratives'.[23] This was a time, in other words, in which political agency was eroded, and the urge to revolution subsided. According to Siebers, not only have 'suspicion, paranoia, and skepticism [. . .] characterized the cold war era', but they also 'in turn preserve[d] the state'.[24]

The following two chapters analyse this drift to scepticism and political pessimism amongst Western writers. Chris Megson's contribution looks at left-wing British drama during the latter half of the twentieth century, and at its increasing disaffection with the ideologies and practices of socialist parties and state systems. Although retaining a faith in libertarianism, playwrights such as Howard Barker, Caryl Churchill and David Edgar came to mistrust the left-wing notion of the Cold War as noble crusade against capitalism, turning to a more complex, despairing portrayal of the crisis and its possible solution. Megson explores in particular their fascination with such peripheral spaces of the Cold War as Eastern Europe, where the binarist logic of superpower rhetoric was unsettled, and where the horrific strategies of superpower ambition were played out. The style of these plays, which exchange chronological naturalism for polyphony, interdeterminacy and non-linearity, mirrors that of the postmodernist fiction investigated in the next chapter. Here, Daniel Cordle argues that American postmodernism, a canonical form of the age, is strongly influenced by nuclear anxiety. Eschewing the overt narratives of nuclear disaster found in science fiction and the thriller, Cordle locates the most effective portrayal of the psychological stress of living with imminent holocaust in the paranoia, lack of closure and linguistic skepsis typifying the work of Don DeLillo, Thomas Pynchon, E.L. Doctorow and others, in which atomic weaponry is rarely mentioned, but the air of constantly deferred catastrophe is powerfully dramatized. As another critic has concluded, the varieties of postmodernism that emerged in Asia, Eastern Europe and the Americas from the 1950s onwards were less a 'self-indulgent formalism' than 'a meaningful response to a historical and literary crisis' and a sincere 'deconstruction of Cold War ideologies'.[25]

Yet postmodernism was not the only literary current to develop after 1945. As central to the multiple expressions of Cold War literature was the socialist realism that attained international stature after its inauguration in Stalinist Russia during the 1930s. Andrei Zhdanov, Stalin's Secretary of the Central Committee and chief spokesman on cultural matters, codified this new realism as the 'specific depiction of reality in its revolutionary development [. . .] combined with the task of ideologically reshaping and educating the toilers in the spirit of socialism'.[26] For Zhdanov, the realist narrative was to be grounded in revolutionary romanticism, rather than verisimilitude, and no longer focused on the bourgeois individual, but on the loyalty of 'socialist man' to the collective and on the collective struggle, through industry, class-consciousness and party loyalty, towards the utopian future. This prescriptive 'Zhdanovism', as it became known, may have dominated Soviet literary life of the 1940s, but over the course of time, as socialist realism was propagated by state-led cultural programmes elsewhere in the Eastern bloc, and simultaneously emerged in France, Italy, Britain and West Germany, it developed into a heterogeneous, innovative form, inflected by national and individual trends. As Michael Scriven and Dennis Tate argue, socialist realism played a crucial role in twentieth-century aesthetics: it had an 'extensive European impact for a good half-century', and also opposed postmodern disillusionment with a more optimistic 'pursuit of [. . .] socialist goals'.[27]

That the expression of political belief and confidence in social progress could overshadow postmodernism is powerfully evidenced by Second and Third World writing. In the next contribution, M. Keith Booker and Dubravka Juraga turn their attention to the commonalities in ideology and intent between African postcolonial literatures and Soviet socialist realism, and call for the same critical respect for the latter that is now awarded the former. Although often dismissed by the Cold War academy as a formally impoverished, ideologically corrupted form, the left-wing historical novels of writers such as Ngugi wa Thiong'o, Maxim Gorky and Alexei Tolstoy demonstrate the power of the Soviet and African literary resistance to Western imperialism and representation, while also censuring, as Booker and Juraga mention, native state systems and national elites. This rich, highly diverse strand of political engagement was simultaneously found in the West. Alan Wald's contribution discusses American left-wing literature of the 1950s: a strong tradition of oppositional commentary that has, like Second World writing, been erased from the literary canon. Setting the work against the backdrop of McCarthyism, Wald surveys the hundreds of authors, working in a multitude of prose genres, who comprised the resistance culture of the 'first cold war', and who used their publications to encourage political dissent in the face of state harassment and imprisonment. In particular, the essay discerns within this 'Un-American Renaissance' a strong African-American contribution which, in such writers as Alice Childress, Julian Mayfield and Shirley Graham, espoused a revolutionary blend of Civil Rights activism, anti-capitalism and feminism. The conclusion of both essays is similar: let's rejuvenate these authors' reputations, and get them read more widely.

The presence of idealism and ideological commitment was even more extensive in national literatures that dealt directly with armed conflict, another core theme. Throughout the embattled Third World, riven by insurrection, civil war and invasion, literature played both social and ideological roles, being committed to educating, politicizing and inspiring a readership, as well as to charting collective experience. The point is crystallised by the lengthiest military conflict of the Cold War, the US engagement in Vietnam, in which some $150 billion was spent between 1954 and 1975 on defeating an indigenous communist movement, involving the deployment of 2,700,000 servicemen and the dropping of ten million tonnes of explosives.[28] As Dana Healy illustrates in her chapter on the North Vietnamese response to the war, it was poetry that proved itself best suited to the exigencies of conflict. A medium easy to write, memorize and distribute on the frontline, poetry was ideal for developing in troops a dedication to the struggle, and for accentuating the military themes of liberation, patriotism, heroism and solidarity, along with the wider topics of national identity and party loyalty. Just as militarism was a shaping influence on the literature of nations at war, it was also prevalent in nations ostensibly at peace. In the following contribution, a study of Maoist theatre, Xiaomei Chen discusses how the Chinese socialist state, in its attempts to consolidate the revolution, frequently made reference during the Cold War to the 'hot wars' of the 1930s and 1940s. In particular, the theatrical production of the Cultural Revolution organised its narratives around the conflict with Japan and the civil war between the Kuomintang and the communists, using their remembered patterns of enmity and national loyalty to incite antagonism towards the Soviet Union and the USA, and to promote support for the extension of Chinese influence through the Third World. The chapter reminds us that Cold War belligerence was both a material and an existential condition, with the absence of war being no insurance against the regimentation and militarization of mass publics, or against images of combat flooding cultural production.

As Healy and Chen reveal, political commitment in the Second and Third Worlds was as much predicated on nationalistic ideologies as it was on communism. This was the product both of the pre-Cold-War independence movements, with decades of anti-imperial opposition coming to fruition in the decolonization of the 1950s and 1960s, and of the contemporary resistance to the political and economic penetration of advanced capitalist nations.[29] Indeed, as one historian argues, it was in 'the indigenous national communism of Russia, Yugoslavia, China, North Korea, Vietnam and Cuba' that 'the most successful and most durable form of communism' was found.[30] The fact that nationalism – and a concomitant critique of national discourse – was a major theme of Cold War literature is emphasized in Marcel Cornis-Pope's analysis of East-Central European writing. The chapter begins by assessing the impact of Soviet 'internationalism' on the satellite states, where national literary traditions were suppressed and a blind fealty to Stalinism was encouraged. Against this homogenizing influence, two core trends emerged in regional literature: the first, a distinct, though xenophobic, nationalism that opposed Soviet-centred communism with an idealization of the homeland; the second, an experimental postmodernism that questioned all forms of legitimizing authority, exposing nationalism and socialism alike to the strategies of irony and deconstruction. Cornis-Pope's underlying point, that nationalism vastly complicated the East-Central European transition to postcommunism, is pertinent to Hazel Pierre's contribution on the imagining of Cuban nationhood. Here, the genre of Cuban autobiography – with its common emphasis on collective, rather than individual, experience – is used to explore the national-socialist ideologies that have informed the islands writing of self and nation since 1959. The chapter begins by outlining the hegemonic, masculinist construction of Cubanness in Fidel Castro's legal testimony, 'History Will Absolve Me' (spoken, 1953). Pierre then goes on to use Cristina García's *Dreaming in Cuban* (1992) to examine how such reductionist imagery has since been subverted through the introduction into the autobiographical text of multiple ethnicities, genders, religions, professions and political stances, their diverse viewpoints complicating the understanding of nationhood and pointing the way to a more inclusive nation space.

In her study of García's work, Pierre also raises the important question of women's position in Cold War societies and literary cultures. A number of critics have argued, cogently, that the twentieth-century prolongation of male authority was ably assisted by Cold War militarism and power politics, with what Ken Ruthven calls its phallocentric iconography of 'science and bombs'.[31] In the USA, for example, there was an extensive 'domestic revival' in the late 1940s and 1950s, with women's return to homemaking and housework being discursively linked – at a time of communist infiltration, nuclear contamination and civil defence planning – with the act of securing the family from the outside world, a 'containment' that 'fus[ed] women's domestic role to the larger national purpose'.[32] In Eastern Europe, as another instance, state socialism allowed little space for the individual woman's rights, and, although a high percentage of women participated in the paid work force, their labour was largely within traditional female fields, lacking economic equality with men.[33] It has even been suggested that the literary engagement with Cold War history is predominantly male. Paul Brians's discovery that, of the thousand or so fictional responses to nuclear war written in the English language, only five per cent are by female novelists, might appear to indicate an overwhelmingly androcentric discourse.[34] Nevertheless, as Brians goes on to mention, women were crucial to oppositional groups and cultures throughout the world, leading the anti-nuclear protests in the West from the 1950s onwards,[35] fighting in liberation movements throughout the Third World, and producing a dynamic, often thematically distinct, literature of resistance.

The topic arises in Mary DeShazer's exploration of South African women's poetry and its attacks, during the 1980s, on the US-sanctioned, ultra-right apartheid state. The essay opens a section of the volume on another pronounced theme of Cold War literature, its critical engagement with state politics. As several contributions have already shown, this was a period in which individual and community came under threat not only from external domination but also from oppressive internal regimes, of both right- and left-wing persuasions. In the South African context, DeShazer details how women were key participants in the street protests spearheaded by the ANC and South African Communist Party, and also key collaborators in the literary movement of dissent. Ranging through four poetry anthologies from the late apartheid era, the chapter outlines the gendered militancy of black women's work, its direct, polemical styles and its concern with motherhood, childbirth, family, female labour and male power, as well as with mobilizing a collective opposition to racism. While such writing was overt in its political radicalism, and often written for performance at mass meetings and protests, Piotr Kuhiwczak's contribution on Eastern European poetry finds work that was altogether more cryptic. Working under totalitarian restrictions, poets on this side of the Iron Curtain, when publishing with the state presses, created a strand of political verse whose strategies were moulded by censorship, developing allusive symbolic frameworks – based for example in classical or naturalistic imagery – that could reach an educated reader while simultaneously evading the censor. Their denunciations of the socialist state contrast to the oppositional thematics that Brian Diemert locates in Graham Greene's work of the 1950s. For this 'anti-American', the US global dominance after 1945 involved far more than Third World interventionism; it was a cultural, ideological and bureaucratic assault on the freedoms and rights of citizens even of allied nations. As Diemert details, the lives of characters in *The Third Man* (1950) and *The Quiet American* (1955), texts typically located in Cold War 'hot spots', find an odd commonality with Greene's own professed experience of espionage, of FBI surveillance, and of suspicion, deceit and human betrayal, both writer and character appearing helpless to resist American cultural and political authority.

Diemert's exploration of Greene's ongoing attempt to find a 'middle ground' in the dichotomous world of the Cold War leads on to the final theme of the volume. The notion of a 'Third Way' – or of a left-leaning, non-materialist politics that challenged Western capitalism without succumbing to the iniquities of Stalinism – was a common pursuit of Western and Eastern bloc literatures. Stephen Spender's assertion, in 1949, 'that neither great power had the solution to the world's problems' was a direct assault on the choice between two '"alternative ways of life"' propounded by the Truman Doctrine,[36] and one that would have struck a chord with many writers around the world. Indeed, for nations in Africa, Asia, Latin America and Eastern Europe, the idea of a neutral space outside US and Soviet 'spheres of influence', as evidenced in the Bandung Conference of African and Asian States and in the non-aligned movement, was a very real proposition, and one that fractures the bipolar conflict into multiple ideological centres. The literary treatment of 'Third Way' politics is addressed by Jean Franco in the final contribution of the collection. Focusing on the Latin American intelligentsia, the essay details the powerful tradition of libertarianism in regional literature, which, in the face of political and cultural interventionism,[37] sought to develop an independent literary aesthetic whose freedom from outside influence would symbolize and assist the cause of independence in the political sphere. Franco surveys the work of Gabriel García Márquez, Angel Rama, Mario Vargas Llosa and Julio Cortázar, amongst others, looking at how the Latin American writers' reference to indigenous languages, faiths and communitarian practices, particularly via magic realism, formed an innovative, though ultimately doomed, attempt to withstand the forces of globalization and military government.

Despite the failure of the project, the power of Latin American literary production, and the influence it wielded in public life, indicates that the analysis of Cold War literature is no esoteric pursuit. In many ways, the crises, inquiries and concerns that literature addressed between 1945 to 1989 are those of our own times, particularly after '9/11', the events of 11 September 2001 which inaugurated hardly a new phase of history, as the media repeatedly claimed, but merely another stage in the consolidation of US hegemony. In the post-Cold-War era, the resurgent neoliberalism, the Manichean worldview, the continual conflict abroad, the militarization of public life and the crushing of dissent, all supported by a 'cravenly servile [...] culture industry',[38] have altered little since the 1980s, and although the terminology may have changed – from 'interventionism' to 'regime change', from 'red threat' to 'global terror' – the political landscape remains the same. The sense of helplessness in the face of globalization also remains, with no 'third way' clearly emerging between the forces of an American-led West and the entity it chooses to confront. Yet in debating the possibilities of resistance, Cold War literature offers a wealth of helpful ideas, especially if one turns from canonized Western writing, which so often reads like a dramatization of political defeat, to the politically engaged, historically contextualized work of the Second and Third Worlds. Here, most powerfully, writers understand human society as something other than given, and understand that this other reality is to be fought for. From its discussions of transnational power, of collective action, of 'the "here and now" of historical reality and its conditions of possibility',[39] the concepts and practices of an updated literature of resistance can be built.

Notes

1 David S. Painter, *The Cold War: An International History* (London and New York: Routledge, 1999), p. 1. In the light of such statistics, Painter adapts Thomas Hobbes to say that 'the Cold War was nasty, brutish, and long' (ibid., p. 118).
2 Noam Chomsky, *Towards a New Cold War: Essays on the Current Crisis and How We Got There* (London: Sinclair Browne, 1982), p. 26.
3 Statistics are taken from Fred Inglis, *The Cruel Peace: Everyday Life in the Cold War* (London: Aurum Press, 1992), pp. 426–7.
4 Ronnie D. Lipschutz, *Cold War Fantasies: Film, Fiction, and Foreign Policy* (Lanham: Rowman and Littlefield, 2001), pp. 83, 173.
5 Mason, *The Cold War, 1945–1991* (London and New York: Routledge, 1996), pp. 73–4.
6 Gaddis, *The Long Peace: Inquiries into the History of the Cold War* (New York and Oxford: Oxford University Press, 1987), pp. 216, 245.
7 Orwell, 'You and the Atom Bomb', in Orwell, *The Collected Essays, Journalism and Letters of George Orwell: Volume IV, In Front of Your Nose, 1945–1950*, ed. Sonia Orwell and Ian Angus (London: Secker and Warburg, 1968), pp. 8–9. I am grateful to David Seed for locating the reference: see Seed, *American Science Fiction and the Cold War: Literature and Film* (Edinburgh: Edinburgh University Press, 1990), p. 1.
8 Orwell, 'You and the Atom Bomb', p. 10. He also talks in the essay of the likelihood of atomic weaponry 'prolonging indefinitely a "peace that is no peace"' (ibid., p. 10).
9 For a definition and a history of the emergence of nuclear criticism see Ken Ruthven, *Nuclear Criticism* (Victoria: Melbourne University Press, 1993), pp. 3–31.
10 See, for example, Woody Haut, *Pulp Culture: Hardboiled Fiction and the Cold War* (1995), Ronnie D. Lipschutz, *Cold War Fantasies: Film, Fiction, and Foreign Policy* (2001) and David Seed, *American Science Ficiton and the Cold War* (1999). Naturally, there are exceptions, and Jean Franco's *The Decline and Fall of the Lettered*

City: Latin America in the Cold War (2002) and Barbara Harlow's *Resistance Literature* (1987) are excellent studies of non-Western Cold War literature.
11 Arif Dirlik, 'The Postcolonial Aura: Third World Criticism in the Age of Global Capitalism', *Critical Inquiry*, 20 (Winter 1994), p. 329.
12 Juraga and Booker, 'Introduction' to Juraga and Booker, eds, *Socialist Cultures East and West: A Post-Cold War Reassessment* (Westport, Conn. and London: Praeger, 2002), p. 3.
13 Ibid., p. 5. As they go on to say, little 'has been done to reassess the legacy of Soviet socialist realism, probably because this legacy is so powerful that it might still pose a threat to the global hegemony of capitalist ideologies' (ibid., p. 6).
14 Ibid., p. 5.
15 Harlow, *Resistance Literature* (New York and London: Methuen, 1987), p. xvi.
16 Ahmad, *In Theory: Classes, Nations, Literatures* (Delhi: Oxford University Press, 1994), p. 93.
17 Juraga and Booker, 'Introduction', p. 5. Elsewhere they add that 'postcolonial scholarship [...] has tended to shy away from an emphasis on the socialist commitment of much postcolonial literature': Juraga and Booker, eds, *Rereading Global Socialist Cultures after the Cold War: The Reassessment of a Tradition* (Westport, Conn. and London: Praeger, 2002), p. 4.
18 Gaddis, *Long Peace*, p. 20.
19 Helena Halmari, 'Dividing the World: The Dichotomous Rhetoric of Ronald Reagan', *Multilingua*, 12: 2 (1993), p. 153; Brett Silverstein, 'Enemy Images: The Psychology of U.S. Attitudes and Cognitions Regarding the Soviet Union', *American Psychologist*, 44: 6 (1989), p. 904.
20 This resurgence of pre-Cold-War orientalism, informed in the US by late nineteenth-century fears of Chinese immigration and economic takeover, reflects the influence on anti-Sovietism of eighteenth- and nineteenth-century Russophobia. See, for example, F.S. Northedge and Audrey Wells, *Britain and Soviet Communism: The Impact of a Revolution* (London and Basingstoke: Macmillan, 1982), p. 156.
21 Philip M. Taylor, 'Through a Glass Darkly? The Psychological Climate and Psychological Warfare of the Cold War', in Gary D. Rawnsley, ed., *Cold-War Propaganda in the 1950s* (London and Basingstoke: Macmillan, 1999), p. 226.
22 Siebers, *Cold War Criticism and the Politics of Skepticism* (New York and Oxford: Oxford University Press, 1993), p. 29.
23 Kaldor, *The Imaginary War: Understanding the East–West Conflict* (Oxford: Basil Blackwell, 1990), p. 112; Alan Nadel, *Containment Culture: American Narratives, Postmodernism, and the Atomic Age* (Durham: Duke University Press, 1995), p. 289.
24 Siebers, *Cold War Criticism*, pp. 29–30. Thomas Hill Schaub views postmodernism as inseparable 'from the politics of paralysis in the postwar period' (Schaub, *American Fiction in the Cold War* (Madison and London: University of Wisconsin Press, 1991), p. 190).
25 Marcel Cornis-Pope, *Narrative Innovation and Cultural Rewriting in the Cold War and After* (New York and Basingstoke: Palgrave, 2001), pp. 6, 4–5.
26 Zhdanov, quoted in Richard Freeborn, *The Russian Revolutionary Novel: Turgenev to Pasternak* (Cambridge: Cambridge University Press, 1982), pp. 246–7.
27 Scriven and Tate, 'Introduction' to Scriven and Tate, eds, *European Socialist Realism* (Oxford: Berg, 1988), pp. 3, 8.
28 Mason, *Cold War*, p. 33.
29 There are commentators who interpret the Cold War as a war 'directed against radical forces in the Third World who had no way of improving the terms under which they participated in the global states system': see Kaldor, *Imaginary War*, p. 97.

14 *Andrew Hammond*

30 Richard Sakwa, *Postcommunism* (Buckingham and Philadelphia: Open University Press, 1999), p. 28.
31 Ruthven, *Nuclear Criticism*, pp. 62–3. As David Dowling indicates, the figure of the male scientist was fundamental to the Cold War imaginary: 'usually allied with the military and political centres of power [these were] men in the know, men with the technology both to cause and to survive a nuclear disaster' (Dowling, *Fictions of Nuclear Disaster* (London: Macmillan, 1987), p. 40).
32 Elaine Tyler May, *Homeward Bound: American Families in the Cold War Era*, rev. edn (1988; New York: Basic Books, 1999), pp. 9, 103.
33 Nanette Funk, 'Introduction' to Funk and Magda Mueller, eds, *Gender Politics and Post-Communism: Reflections from Eastern Europe and the Former Soviet Union* (New York and London: Routledge, 1993), pp. 4–8.
34 Brians, 'Nuclear Family/Nuclear War', in Nancy Anisfield, ed., *The Nightmare Considered: Critical Essays on Nuclear War Literature* (Bowling Green, Ohio: Bowling Green State University Popular Press, 1991), p. 151.
35 Ibid., p. 154.
36 Spender's argument, from *The God that Failed*, is summarized in Alan Sinfield, *Literature, Politics and Culture in Postwar Britain* (Oxford: Basil Blackwell, 1989), p. 93.
37 Gülriz Büken makes the point that 'the export of American popular culture was an indispensable facet of America's economic expansionist policy' and of its attempts to 'disseminat[e] consumerism' (Büken, 'An Argument against the Spread of American Popular Culture in Turkey', in Reinhold Wagnleitner and Elaine Tyler May, eds, *'Here, There and Everywhere': The Foreign Politics of American Popular Culture* (Hanover and London: University Press of New England, 2000), p. 242.
38 William V. Spanos, 'A Rumor of War: 9/11 and the Forgetting of the Vietnam War', *boundary 2*, 30: 3 (2003), p. 31.
39 Harlow, *Resistance Literature*, p. 16. As Harlow goes on to say, 'Whereas the social and the personal have tended to displace the political in western literary and cultural studies, the emphasis in the literature of resistance is on the political as the power to change the world' (ibid., p. 30).

1 The Yellow Peril in the Cold War

Fu Manchu and the Manchurian Candidate

David Seed

In his State of the Union Address for 8 January 1951, President Truman declared: 'Our men are fighting alongside their United Nations allies, because they know, as we do, that the aggression in Korea is part of the attempt of the Russian Communist dictatorship to take over the world, step by step.'[1] This totalizing rhetoric is typical of the discourse of the Cold War, in which no individual conflict can be separated from the worldwide struggle, and which repeatedly exploits polar duality, stark oppositions between us and them, West and East. The 'battle for men's minds', as the Cold War was repeatedly called, was waged through words, through key metaphors and oppositions. As Martin J. Medhurst has explained, 'The currency of Cold War combat – the tokens used in the contest – is rhetorical discourse: discourse intentionally designed to achieve a particular goal with one or more specific audience [. . .]. Cold War weapons are words, images, symbolic actions, and, on occasion, physical actions undertaken by covert means.'[2] Medhurst's argument is specifically applied to the discourse of politicians, which he describes as calculated, end-directed verbal performances. If we extend his approach beyond this material to commentary on the Cold War generally – fictional and non-fictional – we will find the same rhetoric operating. For instance, the repeated references in the 1950s to the 'loss' of China to communism presumes both prior possession and a 'two-world' ideology which found its expression in many contexts, including that of commerce. In 1959 there appeared a report on Western commerce sensationally entitled *The Third World War*. The text opens with a stark warning: 'In every inhabited part of the world the forces of Communism and Democracy are locked together in combat. In this struggle there are no neutral territories.'[3] The notion of warfare is totalized here into a worldwide condition where there are only two ideological positions available.

The polarized rhetoric of the Cold War demonized the communist foe by subtracting cherished Western qualities of individuality and even humanity. The 'new Soviet man' was caricatured as a zombie or robot; the operation of communism was figured by J. Edgar Hoover and others as the spread of a disease in the collective body politic; and in science fiction novels and films of the 1950s perceptions of communist threat are depicted as assault or transformation by pods, slugs, ants and other non-human agencies. Robert Heinlein's *The Puppet Masters* (1951), for example, describes an invasion by extraterrestrial parasites which have to be defeated on Earth and traced back to their source. In case the reader misses the point, Heinlein includes direct comparisons with Soviet communism and draws a stern moral of future vigilance: 'The human race will have to be always on guard.'[4] Ultimacy and emergency are the key notions Heinlein is promoting here, particularly as in the process of take-over the first casualty is the individual consciousness. Indeed, Timothy Melley has explained conspiracy narratives as taking 'individual self-protection' as their starting point. He draws the following conclusion: 'by making diverse social and technological systems enemies of "the self," the conspiratorial views function less as a defence of some *clear* political position than as a defence of individualism, abstractly conceived.'[5] There is no question that the fate of the individual was crucial in Cold War discourse and narratives, but what Melley does not take into account is how an individual can symbolically embody his or her culture. For instance, as we shall see in *The Manchurian Candidate* (1959), the protagonist is seen initially as a war hero; that is, as the embodiment of the nation's pride in its own military. When he is revealed to be an assassin programmed by the communists there are disturbing implications for his national identity which can to some extent be purged by his suicide. It would be helpful, therefore, to think of the individual in this context as carrying different symbolic identifications and also as being the site for an ideological struggle playing itself out on the larger world stage.

The outbreak of the Korean War coincided with the coinage of a word applying the concept of war to the citadel of selfhood: the mind itself. The term 'brainwashing' entered the English language in 1950 to describe the re-education process being carried out by the Chinese communists, but was very quickly applied to the treatment of American prisoners in the Korean War. It was coined by Edward Hunter, a journalist and CIA aide, and promoted from 1953 onwards as a propaganda counter to communist charges that the USA was using biological weapons in Korea. Partly through Hunter's popular account, *Brainwashing* (first published in 1956 and constantly reprinted right through the 1960s), communist practice became demonized as secret, as divorcing words from the consciousness of those prisoners of war who made 'confessions' and as representing a 'political strategy for expansion and control.'[6] Of course the expression is a metaphor combining the mental and the physical, and brainwashing became a potent image in demonizing communist practice. In its applications it always carried connotations of a robotization of the individual. Indeed, within a system applying such a practice, the very notion of individuality ceased to have any meaning and citizens simply became zombies manipulated by their masters. As Hunter wrote, 'The intent is to change a mind radically so that its owner becomes a living puppet – a human robot – without the atrocity being visible from the outside. The aim is to create a mechanism in flesh and blood, with new beliefs and new thought processes inserted into a captive body.'[7] Although brainwashing had been suspected in cases such as that of Cardinal Mindszenty,[8] the concept derived much of its force from its association with Asian communist practice. It was particularly demonized once American prisoners of war started returning home, bringing with them stories of manipulation at the hands of their captors. From the mid-1950s onwards there emerged a series of films and novels dealing with the brainwashing scare, which was taken so seriously that the Eisenhower administration issued a code of behaviour for GIs.[9]

The most famous fictional narrative of brainwashing,[10] Richard Condon's *The Manchurian Candidate* (1959), derived much of its impact, as we shall see, from bringing brainwashing home to the USA. In the year that Condon's novel emerged, the journalist Eugene Kinkead published in book form a report, which had substantially appeared in *The New Yorker* two years earlier, on American prisoners of war in Korea. *In Every War But One* helped promote a perception that the Korean War was unique, not least because a number of POWs had been indoctrinated by the communists and trained to return to America where they would act as enemy agents after a time interval of five or six years. 'The men comprising the group that was uncovered', Kinkead reported, 'were for the most part sleepers',[11] men who had never behaved in a pro-communist fashion. A further complication in identifying these figures arose from the fact that 'the men were instructed to behave in a highly conforming sort of way for a good many years after repatriation, attracting no attention, and certainly not engaging in radical activities'.[12] Point for point, this pattern is repeated in Condon's novel. His protagonist, Raymond Shaw, is an authoritarian figure who finds a job as a journalist in New York after returning from Korea and who shows no interest in politics, radical or otherwise. In fact, he has been so thoroughly brainwashed that his deep-level programming has no connection with his conscious life, except in the working of the cues, or triggers, which will set him in motion as an assassin. The verbal trigger is the phrase 'why don't you spend a little time playing solitaire'; the pictorial trigger is the queen of diamonds playing card.

The Manchurian Candidate conflates the fear of communism with an older image of conspiracy: the Yellow Peril. Yellow Peril narratives date from the late nineteenth century, articulating fears of Chinese immigration and ultimately of the take-over of America. P.W. Dooner's *Last Days of the Republic* (1880) describes with grim relish how millions of Chinese flock to the United States under the guise of coolie labourers and then proceed to take over the country. The result is a total loss of national identity, although, despite the gloom of his subject, Dooner cannot hide his admiration for a 'design too magnificent of conception to be absolutely concealed'.[13] Jack London added his voice to these warnings in his essay 'The Yellow Peril' (published in *Revolution and Other Essays*, 1909), where he identified the 'menace to the Western world' in an awakening China.[14] In his history of this theme of threat to America expressed in a series from novels from 1880 onwards, William F. Wu has shown how Fu Manchu became its supreme embodiment by focusing a whole series of traits associated with Asia rather than China specifically and by possessing a uniquely versatile skill at assassination.[15] Sax Rohmer's novels about Doctor Fu Manchu, which commenced in 1913, gave the Yellow Peril its most famous and melodramatic expression. In the first novel of the series, *The Mystery of Doctor Fu-Manchu* (US title, *The Insidious Doctor Fu Manchu*), his English opponent Sir Denis Nayland Smith describes Fu in the following way:

> 'Imagine a person, tall, lean and feline, high-shouldered, with a brow like Shakespeare and a face like Satan, a close-shaven skull, and long, magnetic eyes of the true cat-green. Invest him with all the cruel cunning of an entire Eastern race, accumulated in one giant intellect, with all the resources of science past and present [...]. Imagine that awful being, and you have a mental picture of Dr. Fu-Manchu, the yellow peril incarnate in one man.'[16]

Fu's features are heavily encoded to give the reader a combination of qualities. Fu is dignified, intellectual and creative, yet at the same time demonic; he embodies his race and is credited with both vision and a certain hypnotic fascination. From the very beginning Fu was presented as a larger-than-life figure which the reader is invited to co-create. As Wu writes, 'By associating Fu Manchu (the hyphen was dropped after the first three novels) with every evil aspect of the Chinese image that existed in the early twentieth century, Rohmer ensured that future Chinese villains would evoke memories of Fu Manchu for many years to come'.[17]

In Rohmer's series this figure represented an unscrupulous and devious intellectualism, which was pitted against Western culture. Fu constantly plans a 'world-change' which will usher in a new order based on oriental models. Rohmer's novels show a struggle of intellect between Fu and Nayland Smith. Both are supremely accomplished shape changers and constantly don different disguises according to the dramatic needs of the particular novels. Most important of all, at those rare points in the later novels where one could kill the other, nothing happens. The opportunity is never used because each figure's role depends on the other's existence. Fu Manchu and Nayland Smith circle round each other throughout the series, constantly re-enacting a dramatic struggle between the threatening alien and the defensive West, which is larger than any individual novel and which can be therefore prolonged indefinitely.

The familiar polarity of Rohmer's novels – Fu Manchu's yellow hordes against the West – was, in theory at least, easily transferable into the totalizing rhetoric of the Cold War. Indeed, allusions to Rohmer's villain recur throughout discussions of Asiatic communism in the Cold War period. When Commander Lloyd M. Bucher of the *USS Pueblo* was captured by the

North Koreans in 1968, his military interrogator was 'like a suave villain out of a Fu Manchu novel'.[18] Rohmer himself changed residence to the USA and consciously revived the Fu Manchu series in the expectation that the Cold War would bring a positive reception from readers. Ironically, when he found his projects for new novels and for the cinema being blocked he began to suspect that he was being 'actively opposed by Communist influence'.[19] And Rohmer has been quoted as saying during the Korean War that Doctor Fu Manchu was 'still an enemy to be reckoned with and as menacing as ever, but he has changed with the times. Now he is against the Chinese Communists and, indeed, Communists everywhere, and a friend of the American people.'[20] In his postwar novels communism sometimes functions like a third term complicating their drama. Indeed, in *The Shadow of Fu Manchu* (1948) Fu himself speaks like a right-wing ideologue: '"My mission is to save the world from the leprosy of Communism,"' he declares to Nayland Smith. '"Only I can do this. And I do it, not because of any love I have for the American people but because if the United States fall, the whole world falls."'[21] In an obvious analogy with the Bomb, the novel's action is grounded in an American development of a device for the transmutation of matter, which could become the ultimate defence weapon (Rohmer has already assimilated the stated US policy about the use of the Bomb) and as such is attracting agents from different countries bent on stealing the blueprint. Nayland Smith anticipates the identification between communism and a virus, which circulated through the 1950s, when he announces that a '"mysterious Eastern epidemic is creeping West"'.[22] His main purpose in this espionage thriller lies in identifying his opponents. In discussing this problem, he considers first Fu Manchu's organization and then that of the communists. When his companion jumps to the conclusion that a Russian has been active, Nayland Smith retorts: '"Why a Russian? Men of influence and good standing in other countries have worked for Communism. It offers glittering prizes. Why not a citizen of the United States?"'[23] The Cold War situation multiplies the forces aligned against each other, although finally Rohmer suppresses this new political complexity in order to preserve the us/them logic of his plot, which resolves itself into the familiar struggle between Fu Manchu and the West. In the end, Fu frustrates the experiment that would verify the efficiency of the super-weapon and flees New York.

The notional distinction between different opponents of the West reaches breaking point in *Emperor Fu Manchu* (1959) where the site for the action has moved to China. The novel dramatizes a conflict centring on the immediate fate of China, where communism is again viewed as the result of invasion or even theft, and features players of different national origins who demonstrate their credentials through their capacity to disguise themselves as Chinese. At this point Rohmer's symbolism approaches contradiction. In the earlier Fu Manchu novels the markers of evil are heightened racial stereotypes of the Chinese. The term 'yellow' thus functions as a catch-all signifier covering the characteristics of cunning, lack of scruple and disrespect for the individual. In Rohmer's prewar novels it is enough for characters to have a 'yellow streak' in their ancestry for them to be stigmatised as sinister alien invaders. Whatever these figures believe, racial determinism triumphs in their classification. In *Emperor Fu Manchu*, however, there have to be good and bad Chinese for the action to make any sense. Rohmer now draws a distinction between Chinese communists and those with a commitment to the Free China movement, in practice those who have so far managed to avoid communist cultural transformation. Further, within the character hierarchy of the novel, the most prominent Chinese usually turn out to be Westerners in disguise. Nayland Smith had started his fictional life as a personification of British doggedness, was then modified into a courtesy American intelligence agent in the 1930s, and reaches his ultimate and least probable transformation in *Emperor Fu Manchu* as a Chinese Buddhist.

As in Rohmer's previous novel, the action of *Emperor Fu Manchu* revolves around a weapon, in this case a Russian facility in southern China developing pneumonic plague. Once again Fu Manchu is presented as fiercely anti-communist ('"my object is to crush Communism"'), but now, in his obligatory meeting with Nayland Smith, he claims that the two men have '"common ground"' in their shared enemy.[24] Smith remains unmoved by this appeal because he has realized that two equally dangerous secrets lie embedded at the heart of the action: the project being pursued in the Russian camp and Fu Manchu's Napoleonic dream of purging China of communism through his secret society, the Si-Fan.[25] Although Fu presents himself as an anti-communist, the novel shows an ironic mirroring between communism and his own organization. Like Stalin, Fu dreams of becoming an autocrat of a new world order; his secret society simply imitates the cultural secretiveness of communist China; and he too claims to possess a super-weapon, one capable of projecting a sound field over a city. When the novel enters science fiction, these similarities become even more marked. Western accounts of Chinese brainwashing had explained the process as a reduction of the individual to an automaton passively obeying the directions of a new master. In *The Shadow of Fu Manchu* the most monstrous figure is a part-African automaton created by vivisection; in *Emperor Fu Manchu* there is a whole group of operatives who collectively represent the ultimate subjection demanded by the emperor-to-be. Fu's 'Cold Men' (called the 'living dead' by the Chinese locals) are Burmese Dacoits reduced to total obedience by an unspecified surgical operation and transformed into grey corpse-like 'necropolites', literally 'dead citizens'.[26] These creatures embody the ultimate subjection to Fu Manchu's post-hypnotic suggestion. Their programming combines medical skill with a mental scrutiny tantamount to telepathy. Once the Cold Men are strapped down on cots, the horrified Western observers are told: '"The most instructive feature of the treatment will now begin. The Master will project to each creature the images appropriate to its particular appetite when it was a normal man. To one, the figure of its enemy; to another, a banquet of its favourite food; to a third, the image of a seductive woman – and so forth."'[27] The echoes in Fu Manchu's clinic of Huxley's *Brave New World* suggest a form of control which actualizes Western premonitions of physical and mental manipulations by the technological nation-state. In Rohmer's novel, Nature reasserts itself when Fu's forces attack the Russian camp; a freak electric storm ruins the Dacoits' programming and they run out of control.

The specific novel which stands behind the melodrama of *The Manchurian Candidate* is *President Fu Manchu* (1936). Here a leading Catholic warns of the impending danger of dictatorship in the USA and his opponents attempt to stifle his voice by both kidnapping and killing him. The domestic political scene is thus established as a conflict between the embattled forces of liberal democracy and a rising tide of demagoguery led by Harvey Bragg and his right-wing League of Good Americans. The novel is set against the background of national graft, naive utopian hopes and the expectation of an American dictatorship (a theme dealt with in Sinclair Lewis's 1935 novel *It Can't Happen Here*). Thus, as usual in Rohmer, the issue at stake is an ultimate one: the fate of the nation. As is also usual in Rohmer, however, the identity of the opposing forces is far from clear. Nayland Smith, now reclassified as 'Federal Agent 56', glosses the mysterious events which are happening in the following way: '"Here's the story of an outside organization aiming to secure control of the country."'[28] To him, the play of domestic politics is little more than smoke screen hiding a larger threat, which is demonized as external and alien (because he has a good idea that Fu Manchu is directing events), and which is conducted on a level almost inconceivable from the viewpoint of conventional politics. Rohmer anticipates postwar images of mind control by showing how Fu incapacitates the liberal Catholic leader's mind, inducing blanks in his memory. Similarly Fu stands behind the suicidally weak performance of another liberal leader when debating politics with Bragg. In both these cases forms of post-hypnotic suggestion operate.

It is the most explicit instance of such suggestion, however, which reveals the strongest link between this novel and *The Manchurian Candidate*. Where the later novel builds up to a climax at a political convention, the corresponding climax in *President Fu Manchu* occurs in the political debate between Bragg and the liberal leader, which takes place in the Carnegie Hall. Immediately before this debate Fu Manchu drugs a local gunman and gives him his final instructions:

> His gaze was caught and held by green compelling eyes, only inches removed from his own. His muscular hands clutched the sides of the bench; he stayed rigid in that pose.
> 'You understand –' the strange voice was pitched very low: 'The word of command is "Asia."'
> 'I understand,' Grosset replied. 'No man shall stop me.'
> 'The word,' Fu Manchu intoned monotonously, 'is "Asia."'

> 'Asia,' Grosset echoed.
> 'Until you hear that word –' the voice seemed to come from the depths of a green lake – 'forget, forget all you have to do.'
> 'I have forgotten.'[29]

Fu's hypnotic powers are shown here firstly in the power play of his gaze and secondly in his repetitive intonation. Just like the Manchurian Candidate, Grosset has been transformed into a passive instrument whose operator is protected by induced amnesia and whose key action is stimulated by a trigger phrase. In *The Manchurian Candidate* the target is the demagogue's only political rival; here the target is the demagogue himself. No sooner has Bragg won the debate than he is gunned down and his place taken by another right-wing politician, one of Fu Manchu's puppets. And, thereby ensuring that no one previously unaware of the conspiracy can learn anything from the assassin, Bragg's bodyguards shoot Grosset on the spot.

President Fu Manchu anticipates *The Manchurian Candidate* in its utter scepticism towards the American public. Both novels show the latter to be superficial, manipulable and all too easily led by party machines. They are fooled into believing that Bragg is the 'greatest statesman since Lincoln';[30] and in both novels post-hypnotic suggestion functions as an analogue for the workings of financial processes. The Catholic leader warns all Americans: '"You are being bought with alien money."'[31] Bragg registers a consciousness at one point of acting a part, of learning a script devised elsewhere, and this consciousness is extended by Condon into a trope expressing the inauthenticity of postwar American political life. Both novelists explore the capacity of conspirators to appropriate cherished national images and slogans for their own purposes. For instance, Fu has constructed a device for converting Daniel Webster's face on an American stamp into his own face. The device scarcely serves any narrative purpose, but functions to remind the reader of the displacements which Fu is attempting. Rohmer shows Fu Manchu exploiting the American underworld in realizing his ambitions; Condon shows an even more ironic congruence of actions between external communist forces and the workings of the American right.

The Manchurian Candidate dates its narrative from 1936 (the year of the Moscow show trials and also of the publication of *President Fu Manchu*), when a process is supposedly started by Stalin's chief of secret police, Beria, to produce the 'perfectly prefabricated assassin' (Condon's phrase).[32] Condon punctuates his narrative with allusions to the Yellow Peril, which are easily assimilated into this melodrama of communist conspiracy. One of the earliest of such references is a yellow carpet used in the special prison camp constructed on the Korean border. This hints towards the character that will form Condon's equivalent of Fu Manchu: the Chinese brainwasher, Yen Lo. He is described in a consciously theatrical scene that finds him expounding his theory of conditioning:

The Yellow Peril in the Cold War   23

> The stage was raised about thirty inches from the floor and was draped with the bunting of the U.S.S.R. and the People's Republic of China. Yen Lo stood behind the centred lectern. He was wearing an ankle-length dress of French blue that buttoned at the side of his throat and fell in straight, comfortable lines. The skin of his face was lapstreaked, or clinkerbuilt, into overlapping horizontal folds like the sides of some small boats, and it was the colour of raw sulphur. His eyes were hooded and dark, which made him seem even older than did the wrinkles. His entire expression was theatrically sardonic as though he had been advised by prepaid cable that the late Fu Manchu had been his uncle.[33]

Condon thematizes the unavoidable theatricality of introducing a character resembling Fu Manchu by representing the occasion as a scene of display. Yen Lo's costume clearly differentiates him from the uniform dress of the communist officials and the colour of his complexion draws the reader's attention to Condon's studied avoidance of the expected term 'yellow' (although 'sulphur' carries equally negative connotations of Hell). Like Fu, Yen Lo is old and wise, the possessor of ancient lore which gives him a superior, ironic poise over the Soviets present. While he does not possess Fu's hypnotic green eyes, the fact that his eyes are hooded sets up a different suggestion of cunning, of hidden purposes; and Condon's term 'dress' suggests a femininity which, we shall see, points towards the second Fu-Manchu-like figure in this narrative.

The Manchurian Candidate conflates Freudian and communist conspiracy. Raymond Shaw's distant enemy is of course Yen Lo, but his real 'operator' – Condon uses the term in both political and psycho-sexual senses – is his mother. In two key scenes she is described as wearing Chinese garments. In the first, she has a bright orange-red house coat (that is, a combination of the two colours symbolizing cultural danger: red and yellow) with a high black Elizabethan collar suggestive of power. At this point she is acting out the role of queen and empress, hence Raymond's trigger-image being the queen of diamonds. In the second scene, her true identity has been revealed:

> Raymond's mother had banged a charge into her arm just before this session of briefing Raymond and it most certainly agreed with her. Her magnetic, perfectly spaced blue eyes seemed to sparkle as she talked. Her lithe, solid figure seemed even more superb because of her flawless carriage. She wore a Chinese dressing gown of a shade so light that it complemented the contrasting colour of her eyes.[34]

Fu Manchu's hypnotic eyes have now reappeared in a colour-echo of Yen Lo's dress. As with Fu, the mother's piercing eyes undercut resistance, and what she lacks in height she compensates for in bearing. She also demonstrates a dependence on drugs similar to Fu Manchu's weakness for opium. This is one of the most important scenes in *The Manchurian Candidate* because here

24 *David Seed*

Raymond receives his instructions on whom he is to kill. As in the corresponding scene in *President Fu Manchu* quoted earlier, Raymond's instructor lowers her voice to ensure that her words penetrate the subject's consciousness. Scenes such as these led the intelligence analyst Walter Bowart to write that the 'techniques he [Condon] described were first perfected and used not by the Chinese or the Communists, but by the United States'.[35] Bowart makes the point that the Cold War produced a curious circularity in the intelligence services of the West. Committed to a worldview where communism had to be demonized as inhuman but also had to be surpassed in psychological warfare, the USA engaged in research which perfected the very techniques they were attacking in the enemy.

In *The Manchurian Candidate* the role of Raymond's mother is created by Condon's displacement of alien threat on to the domestic scene. As Michael Rogin has pointed out, the communist threat (inflected by the Yellow Peril) is brought home, doubly relocated within the USA and within the psyche, as Raymond becomes a 'carrier,' unconsciously enacting the role of an invading agent.[36] The origin of this process is left ambiguous by Condon although the visual imagery associated with Raymond's mother gives the reader a hint of the part she is playing. Elaine Tyler May has described the key role of the home in the USA during the Cold War: 'In virtually all the civil defence publicity, safety was represented in the form of the family.'[37] Within this nuclear family, of course, the mother had a key role to play, but May finds an identification between 'taming fears of the atomic age and taming women', which finds a surprisingly direct confirmation in *The Manchurian Candidate*.[38] Instead of confining herself to support within the home, Raymond's mother has even ventured into active politics, through participation behind the scenes. Thus, the home which should offer Raymond refuge and support proves to be the site of betrayal; and the prime agent of that betrayal is his mother.

The Manchurian Candidate revises Rohmer's narrative of conspiracy in a number of important respects, not least by splitting Fu Manchu into two figures: the planner and the manipulator. Rohmer's gender conservatism is reflected in the fact that women in the Fu Manchu narratives are denied all but minor or romantic roles, whereas in Raymond's mother the category of alien villain has been ironically displaced across national and gender identities to a figure at the heart of the American political establishment. In the novel and even more in its movie adaptation, the consciousness of being used, which is registered intermittently by Fu Manchu's victims, is concentrated in Raymond's fellow officer, Major Marco. He is the one who retains a distorted memory of the indoctrination camp and then heads the investigation into the conspiracy. At one point Marco protests to Raymond: '"What do you think I am – a zombie?"'[39] Ironically, immediately afterwards Marco falls prey again to his recurrent nightmare of Raymond carrying out Yen Lo's instruction to execute two of his fellow POWs. Rohmer builds up a larger-than-life impression of Fu by gradually revealing different kinds of expertise he possesses and by keeping him in the narrative background for the most part. He thus takes on the status of an apparently irresistible force because the reader is never sure which level he is operating on, whether through hypnosis, assassins or some other means. An essential part of Rohmer's narratives always consists of attempts to understand the exact nature of the particular threat posed by Fu. Indeed, sometimes his acts seem to verge on the supernatural. Condon incorporates such a possibility by depicting brainwashing as a new form of demonic possession. Marco feels himself to be struggling with a 'succubus' and explains to Raymond: "'They are inside your mind now [...] and you are helpless. You are a host body and they are feeding on you.'"[40] In *The Manchurian Candidate* the American security forces are presented not only with a new conspiracy but with a new *kind* of threat which they have to gradually come to understand. Condon carefully delays using the term 'brainwashing' until the full ramifications of the plot are beginning to emerge. *President Fu Manchu* presents Fu Manchu's organization as a shadowy mirror image of the FBI, where decisions and power are concentrated in the hands of one man. Hence the final scene of that novel, where a German scientist and Fu Manchu grapple together as they are swept over the Niagara Falls (like Holmes and Moriarty at the Reichenbach Falls), a scene that seems to close off the narrative. In *The Manchurian Candidate*, however, the aggressive alien force remains intact after the death of Raymond. Condon stresses that Raymond was a psychological type and the clear implication is that, although one conspiracy has been foiled, many more could be devised.

Condon took from Rohmer the concept of an ultimate struggle taking place beneath the surface of American national life. For 'Yellow Peril' he substitutes 'communist peril', but the alignment of forces remains unchanged. All characters in *President Fu Manchu* are experts or specialists of some kind, having been given access to areas of knowledge or to the workings of the security services denied to the average citizen. The stakes are high since Fu Manchu is playing for nothing less than the whole world. Nayland Smith grimly warns that "'the map of the world is going to be altered.'"[41] Similarly Raymond's mother instructs him in the need for sacrifice: "'We *are* at war. It's a cold war but it will get worse and worse until every man and woman and child in this country will have to stand up and be counted to say whether or not he or she is on the side of right and freedom, or on the side of the [communist stooges] of this country.'"[42] This totalizing rhetoric narrows options down, imposing compliance on Raymond by sheer force of words. His mother is the supreme tactician of the novel.

The Manchurian Candidate conflates the confrontation of an alien foe with Christian apocalypse. Raymond's mother warns him that the signs tell her: "'Time is going to roar and flash lightning in the streets, Raymond. Blood will gush behind the noise and stones will fall and fools and mockers will be brought down.'"[43] Even during the period when anti-communism peaked there were critics of such apocalyptic or demonic explanations. The sociologist Raymond A. Bauer, for example, was disturbed by popular receptivity to the notion of brainwashing and in 1957 complained: 'A single American soldier converted to Communism could arouse feelings of anxiety and guilt over one's own repressed ideological doubts. Hence, our eagerness to attribute such conversions to the demonic machinations of the Doctors Pavlov and Fu Manchu.'[44]

Bauer's was a rare voice of reason, questioning popular imagery through the medium of an academic journal. However, increasingly from the 1960s onwards the images of conspiracy are parodied in fiction. Drawing on the caricatures of *Dr. Strangelove*, the science fiction writer James Blish burlesques such an apocalyptic mentality in his novel *The Day after Judgement* (1968), where a nuclear holocaust lays waste vast areas of the world. Attempting to identify who has attacked America, Strategic Air Command General McKnight is convinced that the villains are the Chinese because he has been a 'Yellow Peril fan since his boyhood reading of *The American Weekly* in Chicago'.[45] Blish literalizes the American demonization of the enemy by showing the invading forces to be demons. When McKnight launches a futile counter-attack, a goat-headed diabolical form emerges from the nuclear clouds. McKnight has no doubt about the identity of this figure: "'A Chink! I knew it all along!'" and rounding on a colleague, he screams: "'You've sold us out! You were on their side all the time! Do you know into whose hands you have delivered your country? Do you? Do you? [. . .] *That is the insidious Doctor Fu Manchu*!'"[46] Blish shows that the operators of the most sophisticated and, they would say, most rational military system in the world, are themselves swayed by non-rational images which have a destructive momentum of their own. Similarly in William Burroughs's *Exterminator!* (sections composed during the 1960s, published as a single work in 1974), there is a sketch that focuses on a fanatically anti-communist official of the US defence establishment who has a servant named Bently. A mysterious psychological illness seizes other defence officials and conspiracy is suspected, at which point we witness a moment of revelation: 'Alone in the room Bently wipes off the grey features of the perfect servant to reveal himself as the Insidious Doctor Fu Manchu.'[47] Burroughs caricatures conspiracy as theatre, but presents his Fu Manchu figure as a kind of anti-president of the USA calling across his land as it sinks into an entropic death.

Thomas Pynchon's 1973 novel *Gravity's Rainbow* deploys comedy and other effects to probe behind the dualistic mindset which thrives on what he calls the 'ideas of the opposite'.[48] Pynchon draws on the same tradition of Pavlovian experimentation described in *The Manchurian Candidate* and links this tradition with Yellow Peril narratives through the behavioural scientist Edward Pointsman. Not only is the latter an ardent disciple of Pavlov, whom he reveres as the Master; to make the connection clear, he is also the proud possessor of a 'matched set of all the books in Sax Rohmer's great

Manichaean saga'.[49] Pynchon's novel is set in the closing year of the Second World War and he peppers his text with throwaway references to the popular culture of the time, references which include allusions to Fu Manchu. For Pynchon, such images form part of a collective social unconscious which can impact on behaviour unpredictably. Pointsman is a particularly ironic case in point. Although he prides himself on his scientific objectivity, this stance is based on polarities which he has learned from Rohmer's novels. Thus he attempts to read the competition between rival intelligence agencies as an updated version of Rohmer's grand narrative where he or his delegate is playing out the role of Nayland Smith and experiences the most disturbing challenge to ego stability when a subversive, fantastic voice whispers in his ear that he might be able to enact *both* roles: those of Nayland Smith *and* Fu Manchu.[50] In these cases Pynchon, Blish and Burroughs suggest that the melodrama of this figure from popular culture inflects the way officials perceive their nation and the world political situation. They burlesque the Fu Manchu stereotype, but at the same time leave the door ajar to conspiracy.

Of course, conspiracy narratives continue to be published, despite the stereotypes that they contain and despite the changes in global politics. Walter Wager's *Telefon* (1975) describes a group of Soviet 'sleepers' triggered years after their conditioning by a renegade Soviet agent. Richard Condon himself returned to the theme of brainwashing in his 1976 novel *The Whisper of the Axe*, which describes the training of a group of Americans in a secret Chinese camp, in preparation for guerrilla subversion in American cities timed to break out in the centennial year. The camp is run by one Dr Kung, a Chinese from Korea, and the most secret section is the so-called Psychological De-Briefing Area where the surface buildings camouflage an underground facility:

> [The inmates] were dropped sixty feet into the ground by elevators to a large common hospital area that had six cubicles on each side and two projection rooms at each end: four in all. By the time the men reached the lower level they had fallen into an ambulatory hypnotic state from the chemicals that had been contained in their breakfasts. The men were put into separate silent cubicles where two technicians to each cubicle stripped them down and strapped them firmly to steel stretchers.[51]

Once they have been completely isolated, the men undergo a psychological exposure worthy of Fu Manchu: 'Feeding tubes le[d] to bottles containing Chinese-developed preparations (some perfected over centuries, some in recent years), which opened the doors of consciousness and led the interrogators to the truth locked inside the minds of each of the men.'[52] This prolonged interrogation erases the former contents of the captives' minds and prepares them for the final phase of the process: re-education. The phase requires that 'negative lessons be laid down which, if the subject deliberately

28 *David Seed*

chose to transgress the necessities of those lessons, caused extraordinary, instant electric pain to be induced into the central nervous system.'[53] As in *The Manchurian Candidate*, Condon shows these techniques to be an extension of earlier Chinese practice and describes the consciousness of the captives passively as a space to be emptied and refilled.

The Manchurian Candidate drew on an existing tradition of Yellow Peril conspiracy narratives, added the factor of communism and then gave an extra political dimension to the action in its use of Freudian psychology. Its melodrama, however, has not been as divorced from the world of real politics as might be supposed. The propagandist Edward Hunter campaigned tirelessly against the admission of communist China to the United Nations, partly on the grounds of world mental health. In his *Black Book on Red China* (1961), after describing the treatment of Korean POWs, he diagnosed an illness at the heart of the Chinese nation: 'The effect on an entire population of a concentrated programme of brainwashing would inevitably create a national neurosis. The mental upset caused by a single individual is duplicated on a national scale. A nation afflicted with brainwashing would be a mentally sick country, made deliberately so as national policy.'[54] Such a psychological drama plays itself out in *The Manchurian Candidate*, albeit on a smaller scale and with the individual's identification with the nation being more ambiguous. Its version of conspiracy seemed to find literal confirmation in the shooting of President Kennedy, and the film was withdrawn from circulation as a result. More worryingly, the notion of a secret attack on America by covert communist forces evidently continues to weigh with the US Intelligence Council, which in 2002 published a booklet named *Stealth Invasion*, documenting Chinese naval activity. In the best tradition of Cold War warnings, the introduction declares: 'After reading this report few will doubt that the presence of nearly 100 ships of Red China's merchant marine and millions of uninspected containers entering America is a clear and present danger to American lives and property on our home shores.'[55] The emphasis on scale, the designation of China and the general play on revelation throughout the booklet place its rhetoric within the same Cold War tradition as that of *The Manchurian Candidate*.

Notes

1 Truman, '5th State of the Union Address', http://www.geocities.com/americanpresidencynet/1951.htm (accessed 27 September 2004).
2 Medhurst, 'Rhetoric and Cold War: A Strategic Approach', in Martin J. Medhurst, Robert L. Ivie, Philip Wander and Robert L. Scott, eds, *Cold War Rhetoric: Strategy, Metaphor, and Ideology* (Westport, CT: Greenwood Press, 1990), p. 19.
3 Harry Welton, *The Third World War: Trade and Industry – The New Battleground* (London: Pall Mall Press, 1959), p. 1.
4 Heinlein, *The Puppet Masters*, new edn (1951; London: Pan Books, 1969), p. 219.

5 Melley, 'Agency Panic and the Culture of Conspiracy,' in Peter Knight, ed., *Conspiracy Nation: The Politics of Paranoia in Postwar America* (New York: New York University Press, 2002), pp. 60, 61.
6 Hunter, *Brainwashing: The Story of the Men Who Defied It*, new edn (1956; New York: Pyramid Books, 1970), p. 182.
7 Ibid., p. 285.
8 Cardinal Josef Mindszenty, Catholic primate of Hungary, was arrested for treason and imprisoned in 1949. His subsequent acknowledgement of 'guilt' was taken in the West to be the result of brainwashing and the case was widely regarded as symbolizing the hostility of communist regimes to Christianity.
9 For valuable commentary on this context see Susan L. Carruthers, '*The Manchurian Candidate* (1962) and the Cold War Brainwashing Scare', *Historical Journal of Film, Radio and Television*, 18: 1 (1998), pp. 75–94.
10 I discuss many such narratives in Seed, *Brainwashing: The Fictions of Mind Control* (Kent, OH: Kent State University Press, 2004), Chapter 4.
11 Kinkead, *In Every War But One* (New York: Norton, 1959), p. 78.
12 Ibid., p. 78.
13 Dooner, *Last Days of the Republic*, new edn (1880; New York: Arno Press, 1978), p. 123.
14 London's essay combines China and Japan into a common threat. His essay can be found at http://www.readbookonline.net/read/298/8662 (accessed 27 September 2004). London anticipates the symbolism of the Korean War when he crosses the Yalu River from Korea to Manchuria, moving from a quiet agrarian culture into an altogether more threatening one. In the Korean War the Yalu River marked the northern boundary of UN military action, but from the north was the point of access for Chinese troops and Soviet 'advisers'.
15 Wu, *The Yellow Peril: Chinese Americans in American Fiction, 1850–1940* (Hamden, CT: Archon, 1982), p. 167. M.P. Shiel in *The Yellow Danger* (1898) helped create the stereotype of the oriental mastermind intent on destroying the West. There Yen How is a brilliant scientist and a personification of Asia in being half-Chinese and half-Japanese. Further useful historical commentary on this figure is given in 'Fu Manchu and the Yellow Peril' at http://www.illuminatedlantern.com/cinema/features/fumanchu.html (accessed 27 September 2004). Further information on this fiction up to the Second World War can be found in Jess Nevins's 'On Yellow Peril Thrillers', at http://www.violetbooks.com/yellowperil.html (accessed 27 September 2004). Gina Marchetti's *Romance and the 'Yellow Peril': Race, Sex and Discursive Strategies in Hollywood Fiction* (1993) gives valuable commentary on relevant films.
16 Rohmer, *The Mystery of Doctor Fu Manchu*, new edn (1913; London: Allan Wingate, 1977), p. 19.
17 Wu, *Yellow Peril*, p. 174.
18 Bucher, with Mark Rascovich, *Bucher: My Story* (Garden City, New York: Doubleday, 1970), p. 291.
19 Cay Van Ash and Elizabeth Sax Rohmer, *Master of Villainy: A Biography of Sax Rohmer* (London: Tom Stacey, 1972), p. 282.
20 'Sax Rohmer', at http://www.classicreader.com/author.php/aut.88.html (accessed 27 September 2004). Source not given.
21 Rohmer, *The Shadow of Fu Manchu*, new edn (1948; New York: Pyramid Books, 1963), p. 67.
22 Ibid., p. 22.
23 Ibid., p. 118.
24 Rohmer, *Emperor Fu Manchu* (Greenwich, Conn: Fawcett, 1959), pp. 123, 157.
25 Rohmer can set up his narrative only by postulating two Bamboo Curtains, the border of communist China and a mysterious unspecified inner border to Fu

Manchu's ideological heartland in Tibet. Rohmer's geography pulls against history at this point since by 1959 the Chinese communists had already taken over Tibet.
26 Ibid., pp. 99, 147.
27 Ibid., p. 149.
28 Rohmer, *President Fu Manchu*, new edn (1936; New York: Pyramid Books, 1963), p. 23.
29 Ibid., p. 106.
30 Ibid., p. 116.
31 Ibid., p. 215.
32 Condon, *The Manchurian Candidate*, new edn (1959; New York: New American Library, 1960), p. 53.
33 Ibid., p. 46.
34 Ibid., p. 324.
35 Bowart, *Operation Mind Control* (London: Fontana/Collins, 1978), p. 20.
36 Rogin, *'Ronald Reagan,' the Movie and Other Episodes in Political Demonology* (Berkeley: University of California Press, 1987), p. 253.
37 May, *Homeward Bound: American Families in the Cold War Era*, rev. edn (1988; New York: Basic Books, 1999), p. 93.
38 Ibid., p. 95.
39 Condon, *Manchurian Candidate*, p. 130.
40 Ibid., p. 260.
41 Rohmer, *President Fu Manchu*, p. 154.
42 Condon, *Manchurian Candidate*, p. 115.
43 Ibid., p. 161.
44 Bauer, 'Brainwashing: Psychology or Demonology?', *Journal of Social Issues*, 13: 3 (1957), p. 47.
45 Blish, *Black Easter and The Day after Judgement*, new edn (1968; London: Arrow Books, 1981), p. 126,
46 Ibid., p. 192.
47 Burroughs, *Exterminator!* (London: Calder and Boyars, 1974), p.73.
48 Pynchon, *Gravity's Rainbow*, new edn (1973; London: Pan Books, 1975), p. 48.
49 Ibid., p. 631.
50 Ibid., p. 278.
51 Condon, *The Whisper of the Axe* (New York: Dial Press, 1976), p. 136.
52 Ibid., p. 136.
53 Ibid., pp. 136–7.
54 Hunter, *The Black Book on Red China* (New York: The Bookmailer, 1961), p.134.
55 Roger Canfield, *Stealth Invasion: Red Chinese Operations in North America* (Fairfax VA: United States Intelligence Council, 2002), p. 7.

2 The Cold War representation of the West in Russian literature[1]

Andrei Rogachevskii

Over the centuries, Russian attitudes to foreigners have been determined by a number of geo-political and cultural factors (perhaps better qualified as assumptions), which have never replaced and/or counterbalanced one another in keeping with every significant historical change, but rather have continued to co-exist in a state of chaotic syncretism while adding new perceptions to the old ones. Among these assumptions, there are a number worth mentioning. First, one finds an East versus West divide, with nineteenth-century Westernizers, for example, pointing to Western Europe as a role model for Russia, whereas twentieth-century Eurasianists believed that Russia's natural allies should be sought in Asia.[2] Second, there is the North versus South divide, based on a mystical doctrine which claims that the ancestors of today's Russians, the so-called Aryans or Hyperboreans, originating from the mythological country of Hyperborea in the Arctic North, went southward to establish civilizations on their way and contaminated their racial purity in the process. The Aryans or Hyperboreans are juxtaposed to the inferior people of the south, with whom they can live in peace and harmony as long as these southerners yield to Aryan leadership.[3] Third, a sea–land divide has been advanced, by which a 'continental' state, Russia, is supposed to share its core interests with Germany, for instance, as opposed to the 'oceanic' USA and UK.[4] Fourth, there is the linguistic aspect, with nineteenth-century Slavophiles advancing the concept of a Slavonic brotherhood, based on the linguistic and cultural affinity of Eastern, Western and Southern Slavs.[5] Fifth, there is the religious aspect (among brother Slavs, the Orthodox Christian nations, such as Bulgaria, were considered to be much closer to Russia than, say, Polish Catholics; as for non-Slavonic nations in southern Europe, a similar distinction applied to Greeks, on the one hand, and Italians on the other). Finally, the issue of class struggle emerged, a Marxist dogma asserting that the working classes of any nationality have more in common than the working class and the bourgeoisie of the same nationality.

Needless to say, logic has rarely served as a basis for any of the above-named assumptions, whether taken separately or in conjunction with one another. It appears that these assumptions have taken historical reality into account almost as often as they have ignored it (thus, the third assumption seems to be oblivious of the fact that in the first half of the twentieth century Germany and Russia went to war with each other twice, to mention but one obvious discrepancy). The interaction of these, and other, factors has resulted in a complex of self-contradictory, irrational notions (often amounting to stereotypes), all of which are deeply rooted in people's collective subconscious and could be easily appealed to in case of political expediency, whatever that may be. Thus, the shifting Cold War relations between the Soviet Union and the West have been duly reflected in Soviet literature's attitude to the West, which is not monolithic but is mutable and divided.

With the onset of the Cold War, it became necessary for the communist propaganda machine to convince anyone who would care to pay attention that Russia's recent war allies, Great Britain and the United States, had in fact always been Russia's bitter enemies and had tried to use Nazi Germany's military might to defeat the Soviet Union once and for all. As if following the Orwellian maxim 'Oceania has always been at war with Eurasia', Nikolai Shpanov's[6] 900-page novel *Podzhigateli* (*Warmongers*, 1950) sets out to prove that 'people like [Harry] Truman, [John Foster] Dulles and [Averell] Harriman [. . .] not only protected and served as an inspiration to, but also were [fully] behind, the ominous warmongers, namely German and Italian fascists, as well as French and British traitors'.[7] The novel, which forms part of a series that also includes the similarly bulky *Zagovorshchiki* (*Plotters*, 1951), begins in December 1932 and covers all the main events in European history before the Second World War, from Hitler's rise to power, through the Spanish Civil War, to the fall of Czechoslovakia. The prologue and epilogue, however, take place in post-1945 Europe, mostly in Berlin, Prague and the Vatican, with nuclear weaponry heavily dominating the agenda.

True to the spirit of Stalin's regime, with its paranoid spy mania and fake revelations about spurious assassination plots, and to the struggle against 'kowtowing to the West' (*nizkopoklonstvo pered Zapadom*), Shpanov discovers that Marshal Pétain was involved in preparations for the assassination of King Alexander of Yugoslavia and the French Foreign Minister, Louis Barthou, in Marseilles in 1934.[8] Furthermore, Shpanov makes claims that the American diplomat William Bullitt, in collaboration with the Germans, tried to poison President Franklin Delano Roosevelt. He also alleges that Josip Broz Tito, Jean-Paul Sartre and even Admiral Canaris, as well as 'hundreds of thousands of Roman Catholic priests and monks, hundreds of Vatican bishops and dozens of cardinals, all were [. . .] American secret agents'.[9] The Intelligence Service also springs into action from time to time. Thus, Shpanov uncovers an unsuccessful British attempt on the life of the Bulgarian communist Georgi Dimitrov, upon his release from a German prison where he was kept for his alleged part in the 1933 Reichstag fire.[10] This attempt, undertaken to facilitate British access to the oil reserves in Asia Minor and the Caucasus (in the way of which communist Bulgaria, with Dimitrov as a strong leader, would be standing), was masterminded by a special agent called Winfred Row. There is an indication that no other than W. Somerset Maugham served as a prototype for this character, as Row's play, mentioned in Chapter 28 of Part V, is entitled *Shest' shillingov i polnolunie* (*Six Shillings and the Full Moon*),[11] to allude to Maugham's 1919 book *The Moon and Sixpence*. Similarly, a villainous American secret service agent, who poses as Hermann Goering's secretary (and skilfully manipulates his boss),[12] is called MacCronin, 'with the purpose of reminding readers of [. . .] MacCormick, the well-known editor'.[13] The resemblance of these fictional characters to their prototypes is almost imperceptible, though.

It is clear that historical accuracy and even verisimilitude are not among Shpanov's priorities. He forgets, for example, that one of his characters, the floor-polisher Jan Bois, is at first described as a one-armed man, for he later describes him washing his hands.[14] Another character, the journalist Michael Kisch, is wounded in the arm in Chapter 19 of Part III, but is shown effortlessly driving a car, unpacking his suitcase, putting a lantern on a rooftop through a broken window and jotting quickly in a notebook in Chapters 20 and 23.[15] With such a careless attitude to his own narrative, it is hardly surprising that, despite all the fanciful inventions,[16] especially in the secret service department, Shpanov's novel makes an extremely tedious read. As soon as the 'thaw' arrived, Soviet critics branded Shpanov's books a counterproductive 'ideological waste' (*ideologicheskii brak*) because of their cheap schematization,[17] verbosity and general incompetence.[18] A slightly more sophisticated anti-Western propaganda would follow from various authors.

Among them was Daniil Kraminov, who knew the West better than most Soviet writers. He had some English, was attached to the Allied Forces at the Second Front as a war correspondent, regularly visited foreign countries afterwards and even edited the *Za rubezhom* (*Abroad*) weekly. *Pasynki Al'biona* (*Albion's Stepchildren*, 1962) is a novel about a young Soviet *apparatchik*, Leonid Egorshin, who arrives in London in the late 1950s as an employee of an unnamed organization responsible for scientific and cultural contacts between the USSR and the UK. He rents a room and gradually gets to know his British neighbours at the fictional address of All Souls' Close, so named to suggest that, under capitalism, everyone ends up in a *cul de sac* of sorts (the word 'close' could be translated into Russian as *tupik*, which also means 'deadlock'). Among the inhabitants of the close, there is a Mr Backstone, a communist worker (naturally oozing positivity); one Mr Atkins, a small-time shopkeeper (who is pleasant but ultimately petty-bourgeois); a working girl called Barbs, whom Egorshin finds attractive and is trying to court; and a family of Jewish greengrocers, by the name of Gilbert, who are constantly harassed by local members of the Association of True Britons (*Ob"edinenie istinnykh brittov*). This imaginary organization is loosely based on the Union Movement, led by Sir Oswald Mosley from 1947 to 1973. It is obvious that the book was partly inspired by Mosley's unsuccessful attempt, in 1959, to run for a Westminster seat on an anti-immigration (but not an anti-Jewish) ticket.[19] Described ominously as someone whose 'face looked yellow under the street lamps, as if he was a mummy, with two black holes peering from under his thin arched brows',[20] the politician himself makes an appearance at a rally in All Souls' Close, which culminates in a large-scale fistfight between the 'true Britons' and their opponents in the crowd. As one review of the novel points out, judging by the information provided in the book, the residents of All Souls' Close are the only opposition to Mosley known to the reader, and are neither numerous nor powerful enough to mount such a resistance on their own. So 'who are they, these genuine enemies of [neo-]Nazism?',[21] asks the sceptical reviewer. His inference is that Kraminov's account lacks conviction precisely because the British working classes are not yet sufficiently mature to combat reactionary forces actively. After all, adds the reviewer, ordinary British people have only 'started their resolute struggle to free their spirit from the tenets of bourgeois morals'.[22] This review might serve to indicate that, from the point of view of a watchdog of communist morale, Kraminov is a little too optimistic (or maybe insufficiently pessimistic) in his assessment of certain tendencies in British society, and that he should exercise more caution as far as his positive attitudes to Britain are concerned.

Not that Kraminov indiscriminately extols traditional British values when he has a chance to criticize them. To demonstrate the alleged unscrupulousness of British MPs, and thus to diminish the significance of the oldest parliamentary democracy in the eyes of the Soviet reader, he introduces the Crooks family of parliamentarians, which includes a Liberal father, a Conservative son and a Labour son. Such a wide range of political convictions, explains Kraminov, helps the family to run a tobacco business *and* to trade with Spain and Bulgaria successfully (because in the Commons the Conservative MP praises Franco, whereas the Labour MP lends support to the Bulgarian leader Todor Zhivkov). There is also a third son, a student who is too young to enter Parliament, but, when he is older, might as well do so as a communist. The family won't mind. After all, communists control a third of the world and there are many smokers among them.

At first sight, this may seem pure fantasy. However, Kraminov undoubtedly modelled his fictional family on the Liberal MP David Lloyd George (1863–1945) and his children, Gwilym (1894–1967) and Megan (1902–66). In truth, both Gwilym and Megan, who had started out as Liberal activists, drifted away from the party in opposite directions about a decade after their father's death. Still, Kraminov's embellishments, although marked with a touch of malicious intent, seem to fall within the reasonable limits of artistic licence. At least he neither openly discloses the identity of the Crooks's real-life counterparts nor claims that they have all been up to no good on the CIA's payroll, as Shpanov might have done. There is a mild insinuation, though, that Mosley's electoral campaign is being bankrolled by the Americans, as he arrives at All Souls' Close in an American car and his bodyguards are dressed in American jackets.[23] However, Kraminov does not venture any further than that. Hardly a political dove,[24] he clearly prefers hints and exaggerations in his fiction to blatant lies.

It is curious that the poet Evgenii Evtushenko, who enjoys the reputation of a Soviet liberal and a modern Westernizer, is not distinctly different from Kraminov in his representation of contemporary Britain. Just as Kraminov takes the side of the working-class Britons who bear the brunt of bread winning for the nation but who often cannot exercise the same rights as the parasite classes (it is the underprivileged to whom Kraminov figuratively refers in his title as Albion's stepchildren), Evtushenko also feels closer to those who work hard but earn little. Thus, in his poem 'Uriia Gip' ('Uriah Heep'), released in the same year by the same publishing house as Kraminov's novel, Evtushenko reserves special sympathy for 'kind [British] people' (*dobrye liudi*),[25] as he terms them, among whom he mentions a (presumably poor) artist discussing Picasso and Chagall, and unnamed women who walk home, tired after a long day at work. As for the rest, he brackets together posh women in necklaces, tabloid journalists, government informers and neo-Nazi sympathizers, as well as passport control and customs officers, and likens them all to Uriah Heep, the notoriously deceitful character in Dickens's *David Copperfield*. Whether intentionally or not, the British villains in Evtushenko's poem substantially outnumber good British people. In the conclusion, the poet expresses his hopes that, in the future, Russia and Britain might find themselves locked in a friendly embrace, but only after all the Uriah Heeps of the British nation have been buried.[26]

Evtushenko's stance on the USA appears to be milder than that of Kraminov. While Kraminov seems to be suggesting that only the Americans could stoop so low as to finance Mosley's unsavoury campaign, Evtushenko (in his poem 'Amerikanskii solovei' ('The American Nightingale'), published in the same collection as 'Uriia Gip') juxtaposes the disreputable world of American bureaucracy, with its shady deals, loquacious vanity, half-truths, outright lies and shark-like torsos of nuclear warheads, to a nightingale's song which he heard on his 1960 visit to Harvard. Evtushenko goes on to say that American, Russian and other nightingales use the same language and understand each other without any difficulty, so why can't people do the same?[27] At first sight, this might look like a reconciliation offering in the middle of a relentless class struggle. However, upon closer examination, the poem reveals little more than the usual message of Soviet propaganda disguised as the 'Nightingales of all countries, unite!' slogan. In the context of the poem as a whole, the concluding rhetorical question about people being unable to reach understanding places the blame for American–Russian hostility not so much on differences of language but on the aggressive nature of the vain and mendacious US imperialists, who have armed themselves to the teeth. In the light of this statement, it seems truly miraculous that, only two years after Evtushenko's sojourn in Harvard, Khrushchev and Kennedy were able to resolve their differences successfully over the Cuban missile crisis (which had been provoked by the 'peace-loving' Soviet side).

Needless to say, the USA remained Russia's favourite *bête noire* after Krushchev's removal. This image was reinforced in *Chego zhe ty khochesh'?* (*So, What Do You Want, Then?*, 1970), a notorious novel by Vsevolod Kochetov, a one-time head of the Leningrad branch of the Soviet Writers' Union and editor-in-chief of the neo-Stalinist *Oktiabr'* literary magazine.[28] The book tells the story of four foreign nationals (two Americans, one German and one Italian) visiting Moscow on an American- and British-funded trip to put together an illustrated catalogue of Russian icons. This, however, is only their cover story, and their real mission, as the American Portia Brown explains to her colleague, the Italian Umberto Caradonna, is a surreptitious attack on Soviet morals by stimulating

> an intellectual ferment at universities leading to the appearance of unsanctioned journals and leaflets and the shattering of former idols. [...] Those [Western] pop singers that we have seen at the local airport, those who can shake their hips on the stage, are also our weapon. [...] They sexualize the atmosphere in Russia and lure the youth away from civic pursuits and towards an intensely private world of love-making. [...] As a result, Komsomol activities will lose their drive, and Komsomol members' meetings and political indoctrinations will turn into a mere formality. Everything will be only for show, to observe decorum, with a private, sexual and obligation-free life going on behind the scenes. Then, in this society of people who are indifferent to civic virtues, who would not interfere, it will become possible to gradually promote those who prefer the Western system to the Soviet/Communist one, to leadership in various key organizations. This is a long, painstaking process, but it's the only way of dealing with Russia, as things stand.[29]

According to *Chego zhe ty khochesh'?*, the ultimate strategic goal of the West is the destruction of communism (which, for Kochetov, is synonymous with everything that is Russian). This is why the anti-communist crusade is presented in his novel as an anti-Russian crusade, and why the question of national allegiance and patriotism takes priority over the issue of proletarian internationalism. Germans are referred to as 'Russia's oldest [*iskonnye*] enemies' in Chapter 4, and a parallel is drawn between the soldiers of the Bundeswehr and the military might of Wehrmacht in Chapter 5 (symptomatically, East Germany is hardly ever mentioned).[30] In Chapter 23, Americans and Russians are said to have only one thing in common: a lack of manners (*razviaznost'*).[31] As for Russians and Italians, their partial incompatibility is analysed through the failure of a relationship between the Italian intellectual Benito Spada and his Russian wife, Lera. (Admittedly, Kochetov also portrays a group of likeable working-class Italians, perhaps because at the time Italy shared its borders with Eastern bloc countries and thus belonged to the sphere of the bloc's possible expansion.) Although Lera leaves Benito for ideological reasons (a member of the Italian Communist

Party, he criticizes the USSR too much), their story, in Kochetov's opinion, confirms the natural wisdom of Stalin's decree banning marriages between Soviet citizens and foreigners (in force between 1947 and 1956). In his advocacy of racial purity, Kochetov even makes the German member of the subversive team, Herr Klauberg (an ex-Hitlerite), say:

> You, Russians, are so indiscriminate! You'd marry a Japanese, a black woman, whoever ... [...]. You'll live to regret it. Just give it a time, and there won't be any Russians left. Where will they disappear off to? They'll get absorbed by various other nations. You'd better choose Jews as a role model. They have a hard and fast rule – to marry Jews only.[32]

Given the fact that this was written by a man who half-jokingly called himself 'Russia's principal anti-Semite',[33] the degree of confusion in Kochetov's mind should not be underestimated. These and similar statements have raised doubts about his sanity.[34] Also, pronouncements of this kind expressly contradicted both the internationalist aspect of Marxism-Leninism and some of the official USSR foreign and domestic policies of the late 1960s, and, as such, could easily (and legitimately) be termed anti-Soviet. Thus, in his introduction to the Italian translation of Kochetov's novel, the Italian Slavist Vittorio Strada (who, by his own admission, served as a prototype for Benito Spada), claimed that Kochetov had unconsciously written an anti-Soviet and anti-socialist book that discredited the USSR better than any other work, including anything written by anti-communist experts in the West. However, Strada dismisses the widespread theory that Kochetov is an agent provocateur enlisted by the CIA to bring down the Soviet Union and restore monarchy.[35]

Even for the usually timid world of Soviet literary criticism, Kochetov's book was a step too far. One reviewer noted with displeasure that the (autobiographical) character of the writer Bulatov,[36] who single handedly and selflessly rescues Lera from her unhappy marriage to Spada and who, quite literally, delivers a blow to Portia Brown's reputation by slapping her on the posterior,[37]

> appears before the reader as an outstanding personality, who pushes everyone else into the background. This is where the most flagrant discrepancy between real life and the book's concept lies. It is astonishing that in Kochetov's social novel, which focuses on Soviet reality, nothing has been said about the guiding role of the Communist Party in the life of our society! The overblown significance of Bulatov and his actions [*gipertrofiia obraza Bulatova i ego funktsii*] has been caused by the author's desire to somehow conceal this astounding gap.[38]

Shocking as it might appear to both pro-communist and anti-communist readers, Kochetov's book is little more than a mild reprisal of the Stalinist spy mania exemplified by Shpanov. Strictly speaking, *Chego zhe ty khochesh'?* does not belong to the genre of spy thrillers, if only because it 'does not possess the tightly knit plot structure, expected in a spy novel'.[39] However, it arguably succeeds in resurrecting the message that foreigners are to be mistrusted as potential spies. Not unlike Shpanov, Kochetov attracts attention to the inner rivalry among various Western nations, which seem to be united only in their hatred for Russian communism.

When, in the mid-1970s, the political pendulum swung back to peaceful co-existence between capitalist and socialist nations, and the idea of détente was introduced, a CPSU-backed trust-building exercise resulted in the re-emergence of literature promoting the image of foreigners as human beings. Vasilii Aksenov's travelogue 'Kruglye sutki non-stop' ('Round the Clock, Non-stop', 1976) is a case in point. An author whose name in many respects has become synonymous with the revival of Soviet literature during the thaw, Aksenov describes his two-month stay as a visiting professor at the UCLA in 'a hybrid work combining a more or less factual, albeit humorously distorted and impressionistic, account of his sojourn with an inset surreal episodic adventure story that is a mythic incarnation of the spirit of the country'.[40] The latter, termed by its author 'A Typical American Adventure', heavily compensates for the uneventful life on campus that limited the authenticity of Aksenov's American experience (which he expanded only later when he was forced by the Soviets to emigrate).[41] Seemingly short of prototypes, Aksenov casts himself as the adventure's hero, splitting his personality into two, that of benign Moskvich (Muscovite) and of evil Memozov (whose surname ultimately stems from the Latin verb 'to imitate', perhaps underlying the illusory nature of the character). Whatever activity Moskvich is taking part in (generally, the clichés associated with American culture, such as riding a horse in the Wild West or winning a fortune in Las Vegas), Memozov materializes from thin air and tries to spoil all the fun. This rather contrived buffoonery makes one suspect that Aksenov has little of substance to report about his journey. However, for the Soviet reader, who was tired of grey and monotonous existence, even the mention of petrol stations (Esso, Shell and Apollo, 'white and blue, white and red, white and yellow'),[42] let alone the street adverts for Cutty Sark whisky, Rolex watches, Peugeot cars and *Playboy* magazine,[43] was enough to make him or her feel dazzled.

Aksenov's descriptions of a colourful Los Angeles crowd contain what seems to be an unnecessarily high concentration of 'Americanisms'. These appear as either straightforward transliterations or calques: *kar* (car), *er-kondishn* (air conditioner), *khaivei-patrol'* (highway patrol), *sneks* (snacks), *goriachie sobaki* (hot dogs) and so on. It is clear that Aksenov is fascinated by the English language, which he obviously has only recently started to discover for himself (his examples of things American include the mistakenly inverted *diler-uillery* for 'wheeler dealers').[44] There is more to it, however, than just an expansion of the writer's vocabulary. Aksenov is evidently trying to find a common language with the Americans (as if literally following Evtushenko's suggestion made in 'Amerikanskii solovei').[45] It is curious that many of Aksenov's 'Americanisms' are left untranslated and unexplained. The readers are obviously expected either to have some English already or to make an extra effort and pick it up in the process of digesting Aksenov's story; if, that is, they don't simply dismiss the story out of hand. Undoubtedly, this is a test to identify prospective Soviet Westernizers and to rally them behind Aksenov's agenda (in 'Kruglye sutki', he states unambiguously that the 'Western direction is the main one').[46] By contrast, one of Kochetov's characters, Aleksandr Maksimovich Zarodov, is ridiculed by the author when he claims proudly that English has become 'a second state language' in his family and names one room in his large flat a 'sitting room', after the English fashion. '"*Gostinaia* [a guest room], a Russian would say," remarked one of the relatives. [...] "The English don't have such a notion," replied Aleksandr Maksimovich, "They don't invite guests round too often"'.[47] Zarodov's acquisition of a foreign language goes hand in hand with his adoption of alien customs. For Kochetov, needless to say, the idea of a sitting room, as described by Zarodov, is entirely out of keeping with Russia's highly valued communal atmosphere.

It is unsurprising that Aksenov's attempts to go native in the USA, no doubt assisted by the consumption of marijuana,[48] bring him to the conclusion that Americans (American intellectuals, to be precise, because the author hardly had a chance to meet anyone else) are in fact very similar to Russians (or rather Russian intellectuals).[49] They both enjoy long heated discussions, dislike wars, totalitarianism and stool-pigeons, and try to be helpful if you are in trouble. As a way of emphasizing the latter, Moskvich's 'Typical American Adventure' begins when he reads a thank-you note written by a woman who fell down in a LA street and was helped to her feet by a stranger, and ends when Moskvich asks to place a similar note, on his own behalf, all over LA and elsewhere. Predictably, Aksenov comes to the conclusion that 'there is no alternative to Soviet–American mutual respect'.[50] Cleverly mixing 'exotic' attractions (such as brief references to Krishna worshippers and gay parades) with something that looks enticingly familiar, Aksenov reminds the reader that Alaska used to belong to Russia and describes his encounters with Russian émigrés in California. He is careful to mention, however, that although LA feels 'almost like home [*osnovatel'no osvoilsia*], and is nice, soon it'll be time to go where the real home is, and that's extra special nice'.[51] He does not forget to bring up the fact that at his lectures at UCLA he addressed his students as 'comrades', and generally does not flinch from the occasional use of Marxist terminology, such as 'dialectical contradictions' and 'unity of opposites'.[52] In a sense, Aksenov, as he comes across in this travelogue, is little more than a moderate (better educated and more talented) version of Kochetov. They share, for example, a strong dislike for modern-day Slavophiles: in *Chego zhe ty khochesh'?*, Kochetov satirizes the so-called 'village prose' movement, which became something of a Soviet heir to Slavophilism, and in 'Kruglye sutki' Aksenov wages hidden polemics with 'village prose' writers – who were largely language purists – by defending his right to use words borrowed from foreign languages.[53] In the Soviet propaganda arsenal, Kochetov's blunt and uncompromising attacks became the weapon of choice after the 1968 invasion of Czechoslovakia (characteristically, in 'Kruglye sutki', Aksenov says that he has not been in the West since 1967), but in a milder political climate Aksenov's superior art gets a second chance. Paradoxically, Aksenov can occasionally be even more uncompromising than Kochetov. Thus, the sacramental question in the title of Kochetov's book is addressed to a dissolute Soviet youth, who has strayed away from the righteous path of his communist forefathers, by no other than Signor Caradonna, a Russian émigré who fought on the German side in the Second World War and who has had to live under an assumed name for the rest of his life as a consequence. This ex-Nazi collaborator, who has learned the error of his ways, warns the youth that the 'arrival of Western "democracy", with which Western propagandists lure young Russians, means not so much shop-windows full of consumer goods, as the [...] destruction of Russia, first and foremost'.[54] Signor Caradonna asks the youth if he really wants 'the Soviet people to be turned into dust to fertilize European and American fields', and finishes off by saying that there is no alternative: 'either [you'll get] what I've just told you about, or you should do what your people would like you to [that is, return to the communist fold]'.[55] After such an impressive lecture, it is small wonder that the *Literaturnaia Gazeta* reviewer could not get over the fact that in Kochetov's novel 'an old enemy of our country, [...] on the author's whim, becomes a kind of symbol of genuine patriotism, and, to a certain degree, a mentor to the Soviet youth!'[56] Unlike Kochetov, Aksenov is much more unforgiving in his attitude to ex-Nazi collaborators from Russia. When referring to the collaborators who have found refuge in the USA, Aksenov unequivocally states that they 'will hardly succeed in washing themselves clean with American washing powder. Dirt will always remain visible, no matter what disguise such individuals would assume. Any democratic song will sound out of tune if it is performed by a person who at least once sang hosanna to Hitler'.[57]

What also sets Aksenov apart, not only from Kochetov but from everyone else in this survey, is that, wary of the limitations of his first-hand knowledge of the USA, he honestly strives to separate fact from fiction (despite experimenting with the non-fictional genre of travel memoir by introducing phantasmagoric components into it).[58] Perhaps it would not be an exaggeration to suggest that, in general, non-fiction offers its authors less scope for disinformation than fiction, by depriving them of the excuse of poetic licence. In the light of this statement, it would be interesting to examine Vsevolod Ovchinnikov's *Korni duba* (*Oak Roots*, 1980), a purely journalistic account of Britain in the mid- to late 1970s.[59] A sinologist by training, Ovchinnikov worked as a *Pravda* correspondent in the UK from 1974 to

1978, and the book became a research-based medium for his British impressions. From the outset, he advocates an impartial approach, insisting that *Korni duba* is not a regurgitation of preconceived ideas but a careful study of the British 'grammar of life':[60] that is, British perceptions, customs, norms, attitudes and how they influence contemporary socio-political issues. Such impartiality was not easy to maintain, given the fact that the book was published shortly after the Soviet invasion of Afghanistan in 1979. It would be naive to expect too many compliments from Ovchinnikov, who does not fail to mention the British class system, anglocentrism and the overwhelming power of bureaucracy, calling the British educational system a 'gentlemen factory' and the House of Lords an obstacle to social progress.[61] Neither does he forget to mention the homeless, the slums of Glasgow and the Irish question, as well as Scotland Yard's Special Branch keeping tabs on radically minded Britons. On the other hand, these topics were impossible to ignore in any serious analysis of British life at the time (with many of them remaining relevant even now) and quite a few British people would undoubtedly sympathize with Ovchinnikov's critical approach. In addition, he offers a number of insightful (although sometimes slightly idealized) comments on a variety of issues. These include the subtleties of British small talk, the law-abiding nature of British people, their fondness for privacy bordering on loneliness, and even their preference for pets over children.[62] Every chapter is accompanied by an impressive choice of quotations from other writings on Britain – English, French, German, American and Russian (including, unavoidably, Marx, Engels and Lenin) – published over the past two hundred years, which allows the author not only to contextualize British traditions but also to introduce a wide variety of opinions, thereby helping the reader to make up his or her own mind. Notwithstanding this feature, highly irregular in the times of communist censorship and propaganda, the value of *Korni duba* was recognized when, together with two other books by Ovchinnikov, one on Japan and another on the secret story of the atomic bomb, it received USSR's State Prize in 1985. The exact nature of *Korni duba*'s contribution to the Cold War is open to speculation, but its fairly reliable factual basis would leave little to be desired in any time or place.

To sum up, my random but demonstrative samples illustrate that it is virtually impossible to map out a definitive canon that can incorporate the most important features of the Russian Cold War representation of the West. If there was an attempt to create such a canon in the last years of Stalin's rule (comprising, for example, Shpanov's novels obsessed with conspiracy theories), it proved to be unsustainable in the atmosphere of the thaw. Neo-Stalinist attempts to turn the clock back – epitomized by Kochetov, who broadly followed the recipes of the late 1940s and early 1950s and who tried to re-invent a hierarchy of Western countries in accordance with their 'viciousness' (with the USA being the worst and Italy being the friendliest) – fell victim to détente, which promoted a somewhat more inclusive view of foreign nations (such as the one put across in Aksenov's piece). However, both (cautiously) pro- and (dogmatically) anti-Western books, with few exceptions, appear to be either insufficiently researched or simply ill-informed, and tend to tell the reader more about the USSR/Russia's hidden inferiority complex than about everyday life in the West. This complex owes a great deal to a time-honoured tradition stemming from the Westernizers versus Slavophiles controversy,[63] which has repeatedly made Russians vacillate between, on the one hand, an admiration for the West's (comparative) prosperity and efficiency, and on the other a belief in Russia's (alleged) spiritual superiority. Depending on political contingency, it has been relatively easy for Russians (both on the national and on the individual level) to shift from one perspective to another and back again, because the viewpoints are essentially two sides of the same coin.

To play devil's advocate, it is tempting to suggest that the Marxist class approach allowed for a more discerning treatment of the West, because it helped to prevent Russians from xenophobically rejecting other cultures wholesale, whether on the grounds of Orthodox Christianity versus Catholicism and Protestantism, or of Atlanticism versus Eurasianism. From the Marxist point of view, Russia could comfortably fraternize with other nations on the basis of class solidarity. In time, however, such an approach only further added to the confusing continuum of Russian prejudices, because many aspects of Western life became either embraced or dismissed owing not to what was fundamentally right or wrong with the West itself, but to what Russians thought was right or wrong with the Soviet Union. As a result, even a qualified acceptance of so-called Western democratic values, self-professed by a number of Soviet dissidents, would often emerge less from empirical experience than from a rejection of the USSR's ongoing anti-capitalist campaign.[64] In these circumstances, for the curious but disoriented Soviet reader, who did not know who to believe but wanted to find out as much as possible about the controversial West from any sources available, the reasonably sound factual base of Kraminov's and, especially, Ovchinnikov's works would ultimately outweigh in impact and significance the sparkling superficiality of Evtushenko and Aksenov. From this point of view, it appears that, during the Cold War, the best Russian books about the West were arguably written not by those well-disposed but by those well-informed.

Notes

1. I would like to thank Ms Eva Montenegro-Oddo and Dr John Dunn for their invaluable assistance with this project. All translations are mine, unless indicated otherwise.
2. On the Westernizers see, for instance, A.D. Sukhov, *Stoletniaia diskussiia: Zapadnichestvo i samobytnost' v russkoi filisofii* (1998). On the Eurasianists see, for instance, M.G. Vandalkovskaia, *Istoricheskaia nauka rossiiskoi emigratsii: 'Evraziiskii soblazn'* (1997).
3. See Aleksandr Dugin, *Misterii Evrazii* (1996).
4. For more on this topic see A. Dugin, *Osnovy geopolitiki* (1997).

5 On the Slavophiles see, for example, N.I. Tsimbaev, *Slavianofil'stvo: Iz istorii russkoi obshchestvenno-politicheskoi mysli XIX veka* (1986).
6 On Shpanov see the unsigned obituary, 'N.N. Shpanov', *Literaturnaia Gazeta*, 5 October 1961, p. 4; and Kir Bulychev, *Kak stat' fantastom* (Moscow: Drofa, 2003), pp. 87–91.
7 Dymshits, 'Protiv podzhigatelei voiny', *Zvezda*, 9 (1950), p. 181.
8 Shpanov, *Podzhigateli* (Moscow: Molodaia gvardiia, 1950), pp. 315–17.
9 Ibid., p. 894; see also pp. 301, 517, 845 and 847.
10 Ibid., pp. 130–1, 154–5.
11 See ibid., p. 808.
12 See ibid., pp. 165–6.
13 Valentin Kiparsky, *English and American Characters in Russian Fiction* (Berlin: Otto Harrassowitz, 1964), p. 71. For positive heroes in the novel, several prototypes have also been used. The singer Gunther Sinn, for example, has been modelled on Ernst Busch (1900–80); the International Brigade's chief of staff, Ludwig Enkel, on the writer and scholar Ludwig Renn (1889–1979); and General Matrai on the Hungarian writer and politician Mate Zalka (Bela Frankl, 1896–1937).
14 See Shpanov, *Podzhigateli*, pp. 275–7.
15 See ibid., pp. 455, 462–3, 473, 476, 478.
16 Shpanov began his career as a sci-fi author.
17 If a cliché exists then Shpanov would use it, as the following random list of ethnic stereotypes demonstrates: 'Otto saluted and walked away in that special wooden manner which, of all people, is typical of German officers alone' (ibid., p. 122); 'Oh those French women! Otto has never met someone so flippant and so temperamental before' (pp. 157–8); and 'The English should not be imitating anything that comes from the continent. We have our own ways, our own life. The English, my dear, will never be able to feel patriotic about Europe' (p. 319).
18 See, for instance, S. Voitinskii, 'Bez znaniia dela', *Komsomol'skaia Pravda*, 3 October 1957, p. 4; and A. Elkin, 'Kuda idet pisatel' N. Shpanov?', *Komsomol'skaia Pravda*, 21 March 1959, p. 2.
19 For details see Robert Skidelsky, *Oswald Mosley* (London: Macmillan, 1990), pp. 491, 512–14.
20 Kraminov, *Pasynki Al'biona* (Moscow: Molodaia gvardiia, 1962), p. 186.
21 G. Zaostrovtsev, 'Synov'ia i pasynki', *Literaturnaia Zhizn'*, 18 July 1962, p. 3.
22 Ibid., p. 3.
23 See Kraminov, *Pasynki Al'biona*, pp. 189–90.
24 See, for instance, an account of his stance with regard to the Galanskov–Ginsburg affair in Raymond H. Anderson, 'Soviet Reply to Trial Critics', *The Times*, 4 March 1968, p. 8.
25 Evtushenko, 'Uriia Gip', in Evtushenko, *Vzmakh ruki* (Moscow: Molodaia gvardiia, 1962), p. 36, line 4.
26 See ibid., p. 35, lines 1–6; p. 36, lines 3–8, 12–14; p. 37, lines 5–6.
27 See Evtushenko, 'Amerikanskii solovei', in Evtushenko, *Vzmakh ruki*, p. 38, lines 7–8, 13, 23–6; p. 39, lines 1–2, 13–14, 17–18.
28 For more on Kochetov see John Glad, 'Vsevolod Kochetov: An Overview', *Russian Language Journal*, 32: 113 (1978), pp. 95–102. For Kochetov-related epigrams see E. Etkind, ed., *323 epigrammy* (Paris: Sintaksis, 1988), pp. 115–16.
29 Kochetov, *Chego zhe ty khochesh'?* (Minsk: Belarus', 1970), p. 181.
30 Ibid., pp. 31, 46.
31 See ibid., p. 257.
32 Ibid., pp. 373–4.
33 Shtemler, *Zvonok v pustuiu kvartiru* (St Petersburg: Russko-baltiiskii informatsionnyi tsentr BLITs, 1998), p. 191.

34 See Zh. A. Medvedev and R.A. Medvedev, *Kto sumasshedshii?* (London: Macmillan, 1971), pp. 158–9.
35 See Strada, 'Introduzione' to Kočetov, *Ma, insomma, che cosa vuoi?*, trans. Massimo Picchianti and Chiara Spano (Roma: La nuova sinistra, 1970), pp. 16, 21.
36 Incidentally, *bulat* is Russian for 'Damascene steel' and therefore becomes reminiscent of Stalin's surname, which is also derived from a Russian word for 'steel'.
37 Portia Brown is a thinly veiled image of the journalist and editor Patricia Blake. For Blake's interview with Kochetov, which ended by the author putting his hand on her shoulder as a farewell gesture, see Patritsiia Bleik, 'Vstrechi s sovetskimi pisateliami', *Nashi Dni*, 33 (1964), pp. 116–20. In *Chego zhe ty khochesh'?*, Kochetov, who apparently read this émigré publication, transforms this scene into Portia Brown's false claim that the brute Bulatov allegedly slapped her on the backside during the interview. At his next meeting with Portia, Bulatov does slap her for real, in retribution. Portia is said to have German, American and Russian blood in her veins, which, for such a champion of eugenics as Kochetov, is the worst imaginable scenario.
38 Iu. Andreev, 'O romane Vsevoloda Kochetova *Chego zhe ty khochesh'?*', *Literaturnaia Gazeta*, 7 (1970), p. 4.
39 Glad, 'Vsevolod Kochetov', p. 97.
40 D. Barton Johnson, 'Aksenov as Travel Writer:'*Round the Clock, Non-Stop*', in Edward Możejko, ed., *Vasiliy Pavlovich Aksenov: A Writer in Quest of Himself* (Columbus, OH: Slavica, 1984), p. 184.
41 This experience has been reflected upon in Aksenov, *V poiskakh grustnogo bebi: Kniga ob Amerike* (1987).
42 Aksenov, 'Kruglye sutki non-stop', *Novyi Mir*, 8 (1976), p. 57.
43 See ibid., p. 105.
44 Ibid., p. 57.
45 Evtushenko's poetry is quoted in the travelogue as something emblematic of the late 1950s (ibid., p. 70).
46 Ibid., p. 105.
47 Kochetov, *Chego zhe ty khochesh'?*, pp. 235–6.
48 For a full confession to this effect, accompanied by a description of the smoking ritual, see Aksenov, 'Kruglye sutki non-stop', p. 90.
49 Of American authors of his generation, Aksenov even says: 'at our meetings, we looked each other in the eye in a special way, as if trying to discover whether we, by any chance, had been growing together when we were children' (ibid., p. 117).
50 Ibid., p. 122.
51 Ibid., p. 107.
52 Ibid., pp. 73, 70, 88.
53 See the comic figure of the author Savva Mironovich Bogoroditskii in Kochetov's novel, as well as Aksenov, 'Kruglye sutki non-stop', p. 71. For more on the village prose phenomenon see, for instance, Kathleen Parthé, *Russian Village Prose: The Radiant Past* (1992).
54 Kochetov, *Chego zhe ty khochesh'?*, p. 468.
55 Ibid., p. 468.
56 Andreev, 'O romane Vsevoloda Kochetova *Chego zhe ty khochesh'?*', p. 4.
57 Aksenov, 'Kruglye sutki non-stop', p. 112.
58 A justification for this might be found in the following comment: 'America consists of both the real and the mythic, and no absolute line can be drawn between them' (Barton Johnson, 'Aksenov as Travel Writer', p. 190).
59 For an English translation by Michael Basker see Ovchinnikov, *Britain Observed: A Russian's View* (1981).

60 Ovchinnikov, *Korni duba: Vpechatleniia i razmyshleniia ob Anglii i anglichanakh* (Moscow: Mysl', 1980), p. 14.
61 Ibid., p. 110; see also p. 114.
62 See ibid., pp. 45, 59, 71, 76–7, 83, 98, 127, 132, 144, 174, 190, 211–13, 220, 239.
63 See L.I. Blekher and G. Iu. Liubarskii, *Glavnyi russkii spor: Ot zapadnikov i slavianofilov do globalizma i novogo srednevekov'ia* (2003).
64 Paradoxically, when some of these dissidents went into exile and saw for themselves what life beyond the Iron Curtain was like, they began publishing their own critique of the West that was not altogether different from the Soviet counter-propaganda. For a powerful example, see Eduard Limonov's *Eto ia, Edichka* (*It's Me, Eddie*, 1979) and its Soviet reception, outlined in L. Pochivalov, 'Chelovek na dne: Pokinuvshii rodinu – o sebe', *Literaturnaia Gazeta*, 10 September 1980, p. 14. It is not always possible to establish with any degree of certainty whether such people independently verified the credibility of the USSR's anti-Western allegations, or were in fact the KGB's agents of influence.

3 'Is it chaos? Or is it a building site?'
British theatrical responses to the Cold War and its aftermath

Chris Megson

A striking feature of recent Cold War historiography is its insistence on mobilizing terms of reference that derive precisely from the nuts and bolts of theatrical performance. Cold War analysts, working in a spectrum of disciplines ranging from political and diplomatic history to international relations, have conscripted the terminology of theatre to help apprehend the structure, longevity and underlying dynamics of the evolving global conflict. A fairly random overview of recently published studies clarifies this point. John Elsom, for example, contends that the end of the Cold War was marked by a pronounced 'theatricality of [. . .] events'.[1] Douglas Macdonald comments that the conflict was played out in a discrete 'theater of operations' populated, according to Richard Ned Lebow, by erstwhile 'actors'.[2] Noam Chomsky argues that the protagonists of the Cold War often donned 'guise[s]' in order to engage in what John Lewis Gaddis calls 'rhetorical dramatization'.[3] Sean Greenwood refers to the conflict as a diplomatic 'game', while Tony Shaw comments that it might best be understood as a mediatized battle projected in part through 'words and images'.[4]

This widespread acknowledgement of the performative underpinnings of superpower politics is not, of course, unusual but none the less seems to have acquired a particular momentum in retrospective evaluations of the Cold War. This in itself goes some way to explaining the central role that should be accorded to theatrical production in any investigation of cultural activity during this period.[5] For, as this chapter aims to demonstrate, theatre has been uniquely placed to breach the mythologizing rhetoric of the conflict so as to elaborate the underlying and frequently devastating political realities either side of – to coin that most resonantly theatrical motif of geo-political division – the Iron Curtain.

Disillusionment and desire

One of the characteristics of left-wing British drama in the post-1945 period is its articulation of a profound disillusionment with ostensibly socialist parties and state systems – particularly in respect of the former Soviet Union – while at the same time remaining doggedly committed to the desirability of a socialist alternative to the iniquities of Western capitalism. It is a perspective that finds consummate expression in Arnold Wesker's landmark *Chicken Soup with Barley* (1958): 'If the electrician who comes to mend my fuse blows it instead,' argues the indomitable Sarah Kahn at the time of the Soviet invasion of Hungary, 'so I should stop having electricity?'[6] It is, however, the generation of radical playwrights who emerged from the revolutionary events of 1968 – including Howard Brenton, David Hare, David Edgar, John McGrath and Trevor Griffiths – which has responded most insistently, albeit in markedly different ways, to the ideological and political vicissitudes of the late Cold War period. In general terms, this playwriting marks a broad transition from advocating the possibility of revolutionary change in the late 1960s and early 1970s to a more interrogative, at times despairing, approach to socialist ideology and political practice in the ensuing decades.

The growing scepticism about the prospects for revolutionary socialism in Britain can, of course, be contextualized historically in relation to changes in the wider political culture. These changes would include the intensifying disillusionment on the Left with parliamentary politics and British institutions, especially the Labour Party, during the bitter industrial strife of the early 1970s; the inexorable ascendancy of the 'New Right' and Thatcherism in the 1980s; and, finally, the collapse of 'actually existing' state socialism from 1989. It is this historical framework that helps account for the specific theatrical trajectories of those individual playwrights who have attempted to promulgate alternative and oppositional political perspectives in their work. In the mid-1970s, for instance, Edgar rejected the cartoon stereotypes of his early socialist 'agit-prop' plays in favour of social realism, a form that made possible a more complex engagement with individual psychology at a time of retrenchment for the British Left (as evidenced in *Destiny* (1976) and *Maydays* (1983)).[7] Howard Barker gravitated away from the scabrous and satirical style of his early 'State of England' dramas (*Claw* (1975),[8] *The Hang of the Gaol* (1978)) in order to focus, despairingly, on the Labour Party's retreat from socialism (*The Loud Boy's Life* (1980), *A Passion in Six Days* (1983) and *Downchild* (1985)). It is, however, Barker's searing meditations on history, and his eventual outright rejection of ideology, that underpin his uncompromising 'Theatre of Catastrophe': a reformulation of tragedy, developed in the 1980s, which accords a special status to the desiring subject.[9] The ascendancy of Thatcherism was marked by a resurgence of satire, best expressed in the coruscating critiques by Caryl Churchill (*Serious Money*, 1985)[10] and Steven Berkoff (*Sink the Belgrano!*, 1986). In contrast, Brenton's writing in this period endeavoured to set out the contours and complexion of a socialist utopia (*Bloody Poetry* (1984), *Greenland* (1988)).[11]

Given the enormous range of possible case studies, this chapter focuses specifically on the negotiation of late Cold War politics in three plays produced in Britain in the closing stages or aftermath of the conflict: Barker's *The Power of the Dog* (1984), Edgar's *Pentecost* (1994) and Churchill's *Far*

Away (2000).[12] The aim is to explore one of the strategic ways in which the plays have refuted the much-documented binarist logic of Cold War politics: that is, through their evocation of 'marginal', especially Eastern European, spaces. In order to proceed, the early part of the discussion briefly sets out some of the criticisms that have been levelled at so-called Realist interpretations of the Cold War. Realist analyses have promoted a sense of the conflict as a bipolar contest driven by the geo-political interests of respective power blocs. It is a premise of this chapter that the new emphases brought to bear in historical studies of the Cold War throughout the 1990s, emphases that largely challenge the viability of Realist perspectives, find a theatrical accommodation in these examples of playwriting. The theatrical landscapes of these plays are 'deterritorialized', transitory and uncertain; on the margins of the 'bipolar' conflict, they are established as peripheral but liminal zones wherein the grip of Cold War ideology is potentially unsettled. One of the distinctive qualities of live theatrical performance is its capacity to *spatialize* its metaphors; on this basis, I will consider how these plays negotiate theatrical worlds that illuminate the 'human cost of power politics' as well as the possibilities and horrors that have attended the emergence of the new Europe since 1989.[13]

Beyond Realism

The most astute analyses of the Cold War in the past few decades have derived from developments in international relations theory. Many of these interventions have been concerned to map the trajectory from so-called orthodox to revisionist, or indeed post-revisionist, interpretations of the Cold War and, in particular, to challenge the critical endeavour to isolate its presumed 'origins'. Lebow usefully summarizes the four dominant and sometimes interchangeable 'generic explanations' for the Cold War: the Realist position, which conceives of the conflict as a competitive 'power struggle' between nation states that intensified because of the 'bipolar structure of the post-war world'; the 'ideas' explanation, which contends that the Cold War was primarily an ideological conflagration emanating from the Bolshevik Revolution; the 'domestic politics' explanation, which interprets the Cold War in terms of leaders' aspirations to extend their control of domestic agendas; and, finally, the 'leaders' explanation which ascribes key significance to the actions and personalities of individual politicians.[14] He concludes that this unremitting search for causality has tended to efface the importance of process and interdependency in the vast transnational ecosystem of the Cold War.

In a similar vein, Gaddis argues that the fall of communism has opened up an opportunity for a wholesale rethinking of the familiar methodologies that have tended to hold together Cold War histories.[15] Specifically, his concern is that historians and theorists need to develop diachronic explanations that can properly account for the evolving ecology of the Cold War, its changing structures and processes across space and time. In this respect, it is arguably the Realist position that has come under the most intensive scrutiny since the fall of the Berlin Wall. Realist understandings of the Cold War gathered momentum in the 1940s, predicated on the forceful injunction set out in the Truman doctrine, the founding shibboleth of bipolarity: 'At the present moment in world history nearly every nation must choose between alternative ways of life.'[16] Classic Realism is indelibly identified with Hans J. Morgenthau's resounding dictum that 'All states pursue their national interest defined in terms of power'.[17] Robin Brown, in his insightful reflections on Realism, notes the signal importance of Kenneth Waltz's book *Theory of International Politics* (1979), which rose to prominence as one of the cornerstones of a resurgent neo-Realism in the 1980s; for Waltz, Brown argues, 'the crucial factor in the international system is the distribution of power which is determined by the number of poles or great power states existing at any one time'.[18] In this regard, Realism provides one way of accounting for the perceived stability and longevity of the Cold War, as well as for the systemic polarisation of nation states during this period.

From the vantage point of Realism, the Cold War thus appears as a symmetrical bipolar organisation of global power that produced a period of stability, what Gaddis notoriously glossed, in 1986, as 'the long peace'.[19] '"The Long Peace"', in the words of Yale Ferguson and Rey Koslowski, became 'indicative of an institutionalization of the practices of Cold War bipolarity and thereby itself became part of the edifice of Cold War culture'.[20] Realist studies of the Cold War tend to draw attention to the commonalities in structure and strategy of the two superpowers which underlie their repeated rhetorical iteration of the ideological differences that divide them. Realism, therefore, reifies bipolarity, structural continuity and the importance of nation-states in a much-documented 'hegemonic stability thesis' that is held to have guaranteed a level of global security in the ascendant nuclear age.[21]

However, Realist theoretical paradigms have been challenged from a range of critical positions over the past two decades. Drawing variously on the insights of poststructuralism and postcolonialism, these writings have embarked on, in the words of Greenwood, a 'depolarization of Cold War history', reframing the conflict in ways that expose its scale, impact and interconnectedness.[22] Richard Crockatt, for instance, argues that the Realist 'definition of structure excludes consideration of interaction', what Odd Arne Westad describes as 'the social and cultural context within which a state acts'.[23] David Reynolds argues that the Cold War was constituted not by monolithic blocs of power suspended in structural symmetry but rather by manifold polarities, zones of marginality, that exerted myriad influences and pressures at the regional or local level.[24] Indeed, Walter LaFeber has questioned the very idea of a singular and monolithic 'Cold War', arguing that no fewer than four 'Cold Wars' were overlapping simultaneously.[25]

A related challenge to Realism has focused on what might be called geo-political tectonics and, in particular, on the decline of the nation-state. Gaddis suggests that the Cold War will be remembered 'not so much as a clash among superpowers, but as the point at which the long ascendancy of the state reached its peak and began to wane'.[26] Martin Walker, too, contends that the 'real significance' of the Cold War was 'to play the role of the catalyst in the creation of the extraordinary global economy which will dominate our future'.[27] The Realist model of a balance of power predicated on the autonomy of the nation-state has since been invalidated by 'new actors and new issues' that have, according to Brown, been unleashed in the era of post-Cold-War globalization.[28] These new 'actors' include 'terrorists, multinational corporations, intelligence agencies and drug dealers' that operate across borders and on a global scale; the ascendant 'new issues' are 'pollution, overpopulation, nuclear proliferation, resource depletion and poverty'.[29] Focusing on the late Cold War period, his important contention is that orthodox Realism cannot properly accommodate the decline in the nation-state of which these deleterious 'issues' are symptomatic.

This widespread project in international relations theory to apprehend the significance of 'interaction' and interdependency under the radar of bipolar hegemony finds, I argue, a striking theatrical corollary in the plays foregrounded in this chapter. Each of them, in discrete ways, galvanizes the elements of theatrical performance to excoriate the underlying dynamics of the conflict. In dismembering orthodox narrative structures, in focusing on the desperate attempts of individuals to escape the overweening carapace of Cold War ideology and in presenting stage worlds that are hauntingly peripheral and 'deterritorialized', these interventions up-end the demarcated bipolarities of Realist discourse. In so doing, they enact a sceptical and questioning theatrical 'depolarisation' of the conflict that elaborates a more complex and ambivalent view of Cold War political realities.

The Power of the Dog

> 'The cold war' is tricky because it is both metaphor and not metaphor. Its meaning hovers uncertainly between war and war-like. Absolute hostility, the antithesis of peace, is coupled with the absence of real war. 'Interaction' freezes, or is reduced to ideological and political monologues, the polarity marked by immobility and frigidity. [. . .] Real war, meanwhile, is displaced beyond the militarized heartlands onto the 'periphery', articulated in regional and local conflict which often had little to do with the polarity as such. Thus the cold war appears in spaces of a third kind as militarization and death, as crushing effects [. . .].[30]

For Anders Stephanson, the major impact of the Cold War was experienced at the margins, in peripheral locales strategically distanced from the 'ideological and political' posturing played out at the respective poles of the conflict. His comments provide a useful starting point for understanding Barker's theatrical strategy in *The Power of the Dog*, a play first produced in 1984 at the time of the 'neo-Realist' ascendancy.[31] The mission of the play, according to one critic, is to 'present a slice of modern European history and to anatomise various modes of historical record and presentation'.[32] It is a work of scatological and imaginative historical speculation that wilfully eschews the imperatives of documentary realism. Barker has noted that 'what makes my historical plays genuinely historical, as opposed to being picaresque in any way, is that they refer to a sort of unspoken historical perspective, which is a kind of popular mythology'.[33] For Barker, the devastating events of the Second World War, and the brutal cauterisation of Europe in its aftermath, constitutes a 'secret history' that has been subsumed in Cold War mythology.[34] The play is set in the closing stages of the Second World War, as the Russians march into Europe; subtitled 'Moments in History and Anti-History', it consists of eleven jagged scenes that shuttle back and forth from the splendour of the Kremlin to a devastated hinterland 'somewhere in the Polish Plain' (9).

The opening scene unfolds as a bizarre re-enactment of the infamous 'percentages agreement' brokered by Churchill and Stalin in Moscow, October 1944.[35] McGroot, a caustic Scottish comedian and juggler, has been summoned to perform in the Banqueting Hall of the Kremlin as a paranoid Stalin and increasingly drunken Churchill carve up Eastern Europe on the back of an envelope. The scene gains its theatrical potency not only from McGroot's cod-philosophical asides ('History! A will tell ye wha' history is, it's a woman bein' raped by ten soldiers in a village in Manchuria ...' (4)) but also from the largely unsuccessful struggle of two translators to accurately interpret the portentous exchanges of the statesmen:

STALIN: It is a sad fact that I cannot meet a woman on a train unless both the woman and the train are commandeered for me. But of course that entirely removes the significance of the occasion. Accident, which is the essence of experience, has been eliminated from my life ...
ENGLISH INTERPRETER: He says, such opportunities don't ... come his way that often ...
STALIN: Has Churchill ever met a beautiful woman on a train?
ENGLISH INTERPRETER: He asks – the connotations are humorous – if you, Churchill, have encountered a lady in a railway compartment –
CHURCHILL: I have met my wife.
SOVIET INTERPRETER: He says he has met Mrs Churchill –
(*MOLOTOV bursts out laughing*)
CHURCHILL: What is so amusing about my wife? (5)

Following these botched and infelicitous exchanges, the two leaders quickly proceed to haggle over the spoils of victory. With manic impropriety, Churchill and Stalin engage in a frenzied land-grab, redrawing the cartography of a new Europe that is to be clinically bifurcated along an East/West axis. It is a scene that, according to one reviewer, neatly encapsulates the 'obscenity of authoritarianism'.[36] The politicians are intoxicated with drink or their own iconicity ('Good night, you foul genius ... Good night ...', is Churchill's telling parting shot to Stalin (8)); they speak a loquacious, inflated prose that confounds the attempts of translators to make sense of it, and they cherry-pick the nation-states of Europe with a blithe insouciance.

Scenes in the Kremlin are juxtaposed with a series of fraught episodes set in the wastelands of Poland. The sweep of the Polish plain functions as a metonym for a devastated Europe, and specifically for one of those liminal zones that, as Stephanson put it, mark the geopolitical 'periphery' of the Cold War. The landscape is punctuated by mass graves, hanging bodies and wandering diaspora, the residual flotsam of unspeakable catastrophe. Here, the aftershocks of war are experienced as raw and visceral: a former Hungarian fashion model bargains to retrieve the dead body of a woman she presumes to be her missing sister; a Russian infantrywoman slides into apoplexy as she attempts, unsuccessfully, to film in an unmediated way the unending horrors of war, and another finds her commitment to Party discipline eroded by her overwhelming sexual desire for a Russian soldier. Elsewhere, an officer castrates himself in inconsolable despair and a group of Soviet troops engage in pseudo-mystic ritual incantations in an attempt to loosen the tentacular grip of Party dogma. Meanwhile, back in his Moscow citadel, Stalin ruminates quixotically on the devastation of Europe:

> [...] Is it chaos? Or is it a building site? A building site, to the uninitiated, is the essence of chaos, but to the foreman, merely the first stage of the plan. I am the foreman, and Lenin made the plans. Of course, if you are sitting in a puddle with raw, bloody feet, it is hard to appreciate the beauty of the structure. (28)

The double-edged response from Zdhanov, the Soviet intellectual who is party to this meditation, unlocks the primary trope of Barker's play: 'No one misses History. Whether he sees its purpose or not' (28).

Tony Dunn notes that the structure of *The Power of the Dog* 'links the heights with the depths of the power structure' by focusing 'on the "middle strata", the men and women who have to do history's dirty work'.[37] Yet, in spite of his unremitting focus on the destabilizing effects of war, a latticework of desire infuses Barker's dramatic writing, one that propels his protagonists towards a self-expression that has the potential to rupture the prescriptive straitjacket of ideology. In a memorable scene, Arkov, a Russian officer, encounters Gloria, a former SS apparatchik who has been flushed from her hiding place after the German retreat. Attempting a gesture of unprovoked compassion, he urges her to remove her uniform to avoid being shot on sight by the Russian military. As he presses towards her, Gloria takes off her clothes resignedly, assuming that he is intent on rape. It is at

'Is it chaos? Or is it a building site?' 53

this point that Arkov, in a frenzy of utter desperation, shoots off his penis. The scene concludes with his forlorn plea to her: 'Trust now ... trust ...' (25). In a moment of parallel intensity towards the end of the play, Sorge, a Russian officer, tentatively expresses his longing for Ilona, the Hungarian refugee: 'When I set eyes on you ... the mud splashed on your calves and your crushed shoes I felt – how pure she is ... through all this clamour she walks untouched ...' (39). In Barker's world, desire is the antithesis of stultifying ideology; it is the volatile agency that makes the transformation of self and others possible.

Barker locates his profound and radical disillusionment with political ideology in the context of Cold War stagnation but, none the less, *The Power of the Dog* gives rich expression to the redemptive power of individual desire. For Barker, the play gestures towards 'the capacity of individuals for alternative experience and private history, which both dives under and is swamped by collective politics'.[38] In this respect, the frenzied and atomized interactions that are staged in the maelstrom of the Polish plain offer a reverse perspective on the global mayhem triggered, with monstrous whimsy, in the Kremlin. Cumulatively, the effect is to turn the Realist shibboleth of 'hegemonic stability' on its head: for Barker, chaos, not stability, is both the premise and precondition for an emergent bipolar world that is incubated on the back of an envelope.

Pentecost

> Communism was a sort of Esperanto, trying to create a perfect language without any of the difficulties or problems existing in language.[39]

Edgar's response to the end of the Cold War was to write a triptych of plays that examine the emergence of nationalism in the former satellite Soviet republics; collectively, they dramatize the transition, as it were, from 'post-Communism [to] coca-colonialism'.[40] Each of the plays takes place in a fictionalized country situated precariously on the boundary between East and West. This enables Edgar to transcend the imperatives of theatrical documentary in order to probe the complex processes of identity formation in formerly 'peripheral' territories emerging from the shadow of the Cold War. *The Shape of the Table* (1990) takes place in a baroque palace in an unspecified Eastern European state. In the play, politicians and activists debate the revolutionary changes affecting their country while the talismanic diplomatic table – around which much of the action coheres – becomes a motif for the possible territorial configurations that may transpire. *The Prisoner's Dilemma* (2001) focuses on the fictional ex-Soviet republic of Khavkhazia that, in the aftermath of the Cold War, is riven with escalating internal conflict. The series of labyrinthine negotiations staged in the play spotlight the frustrations of diplomatic and humanitarian activity in a country ravaged by a war in which the West is fully implicated. *Pentecost* (1994),[41] heralded by one critic as 'the first play to tackle head-on the problems created by the disintegration of Communism',[42] questions the viability of cohesive national identity when states are subject to a welter of external forces that stretch beyond territorial boundaries.

The play is set inside an abandoned church in an unnamed country that occupies a corner of south-eastern Europe. Like Barker, Edgar locates his play in a marginal territory that has endured the full and violent force of recent European conflict. In an early scene, Gabriella, the curator of the National Museum, climbs a ladder and begins to dismantle one of the ancient church walls, brick by brick. The markings underneath expose a palimpsest of history: the building most recently served as a warehouse for the storage of potatoes; prior to this it was a 'Museum of Atheism and Progressive People's Culture', a Nazi 'transit' depot, a Catholic church, an Orthodox church, a Turkish mosque during the period of Ottoman rule and, earlier still, a stable for Napoleon's horses (5). In the cautionary and fragmented words of Bojovic, the combative Orthodox priest who flexes his impeccable nationalist credentials in the opening scenes:

> there is something you must understand about this country. It will always prove last barrier. To Russia from above, to Muslim from below. As has always been, way back into Byzantine days. You stand on Europe's battlement. Take care. (24)

The play begins as a cultural 'whodunit', with Gabriella and Oliver, an English art historian, examining a fresco that has been uncovered behind what Edgar describes as a 'large heroic revolutionary mural' in the church (xx). This fresco demonstrates sophisticated techniques of perspective that might feasibly predate Giotto. It is quickly pointed out that this discovery has seismic implications, throwing into question the genealogy 'of universal European man' (75). In the first half of the play, the fresco is placed at the centre of torrid political discussion and competing factional interests: Orthodox and Catholic priests, nationalists, a government minister and a bullish American art historian each present different perspectives on the spiritual, cultural or economic value of the painting to a beleaguered nation emerging from the deep freeze of the Cold War. 'Questions of attribution', as one reviewer noted, 'become questions of acquisition and identity.'[43]

Prior to the ending of Act One, however, the church is suddenly invaded by a motley collection of armed refugees who are seeking asylum in the West: Afghan, Mozambican and Russian men alongside Bosnian, Roma, Kurdish, Palestinian and Sri Lankan women. These insurgents take the other characters hostage and set about using the fresco as a bargaining chip in their attempt to gain asylum. This structural upheaval operates as the fulcrum of the play, transforming its complexion by focusing audience attention on issues of narrative, language and cultural exchange in Europe.

'*Is it chaos? Or is it a building site?*'   55

In Act Two, in a scene that recalls the Biblical provenance of the play's title, the refugees share aspects of their disparate cultural inheritance by exchanging folk tales, songs and stories. They speak in different languages, communicating by gesture and a scattergun of references plucked from Western popular culture. Finally, however, as the charged atmosphere intensifies, armed commandoes burst through the wall, wrecking the fresco and 'liberating' the church from occupation. As shots are fired, a number of the key characters are killed or wounded. This melodramatic final sequence serves to inscribe a clear political and iconic resonance in the image of a wall that is demolished. In spite of the violence, however, the ending of the play is gently upbeat as the original detective story reaches its denouement. It is suggested that the fresco was painted by an Arab exile travelling westwards in the early thirteenth century, 'from what perils we cannot imagine' (98). It is this conjecture that leads Leo, the American art historian, to articulate the central thesis thematized in the play: 'That basically, we are the sum of all the people who've invaded us. We are, involuntarily, each other's guests' (104). In its focus on refugees, ethnic insurgency and hostage taking, *Pentecost* is certainly prescient in its anticipation of the wider political repercussions of the Soviet meltdown. It presents a marginalized territory of the former Eastern bloc struggling to assert a national identity in the face of those myriad 'new actors and new issues', identified by Brown earlier, that confound territorial borders in a globalized era. Yet, in one sense, it has always been thus. Cultural purity, for Edgar, is an illusion preserved in aspic by the hermetic insularity of Cold War ideology and which, since 1989, has erupted into cantankerous nationalism and a xenophobic demonization of the 'other'. The sharing of songs, rituals and narratives in the play, coupled with Leo's remarks in the closing moments, open up the possibility of a new Europe defined, instead, by pluralism, cultural fluidity and hybridity. In placing this pluralism within a historical frame through the device of the artistic whodunit, Edgar delicately asserts more than a residual vestige of socialist commitment. As one critic put it, *Pentecost* 'celebrates the diversity of self-expression in a postmodern culture that goes beyond cold war polarities'.[44]

Far Away

> I'm desperately concerned that we are about to walk into the next millennium with no firm set of ways of looking at the world that aren't terrifying, that the only grand narratives still on the block are Christian fundamentalism and nationalism and that very extreme form of free marketeering that shades so interestingly into authoritarianism wherever you push it.... The left and indeed the liberal centre, is confused and has no model which particularly works. I think that's very scary in ... a situation where new countries with great hopes are emerging and coming up against sinister realities.[45]

Edgar's concerns about the political fall out of the Cold War resonate precisely with some of Churchill's theatrical preoccupations during this period which have endeavoured to give these 'sinister realities' a dramatic expression. Her play *Mad Forest* (1990) negotiates the impact of the Romanian revolution on two families; it concludes uneasily with a cornucopia of individual voices that inflect different perspectives on the country's emergence from communist rule. Ten years later, *Far Away* (2000) offers an altogether more apocalyptic vision of a world that has been terminally dislocated by partisan conflict.[46] The play was first performed in the immediate aftermath of the Kosovan war, a few months after the second Russian invasion of Chechnya, and in the same month that Slobodan Milošević was toppled in Serbia. Shortly after the production transferred into London's West End, Macedonia launched a campaign against Albanian insurgents seeking to divide the country into ethnic zones. The subject matter of the play triggers wider socio-political connotations without making its referentiality explicit or reducible.

Churchill's characteristic procedure in *Far Away* is to eliminate causality from the audience's experience of the violence that is either depicted or suggested. This is achieved through a patterning of dialogue that unfolds in short, pared-down sentences, embedding the violent social context of the play within a seductive tapestry of the 'everyday' that embraces the mundane and the startlingly surreal in equal measure. This is discernible when, towards the end of the play, one of the characters, Todd, protests his military credentials with moody defensiveness:

> I've shot cattle and children in Ethiopia. I've gassed mixed troops of Spanish, computer programmers and dogs. I've torn starlings apart with my bare hands. And I liked doing it with my bare hands. So don't suggest I'm not reliable. (40)

In spite of the outlandish remarks, the tenor of the dialogue throughout is understated, jolting the audience to accept its propositions at face value. The settings of *Far Away* are similarly downplayed and the text is furnished with minimal detail: the first and third acts unfold in 'Harper's house' which is situated in a remote rural area (9); the second act is located in the apparently unremarkable environs of a 'hat makers' (22). As its title indicates, the play takes place in one of Stephanson's outlying 'spaces of a third kind': a marginal territory, at once anonymized and curiously banal, that is convulsed by an intensifying and unexplained violence that seems to have its origins in a notional, indeterminate 'elsewhere'.

In Act One, a young girl, Joan, is lodging with her aunt, Harper, and questions her about some strange disturbances outside that have kept her awake. Each time Harper attempts to rationalize what Joan has seen or heard, her niece counters with another observation that dissolves the veracity of Harper's explanations:

JOAN: I heard a noise.
HARPER: An owl?
JOAN: A shriek.
HARPER: An owl then. There are all sorts of birds here, you might see a golden oriole. People come here especially to watch birds and we sometimes make tea or coffee or sell bottles of water because there's no café and people don't expect that and they get thirsty. You'll see in the morning what a beautiful place it is.
JOAN: It was more like a person screaming.
HARPER: It is like a person screaming when you hear an owl.
JOAN: It was a person screaming. (12)

It becomes clear that Joan has witnessed the night-time arrival of a lorry full of beaten and bloodied men, women and children; she has seen her uncle hit these prisoners with a metal stick and herd them into a hut to await transportation the following morning. Harper tries to reassure Joan, saying that her husband was attacking only traitors in the group while attempting to help the others escape from an enemy. She tells Joan that what she has seen must remain a secret: 'You're part of a big movement now to make things better. You can be proud of that' (20).

The second act takes place 'several years later' (22) and comprises seven short scenes. Joan is now working as a hat maker alongside her colleague, Todd. They are preparing outlandish hats that will be judged in a forthcoming parade. While working, they moan about the corrupt management and poor pay and conditions. By the fourth scene, their hats have reached 'enormous and preposterous' proportions (28). The fifth scene consists of a single stage direction that ruptures the play in one appalling image:

Next day. A procession of ragged, beaten and chained prisoners, each wearing a hat, on their way to execution. The finished hats are even more enormous and preposterous than in the previous scene. (30)

In the ensuing scene, Joan is ecstatic to have won the hat competition. Her only regret is that the hats are ephemeral and so few of them are preserved for posterity: 'it seems so sad', she opines, 'to burn them with the bodies' (31). This entire sequence attains mesmerising theatrical force, not from disputation or argument but from its uncompromising distillation of a political condition, a condition that Elaine Aston describes as the 'ever-widening gap between people's everyday lives and the political'.[47] It is a gap that finds a dramatic visual corollary in the image of the fetishized hats that garland the heads of those doomed prisoners as they trudge towards execution, as well as in Joan's apparent acceptance of the violence that she questioned innocuously as a child in Act One.

The structure of *Far Away* thus maps a trajectory from localized, partisan violence that is hidden from view in Act One to state-sanctioned mass murder that has become normalized as public spectacle by the middle of the play. In Act Three, however, which again takes place 'several years later' (34), the violence has escalated beyond measure. Joan, now married to Todd, has returned to her aunt to seek temporary refuge from an unending war. The atmosphere is fraught because Harper is nervous that Joan's presence will compromise her own safety. The battle outside is global and all-consuming: we learn that wasps have turned on horses, butterflies are on the offensive, mallards have aligned with Koreans, dentists are not to be trusted any more and babies are being murdered by cats who 'have come in on the side of the French' (35). The play concludes suddenly with a speech from Joan in which she explains what she has seen on the road from war. It includes the following:

> The rats are bleeding out of their mouths and ears, which is good, and so were the girls by the side of the road. It was tiring there because everything's been recruited, there were piles of bodies and if you stopped to find out there was one killed by coffee or one killed by pins, they were killed by heroin, petrol, chainsaws, hairspray, bleach, foxgloves, the smell of smoke was where we were burning the grass that wouldn't serve. The Bolivians are working with gravity, that's a secret so as not to spread alarm. But we're getting further with noise and there's thousands dead of light in Madagascar. Who's going to mobilise darkness and silence? (43–4)

It is a speech that represents the final word in post-Cold-War dystopia. Relentless violence on a limitless scale has consumed the physical universe, and arbitrary conflicts are fuelled by the configuration and endless reconfiguration of allegiances. The need to recruit, to randomly align, has engendered a world of multiple polarities bent on annihilation. The discomforting domestic setting of Acts One and Three affords no material or emotional consolation for any of the characters. Instead, it has become equivalent to a fortress, a checkpoint, where even visiting relatives are a potential threat to security. We learn that television has become a showcase for 'trials', the staff canteen a place of lurking surveillance (26). The three-act structure of *Far Away* charts a remorseless amplification from the local and domestic to the global and universal. Dispensing with origins, history and causality, the play dramatizes the absolute antithesis of Realist 'hegemonic stability'. Instead, Churchill places the focus squarely on violence that, virus-like, spreads from a rural enclave in Act One to consume the whole world by Act Three. The effect of this on an audience is intensified by the relatively short duration of the play (the original production at the Royal Court Theatre lasted fifty minutes). The abrupt ending, affording no conventional resolution, is wholly attuned to a theatrical experience characterized throughout by deep foreboding and sharp pessimism. *Far Away* calibrates – with dazzling theatrical economy – a range of contemporary anxieties, not only about the global resurgence of internecine strife in the tumultuous aftermath of the Cold War but also about the capacity of those not directly affected to remain inoculated from its desolating effects.

Conclusion

The theatrical evocation of 'spaces of a third kind' in these plays places the emphasis on personal and collective identity in a state of flux, where individuals struggle towards new paradigms of self and mutual understanding. Both Barker and Edgar articulate an insistent yearning for the 'other' that confounds the hermetic reflexes of a Europe divided by Cold War ideology. Churchill, meanwhile, presents a nightmarish dramatic world with proliferating and irrational violence as its structuring principle. Collectively, these plays challenge the logic of Realist conceptions of Cold War bipolarity, with its attendant notions of 'hegemonic stability' and 'balance of power', by exploding the parameters of theatrical realism: localized documentary specificity is jettisoned in favour of expansive, abstracted landscapes that function as metaphors for Cold War political realities that are far more complex and intractable. The emphasis throughout is on mordant political scepticism, but the result is a series of compelling theatrical provocations that explore the impact of the Cold War at the level of individual experience, and attempt to recontextualize aspects of its history and abiding legacy.

Notes

1. Elsom, *Cold War Theatre* (London: Routledge, 1992), p. 161.
2. Macdonald, 'Formal Ideologies in the Cold War: Toward a Framework for Empirical Analysis', in Odd Arne Westad, ed., *Reviewing the Cold War: Approaches, Interpretations, Theory* (London: Frank Cass, 2000), p. 186; Lebow, 'The Rise and Fall of the Cold War in Comparative Perspective', in Michael Cox, Ken Booth and Tim Dunne, eds, *The Interregnum: Controversies in World Politics 1989–1999* (Cambridge: Cambridge University Press, 1999), p. 38.
3. Chomsky, *World Orders, Old and New* (London: Pluto Press, 1997), p. 81; Gaddis, 'The Cold War, the Long Peace, and the Future', in Michael J. Hogan, ed., *The End of the Cold War: Its Meaning and Implications* (Cambridge: Cambridge University Press, 1992), p. 23.
4. Greenwood, *Britain and the Cold War, 1945–91* (Basingstoke: Macmillan, 2000), p. 190; Shaw, *British Cinema and the Cold War: The State, Propaganda and Consensus* (London: I.B. Taurus, 2001), p. 1.
5. Indeed, Westad indirectly presses this point: 'increasingly important in our understanding of [Cold War] history is its visual representations'. See Westad, 'Introduction' to Westad, ed., *Reviewing the Cold War*, p. 18.
6. Wesker, *Chicken Soup with Barley*, in Wesker, *The Wesker Trilogy*, new edn (1960; Harmondsworth: Penguin, 1987), p. 73.
7. *Destiny* is published in Edgar, *Plays: One* (1987), *Maydays* in Edgar, *Plays: Three* (1991).
8. *Claw* is published in Barker, *Collected Plays: Volume One* (1990).
9. Barker sets out the principles of his 'Theatre of Catastrophe' in Barker, *Arguments for a Theatre* (1989).

10 *Serious Money* is published in Churchill, *Plays: Two* (1990).
11 Both plays are published in Brenton, *Plays: Two* (1989).
12 This is, of course, a highly selective list of plays. There have been a great number of plays written and performed in Britain throughout, and in the aftermath of, the Cold War that have engaged directly with the politics and history of the conflict, or that have thematized its concerns in a varied range of styles. Readers are referred to the plays listed above, and also to Elsom's *Cold War Theatre* for a wide-ranging historical survey.
13 The comment is taken from Patrick Carnegy's review of Peter Whelan's Cold War play, *A Russian in the Woods* (2001), published in the *Spectator* (7 April 2001) and reproduced in *Theatre Record*, 21: 7 (26 March–8 April 2001), p. 442. Interestingly, this play is also set in a splintered, transitory environment: a dilapidated army education centre, formerly a luxurious villa, in Charlottenburg, which itself is part of the British zone of a divided Berlin in 1950.
14 Lebow, 'Rise and Fall of the Cold War', pp. 21–4.
15 Gaddis, 'On Starting All Over Again: A Naïve Approach to the Study of the Cold War', in Westad, ed., *Reviewing the Cold War*, pp. 27–42.
16 Truman, quoted in Ralph B. Levering, *The Cold War: 1945–1987*, 2nd edn (1982; Arlington Heights, Illinois: H. Davidson, 1988), p. 30.
17 Morgenthau, quoted in Yale Ferguson and Rey Koslowski, 'Culture, International Relations Theory, and Cold War History', in Westad, *Reviewing the Cold War*, p. 155.
18 Brown, 'Introduction: Towards a New Synthesis of International Relations', in Mike Bowker and Robin Brown, eds, *From Cold War to Collapse: Theory and World Politics in the 1980s* (Cambridge: Cambridge University Press, 1993), p. 4.
19 For an interesting critique of Gaddis's position see Richard Crockatt, 'Theories of Stability and the End of the Cold War', in Bowker and Brown, eds, *Cold War to Collapse*, pp. 59–81.
20 Ferguson and Koslowski, 'Culture, International Relations Theory, and Cold War History', in Westad, *Reviewing the Cold War*, p. 171.
21 See Brown, 'Introduction', p. 6.
22 Greenwood, *Britain and the Cold War*, p. 3.
23 Crockatt, 'Theories of Stability', p. 63; Westad, 'Introduction', p. 8.
24 Reynolds, 'Beyond Bipolarity in Space and Time', in Hogan, ed., *End of the Cold War*, pp. 245–56.
25 LaFeber, 'An End to *Which* Cold War?', in Hogan, ed., *End of the Cold War*, pp. 13–19. For LaFeber, the following four interconnected Cold Wars shared deep historical roots and together reached 'maturity' in the post-1945 period: the battle between the United States and European countries about the future direction of Europe and the nature and extent of American involvement in Europe (p. 14); the 'struggle between the world's commercial centers and the outlying countries that provide the markets and raw materials' (p. 16); the conflict within the United States over the increasing executive dominance of foreign policy (p. 17); and finally the stand-off between the United States and the USSR (p. 18).
26 Gaddis, 'Starting All Over Again', p. 37.
27 Walker, *The Cold War and the Making of the Modern World* (London: Fourth Estate, 1993), p. 355.
28 Brown, 'Introduction', p. 3.
29 Ibid., p. 3.
30 Stephanson, 'Fourteen Notes on the Very Concept of the Cold War', http://www.h-net.msu.edu/~diplo/stephanson.html (accessed 2 September 2003).
31 Barker, *The Power of the Dog* (London: John Calder, 1985). All subsequent page

'Is it chaos? Or is it a building site?' 61

references from the play are taken from this edition. The production, directed by Kenny Ireland, was first performed on 14 November 1984 at the Royal Lyceum Theatre, Edinburgh, by the Joint Stock Theatre Company.
32 Christopher Edwards, review of *The Power of the Dog* in the *Spectator* (2 February 1985), reproduced in *London Theatre Record*, 5: 2 (16–29 January 1985), p. 68.
33 Barker, 'Oppression, Resistance and the Writer's Testament', interviewed by Finlay Donesky, *New Theatre Quarterly*, 11: 8 (November 1986), p. 338.
34 Ibid., p. 338.
35 At this meeting, the two leaders negotiated a postwar settlement that focused on control of Eastern Europe (including Romania, Greece, Yugoslavia, Hungary and Bulgaria). With brutal decisiveness, they determined the percentage of control that each victorious party would exercise in each country. Churchill scribbled the final breakdown on half a sheet of paper and Stalin acceded by placing a large tick on it. In his reflections, Churchill describes the moments that followed: 'The pencilled paper lay in the centre of the table. At length I said, "Might it be thought rather cynical if it seemed we had disposed of these issues, so fateful to millions of people, in such an offhand manner? Let us burn the paper." "No, you keep it," said Stalin.' Churchill, quoted in Martin McCauley, *The Origins of the Cold War, 1941–1949*, 2nd edn (1983; Harlow: Longman, 1995), pp. 118–19. A number of reviewers of Barker's play mistakenly hold this scene to be a parody of the Yalta Conference (which took place in March 1945) rather than the earlier Moscow meeting. This is probably because the explosive issue at Yalta was Poland, where Barker sets much of the action of his play. For Barker, Poland has a strategic and emblematic significance as the unwitting crucible of postwar bipolarity, a peripheral territory luckless enough to have found itself at the epicentre of grotesque geopolitical squabbling.
36 Michael Billington, review of *The Power of the Dog* in the *Guardian* (28 January 1985), reproduced in *London Theatre Record*, 5: 2 (16–29 January 1985), p. 65.
37 Dunn, 'The Real History Man: Howard Barker's Plays for Spring 1985', *Drama – The Quarterly Theatre Review (TQTR)*, 155 (Spring 1985), p. 10.
38 Barker, *Arguments for a Theatre*, 3rd edn (1989; Manchester: Manchester University Press, 1997), p. 200.
39 Edgar, quoted in Susan Painter, *Edgar the Playwright* (London: Methuen, 1996), p. 150.
40 Michael Billington, review of *Pentecost* in the *Guardian* (17 June 1995), reproduced in *Theatre Record*, 15: 12 (4–17 June 1995), p. 749.
41 Edgar, *Pentecost* (London: Nick Hern Books, 1995). All subsequent page references from the play are taken from this edition. The production, directed by Michael Attenborough, was first performed on 12 October 1994 at the Other Place Theatre, Stratford-upon-Avon, by the Royal Shakespeare Company.
42 Bill Hagerty, review of *Pentecost* in *Today* (16 June 1995), reproduced in *Theatre Record*, 15: 12 (4–17 June 1995), p. 751. Hagerty implies that *Pentecost* is the first *British* play to engage with the meltdown of the Soviet bloc. In fact, this is inaccurate. As I have noted, Edgar's *The Shape of the Table* was produced in 1990. Readers are also referred to Tariq Ali and Howard Brenton's *Moscow Gold* (1990), Caryl Churchill's *Mad Forest* (1990) and Brenton's *Berlin Bertie* (1992), all of which engage directly with the personal and political ramifications of the collapse of communism.
43 James Christopher, review of *Pentecost* in *Time Out* (14 June 1995), reproduced in *Theatre Record*, 15: 12 (4–17 June 1995), p. 751.
44 Aleks Sierz, review of *Pentecost* in *Tribune* (16 June 1995), reproduced in *Theatre Record*, 15: 12 (4–17 June 1995), p. 748.
45 Edgar, quoted in Painter, *Edgar the Playwright*, p. 159.
46 Churchill, *Far Away* (London: Nick Hern Books, 2000). All subsequent page

references from the play are taken from this edition. The production, directed by Stephen Daldry, was first performed on 24 November 2000 at the Royal Court Theatre, London.

47 Aston, *Caryl Churchill*, 2nd edn (1997; Tavistock: Northcote House, 2001), p. 116.

4 Beyond the apocalypse of closure

Nuclear anxiety in postmodern literature of the United States

Daniel Cordle

> There is only one question: When will I be blown up?
> William Faulkner, 10 December 1950[1]

Near the beginning of the Cold War, on accepting the Nobel Prize for Literature, William Faulkner spoke of the future of fiction. Concerned by the insistence with which new fears of nuclear oblivion pressed themselves on the contemporary imagination, he worried that the true subject of literature, 'the problems of the human heart in conflict with itself', would be forgotten.[2] Yet nearly forty years later, in the final years of the Cold War, Martin Amis commented with astonishment and concern at 'how little the mainstream [of literature] has had to say about the nuclear destiny'.[3]

This chapter interrogates the seeming absence of nuclear fear from 'mainstream' literature. After sketching the way in which Cold War nuclear fears became established early in the second half of the twentieth century, it turns its attention to the postmodern literature that emerged after this time. Although it concentrates on those rare texts where nuclear anxiety is a central concern, and on identifying some key tropes in such texts, it suggests how the form and content of a broader body of postmodern literature might be read in terms of the nuclear context. For example, the overwhelming sense of paranoia apparent in much postmodern fiction, along with the frequent deferral of closure and a concentration on the fraught relations between language and reality, are analogous, in meaningful ways, with the psychological impact of nuclear anxiety.

The emergence of Cold War nuclear fears

It is not hard to see why Faulkner worried that the nuclear question would predominate in literature. When he rose to make his speech at the mid-point of the century, he was addressing a world that was increasingly cognizant of the Cold War threat. The boundaries of conflict and stand-off that would define the following forty years were already being drawn, and it was clear that atomic weapons would set the template for international relations between the emerging superpowers. In the five years since the end of the Second World War, Europe had rapidly fractured along fault lines which were given their abiding image by Winston Churchill's 1946 declaration that an 'iron curtain has descended across the continent'.[4] Berlin, a divided city at the heart of a divided continent, had already experienced the blockade and airlift that was the first in a series of crises in its Cold War history. NATO had been formed in 1949 and would find its Eastern bloc antagonist formalized in the shape of the Warsaw Pact six years later. It was clear, too, that Cold War antagonisms, though centred on Europe, would be imprinted on conflicts around the globe: the Korean War had begun a few months earlier, and Mao Zedong was leading communist forces in the newly declared People's Republic of China.

Also apparent was the importance of nuclear technologies to the period, and Americans were well aware of the power of the new weapons. Not only had the bomb produced a remarkably swift end to hostilities with Japan in 1945, but John Hersey's brutal documentary depiction of the destruction of Hiroshima had taken over a whole issue of *The New Yorker* on 31 August 1946, and was subsequently widely disseminated in serialized newspaper accounts and in book and radio versions.[5] As Faulkner made his speech it was just over a year since the Soviet Union had successfully tested its first atomic device, and only a month before President Truman would order the construction of the much more powerful hydrogen bomb. In the following decade, images of bomb tests would appear on the cover of *Life* magazine, concerns would emerge about the environmental impact of nuclear explosions, schoolchildren in the United States would learn to 'duck and cover' in civil defence drills, and the technological race with the Soviet Union would produce outcries over a 'bomber gap' and a 'missile gap', which were exploited by John F. Kennedy in the 1960 presidential election.[6] The 1950s were also to see the emergence, albeit centred more in Europe than in America, of anti-nuclear pressure groups. (Interestingly, next to Faulkner at the Nobel Prize presentation ceremony sat Bertrand Russell, who later became a president of CND before breaking away to join the more radical Committee of 100.)

By the end of the 1950s, the nuclear threat was firmly established as a defining feature of Cold War life. By the early 1960s the strategy of Mutual Assured Destruction had emerged: absolute annihilation held in abeyance as a deterrent to direct confrontation between the United States and the Soviet Union. Although in the period between the Cuban Missile Crisis and the early 1980s nuclear issues became less prominent (perhaps because more tests took place underground; perhaps because issues such as Civil Rights and Vietnam assumed centre stage), by the beginning of the 1960s global nuclear conflict had been firmly established in the public imagination as a possible outcome of the Cold War. Furthermore, the popular image of this war was as a cataclysm that would destroy civilization and probably also end human life on the planet.[7]

Where, then, was the literature of this nuclear age? Certainly there *is* a body of literature where the bomb features prominently. Writing in 1990, Paul Brians identified 'over a thousand depictions of nuclear war and its aftermath' in English.[8] However, nuclear issues tend to be confined to the ghettos of science fiction and the Cold War thriller: as Martin Amis put it, when pointing out the paucity of mainstream coverage of nuclear issues, 'about one SF novel in four is set beyond the holocaust'.[9] Where this literature does deal directly with nuclear issues there is an understandable tendency – for reasons of narrative interest and suspense – to make nuclear conflict, its consequences or its narrow aversion, the primary focus. The emphasis is on closure: on a nullification of the immediate danger, as in the nuclear thriller, or on a depiction of nuclear conflict which removes, however horribly, the psychological tension of waiting for the bomb.

Yet the signature Cold War experience is not nuclear conflict but suspense: the *threat* of conflict which is never quite realized. The texts identified by Brians stem from such suspense, but that suspense is itself almost always, in narrative terms, resolved and removed through the apocalypse of closure. Jean Baudrillard writes, of the postmodern simulacrum, that it involves 'substituting signs of the real for the real itself', and we might see this as a process at work in nuclear disaster fictions.[10] Their representation of the 'real' stands in for the conflict itself, which is perpetually deferred and absent during the Cold War. (Baudrillard is much less convincing when he writes of nuclear war directly in his essay 'Fatal Strategies'. His argument that the excess of destructive power abolishes both 'any space for warfare' and 'the possibility of spectacle' (because there would be no vantage point from which to view a nuclear war) is an original way of saying something unoriginal and dangerous: that Mutual Assured Destruction is a rational mechanism for the preservation of peace.)[11] What disaster fictions inevitably misrepresent is the everyday experience of living with the bomb, and this is precisely because they focus on those moments when that experience ceases to be everyday.

Direct depictions of what it is like to live with the threat of the bomb – and the psychological and cultural consequences of living with that threat over an extended period of time – are much more rare, and are only occasionally noted by literary criticism of the period. The self-styled 'nuclear criticism' of the mid-1980s to the early 1990s provided a welcome and productive approach to the depiction of nuclear issues in language and literature, but it too concerned itself with fictions about the lead up to war, about the war itself or about the post-holocaust environment, largely because of the pressing political environment in which it was produced.[12]

The literature of nuclear anxiety

Where might we look, instead, for depictions of the Cold War state of suspense and of the impact of living with the permanent threat of nuclear conflict? While the nuclear disaster fiction identified by Brians may have its roots in the ongoing suspense of the Cold War (as well as in a more prosaic sensationalism), the true picture emerges when we look not for depictions of disaster but for depictions of nuclear anxiety, as are found in a range of postmodernist texts. Very occasionally, as in Tim O'Brien's *The Nuclear Age* (1985), this is an overt subject of a novel. More frequently, it is represented by minor characters, scenes or themes, as in E.L. Doctorow's *The Book of Daniel* (1971), Don DeLillo's *End Zone* (1972), Robert Coover's *The Public Burning* (1977), Thomas Pynchon's *Gravity's Rainbow* (1973) or Leslie Marmon Silko's *Ceremony* (1977). Sometimes, too, it may emerge in an even more muted form, where an anxiety is expressed that is contiguous with nuclear fears, but whose origins are not named, as in Don DeLillo's *White Noise* (1984) and Paul Auster's *The Country of Last Things* (1987). This list is not, of course, comprehensive, but it indicates where a literary criticism interested in teasing out the representation of nuclear anxiety might begin its work.

The generally muted, or displaced, representation of nuclear anxiety in these texts is a more accurate depiction of the Cold War mentality than the sensational (though how could they be otherwise?) treatment of the end of the world in nuclear disaster fictions. After all, despite moments of palpable fear, such as the Cuban Missile Crisis of 1962, in other periods the nuclear threat seemed either a distant possibility or, through familiarity, faded into the background, drowned out by the cacophony of everyday life. Some psychologists have argued that there is a psychological reason why nuclear fears are often not directly acknowledged. In *Indefensible Weapons* (1982), a speculative but influential book co-authored with Richard Falk, Robert Jay Lifton extrapolates from his work with the traumatized survivors of Hiroshima to argue that the general process by which people comprehend and learn to live with the threat of the bomb involves a 'psychic numbing': a suppression of terror that preserves the illusion of normality.[13] For Lifton, nuclear weapons are rarely at the forefront of people's minds but lurk, instead, in the background, as 'the context of our lives, a shadow that persistently intrudes upon our mental ecology'.[14] As with our mental ecology, it is reasonable to suppose that nuclear fear also seeps into our cultural and literary ecology through the food-chain of virtual constructs that our minds use to process the world. The possibility of nuclear war might not overwhelm us, but it is a potential future that has to be assimilated. It is just such an assimilation that takes place in those texts I have designated nuclear anxiety fictions.

Lifton singles out vulnerability as the 'central existential fact of the nuclear age',[15] and it is largely in the portrayal of specific sorts of vulnerability that these texts engage with nuclear anxiety. Particularly threatened are domestic spaces and the 'nuclear' family units with which they are associated. Danger is often configured in terms of an agoraphobic fear of death coming from above, and the individual's sense of vulnerability frequently finds expression in images of desired womblike spaces and in disillusionment with, and suspicion of, political activism. Also notable is the sense in which the threat is seen to be posed by something that comes with little or no warning (as in the cliché of the 'four-minute' warning that could have presaged nuclear war in Britain): an alternative reality, hovering behind the apparent normality of everyday life, constantly threatens to break through. Everyday life is thus rendered absurd, and it is with this sense of the grimly absurd that postmodern forms make great play.

William, the narrator of O'Brien's *The Nuclear Age*, voices this vulnerability most clearly. He is one of those christened the 'nuclear-haunted' generation by Michael Mandelbaum: the generation born between 1940 and 1950, for whom images of atomic and hydrogen bomb tests were familiar from newspapers and newsreels, who participated in 'duck and cover' air raid drills, and whose maturation and first cognition of death coincided with the period in which nuclear anxieties were to the fore of public consciousness.[16] His fear is meant to be extraordinary, but brings home the accommodations and denials everyone has to make in order to avoid being paralysed by terror. Published in 1985, the novel imagines the Cold War to be under way a decade later, when, one night, William suffers a recurrence of adolescent nuclear fears and, in the grip of this midnight terror, abandons the marital bed to begin digging a bomb shelter in the garden. Telling the story of his life as he digs the hole in the garden, William recalls the comfort he felt as a child, sleeping in a homemade shelter: 'Cozy and walled in and secure [. . .]. I'll even admit that my motives may have been anchored in some ancestral craving for refuge [. . .]. The mole in his hole. The turtle in his shell.'[17]

Although William does not mention it, the turtle in his shell recalls possibly the most famous United States civil defence film of the Cold War, in which Bert the Turtle enjoined schoolchildren to 'duck and cover' in the event of a nuclear explosion. A similar yearning to achieve safety, by falling flat or burrowing into the ground, is a recurrent preoccupation when nuclear anxiety appears in fiction. In *Underworld* (1997), Don DeLillo's elegiac, retrospective depiction of the Cold War, Matty feels 'snug and safe here on the floor' during an air raid drill at school.[18] Similarly, in Doctorow's *The Book of Daniel*, a family friend, Ben Cohen, is singled out for affection by Daniel because of his job in the subway:

> [A] really fine job. You're underground in a stronghold that has barred windows, and a heavy steel door that locks from the inside [. . .]. If a bomb drops, you probably won't even feel it. If there's a storm, you don't get wet.[19]

This protection from bomb and storm is in stark contrast to Daniel's family home which is, in a characteristic Cold War image, strikingly vulnerable:

> It was the way the wind could sweep up the hill over the schoolyard right at his house and, during a storm, actually make the inside wall

near the front door wet that alarmed Daniel. The sky offered no protection, it was too open.[20]

Similarly, Slothrop, in Pynchon's *Gravity's Rainbow*, fears that death will drop seemingly from nowhere. Although his terror is of the V-2 bombs that seem to pursue him around Second World War London, the novel makes clear that this preoccupation with rocketry has a nuclear dimension in its closing scene, when a nuclear missile is poised, at the moment before impact, above the cinema in which the reader is imagined to sit.

Scurrying for cover is often associated in these texts with a turning away from political activism and a disbelief in, if not suspicion of, the efficacy of individual action. William's shelter digging, in *The Nuclear Age*, coincides with his rejection of the radical political activism of his contemporaries ('no more crusades',[21] he says, as he begins to dig his hole). In *The Book of Daniel*, Daniel's scepticism about political action is contrasted with his sister's involvement in the protest movements of the 1960s. The impotence of both William and Daniel, emasculated by their perceived inability to resist the huge social and political forces that operate upon them, is associated with their angry, aggressive and abusive relationships with their families. Powerless in their public lives, they visit their subjugation upon their wives and children: William ties up and nearly kills his wife and daughter, and Daniel treats his family sadistically, as when he threatens his wife with a car cigarette lighter or takes a game of throwing his son in the air to the point where the boy is terrified.

There is, in these books, an ambiguous relation to political action, a feature viewed by Linda Hutcheon as a characteristic of postmodernism. As she points out, the critique found within postmodern art is bound up with 'its own *complicity* with power and domination, one that acknowledges that it cannot escape implication in that which it nevertheless still wants to analyze and maybe even undermine'.[22] Nuclear anxiety texts show an acute awareness of the way in which personal and domestic relations and spaces become heavily politicised by external forces. However, they also show individual subjectivities to be so overwhelmingly forged by discourses and powers outside themselves that scope for effective individual action is severely limited. In demonstrating the reach of the political, they both expose and criticise the actions of power and, paradoxically, simultaneously enact the difficulty, if not impossibility, of resisting power. This is, of course, to do as much with the grand scale of Cold War politics, and the far-reaching impact of capitalism, as it is with the threat of nuclear annihilation. Pynchon's paranoid fiction, especially its construction of the mysterious 'They' who manipulate Slothrop in *Gravity's Rainbow*, probably best exemplifies this generalized sense of the intricacy and scope of the actions of power. It can, however, equally be found in DeLillo (in the webs of language, culture and convention that map out the conversations of the Gladney family in *White Noise*, for example), in Coover (where, in *The Public Burning*, Uncle Sam is a vulgar distortion of a cartoon hero, fighting the communist forces of the 'Phantom' and speaking directly to Richard Nixon) and even in a forerunner of postmodernist fiction like, from 1961, Joseph Heller's *Catch-22* (where Yossarian discovers that there is no centre to the malignant structures of power of which he becomes aware).

In the nuclear context, this immanence of power is enacted through a concern with the contamination of domestic and bodily spaces. After the dawn of the nuclear era, the pollution of the environment by radiation quickly became a key element in the mythology of atomic weapons. Only a year after the dropping of the Hiroshima bomb, Hersey was able to exploit, for dramatic effect, the gulf in knowledge between the residents of the city in 1945 and his readers, who had, in the succeeding twelve months, swiftly become familiar with the effects of radiation. When, in *Hiroshima*, people are seen vomiting at the side of a road out of town, and when X-ray plates are found to have been mysteriously exposed in the city's Red Cross hospital, Hersey need offer no comment for his readers to guess the cause of these phenomena.[23]

Civil defence literature also played up this idea of contamination. A revealing 1954 short film, *The House in the Middle*, spins its narrative about nuclear preparedness around footage of three houses being subjected to bomb tests.[24] Two are untidy in various ways (unpainted, papers lying around, and so on) and are swiftly destroyed, but the third, the eponymous House in the Middle, is clean and much more resistant to bomb damage and fire. Here, doing the domestic chores is viewed as a part of being American, while dirtiness is un-American (and, of course, early in the 1950s the House Un-American Activities Commission was busy rooting out suspected communists, who were also popularly characterized as a dirty infection of the body politic). These sorts of motifs soon entered literature of the bomb. Judith Merril's important 1950 disaster fiction, *Shadow on the Hearth*, about a woman, Gladys, trying to hold her family together after an atomic attack on New York, is full of details of domestic routine, particularly about the securing of doors and windows and the cleaning of their suburban house. Although a contemporary reviewer described the novel as 'chintzy' in this respect, he missed entirely the novel's complex narrative about the way in which the nominally apolitical domestic space becomes compromised.[25] Gladys spends the entire novel trying to secure her home from threats that come from the outside – radiation, looters, sexually threatening authority figures – only for her daughter to contract radiation sickness from the toy horse she cuddles for comfort in bed. Merril's narrative, traditional in so many ways, prefigures the unresolved nuclear anxiety of some postmodern texts: the nuclear emergency is over at the end of the book, but Gladys is left wondering, 'Would anything ever be safe again?'[26]

The home is configured in US culture as a domain of normality, the family unit and the pristine suburban or small town house offering the illusion of protection from outside threats. William's decision, in *The Nuclear*

Age, to abandon the family home is therefore significant. When he starts to dig his bomb shelter, he contrasts the house, which smells of 'Windex and wax', with his hole in the garden, and comments that 'Safety can be very messy'.[27] Later in the novel he imagines a reunion of his once-radical college contemporaries in which they cease to sing protest songs ('*Give peace a chance*') in favour of advertising jingles about cleaning products ('*Mr. Clean will clean your whole house, and everything that's in it*').[28] Consumerism is implicated here, cleansing products being sold on the promise of a pristine home and, by implication, the illusion of safety they offer, suppressing consciousness of the dirty political reality of the missiles poised around the globe.

In a passage of DeLillo's *Underworld*, entitled 'October 8, 1957', this association between domestic cleanliness – the home as safe refuge – and the Cold War threat is developed in a striking way.[29] Erica Deming, on whom the passage concentrates, goes through the stereotypical actions of a suburban housewife, doing ingenious things with Jell-O and cleaning the house. Outside, her husband, Rick, simonizes their car. Their son, Eric, is in his bedroom. Despite these comforting routines of family life (which, the peaceful scene outside the window suggests, are replicated throughout the street), Erica feels strangely disturbed. Initially, it is only small remarks that suggest her anxiety is associated with the intrusion into her home of Cold War anxieties. The Jell-O chicken mousse that Erica makes is described as 'strontium white', and her son is hidden away in his room upstairs because he is masturbating into a condom that reminds him of his favourite weapons system, the Honest John.[30] Over dinner, Erica realises the source of her unease when the conversation turns to Sputnik, recently launched by the Russians, that is orbiting above them. As with William's fear of exposure in *The Nuclear Age*, and Daniel's awareness of the vulnerability of his home to storm damage in *The Book of Daniel*, the Cold War experience is presented as one of feeling perpetually under threat, particularly through the fragility and permeability of the domestic environment. Importantly, Erica attempts to counter her anxiety by indulging, all the more keenly, in domestic routine: 'Doing things with Jell-O was just about the best way to improve her mood', we are told, and she tries to 'lift her spirits by doing something for the church social'.[31] Most significantly, she cleans the house, although even this recourse is doomed, for Erica's futuristic vacuum cleaner reminds her of the satellite flying above. Indeed, just as domestic spaces are compromised, so too are bodily ones. Erica treasures the way her gloves protect her hands from food scraps and germs while doing the washing up, but one of her gloves is missing, borrowed, she thinks, by Eric for reasons about which she is 'afraid to ask'.[32] Just as Gladys's daughter is made ill by the radioactive toy horse lurking in the home, so Erica's attempts to banish germs do not quench her anxiety, and nor can she keep out of her mind her son's emerging and secretive sexuality.

We might, then, see the home as the locus on which dynamics related to the anxiety of the time centre. A strong discourse of infection is thus linked to the insidious impact of Cold War fears, with the house, the family and even the body being compromised by threats from the outside. Literally fragile in the face of nuclear blast, and permeable in the face of atomic fallout, they are also metaphorically fragile, permeable to the creeping anxiety of the age.

In other words, threatening to break through the façade of the everyday is the fear that a terrible alternative reality will swiftly impose itself. Very often, nuclear anxiety is expressed in terms of the consciousness that what we experience as normal might suddenly flip over to be replaced by an entirely different mode of reality. Jonathan Schell expresses this clearly in a powerful environmentalist tract about the nuclear threat that was, like Hersey's *Hiroshima*, first published in *The New Yorker*, before going on to sell widely as a book: 'Now we are on our way to work, walking through the city streets, but in a moment we may be standing on an empty plain under a darkened sky looking for the charred remnants of our children.'[33] Even in anticipation, before the first bomb was built, nuclear threat was imagined in terms of a sudden and unprecedented attack on normality. Richard Rhodes describes in his impressively detailed book *The Making of the Atomic Bomb* the physicist Enrico Fermi looking out from his office over the teeming streets of late 1930s Manhattan: 'He cupped his hands as if he were holding a ball. "A little bomb like that", he said simply, for once not lightly mocking, "and it would all disappear".'[34] This awareness that the bomb makes such a radically and rapidly changed world possible, even imminent, is singled out by Robert Lifton as the key aspect of Cold War experience. 'Above all', he says, 'we all live a double life.'[35]

The psychological juxtaposition of two worlds produced by nuclear anxiety (the one we are in and the one threatened by nuclear war) means that fictive worlds collide abruptly with 'real' ones. Postmodern literature is particularly attuned to such collisions of mutually incompatible realities. As Brian McHale argues, it is a literature defined by its preoccupation with ontological concerns, and thus deals with questions such as:

> What happens when different kinds of world are placed in confrontation or when boundaries between worlds are violated?; What is the mode of existence of a text, and what is the mode of existence of the world (or worlds) it projects?[36]

Similar questions are thrown up when the 'double life' of Cold War experience is represented. By positing an anxiety about a projected alternative world (the world that would result from a nuclear confrontation), nuclear anxiety texts, in moments at least, put the other reality (that of everyday life) under negation. McHale's juxtaposition of questions about worlds with questions about texts is pertinent here. For McHale, as for other critics of postmodernism, the world is essentially a textual construct, read by each of us through a grid of cultural references. In its concern with the cusp between alternative futures, nuclear anxiety literature involves a particularly interesting cross-fertilization of the relations between texts and worlds. As is often commented upon, the nuclear future exists only in art; were it to come to pass, representations, and even consciousness, of it may not be possible.[37] It exists, therefore, only in the future conditional tense, and yet its threat to become present lingered throughout the Cold War. It was, as Lifton puts it, 'the context for our lives'.[38] Because of its refusal to go away, it frustrated closure. To reproduce the anxiety of the age accurately, literature needs similarly to refuse this resolution, and, of course, it is precisely in the frustration of our impulse to closure that postmodern texts excel.

The end of O'Brien's *The Nuclear Age*, in which William learns to live with his nuclear fear, is particularly interesting. Rather than the climactic nuclear holocaust he had imagined (and the more personal holocaust of murder with which he had threatened his family), we get the anticlimax of things not happening. Moreover, the novel presents this as a false resolution: William's return to normal life is a willing self-deception, a comforting fiction of security that represses consciousness of nuclear danger. Crucially, the subject of the novel – nuclear anxiety – cannot be resolved; it can only be denied. It is worth quoting in full the closing sentence of William's narrative to illustrate this:

> I will live my life in the conviction that when it finally happens – when we hear that midnight whine, when Kansas burns, when what is done is undone, when fail-safe fails, when deterrence no longer deters, when the jig is at last up – yes, even then I will hold to a steadfast orthodoxy, confident to the end that E will somehow not quite equal mc^2, that it's a cunning metaphor, that the terminal equation will somehow not quite balance.[39]

William suppresses consciousness of one reality in order to continue with the other; 'normal' life is rendered absurd when the alternative is contemplated. It is a denial which rests on a linguistic sleight of hand, turning $E = mc^2$, the equation which predicts the massive release of energy that occurs during fission, into a metaphor, on the assumption that metaphors are entirely disconnected from reality. At the beginning of the novel, William's assertion of the nuclear threat rested on his denial of metaphor: 'No metaphors, the bombs are real.'[40] At the end, he embraces the metaphoric power of the science behind the bomb, as though this will make the threat less real. However, a third position emerges from the text, although William does not realize it: both the bombs and the metaphors are real; it is not a choice between one and the other. This is indicated by the poems that William's wife, Bobbi, pens to him, which are an important and recurring feature of the novel. Taking terms associated with nuclear technology and Cold War international politics, such as 'Fission' and 'The Balance of Power', she spins poems about their troubled marriage. These are powerful metaphors for domestic crisis, but they also indicate how the language of power and control, and the way of thinking that accompanies it, permeates society from the macrocosm of international politics to the microcosm of the family unit. It suggests a vulnerability of personal lives to outside influences, similar to that experienced by Gladys in *Shadow on the Hearth* and Erica in *Underworld*.

The focus in *The Nuclear Age* on language as a particularly fraught and contested issue in the representation of nuclear anxiety is reproduced in DeLillo's novel *End Zone*. At a remote college in the Texan desert, a disaffected American football player, Gary Harkness, recalls what happened when he began to read obsessively about nuclear war:

> I became fascinated by words and phrases like thermal hurricane, overkill, circular error probability, post-attack environment, stark deterrence, dose-rate contours, kill-ration, spasm war. Pleasure in these words. They were extremely effective, I thought, whispering shyly of cycles of destruction so great that the language of past world wars became laughable, the wars themselves somewhat naive.[41]

The insubstantial language of nuclear strategy becomes real here, rendering terrible reality ('past world wars') itself unreal. This ambiguity – the way in which words are insubstantial, slippery and ephemeral at the same time as they are weighty, present and significant – speaks partly to the postmodern concern with the charged connections between language and reality. Yet it takes on further significance in an anxious nuclear age, for a world that no one has experienced, and that exists only in words, can suddenly and terribly come to pass, negating everyday experience.

Where nuclear holocaust is directly represented in these texts, it is in terms of this doubleness that shadows everyday life. In *End Zone*, a nuclear device explodes high over Brussels, there is a rapid escalation of responses, and cities, including Washington, New York and Los Angeles, are destroyed. In *The Nuclear Age*, William looks out of his airplane window to see nuclear explosions lighting up the United States from east coast to west. Yet these iconic Cold War images of the end of the world in nuclear cataclysm are fictions within fictions: in the first, Gary is playing a war game with a military strategist, and in the second William is hallucinating. What distinguishes these books from more conventional nuclear disaster fictions, then, is that the images of the end (mushroom clouds, flattened cities) are placed under elision: we are not expected to suspend disbelief and assume they are happening. They play with different sorts of closure – particularly the terminal closure of nuclear war – but their actual endings are anticlimactic (William simply ceases to be frightened of war; Gary is taken to the infirmary).

Douglas Coupland's short story 'The Wrong Sun' (1994), published after the end of the Cold War but strongly rooted in its sensibilities, makes the doubleness of nuclear anxiety and the deferral of closure its central structuring principles. Both are rooted in an emphatic sense of fragmentation. The story is split into two sections, and the first, 'Thinking of the Sun', recounts episodes of momentary nuclear terror in the narrator's life, such as hearing a siren, and expecting a bomb to drop when a jet passes over his school. Although there is some sense of community here – he claims that they are widely shared experiences[42] – the effect of recounting these episodes is to produce the impression of a life fragmented by the sporadic images of a nuclear end that intrude upon the consciousness. Each brief moment of anticipation of the end is left unresolved: something is expected, but does not happen; ordinary life continues until the expectation of a nuclear flash intrudes again. The sense of fragmentation is carried over into the second section, 'The Dead Speak'. Multiple, disconnected narrators describe the moment when their ordinary lives – 'I was by the fridge in the kitchen when it happened'; 'I was having my hair done when it happened'; 'I was at the mall when it happened'[43] – are suddenly interrupted as they are killed by an unexpected nuclear explosion. There is resolution of a sort here: the bombs drop and lives are ended. However, there is no lead up to, or consequences beyond, these moments; they are endings without beginnings. Furthermore, because 'The Dead Speak' is counterpointed with 'Thinking of the Sun', and no master narrative connects or mediates between them, Coupland's story gives a very strong sense of Cold War experience as one of a 'double life'. Both the main possible outcomes of the Cold War nuclear stand-off – the bombs drop; the bombs do not drop – are presented as equally viable possibilities.

Nuclear anxiety is the main subject of O'Brien's *The Nuclear Age* and Coupland's 'The Wrong Sun', and is also one of the central features of *End Zone*. In the other postmodern fictions cited in this chapter, rather than forming the foregrounded focus of the text, nuclear anxiety erupts out of the background. *The Book of Daniel*, for instance, produces a fictionalized account of the impact of the political atmosphere of the United States on the children of the Rosenbergs, executed for allegedly passing atomic secrets to the Russians. Similarly, Silko's *Ceremony*, although set in the New Mexico desert not long after it became the site for the testing of the first atomic bomb, is more directly concerned with the challenge posed to Native American subjectivities and perspectives than it is with Cold War fears. Nevertheless, in these texts and others like them, although direct representation of nuclear anxiety may be downplayed, associated anxieties are very strongly represented: *The Book of Daniel* is preoccupied with the exposure of the family unit to violent, destructive forces, as discussed above, and *Ceremony* is suffused with images of contamination of the land, the body and the mind.[44]

It is in these culturally powerful images of exposure and contamination, and in the sense of living in end times, that nuclear anxiety makes itself felt. The perpetual deferral of the nuclear outcome, and the concomitant sense of an alternative reality that is poised behind the everyday, waiting to assert itself, cause problems for realist narratives wedded to a teleological structure, because during the Cold War there was no resolution of the fear. Postmodern narratives, on the other hand, in their tantalizing refusal of traditional modes of closure, in their sense of the absurd and in their preoccupation with language games, inflect the anticipatory anxiety of the Cold War era peculiarly well. Such representations are rarely direct, and have been little commented on, but the texts discussed above provide a starting point from which a more comprehensive analysis of the impact of nuclear anxiety on postmodern culture might proceed.

Notes

1 Faulkner, 'The Stockholm Address', in Frederick J. Hoffman and Olga Vickery, eds, *William Faulkner: Three Decades of Criticism* (New York: Harbinger, 1960), p. 347.
2 Ibid., pp. 347–8.
3 Amis, 'Introduction: Thinkability', in Amis, *Einstein's Monsters*, new edn (1987; London: Vintage, 2003), p. 23.
4 Churchill, quoted in Oliver Edwards, *The USA and the Cold War: 1945–1963*, 2nd edn (1997; Oxon: Hodder and Stoughton, 2002), p. 28.
5 For details of the cultural reception of Hersey's *Hiroshima* (1946) see Paul Boyer, *By the Bomb's Early Light: American Thought and Culture at the Dawn of the Atomic Age*, 2nd edn (London: University of North Carolina Press, 1994), p. 204.
6 Atomic explosions were *Life*'s cover story on 27 February 1950, 19 April 1954 and 20 July 1962. When Kennedy took power he discovered that the Soviets' technological superiority was a chimera.
7 The most famous image of nuclear war as the end of the world comes in Nevil Shute's 1957 novel *On the Beach*, which was also made into a successful film, but the suggestion that a war between the United States and the Soviet Union would end human life recurred frequently until the end of the Cold War.
8 Brians, 'Nuclear Family/Nuclear War', *Papers on Language and Literature: A Journal for Scholars and Critics of Language and Literature*, 26: 1 (1990), p. 151. Brians's book, *Nuclear Holocausts: Atomic War in Fiction 1895–1984* (1987) is a comprehensive guide to this fiction. Notable examples of nuclear disaster literature are Nevil Shute's *On the Beach* (1957), Walter Miller's *A Canticle for Leibowitz* (1959) and Russell Hoban's *Riddley Walker* (1980).
9 Amis, 'Introduction', p. 23.
10 Baudrillard, 'Simulacra and Simulations', in Baudrillard, *Jean Baudrillard: Selected Writings*, ed. Mark Poster, trans. Jacques Mourrain (Cambridge: Polity Press, 1988), p. 167.
11 Baudrillard, 'Fatal Strategies', in Baudrillard, *Jean Baudrillard*, pp. 190, 202.
12 Some good examples of nuclear criticism, and fine introductions to nuclear war fiction, are: Nancy Anisfield, ed., *The Nightmare Considered: Critical Essays on Nuclear War Literature* (1991), Paul Brians, *Nuclear Holocausts: Atomic War in Fiction, 1895–1984* (1987); I.F. Clarke, *Voices Prophesying War: Future Wars 1763–3749* (1966); Joseph Dewey, *In a Dark Time: The Apocalyptic Temper in the American Novel of the Nuclear Age* (1990); David Dowling, *Fictions of Nuclear Disaster* (1987); Patrick Mannix, *The Rhetoric of Antinuclear Fiction: Persuasive Strategies in Novels and Films* (1992). A special edition of *Papers on Language and Literature: A Journal for Scholars of Language and Literature*, 26: 1 (1990), devoted to nuclear fiction and nuclear criticism, is also a valuable guide to the subject.

76   *Daniel Cordle*

13 Lifton and Falk, *Indefensible Weapons: The Political and Psychological Case Against Nuclearism* (New York: Basic Books, 1982), pp. 99, 101, 103–4. Here, and elsewhere, I speak of the ideas as Lifton's because they come from the section of the book on psychology for which he took primary responsibility. For objections to Lifton's argument, see Ofer Zur, 'On Nuclear Attitudes and Psychic Numbing: Overview and Critique', *Contemporary Social Psychology*, 14: 2 (1990), pp. 96–118.
14 Lifton and Falk, *Indefensible Weapons*, p. 3.
15 Ibid., p. 23.
16 Mandelbaum, *The Nuclear Revolution: International Politics before and after Hiroshima* (Cambridge: Cambridge University Press, 1981), p. 209.
17 O'Brien, *The Nuclear Age*, new edn (1985; London: Flamingo, 1987), p. 312.
18 DeLillo, *Underworld*, new edn (1997; London: Picador, 1998), p. 728.
19 Doctorow, *The Book of Daniel*, new edn (1971; London: Picador-Pan, 1982), p. 45. Cohen makes only one more appearance in the novel, but again the protection his job affords him is mentioned: 'He had come directly from work from the subway where it was his job to make change and which protects him from the atom bomb' (ibid., p. 126).
20 Ibid., p. 92.
21 O'Brien, *Nuclear Age*, p. 8.
22 Hutcheon, *The Politics of Postmodernism* (London: Routledge, 1989), p. 4.
23 Hersey, *Hiroshima*, rev. edn (1946; London: Penguin, 1985), pp. 47, 74.
24 This film can be viewed at the Prelinger Archives, an excellent resource of short public service and other films (http://www.archive.org/movies/prelinger.php (accessed 29 April 2004)).
25 Charles Poore, 'Books of the Times', *New York Times*, 15 June 1950, p. 29.
26 Merril, *Shadow on the Hearth* (New York: Doubleday, 1950), p. 275.
27 O'Brien, *Nuclear Age*, p. 6.
28 The italics appear in the original text. Ibid., p. 131.
29 DeLillo, *Underworld*, pp. 513–21.
30 Ibid., pp. 514–15, 516. In the 1950s there was a public health scare over the appearance in milk of strontium 90 from bomb tests.
31 Ibid., pp. 514, 520.
32 Ibid., p. 519. Another striking image of the link between sexuality, repression and Cold War politics is produced by Robert Coover, who presents us with a scene in which Richard Nixon masturbates as he thinks about Ethel Rosenberg (who is awaiting execution for allegedly passing atomic secrets to the Russians): Coover, *The Public Burning*, new edn (1977; New York: Grove, 1998), p. 318.
33 Schell, *The Fate of the Earth* (London: Pan, 1982), p. 182.
34 Rhodes, *The Making of the Atomic Bomb*, rev. edn (1986; London: Penguin, 1988), p. 275.
35 Lifton and Falk, *Indefensible Weapons*, p. 52.
36 McHale, *Postmodernist Fiction* (New York: Methuen, 1987), p. 10.
37 Schell is particularly good on this: 'If it wishes to truthfully reflect the reality of its period, whose leading feature is the jeopardy of the human future, art will have to go out of existence, while if it insists on trying to be timeless it has to ignore this reality [. . .] and so, in a sense, tell a lie' (Schell, *Fate of the Earth*, p. 165).
38 Lifton and Falk, *Indefensible Weapons*, p. 3.
39 O'Brien, *Nuclear Age*, p. 312. Other critics see William's final vision to be a positive affirmation of a way forward. For instance, Jacqueline Foertsch, in an otherwise excellent article, sees it as allowing William 'to rebuild in the direction of secured physical well-being *and* mental health': Foertsch, 'Not Bombshells but Basketcases: Gendered Illness in Nuclear Texts', *Studies in the Novel*,

31: 4 (1999), p. 475. There is not room, here, to explore fully my objections to this sort of reading, but what it misses out is the extent to which William's final vision is presented as self-deceiving.
40 O'Brien, *Nuclear Age*, p. 4.
41 DeLillo, *End Zone*, new edn (1972; London: Penguin, 1986), p. 21.
42 I refer to the narrator as male because the little he reveals about himself – that he lives in Vancouver; that he went to art school – aligns him very closely with Coupland himself.
43 Coupland, 'The Wrong Sun', in Coupland, *Life after God*, new edn (1994; London: Simon & Schuster, 1999), pp. 89, 91, 95.
44 Tayo, the central protagonist, returns from fighting in Japan to his homeland, the site of the A-bomb tests in the New Mexico desert. The novel traces Tayo's psychological disintegration, linking it to the contamination and sickness of the land.

5 The Reds and the Blacks
The historical novel in the Soviet Union and postcolonial Africa[1]

M. Keith Booker and Dubravka Juraga

In an important, though highly controversial, article from 1986, Fredric Jameson argues the value to 'First World' intellectuals of close and careful analysis of 'Third World' literature, which for Jameson still has access to certain kinds of social experience that have been made almost entirely unavailable in the West as a result of the homogenizing effects of the postmodernist culture of late capitalism.[2] Jameson's article is now remembered (and often criticized) mostly for its elaboration of the notion that 'national allegory' may be the necessary mode of Third World literature. Meanwhile, his more fundamental point – that the Third World is an important source of new cultural energies in the era of late capitalism – is now almost forgotten, but only because it has been so widely accepted as to appear obvious. The two intervening decades have seen a veritable explosion in postcolonial studies, leading to a widespread acceptance of the notion that close and careful study of non-Western texts is not only rewarding but essential for anyone who would seek to understand world culture at this juncture in history. Among other things, by learning to understand that cultural phenomena such as the African novel may operate according to aesthetic principles different from those that have typically governed the central texts of the Western canon, we have gained a much better understanding of the historicity of aesthetic criteria in general while learning to challenge the traditional claim of universality that has long underwritten Western bourgeois aesthetics.

The new respect being paid these days to postcolonial cultural phenomena such as the African novel was not gained without a difficult struggle in which a long legacy of colonialist stereotypes had to be overcome. Meanwhile, other cultural phenomena that challenge the hegemony of Western bourgeois aesthetics have still not overcome similar stereotypes. For example, it remains conventional in the West to dismiss most of the massive cultural production of the Soviet Union (especially that which falls under the rubric of socialist realism) as so much ideological tripe, as an unfortunate detour from the literary into the political that resulted in more than half a century of cultural impoverishment in which the once-mighty Russian cultural apparatus produced essentially nothing of any real value. Régine

Robin's well-known characterization of socialist realism as an 'impossible aesthetic' is only one of the more diplomatic dismissals of Soviet literature, the study of which was, for an entire generation, dominated by the early Cold War diatribes of such strident anti-Soviets as Marc Slonim and Gleb Struve.[3] Even Katerina Clark's *The Soviet Novel*, perhaps the most objective Western study of socialist realism to be produced during the Cold War, tends to concentrate on the identification of stereotypes and master plots in socialist-realist novels, never really questioning the notion that socialist realism is governed by such devices or asking whether these devices are really any more restrictive than the Western notion of literary conventions.[4]

Of course, numerous studies from within the Soviet Union have pointed out the richness of the achievements of Soviet culture, while also attempting to explain the ways in which socialist realism operates according to an aesthetic of its own that is in many ways radically different from that of the Western bourgeois novel.[5] But these studies have generally been dismissed in the West as examples of the same degraded descent into 'ideology' that made socialist realism itself such a presumably reprehensible phenomenon. Meanwhile (perhaps predictably), by the time of *perestroika*, Western aesthetics, like many artefacts of Western bourgeois ideology, had gained considerable purchase in the Soviet Union. Prominent Soviet critics such as Evgeny Dobrenko began to characterize socialist realism in many of the same terms that had long been used in the West, though at least with the advantage of apparently having actually read the works they were deriding, something that could not always be said for their Western counterparts.

One would hope, in the aftermath of the fall of the Soviet Union, that we can now begin to assess the achievements of Soviet culture in a more measured and objective fashion, and there are some signs that the early steps of such a reassessment are under way. One might note, for example, the recent special edition of *South Atlantic Quarterly* (edited by Dobrenko and Thomas Lahusen), in which many of the contributors are at least willing to admit that socialist realism is worthy of detailed study as a legitimate aesthetic system rather than simply being dismissed as an unfortunate consequence of Stalinist-Zhadonivite totalitarianism.[6] For example, in his own essay in that volume, Dobrenko concludes that the aesthetics of socialist realism arose in response to the popular tastes of the Soviet reading public rather than being dictated by the Stalinist bureaucracy, a truism of Western Sovietology that Dobrenko characterizes as ludicrous.[7] The present chapter seeks to contribute to the reassessment of Soviet culture by exploring some of the many parallels between Soviet socialist realism and African postcolonial literature, with the corollary suggestion that socialist realism deserves some of the same kinds of respect that have been afforded postcolonial literature in recent years. In particular, we will focus on the central importance of the historical novel in both Soviet postrevolutionary and African postcolonial literature.

To an extent, of course, the parallels between Soviet literature and African literature are obvious. Ironically, they have already been recognized in the Western rhetoric of the Cold War, which often employed colonialist stereotyping to describe the Soviets as non-Western primitives. Thus William Pietz notes that the mapping of certain traditional Orientalist stereotypes on to the Russians not only helped to 'justify the practical policy of containment, but it contributed to a new theory of the neurotic psychological basis of all "ideology", that is, of all left political argument'.[8] Further, such stereotyping was offered as an explanation for the 'component of state-backed social terror so prominent in twentieth-century European history'.[9] It is certainly the case that Sovietology was a well-elaborated discourse in the sense meant by Foucault and in the way associated by Said with Orientalism. That is, Sovietology tells us very little about what was actually going on in the Soviet Union but a great deal about the fears and fascinations of the West.

In this context, the most obvious similarity between African and Soviet fiction is that they are both inherently political and that the authors of both recognize the specifically political nature of their attempt to contribute to the construction of new cultural identities in their respective societies. The overtly political nature of Soviet socialist realism contributed, during the Cold War, to the institutionalization of New Critical and other formalist approaches in the Western academy. Such approaches declared a formally complex (if historically disengaged, at least according to formalist critics) modernism the epitome of high literary art and consigned any political art to the debased category of propaganda.[10] Of course, such scholars themselves repeat (if unwittingly) a central technique of *Western* propaganda during the Cold War, in which a once-disreputable (or, at best, irrelevant) but now newly enshrined modernism was opposed to a presumably simplistic socialist realism as evidence of the greater cultural openness and sophistication of the enlightened West in comparison with the benighted Soviet Union.[11] This discourse contributed in obvious ways to the promulgation of the widely held view (especially among Western Sovietologists, whose *raison d'être* was, after all, the exposure of the poverty of Soviet culture) that socialist realism was incapable of producing genuine literature.[12] Yet many, and probably most, of the Soviet novels that might be categorized as socialist realism are not only formally sophisticated but also ideologically complex and ambivalent, supporting the Soviet regime no more unequivocally and uncritically than most Western novels support capitalism.[13] Meanwhile, the works of such pro-Soviet writers as Maxim Gorky, Mikhail Sholokhov, Valentin Kataev and Andrei Platonov have obvious literary merit, even from the standpoint of Western aesthetics. What is important to recognize, however, is not that socialist realism can be justified on the basis of Western aesthetics, but rather that it is based on aesthetic premises that are different from (and largely opposed to) those that inform bourgeois notions of literary 'quality'.

The same might be said for postcolonial African literature, which provides such a clear demonstration that art cannot be separated from the social world and that aesthetic criteria are not universal and timeless, but arise in response to specific historical conditions and developments. As Chinua Achebe angrily suggested in a lecture on the relationship between art and society in the postcolonial world, the close connection between literature and politics in that world makes it clear that 'art for art's sake is just another piece of deodorised dogshit'.[14] Yet such criteria have frequently been applied to African literature. The prominent African critic Abiola Irele, for example, notes that African critics have felt pressure to conform to Western formalist approaches to literature in order to establish that African literature is worthy of serious critical attention. Thus, critics of African literature have been hesitant to discuss the social and political implications of literature because of Western tendencies to declare such discussions primitive by definition. For Irele, however, socially engaged readings of African literature are essential:

> The manifest concern of the writers to speak to the immediate issues of social life, to narrate the tensions that traverse their world – to relate their imaginative expression to their particular universe of experience in all its existential concreteness – this seems to me to leave the African critic with hardly any choice but to give precedence to the powerful referential thrust of our literature.[15]

Similarly, in his excellent introduction to the West African novel, Emmanuel Obiechina repeatedly emphasizes the social and political engagement of such novels, which are often overtly didactic in their attempt to convince their readers to support certain specific political ideas:

> Because the West African novel has risen at a time when large-scale social and economic changes are taking place, the writers show an almost obsessive preoccupation with the influence of these conditions. This is the condition of life; these are the ways in which people feel its pressure; these pressures demand expression.[16]

Perhaps the most powerful response to Western-style formalist criticism of African literature has come from the Nigerian critics Chinweizu, Onwuchekwa Jemie and Ihechukwu Madubuike. In their controversial but important book *Toward the Decolonization of African Literature*, these three critics review in detail the work of Western commentators such as Eustace Palmer and Charles Larson (in many ways the Slonim and Struve of African literature) in order to reveal the assumption of Western cultural superiority that lies behind the work of such commentators, even when they are ostensibly attempting to serve as advocates for the value of African literature. Chinweizu, Jemie and Madubuike have been especially influential for their impassioned insistence that critics of African literature should pay close and serious attention to the role played by African oral traditions in the development of modern African literature. To emphasize the dialogue between

African and European literature at the expense of ignoring the specific Africanness of African literature is for these critics merely a subtle continuation of the European colonial domination of Africa. At the same time, Chinweizu and associates are perfectly aware that African writers have been influenced by Western models, so that the African novel is always a complex hybrid cultural phenomenon that combines both Western and African cultural perspectives. They thus point out that 'the African novel is a hybrid of the African oral tradition and the imported forms of Europe, and it is precisely this hybrid origin which needs most to be considered' when judging the effectiveness of African novels.[17]

While Chinweizu and his collaborators have sometimes been criticized as extremists, their point has largely been won in the Western academy, which now routinely acknowledges that African aesthetic criteria may differ from Western ones and that African novels should be judged by the former, not the latter. Soviet socialist realism, after nearly half a century of intensive ridicule and scorn at the hands of Western critics, has not been so fortunate. Yet many of the reasons why we should avoid the blind application of Western aesthetic criteria to African novels also suggest that we should avoid the wholesale application of bourgeois aesthetic criteria to postrevolutionary Soviet novels. For one thing, much African postcolonial literature is also postrevolutionary in that it focuses on the process through which numerous African nations gained their independence through anticolonial revolutions. Thus, the novels of the radical Kenyan novelist Ngugi wa Thiong'o, especially *Devil on the Cross* (1982) and *Matigari* (1987), focus centrally on a hoped-for future revolution, in ways that often recall Russian works such as Maxim Gorky's *Mother* (1907). In addition, Ngugi's novels from *A Grain of Wheat* (1967) to *Matigari* draw important energies from the Mau Mau rebellion against British rule in the 1950s, while the Mau Mau are also central to numerous other Kenyan novels, including Charles Mangua's *A Tail in the Mouth* (1972) and Meja Mwangi's *Carcase for Hounds* (1974) and *Taste of Death* (1975). Similarly, Zimbabwean novels such as Chinjerai Hove's *Bones* (1988) and Shimmer Chinodya's *Harvest of Thorns* (1989) deal with the long and difficult Zimbabwean war of liberation from white rule, while Pepetela's *Mayombe* (1984) focuses on the Angolan war of independence from Portuguese rule. Such war novels recall the central importance of the Great Patriotic War (the Second World War) in major socialist realist works such as Anatoli Ivanov's *The Eternal Call* (1971–7), Alexander Fadeyev's *The Young Guard* (1945), Boris Polevoi's *Story of a Real Man* (1946), Yuri Krymov's *Tanker Derbent* (1938) and Konstantin Simonov's *Days and Nights* (1944). But African novels of anticolonial war even more directly recall the prominence of the Civil War of 1917 to 1920 in early Soviet socialist realism, with such important works as Dmitry Furmanov's *Chapayev* (1923), Sholokhov's *Quiet Flows the Don* (1928), Alexander Serafimovich's *The Iron Flood* (1924), Fadeyev's *The Rout* (1927), Nikolai Ostrovsky's *How the Steel Was Tempered* (1932–4) and Alexei Tolstoy's *The Ordeal*

(1919–41) focusing centrally on that crucial early moment in Soviet history. Civil wars are also important in African fiction, though sometimes in a more sombre way, especially in the numerous works – Wole Soyinka's *Season of Anomy* (1973), Elechi Amadi's *Estrangement* (1986), Buchi Emecheta's *Destination Biafra* (1982), Festus Iyayi's *Heroes* (1986) – that deal with the Nigerian–Biafran Civil War of 1967 to 1970.

In addition to such general and thematic parallels, it should not be forgotten that many postcolonial African writers have been directly influenced by Soviet and Russian culture, and by Marxism in general. The African philosopher and novelist V.Y. Mudimbe notes that, while African thought from the 1930s to the 1950s was informed by a number of important influences, Marxism was clearly the most important of these.[18] Further, Mudimbe notes that (while he himself works from a somewhat Foucauldian perspective) Marxism, along with a more general critique of imperialism, remains the most vital force in African philosophy to this day. Figures such as Aimé Césaire, Leopold Senghor, Kwame Nkrumah and Julius Nyerere all made important contributions to the attempt to adapt socialism to an African context. Meanwhile, as critics such as Emmanuel Ngara and Georg Gugelberger have noted, Marxism has had an important influence not only on African philosophy and politics but also on African literature, which is, in fact, inseparable from African philosophy and politics.[19] Ngugi is perhaps the best known example of this phenomenon, and it is telling that Ngugi, when listing the novelists who had the greatest influence on his own development as a writer, includes such Russian figures as Nikolai Gogol, Fyodor Dostoevsky, Leo Tolstoy, Gorky and Sholokhov, in addition to Honoré de Balzac, William Faulkner and the Caribbean novelist George Lamming.[20] One should not underestimate the direct role played by Soviet support in the growth of postcolonial African culture. Ousmane Sembène, after all, became the father of African cinema only after he had studied at the Moscow Film School, while writers such as Ngugi and Iyayi worked and studied in the Soviet Union with the official support of the Soviet government. In fact, the Soviet Union provided extensive moral and material support to many of the African writers who were just beginning to develop their craft in the early years of nominal independence from colonial rule, while Russian writers, including Soviet ones, provided important models for novelists who were seeking new forms that might escape the domination of the West.

That the historical novel would be central to such a project might be predicted from Georg Lukács's classic argument, in *The Historical Novel*, that the great historical novels of the nineteenth century are the quintessential expressions of literary realism and of the ideology of the bourgeoisie in the early days of their rise to power in Europe.[21] Indeed, Lukács makes these comments in a context in which he is urging socialist writers to follow the example of their bourgeois predecessors. For Lukács, in short, history is the special province not of the bourgeoisie, but of whatever revolutionary class happens to be the principal agent of historical change at any given point in time. By the twentieth century, Lukács argues elsewhere, 'the road to socialism is identical with the movement of history itself'.[22] History, long used by the bourgeoisie to legitimate their new power in modern Europe, becomes for Lukács the principal grounds upon which bourgeois hegemony can be challenged. Soviet writers seemed to agree, and one of the distinguishing features of Soviet socialist realism is its sense of itself as a postrevolutionary literature that participates in and draws its energies from a revolutionary process of historical transformation.

For Lukács (as for anyone with a genuinely dialectical sense of history) there is no contradiction between his belief that modern socialist writers need to look for models in the work of nineteenth-century bourgeois writers such as Walter Scott and Balzac and his conviction that socialism is part of an ongoing historical transformation that will ultimately render moot the earlier historical victory of the bourgeoisie. After all, the revolutionary victory that bourgeois history is designed to narrate is, in Marxist thought, merely a stage in a longer historical process that ultimately leads to the triumph of socialism. In addition, the whole phenomenon of Soviet socialist realism represents an attempt to contest the bourgeoisie on what had earlier been their own ground and to struggle for control of the historical representation of the Soviet project. It is no accident, for example, that so many of the greatest works of socialist realism (*Quiet Flows the Don*, Gorky's *The Life of Klim Samgin* (1927–36), Alexei Tolstoy's *Peter the First* (1929–45)) explicitly belong to the genre of the historical novel or that other leading socialist realist works (*Mother*, *How the Steel Was Tempered*, Feodor Gladkov's *Cement* (1925)) are so intimately engaged with history that they can rightly be considered historical novels, even when they (like the novels of Balzac) are essentially located in the present. One of the central insights of a revolutionary history is that history occurs not just in the past, but in the present and the future.

But Soviet socialist realists are not the only twentieth-century writers who have attempted to overcome and move beyond the imposing tandem tradition of bourgeois aesthetics and bourgeois history. For example, given the material impact of colonialism on African history and the symbolic impact of colonialist historiography on the African imagination, it is obvious that history is a crucial area of contestation for African writers who seek to wrest control of their cultural identities from the metropolitan centre of Europe. It is thus not surprising that African writers have also quite often employed the historical novel as part of their programme to generate new postcolonial African cultural identities that transcend this inherited tradition of European bourgeois historiography and that escape definition by the colonial past. For example, each of Ngugi's novels focuses on a particular moment in the history of Kenya, and together his novels, ranging from *The River Between* (1965) to *Matigari*, constitute a sweeping historical narrative that tells the story of Kenya from the early days of British colonization to the contemporary postcolonial period, focusing on the strong Kenyan tradition of resistance to oppression. Indeed, Ngugi has openly proclaimed that Kenyan history provides the principal inspiration for his fiction, especially in the sense that 'the Kenyan peoples' struggle against foreign domination' is the 'one consistent theme' of this history over the past 400 years.[23] In a similar (if less politically specific) manner, Achebe, in works such as *Things Fall Apart* (1958), seeks to provide his African readers with a realistic depiction of their precolonial past, free of the distortions and stereotypes imposed upon that past in European accounts. Meanwhile, Achebe's novels, from *Things Fall Apart* to *Anthills of the Savannah* (1987), collectively trace the colonial and neocolonial history of Nigeria. Other representative examples of African historical novels include Nadine Gordimer's intense engagement with the history of apartheid in South Africa in works such as *Burger's Daughter* (1979) and *A Sport of Nature* (1987),[24] Sembène's dramatization of a 1947–8 railway strike in French colonial Africa in *God's Bits of Woods* (1960), M.G. Vassanji's imaginative retelling of the history of Tanzania in *The Gunny Sack* (1989), Nuruddin Farah's elaboration in his trilogy 'Variations on the Theme of an African Dictatorship' (1979–83) of the Siyad Barre period in Somalia, Ben Okri's attempt to capture the spirit of modern Nigerian history through an Africanized magical realism in *The Famished Road* (1991), Yambo Ouologuem's somewhat notorious depiction of African history as a never-ending cycle of abject violence in *Bound to Violence* (1968) and Ayi Kwei Armah's *Two Thousand Seasons* (1973), a more positive and mythic version of African history (written partially in response to Ouologuem).

The centrality of history in both Soviet and African novels arises from a number of sources, not the least of which is the fact that both Russians and Africans have long had to face the systematic exclusion of their cultures from Western European bourgeois narratives of history. In the case of Africa, this exclusion has received considerable attention in recent years and is now well known. Ngugi, for example, notes that the people's history of anticolonial struggle on which his work so centrally depends is virtually absent from 'official' histories of Kenya, which continue even in the era of nominal independence to see the central event of recent Kenyan history not as resistance to colonization but simply as colonization itself. Such histories thus take their cue from the long and woeful tradition of colonialist historiography, which played a central role in the European colonial domination of Africa by envisioning Africa as a timeless place without history, mired in the primeval past and unable to move forward until the European colonizers brought new energies and new knowledge to the continent. Catherine Coquery-Vidrovitch describes this phenomenon, noting that

> colonialist histories have long perpetuated the myth of a sub-Saharan Africa conquered fairly easily and profiting from pacification [...]. The local populations, according to these histories, were finally delivered by the 'colonial peace' from the internal struggles of little local rulers

forever raiding their neighbors' territories in search of slaves or livestock.[25]

Mudimbe notes that such histories 'speak neither about Africa nor Africans, but rather justify the process of inventing and conquering a continent and naming its "primitiveness" or "disorder," as well as the subsequent means of its exploitation and methods for its "regeneration".'[26] It is little wonder, then, that Ngugi sees history as a crucial ground upon which contemporary African writers must challenge the cultural legacy of colonialism. In particular, the recovery of the Kenyan history of anticolonial resistance becomes a central project of Ngugi's postcolonial fiction, which thereby seeks to help provide his fellow Kenyans with a useable past upon which to build a viable present and future.

The colonialist historiography opposed by Ngugi relies on a polar opposition between Europe and the rest of the world of a kind that has been identified by Edward Said as central to 'Orientalist' (and, by extension, Africanist)[27] discourses as a whole. Indeed, for Said, Europe centrally depends for its cultural identity on 'the idea of European identity as a superior one in comparison with all the non-European peoples and cultures'.[28] On the other hand, Europe itself is not nearly so monolithic as Said seems to imply, and the 'Europe' he describes in *Orientalism* is really Western Europe, which began in the Enlightenment to develop a sense of itself in terms of its self-proclaimed moral and cultural superiority not only to non-Europeans but to Eastern Europeans as well.[29] The resulting image of Eastern Europe (with a special focus on areas such as Russia and the Balkans) as a primitive and barbaric land ruled by despots and peopled by half-savage tribesmen clearly resonates with colonialist visions of Africa while also providing crucial background for much of the Western rhetoric of the Cold War, which can be seen in retrospect to have been fuelled not only by a capitalist terror of communism but also by racialist fears of Eastern European primitivity. Meanwhile, Orientalist fears of Russia (which, after all, extends east of China) are linked in an especially direct way to colonialism, as when the British consistently justified the nineteenth-century expansion of their empire on the grounds that such expansion was necessary to counter the menace of Russian expansionism.[30]

Western European discourse about Russia often envisioned the Russians as a people without history, much in the way Africans are pictured in colonialist histories. Nineteenth-century Russian writers such as Alexander Pushkin, Gogol, Dostoevsky and Leo Tolstoy were thus in much the same marginalized position with regard to history as Africans writers such as Ngugi would later be. For example, in his influential study of the fiction of Dostoevsky, Michael Holquist argues that the fragile and unstable identities of Dostoevsky's characters reflect the way in which a sense of existing outside the mainstream of European history led to an uncertain sense of cultural identity in nineteenth-century Russia as a whole. Despite the strength of nineteenth-century Russian literature, Holquist suggests that 'doubts about the existence of a national literature, not pious affirmations of Russian culture, carried the day in the early nineteenth century'.[31] He then illustrates this point with reference to the work of nineteenth-century thinker Pyotr Chaadaev, noting that Chaadaev's work

> cut to the heart of all doubts about the history of particular Russian institutions, political as well as cultural, by declaring, in effect, the Russians had no history at all: 'Historical experience does not exist for us. Generations and ages have passed without benefit to us. With regard to us it is as if the general law of mankind had been suspended [. . .].' He goes on to speak of the Russians as 'being somehow out of time.'[32]

Holquist further observes that the attempts of Dostoevsky's characters to employ narrative as a means to develop a viable sense of self parallel the broader nineteenth-century Russian project of developing historical narratives to supply a viable sense of national identity. Indeed, for Holquist, literature in general functions as a particularly important site for attempts to establish a stable Russian cultural identity in the nineteenth century. As a result, 'history was more often than not in Russia equated with literary history'.[33] Meanwhile, though writers like G.R. Derzhavin and N.M. Karamzin had already struggled to find a Russian literary voice, the special exigencies of Russian history left early nineteenth-century writers such as Pushkin and Gogol with virtually no native Russian literary tradition upon which to draw. Such writers were thus forced to try to create their own traditions and conventions, attempting to avoid domination by the conventions of the West while at the same time seeking recognition and respect from their Western counterparts.

In this sense, the situation of nineteenth-century Russian writers directly anticipates that in which postcolonial writers have found themselves in recent decades. Typically working in European languages and genres, writers from Africa, Asia, South America and the Caribbean have struggled for respect from a powerful Western world still dominated by the old Enlightenment notion that the ability to read and write is a prerequisite of genuine humanity. Yet postcolonial writers, while having to demonstrate that they can write on the terms of the West, have at the same time had to try to contribute to the development of new postcolonial cultural identities that go beyond the past legacy of colonial domination. In many ways, of course, the cultural and historical situation of Russia in the nineteenth century differs substantially from that of postcolonial Africa. In particular, while many nineteenth-century Russians, following in the footsteps of Peter the Great, were struggling to enter an Enlightenment from which they had largely been excluded, postcolonial Africans are still struggling to deal with the consequences of an Enlightenment that was forcibly thrust upon them during the era of colonialism. Nineteenth-century Russian writers and postcolonial African writers in this sense have very different cultural projects, though it should also be recalled that major figures such as Gogol and Dostoevsky sided firmly with the 'Slavophiles' in the Manichean culture wars that raged in their society, railing against Western influence as a moral and spiritual contamination of the 'true' (Christian Orthodox) Russia.

In many ways, then, the Russian writers whose historical situation most resembles that of postcolonial African writers are not nineteenth-century figures such as Pushkin and Dostoevsky but postrevolutionary socialist writers such as Gorky, Sholokhov and Alexei Tolstoy. After all, Soviet literature is itself in a sense postcolonial. The period from Peter the Great to the October Revolution can be seen as a sort of quasi-colonial era in which Russia was economically exploited by the emergent capitalism of the West and at least to an extent dominated, if not literally by Western European powers, then figuratively by the imperialistic discourse of the Western Enlightenment, which pronounced itself the universal epitome of modernity, thus consigning everything else to the ashcan of primitivity and inferiority. The two-stage nature of the Russian Revolution, meanwhile, encapsulates the process by which Russians sought to overcome this legacy. The March Revolution can then be seen as a necessary break with the feudal past of tsarist Russia, while the October Revolution takes this process further into an anticolonial rejection of the Western bourgeois ideology that had gradually seeped into Russia and which, from March to October of 1917, was momentarily triumphant. In short, the two Russian Revolutions together constitute precisely the double movement toward emancipation that Frantz Fanon saw as necessary in colonial Africa: first independence from white European rule; then, class-based revolution to overturn the indigenous bourgeoisie who would inevitably come to power at the moment of decolonization.[34]

The relevance of Fanon's work to the postrevolutionary Soviet situation (and to postrevolutionary Soviet literature) can be clearly seen in Gorky's *Klim Samgin*, surely one of the most important literary works to have been produced in the Soviet Union, though one that has not been widely read in the West, despite Gorky's relatively (compared to other Soviet writers) positive reputation there, no doubt partially because of the massive length of this four-volume, three-thousand-page opus. *Klim Samgin* is somewhat unusual among major Soviet postrevolutionary works because of its bourgeois protagonist and its focus on the historical period prior to the October Revolution. Indeed, this massive work, the centrepiece of Gorky's postrevolutionary writing, has very little in common with the Western stereotype of the socialist realist novel (with its presumably obligatory supersocialist positive hero and its formulaic happy ending as all conflicts are resolved in the interest of progress toward socialism), despite Gorky's unchallenged status as the father of Soviet socialist realism. As a matter of fact, all of Gorky's novels differ substantially from the stereotypical Western view of socialist realism, as in fact do most Soviet novels, demonstrating the facticity of the stereotype, which in retrospect appears to be simply another example of Western Cold War propaganda, of a piece with paranoid and hysterical visions of communist hordes overrunning the West, raping and pillaging along the way.

Klim Samgin is a crucial work of socialist realism that demonstrates the historical necessity of the Russian Revolution by detailing, in epic proportions, the aborted birth of the Russian bourgeoisie, struggling for influence and power at the end of the nineteenth century and beginning of the twentieth. In this sense, Gorky follows directly in the footsteps of bourgeois historical novelists such as Scott, precisely as Lukács would advise. For Lukács, 'the great novels of world literature, in particular those of the nineteenth century, portray not so much the collapse of a society as its process of disintegration, each one embracing a phase of this process [...]. The essential aim of the novel is the representation of the way society moves.'[35] Thus, Scott's novels narrate the sweeping away of a whole way of life in feudal, clan-dominated Scotland, treating this old way sympathetically while nevertheless treating its demise as inevitable and as no particular cause for nostalgia, much in the way Sholokhov's *Quiet Flows the Don* narrates the demise of rural Cossack society as Russia moves toward socialism. Meanwhile, if Scott depicts the demise of feudal Scottish society as the necessary historical prerequisite for the rise of British capitalism, *Klim Samgin* narrates the disintegration of bourgeois society in Russia, even before it fully came into being. Gorky thus not only echoes Scott but anticipates the postcolonial situation as well. The central insight of *Klim Samgin* is that the emergent Russian bourgeoisie were already prematurely decadent, much in the way Fanon envisions the premature decadence of the postcolonial African bourgeoisie, who come to power far too late in history and thus become little more than a feeble echo of the rise of their Western European predecessors, thereby demonstrating the validity of Marx's famous observation (in *The Eighteenth Brumaire*) about the inevitable repetition of historical events, first as tragedy, then as farce. *Klim Samgin* is abundantly clear in its searing portrayal of the decadence of the emergent bourgeoisie in pre-Soviet Russia, among other things thereby giving the lie to the standard Western fantasy that Russia would now be a modern, affluent democracy if only the Kerensky government had been allowed to run its course without the rude interruption of Lenin and the Bolsheviks.[36] Moreover, Gorky makes his revolutionary point inescapable when he has his protagonist symbolically drop dead at the moment of Lenin's triumphant arrival in St Petersburg on his way to power, thus announcing the death of the bourgeois alternative and the birth of the socialist one.

In comparison, one might cite a text such as Armah's *The Beautyful Ones Are Not Yet Born* (1969), which employs an overtly Fanonian perspective to detail the woes of postcolonial Ghana, but which ends with the positive image of a potential utopian future in which the 'beautyful ones' will be born at last, as the book's nameless (and thus highly allegorical) protagonist spots a bus that bears a picture of a flower (a traditional symbol of rebirth) surrounded by a legend that is repeated in the book's title.[37] As Neil Lazarus puts it, Armah's purpose in the book is 'to describe the preconditions of and prevailing constraints to change. The novel is formulated upon the premise that it is only by knowing one's world, by seeing it for what it is, that one can ever genuinely aspire to bring about its revolutionary transformation.'[38] Lazarus here is making the point that Armah's work resembles the Marxist plays of Bertolt Brecht, but Gorky might provide an even more direct analogy. Not only does the message of *The Beautyful Ones* resemble that of *Klim Samgin* in important ways, but the title and the associated message of Armah's novel are directly anticipated near the end of Gorky's autobiographical *My Universities* (1923), when the enlightened peasant Barinov tells the young Gorky, 'Evil men are the truth, but where are the good ones? Not even invented yet, oh no!'[39]

Of course, Armah is hardly alone among African writers in having been strongly influenced by Fanon, who has also provided the most important theoretical basis for the political vision of Ngugi. Indeed, the crucial impact of Fanon (and of Marxist thought in general) on postcolonial African writers is well known. Sembène, Iyayi and Alex La Guma are only the first of many names (in addition to Armah and Ngugi) that come to mind to illustrate this phenomenon. On the other hand, *Klim Samgin* and other postrevolutionary Russian texts differ substantially from African novels of postcolonial decadence in the sense that Soviet writers like Gorky can rely on the Russian Revolution as background, thus placing them, as it were, one step ahead of their African counterparts in the Fanonian narrative of revolutionary history. Moreover, if Soviet novelists end up at a different point along the narrative of history than do African ones, it is also the case that Russians first entered the flow of history (in the Western European, bourgeois sense) in a very different way than did Africans. In Africa, 'history' first arrived aboard slaving ships and in the persons of Christian missionaries dedicated to the destruction of indigenous African culture and religion. In Russia, this process began in a more positive fashion with the attempts of Peter the Great, beginning at the end of the seventeenth century, to transform his still-medieval Russia along lines suggested by the Western Enlightenment. Peter's project did in fact bring great changes to Russian society, though these changes were staunchly resisted by many elements of Russian society (especially the Orthodox Church), while Russia's participation in the cultural and political life of Europe remained marginal and secondary at best. Meanwhile, the radical rupture in the flow of Russian history effected during Peter's reign separated Russians from their own native cultural and political traditions as well, eventually contributing to the nineteenth-century Russian sense of historical estrangement described by Holquist.

Not surprisingly, both Russian and African historical novels have frequently dealt with this moment of entry into Western history. For example, Peter's attempts to transform Russia provide the subject matter for Alexei

Tolstoy's historical novel *Peter the First*, described by K. Zelinsky as being (along with *Quiet Flows the Don*) one of the two 'peaks of Soviet fiction'.[40] *Peter the First* provides a vivid evocation of the texture of Russian life in the dark and barbarous time of its eponymous protagonist, capturing very well the complexity and contradictions of this crucial turning point in Russian history. *Peter the First* presents characters from all layers of Russian society, which is depicted as an intricately interrelated totality, very much in the way described by Lukács as a crucial project of the greatest historical novels. Indeed, it is clear that Russia as a whole is the true protagonist of the text, though Peter himself is certainly the book's central character in the traditional sense. And, though Tolstoy is careful to avoid depicting Peter's attempted revolution as a sort of allegorical anticipation of the Soviet project, he does make clear Peter's status as a predecessor to the Bolsheviks and as a modernizer who helped to take a primitive Russia one step closer to the day when the Soviet Union might become a historical possibility. Peter, though presented in anything but a simplistic way, is thus portrayed in an essentially positive light, as is his modernizing project.

Meanwhile, African novels about the beginnings of European domination in Africa are legion. Ngugi's *The River Between* is a good example of a novel that treats this process from a complex perspective that is staunchly anti-colonial while refusing to endorse a nostalgic return to the precolonial past. History, for Ngugi, moves only forward. Ouologuem's *Bound to Violence* also pays attention to the first moments of European rule in Africa, but presents a much more pessimistic vision of African history as a never-ending cycle of violence in which the period of European colonization is merely one stage. Armah's *Two Thousand Seasons* employs a similarly broad scope, acknowledging indigenous contributions to the baleful history of violence in Africa but also including a strong utopian element that retains hope in a better future based on the communal 'way' of traditional African society. However, Tolstoy's vision of Peter's reforms as a progressive step forward might be contrasted with a text such as *Things Fall Apart*, the Yeatsian title of which indicates the traumatic and essentially destructive nature of modernization in colonial Africa. As opposed to the dynamic world-historical figure of Peter the Great, Achebe's novel features the tragic hero Okonkwo, whose demise mirrors that of traditional Igbo society in which he had formerly been a leading figure. Achebe has made it clear that his principal purpose in the book was to provide African readers with a realistic depiction of their precolonial past, free of the distortions and stereotypes imposed upon that past in European accounts. The Africans of Achebe's book live not in primitive savagery but in a sophisticated society 'in which life is rounded and intricate and sensitively in correspondence with a range of human impulses. It admits both the aristocratic and the democratic principles. It is a life lived by a dignified clan of equals who meet together in an Athenian way.'[41]

Achebe's reminders that precolonial African societies functioned in such sophisticated ways are, of course, valuable to both African and Western readers. Meanwhile, Achebe also reminds us that the coming of European 'civilization' had disastrous consequences for traditional Igbo culture and was (especially with the added perspective of nearly forty years of postcolonial history) the prerequisite for a movement toward not a golden future but the miseries of the Biafran War and the subsequent Nigerian military dictatorships. On the other hand, however tragic the consequences of European colonization for Igbo culture, it might also be argued (as Michael Valdez Moses has in fact done) that, sharp though Achebe's critique of colonialism may be, Achebe ultimately accepts the historical inevitability of modernization in a mode that shows a fundamental agreement with 'the historicist legacy of Hegel's thinking'.[42] Viewed in this way, *Things Fall Apart* also begins to resemble the historical novels of Scott, with the demise of Igbo culture as narrated by Achebe paralleling the fall of Scottish clan culture as narrated by Scott (or, for that matter, the demise of Russian cossack culture as narrated by Sholokhov). In all three cases, the destruction of an older culture paves the wave for the onslaught of modernity, though Scott and Sholokhov ultimately endorse this process as a necessary step toward the triumph of modernity in their respective societies, while Achebe describes the process from the perspective of a defeated adversary of modernity.

In this sense, Soviet writers, following in the wake of a successful socialist revolution, are closer to Scott than are African writers like Achebe, though it is also the case that postrevolutionary Soviet writers work at a time when the historical victory of socialism is anything but assured and when they must therefore to some extent anticipate the future in their vision of history. Numerous African novels also feature strong utopian components that must of necessity be located in the future. The African writer who most resembles Soviet ones in this regard is probably Nadine Gordimer, especially in *A Sport of Nature*, which envisions the end of apartheid in a way that would quite soon be realized. Meanwhile, the complexity of the relationship between African and Soviet writers with respect to their engagement with history mirrors the complexity of the phenomenon of modernity itself. On the one hand, one can see the Soviet Union as the culmination of the Enlightenment and therefore as a phenomenon to be grouped with the 'West' in opposition to African and other non-Western cultures. On the other hand, one can see the Soviet Union as belonging to the same category of these non-Western cultures, long excluded from the Enlightenment and attempting to compete with the West in the global political and economic marketplace.

The recent collapse of the Soviet Union, of course, is an event that casts new light on the phenomenon of modernity in Russia, though the exact implications of this event are yet to be determined. For example, if one believes, with John Gray, that the attempt to build a socialist state in the Soviet Union was 'the greatest rationalist project in human history' and 'one of the Enlightenment's most stupendous constructions', then surely the demise of the Soviet state casts significant doubt on the inevitable historical triumph of modernity. Gray believes that, eventually, 'the Soviet collapse will be seen not as another surge in an irresistible movement of Westernization but as the beginning of the world-historical reversal of that movement'.[43] This collapse, then, 'is probably best interpreted not, fortunately, as a victory for Western capitalism, but instead as a decisive moment in the global counter-movement against Westernization, now underway in many parts of the world, in which Occidental ideologies are repudiated and Western models of social life spurned'.[44] For Gray, in short, the Enlightenment is a bust, and the best hope for the future lies in non-Occidental cultures, though he is also worried that the global reach of the Enlightenment project may have already contaminated many of these cultures with 'the radical modernist project of subjugating nature by deploying technology to exploit the earth for human purposes'.[45]

Gray's analysis of recent events as a victory of the various indigenous non-Western cultures of the former Soviet Union over the modernizing drive of the central Soviet state needs to be examined in the light of numerous complicating factors, not the least of which is that the collapse of the Soviet Union seemed to radiate outward from Moscow itself, eventually reaching Kazakhstan and Turkmenistan, but hardly originating there. On the other hand, Gray's belief that the fall of the Soviet Union signalled a major turning point in world history is shared by numerous scholars with whom he might otherwise agree about very little, suggesting the crucial importance of an understanding of the Soviet experience (and, presumably, of Soviet culture) to anyone who would seek to understand the course of modernity in the twentieth century. For example, Gray's vision of Soviet culture as a product of the Enlightenment in many ways recalls Theodore Von Laue's 1987 *The World Revolution of Westernization*, in which Von Laue figures the history of the twentieth century as the story of the worldwide triumph of 'Westernization', which can be taken as roughly synonymous with modernity. For Von Laue, the Soviets may indeed have provided the most important opposition to Westernization, but they themselves actually represented a Westernizing force of an only slightly different kind. However, Von Laue, though not entirely sanguine about the prospects of a thoroughly Westernized world, differs from Gray in that he sees no particular reason why Westernization must, or should, come to an end.[46] In this sense, Von Laue anticipates Francis Fukuyama's post-Cold-War notion that we have reached 'the end of history' and that all that remains is a minor mopping-up operation in which Western capitalism and 'democracy' will assert their global and permanent hegemony.[47]

Gray, in fact, responds directly to Fukuyama in much of his recent work, declaring Fukuyama's vision an 'absurdist' model of history.[48] Indeed, Fukuyama's notion of history can be challenged on numerous counts, including the common-sense reminder of the historian John Lukacs that we are certainly living at the end of a century, but that this hardly constitutes the end of history altogether. Lukacs even grants that we are living at the beginning of the end of the Modern Age, but for him this constitutes anything but the beginning of an eternity of capitalist and democratic triumph. Lukacs, of course, has his own limitations. For one thing, he sometimes lapses into a rather crude anticommunism, despite his own characterization of American anticommunists as crudely opportunistic. He thus hardly mourns the passing of the Soviet Union, but he also believes that both capitalism and democracy (Fukuyama's key terms) have passed their peak and have taken on sinister and oppressive aspects, including a tendency toward rule by mass taste that for Lukacs contrasts with the more genteel and civilized values of earlier days, when bourgeois hegemony was still tempered by aristocratic virtues such as 'high-mindedness and generosity' and the 'primacy of a sense of honor over that of a passion for fame'.[49]

For Lukacs, the story of the twentieth century is not the opposition between capitalism and communism but a competition among nations not all that different from the nationalist inclinations of the nineteenth century. He thus argues that the Cold War remained cold largely because the Russian and American peoples had no historical nationalist antipathies between them.[50] This emphasis may partially reflect Lukacs's desire to discount the importance of communism as a force in modern world history, but in some ways it resembles Eric Hobsbawm's recent argument that, in retrospect, we will eventually see the major event of the twentieth century as the culmination of 'the seven or eight millennia of human history that began with the invention of agriculture in the stone age, if only because it ended the long era when the overwhelming majority of the human race lived by growing food and herding animals'.[51]

Hobsbawm's vision of history is based on an essentially Marxist notion of the movement of history as shifts in mode of production, though Hobsbawm considerably lengthens his historical vision by locating the beginnings of the movement toward modernity in the Stone Age rather than in the Renaissaance. Hobsbawm, meanwhile, believes that Marxism is still a legitimate alternative to capitalism, even after the fall of the Soviet Union. In particular, while Hobsbawm argues that the Russian Revolution was far and away the most important single historical event of the twentieth century, he does not see the twentieth century as centrally informed by the opposition between capitalism and communism. Nor does he see the failure of the Soviet Union as an indictment of socialism per se. He concludes that Lenin and the other leaders of the Bolshevik Revolution initially had no illusions that they could build socialism in the Soviet Union alone, but instead staked their hopes on a belief (not at all far-fetched in the context of the times) that their revolution might trigger working-class revolts in Germany and other advanced industrial countries. That broader revolution, however, was not to be, and, though the triumphs of the Red Army in the Second World War would lead to the spread of Soviet influence over much of Eastern and Central Europe and the long-suffering Chinese communists would complete their long march to power soon afterward, the Bolshevik commitment to socialism remained for decades limited to the Soviet Union itself and never involved a concentrated effort at imperial expansion. Even this commitment had to do more with theory than with practice. Thwarted in their initial plans to export revolution worldwide, the Soviet communists had little choice but to set about the desperate project of building socialism in the huge, impoverished and unruly political entity that was the Soviet Union. Recognizing that this could not be done in a poor, backward country, the Soviets set forth on an astonishingly ambitious (and sometimes ruthless) campaign of rapid modernization based on a combination of 'an all-out offensive against the cultural backwardness of the notoriously "dark," ignorant, illiterate, and superstitious masses with an all-out drive for technological modernization and industrial revolution'.[52] This project was not without its successes. As Hobsbawm points out, Soviet economic policies 'turned the USSR into a major industrial economy in just a few years and one capable, as Tsarist Russia had not been, of surviving and winning the war against Germany in spite of the temporary loss of areas containing a third of her population and, in many industries, half the industrial plant'.[53]

Moreover, Soviet policies provided a social safety net unheard-of in the centuries of tsarist rule, while in education the 'transformation of a largely illiterate country into the modern USSR was, by any standards, a towering achievement'.[54] Nevertheless, the intense emphasis on modernization under Stalin meant that the socialist project of social and political emancipation had to take a back seat. The ultimate result was that Stalinism became a model not for building socialism (which it failed to do) but for modernizing societies that were (by the standards of the Western Enlightenment) culturally and economically backward. This fact establishes still another point of contact between the postrevolutionary culture of the Soviet Union and the postcolonial culture of Africa, where numerous leaders, understanding the development potential of Stalinist central planning, turned precisely to that system as a model in their attempts to build postcolonial societies that could successfully compete in the global political and economic marketplace. Even overtly capitalist 'developing' nations (South Korea is perhaps the key example) turned to central planning in building their new economies, while ostensibly socialist countries (of which there were so many in the early postcolonial era in Africa) were understandably even more likely to look to the Soviet model for guidance.

It is also not surprising that those involved in the attempt to develop new cultural identities in the postcolonial world have often turned to the Soviet experiment for models, not only because of the parallels we have already discussed between postrevolutionary culture and postcolonial culture but also because of the important role played in Soviet cultural production by non-European cultures. Indeed, one potential problem with Gray's analysis of the Soviet collapse is his failure to address the fact that Soviet culture in its last few decades was so greatly enriched by the contributions of various 'national' literatures at a time when mainstream Russian literature was in a definite period of decadence and decline. Thus, while Russian writers such as Anatoli

Ivanov and Konstantin Simonov continued to produce important works of socialist realism in the classic mode of the 1930s, perhaps the most exciting energies in Soviet literature following the Second World War came from writers such as the Kazakh Mukhtar Auezov and the Kirghiz Chingiz Aitmatov.[55] It is thus no surprise that, as early as 1948, the Indian writer Kumar Goshal was urging colonial peoples all over the world to look to the literatures of the Soviet Central Asian Republics as models for their own early attempts to develop indigenous literatures, just as postcolonial writers have often looked to Soviet literature for inspiration ever since.[56]

Among other things, the direct influence of Soviet culture on postcolonial culture suggests that Jameson's Manichean opposition between First World and Third World cultures in his 1986 'Third-World Literatures' essay needs to be mediated by a consideration of the important role played by Second World literature, which somehow vanishes from Jameson's account almost entirely, even though some of his central examples of Third World literature are works by Marxist-influenced writers such as Sembène and the Chinese Lu Hsun. But the various connections and parallels between Soviet postrevolutionary literature and African postcolonial literature also suggest that Jameson's insistence that First World intellectuals should pay more attention to Third World literature goes for Second World literature as well. In recent years, many Western scholars have gained important new insights into literature, history and the relationship between the two by studying postcolonial literatures, and that trend promises to continue for the foreseeable future. Soviet socialist realism might yield similar dividends if we can only overcome our lingering Cold War Stalinophobia and allow it to do so.

Notes

1 This essay previously appeared in Dubravka Juraga and M. Keith Booker, eds, *Socialist Cultures East and West: A Post-Cold War Reassessment* (Westport, Conn., and London: Praeger, 2002), pp. 11–30. Reprinted with permission.
2 Jameson, 'Third-World Literature in the Era of Multinational Capitalism', *Social Text*, 15 (1986), pp. 65–88.
3 Robin, *Socialist Realism: An Impossible Aesthetic* (1992); Slonim, *Modern Russian Literature from Chekhov to the Present* (1953); Struve, *Soviet Russian Literature 1917–50* (1951). On the obvious bias of Western Sovietologists see Albert Beliaev, *The Ideological Struggle and Literature: A Critical Analysis of the Writings of U.S. Sovietologists* (1975).
4 Clark, *The Soviet Novel: History as Ritual* (1981).
5 Some of the most important of these studies available in English include Yuri Barabash, *Aesthetics and Politics* (1968); Dmitry Markov, *Socialist Literatures: Problems of Development* (1975); A. Ovcharenko, *Socialist Realism and the Modern Literary Process* (1968); and Avner Zis, *Foundations of Marxist Aesthetics* (1976).
6 Lahusen and Dobrenko, eds, *Socialist Realism without Borders*, special number of *South Atlantic Quarterly*, 94: 3 (1995).
7 Dobrenko, 'The Disaster of Middlebrow Taste, or, Who "Invented" Socialist Realism', *South Atlantic Quarterly*, 94: 3 (1995), pp. 773–806.

8 Pietz, 'The "Post-Colonialism" of Cold War Discourse', *Social Text*, 19–20 (Fall 1988), p. 69.
9 Ibid., p. 69. For more on the colonialist sources of Western Cold War rhetoric see M. Keith Booker, *Colonial Power, Colonial Texts: India in the Modern British Novel* (1997).
10 A substantial body of leftist literature by American and British writers was similarly consigned to subliterary status and is only now, after the end of the Cold War, being resurrected by Western critics. On American leftist literature in this regard see Barbara Foley, *Radical Representations: Politics and Form in U.S. Proletarian Fiction, 1929–1941* (1993); Cary Nelson, *Repression and Recovery: Modern American Poetry and the Politics of Cultural Memory, 1914–1945* (1989); and Alan Wald, *Writing from the Left: New Essays on Radical Culture and Politics* (1994). On British leftist literature see Andy Croft, *Red Letter Days: British Fiction in the 1930s* (1990); Pamela Fox, *Class Fictions: Shame and Resistance in the British Working-Class Novel, 1890–1945* (1994) and H. Gustav Klaus, ed., *The Socialist Novel in Britain: Towards the Recovery of a Tradition* (1982). On potential parallels between the African historical novel and the historical novels of the Western left see M. Keith Booker, 'The Historical Novel in Ayi Kwei Armah and David Caute: African Literature, Socialist Literature, and the Bourgeois Cultural Tradition', *Critique*, 38: 3 (1997), pp. 235–48.
11 See, for example, Huyssen for a suggestion that modernism was 'domesticated' for just such purposes in the 1950s and 'turned into a propaganda weapon in the cultural-political arsenal of Cold War anti-communism': Andreas Huyssen, *After the Great Divide: Modernism, Mass Culture, Postmodernism* (Bloomington: Indiana University Press, 1986), p. 190.
12 We have sometimes fallen into the same trap ourselves. See, for example, Booker and Juraga, *Bakhtin, Stalin, and Modern Russian Fiction: Carnival, Dialogism, and History* (1995), which essentially proceeds according to the common Western assumption that Russian exile and émigré writers are more interesting than Soviet writers of socialist realism.
13 This was especially the case before the Second World War. During the war, of course, there was little overt criticism of the Soviet system in Soviet literature, just as the radical critique of capitalism that characterized British and American leftist literature of the 1930s was essentially silenced during the war. After the war, Soviet socialist realism never regained its momentum, going into an era of decadence and decline that, in retrospect, foreshadows the fall of the entire Soviet system.
14 Achebe, *Morning Yet on Creation Day* (London: Heinemann, 1975), p. 29.
15 Irele, *The African Experience in Literature and Ideology* (Bloomington: Indiana University Press, 1990), p. xiv.
16 Obiechina, *Culture, Tradition and Society in the West African Novel* (Cambridge: Cambridge University Press, 1975), p. 35.
17 Chinweizu, Jemie and Madubuike, *Toward the Decolonization of African Literature: African Fiction and Poetry and Their Critics* (Washington, DC: Howard University Press, 1983), p. 8.
18 Mudimbe, *The Invention of Africa: Gnosis, Philosophy, and the Order of Knowledge* (Bloomington: Indiana University Press, 1988), p. 90.
19 Ngara, *Art and Ideology in the African Novel: A Study of the Influence of Marxism on African Writing* (1985); Gugelberger, ed., *Marxism and African Literature* (1985).
20 Ngugi, *Decolonising the Mind: The Politics of Language in African Literature* (London: James Currey, 1992), p. 76.
21 Lukács, *The Historical Novel* (1937).
22 Lukács, *The Meaning of Contemporary Realism*, trans. John Mander and Necker Mander (1957; London: Merlin, 1963), p. 101.

23 Ngugi, *Moving the Centre: The Struggle for Cultural Freedoms* (London: James Currey, 1993), p. 97.
24 For an excellent study of the engagement of all of Gordimer's fiction with South African history see Stephen Clingman, *The Novels of Nadine Gordimer: History from the Inside* (1986).
25 Coquery-Vidrovitch, *Africa: Endurance and Change South of the Sahara*, trans. David Maisel (1985; Berkeley: University of California Press, 1988), p. 66.
26 Mudimbe, *Invention of Africa*, p. 20.
27 Christopher Miller notes that Said's description of Orientalism can be extended to Africa, but argues that, while Africanist discourses are very similar to the Orientalist discourses described by Said with regard to European visions of the Middle East, European visions of Africa include an additional dose of darkness, primitivity and mystery (Miller, *Blank Darkness: Africanist Discourse in French* (Chicago: University of Chicago Press, 1985), pp. 14–23).
28 Said, *Orientalism* (New York: Vintage-Random House, 1979), p. 7.
29 On these 'Orientalist' visions of Eastern Europe see Maria Todorova, *Imagining the Balkans* (1997) and Larry Wolff, *Inventing Eastern Europe: The Map of Civilization and the Mind of the Enlightenment* (1994).
30 On the ways in which British fears of the Russians in the nineteenth century provided background (and vocabulary) for American fears of Russia in the Cold War see Booker, *Colonial Power*, pp. 171–99.
31 Holquist, *Dostoevsky and the Novel* (Princeton: Princeton University Press, 1977), p. 13.
32 Ibid., p. 14.
33 Ibid., p. 28.
34 Fanon, *The Wretched of the Earth* (1961).
35 Lukács, *Historical Novel*, p. 144.
36 For a similar insight in relation to the emergent bourgeois society of interwar Yugoslavia see Miroslav Krleza's *Zastave* (Banners, 1976), a massive four-volume historical novel that is in many ways a sort of Balkan *Klim Samgin*. On *Zastave* as a historical novel see Dubravka Juraga, 'Miroslav Krleža's *Zastave*: Socialism, Yugoslavia, and the Historical Novel', *South Atlantic Review*, 62: 4 (Fall 1997), pp. 32–56.
37 Armah, *The Beautyful Ones Are Not Yet Born* (London: Heinemann, 1969), p. 183. This flower image links up with the earlier reminder by the book's allegorical 'Teacher' that 'out of the decay and the dung there is always a new flowering' (ibid., p. 85).
38 Lazarus, *Resistance in Postcolonial African Fiction* (New Haven: Yale University Press, 1990), p. 48.
39 Gorky, *My Universities*, new edn, trans. Ronald Wilks (1923; London: Penguin, 1979), p. 157.
40 Zelinsky, *Soviet Literature: Problems and People*, trans. Olga Shartse (c. 1969; Moscow: Progress Publishers, 1970), p. 103.
41 William Walsh, *A Manifold Voice: Studies in Commonwealth Literature* (New York: Barnes and Noble, 1970), p. 49.
42 Moses, *The Novel and the Globalization of Culture* (New York: Oxford University Press, 1995), p. 108.
43 Gray, *Enlightenment's Wake: Politics and Culture at the Close of the Modern Age* (London: Routledge, 1995), p. 63.
44 Ibid., pp. 178–9.
45 Ibid., p. 178.
46 Von Laue, *The World Revolution of Westernization: The Twentieth Century in Global Perspective* (1987).
47 Fukuyama, *The End of History and the Last Man* (1992).

48 See the chapter on Fukuyama in Gray, *Post-liberalism: Studies in Political Thought* (London: Routledge, 1993), pp. 245–50.
49 Lukacs, *The End of the Twentieth Century and the End of the Modern Age* (New York: Ticknor and Fields, 1993), p. 287.
50 Ibid., p. 33.
51 Hobsbawm, *The Age of Extremes: A History of the World, 1914–1991* (New York: Pantheon, 1994), p. 9.
52 Ibid., p. 376.
53 Ibid., p. 382.
54 Ibid., p. 382.
55 On the impressive growth of national literatures during the Soviet years see Georgi Lomidze, *National Soviet Literatures: Unity of Purpose* (1978).
56 Goshal, *People in the Colonies* (1948).

6 Marxist literary resistance to the Cold War

Alan Wald

McCarthyite memory hole

On the morning of 20 June 1951, a hundred FBI agents poured out of the Foley Square Federal Building in Manhattan at dawn, buttoned up their grey trench coats and bounded into a fleet of waiting Buicks. Spreading throughout New York City in a well-orchestrated operation, they surrounded twenty private homes, burst into bedrooms and dragged 16 Communist Party leaders off to jail under the Smith Act charge of conspiring to teach the overthrow of the US government.[1] This was the second group of top Party functionaries to be arrested under the Act.

Among them was V.J. Jerome, Chairman of the Party Cultural Commission and editor of the Party's theoretical journal, *Political Affairs*.[2] A month later, Jerome was temporarily released after bail was posted by six individuals. Those six names were immediately published in the *New York Times* and elsewhere.[3] Such public exposure was a very effective means of intimidating others from providing support to alleged subversives such as Jerome; all six would now have good reason to fear that they themselves might be targeted next for blacklisting and other harassment. Thus the individuals who publicly put up bail tended to be those already victimized by McCarthyism, or else individuals of unusual political courage.

The six in the case of Jerome's bail were Alice Jerome, wife of the Party cultural leader and director of a nursery school; the Reverend E. White, a left-wing minister; Herbert Aptheker, the Communist Party historian who worked with Jerome on *Political Affairs* and who was already blacklisted; Howard Fast, the best-selling Marxist novelist who himself served a prison sentence for non-cooperation in naming names the year before, and who was also already blacklisted from publishing and from speaking on university campuses; Waldo Salt, the communist screenwriter who had been subpoenaed by the House Un-American Activities Committee (HUAC) to Washington, DC, in 1947, just after making a film based on Howard Fast's short stories called *Rachel and the Stranger*, and who was now, too, blacklisted; and Barbara Giles, a Louisiana-born writer and critic who had authored a successful Southern historical novel of turn-of-the-century racism just four years earlier, and who served in various editorial capacities on communist publications such as the *New Masses* and *Masses & Mainstream*.

In the fifty years since that dramatic moment, the persecution of suspected communists in the Cold War McCarthyite witch-hunt era has become increasingly regarded as shameful. Even the attacks upon real live, up-front, 'card-carrying' communists such as Jerome, Fast, Aptheker, Salt and Giles are frequently seen as almost as bad, although, regrettably, most books and films critical of the blacklist and persecutions still tend to focus on the cases of individuals falsely accused of communist membership, not the 'real' Reds.[4]

More positively, the reputations of a select few of these persecuted communists were eventually restored after a decade or more of attempted erasure. Aptheker, for example, achieved national recognition through his devoted work as the literary executor of W.E.B. Du Bois and was offered, as he approached retirement age, a university position on the West Coast. Howard Fast, the best-known communist writer of the witch-hunt era, struggled at first to rebuild his career. Yet when the publishing house of Little, Brown & Co. revoked, for political reasons, the contract for *Spartacus* (1951), the novel he began in prison, Fast produced it on his own Blue Heron Press to become perhaps the only self-published best-seller in literary history. Waldo Salt made a big comeback in film with *Midnight Cowboy* (1969), *Serpico* (1973), *Day of the Locust* (1975), *Coming Home* (1978) and other hits and award nominations. Even the Party functionary, Jerome, now gets ritualistic entries in histories of the US communist movement, and Lillian Hellman tells a few amusing anecdotes about Jerome's prison experiences in *Scoundrel Time* (1976), based on information she received from Jerome's friend and prison mate, communist mystery writer Dashiell Hammett.

However, it is symptomatic that Barbara Giles, the mysterious Red Lady Novelist from Louisiana, still remains lost to literary history. In 1992, Louisiana State University Press published a 350-page reference book of *Louisiana Women Writers* containing 'A Comprehensive Bibliography'. Yet there is not a word on Giles or her 550-page 1947 anti-racist novel *The Gentle Bush*, published by Harcourt, Brace and Company to reviews in the *New York Times* and other prominent papers. Nor is there any mention of her substantial Marxist literary criticism on Southern writers, which is rather unique for that period in the history of US criticism, and some of which is indexed in the Union Catalogue. In contrast, there are abundant references to many women who wrote much less and whose personal associations with Louisiana are not nearly as substantial.[5] Perhaps, then, the invocation of Giles's obscure name and erased career is a fitting way to begin the arduous task of moving toward a reconstitution, in the appropriate genres and regional histories, of the literary practice of the hundreds of 'lost' US left-wing cultural workers who resisted McCarthyism through their writings and actions.

102 *Alan Wald*

The Un-American Renaissance

The radical anti-witch-hunt resistance culture of the late 1940s and 1950s might be thought of as 'The Un-American Renaissance'. However, a survey of the most recent scholarship suggests that the 1940s and 1950s era as a whole – not just its left-wing or African-American component – remains relatively unexplored in US cultural history. Ironically, like canonical depictions of the nineteenth-century American Renaissance, the high Cold War period is represented in conventional academic scholarship as dominated by a relatively few white male figures depicted as heroic transgressors of literary convention. Receiving most attention are Norman Mailer, Saul Bellow, William Styron, J.D. Salinger, John Updike, Bernard Malamud and John Cheever. These are joined by a smattering of deradicalized African-Americans (the ex-pro-communists Ralph Ellison and James Baldwin) and an occasional token woman, such as the so-called 'Southern Gothic', Flannery O'Connor.[6]

This failure to grasp the totality of the un-American Renaissance is true even among the canon revisionists of recent decades. If one examines, for instance, the recent *Columbia Literary History of the United States* (1988), *Columbia History of the American Novel* (1991) and the *Columbia History of American Poetry* (1993); collections such as *Toward a New American Literary History* (1980) and *Reconstructing American Literary History* (1986); and the most impressive college-level anthologies such as the *Heath Anthology of American Literature* (1990), the culture of the high Cold War is never confronted head-on. Rather, the epoch is dissolved into less incisive categories such as 'Issues and Visions' and 'The American Self'.[7] These rubrics have the welcome advantage of allowing voice to a range of multicultural, female and working-class experiences, but at the expense of some coherency from a historicizing point of view. Missing from canon revision to date is a much-needed interpretation of the two most neglected and misunderstood decades of twentieth-century US literature, the late 1940s and the 1950s.

To re-establish this moment, scholars must return to memory dozens of extraordinarily talented writers who have 'disappeared' from cultural history, while reassessing scores of others who have been misread owing to the curtain of secrecy descending over activities of the literary left during the Cold War. Conceptually, such a reconstitution of the literary left as a continuous, rather than an episodic, feature of US culture will suggest new approaches for analysing and assessing the interrelationship of politics and art. The categories of region, gender, race, ethnicity and sexual orientation will need to be reconfigured to an extent, outdistancing all earlier scholarship on the literary left.

Finally, such new research will need to be partly collective biography, telling an important human story of writers who made many sacrifices, including loss of jobs, forced relocation to other countries, prison terms, the risking of their necks in violent confrontations with right-wing mobs and, in some cases, death on the battlefield in Spain, all for a new world that they would never see. The conclusions of such research will be of special interest in the light of some of the new assessments underway of the US intellectual left resulting from the opening of archives and other sources in the former USSR that concern US radicalism.

To date, however, the decades of the 1940s and 1950s have received only a cursory overview in a number of traditional histories of the literary left by Daniel Aaron (*Writers on the Left*, 1961), James Gilbert (*Writers and Partisans*, 1968) and Walter Rideout (*The Radical Novel in the United States*, 1956). All of these go from the turn of the century to the McCarthy era, but invariably centre on the 1930s. Beyond these standard works, nearly every other study of literary radicalism, whatever its merits, tends to treat 'the thirties' as the main unit with minimal consideration of the fate of that generation and tradition in later decades. This includes excellent books by Marcus Klein (*Foreigners*, 1981), Paula Rabinowitz (*Labor and Desire*, 1991) and Barbara Foley (*Radical Representations*, 1993). Thus far, the only general literary history to cover the 1940s with any attention to the left is Chester Eisinger's *Fiction of the Forties* (1963). Most of the books about the politics and literature of the 1950s, such as the fine ones by Thomas Schaub (*American Fiction in the Cold War*, 1991) and Stephen Whitfield (*The Culture of the Cold War*, 1991), are limited either to the assault on the left or to a few well-known authors, such as Ellison, Mailer or famous 'Beats' such as Jack Kerouac.

A few helpful exceptions to the 1930s-fixated treatment of the left include two short but brilliant poetry studies by Cary Nelson (*Repression and Recovery*, 1989) and Walter Kaladjian (*American Culture between the Wars*, 1994), and a recently published dissertation by Alan Block called *Anonymous Toil* (1992), which expand the temporal boundaries somewhat. There are also a number of excellent biographies of writers tracing their entire careers, the most extraordinary of the last few years being Douglas Wixson's *Worker-Writer in America* (1994) about Jack Conroy. But these necessarily lack a comparative dimension and treat in detail only better known figures.

In contrast, to reconstruct the left of the 'Un-American Renaissance' one requires 'bottom up' studies that begin with an empirical base of the approximately 300 writers who evidenced substantial sympathy for left-wing (that is, pro-communist, socialist, Trotskyist, anarchist and hybrid) causes at various times in the decades following the Russian Revolution. Such an approach to the literary left differs significantly from that discussed in the previously existing studies. It is not that earlier books are factually 'wrong' (although a few are), but that much of even the very best of such scholarship is limited by a 1939 cut-off date; a relatively small cast of characters; a narrowness in coverage by region, gender, race, ethnicity and sexual orientation; and, most of all, by the assumption that left-wing literature must assume certain recurring forms, such as strike novels, proletarian novels, novels of socialist conversion and so forth. The problem is that most of the 'writers on the left' who form the 'canon' in most of the existing scholarly works are primarily figures formed in the 1920s, but who came to prominence in the 1930s. Actually, the majority of writers influenced by left-wing ideas were young in the 1930s, launching their literary careers in the 1940s or early 1950s. By then, the left tradition had passed through the 'moments' of 'proletarian literature' and 'Popular Front culture', transcending as well as incorporating elements of both to create new blends.

There was also a revolution in paperback publishing and mass culture, soon followed by the anti-communist repression of the Cold War. Thus the characteristic forms of literary production in fiction for left-wing writers in the Un-American Renaissance moved toward the popular novel (as can be seen in novels by David Alman, Ben Appel, Robert Carse, Vera Caspary, Ring Lardner Jr, Alfred Maund, Sam Ross, George Sklar); science fiction (Frederik Pohl, Cyril Kornbluth, Donald Wollheim, Isaac Asimov, Judith Merril, Mack Reynolds); detective or thriller fiction (Guy Endore, Julius Fast, Kenneth Fearing, Robert Finnegan, Ed Lacy); pulp fiction (William Lindsay Gresham, Jean Karsavina, Jim Thompson); historical fiction (Barbara Giles, Mari Sandoz, Henrietta Buckmaster, William Blake, Howard Fast, Truman Nelson); children's and young adult literature (Arna Bontemps, Mary Elting, Shirley Graham, Milton Meltzer); and popular science for young people (Irving Adler, Millicent Selsam).

Some novelists, of course, continued the tradition of proletarian or radical literature (Philip Bonosky, John Sanford, Philip Stevenson, Albert Maltz, Alvah Bessie). In poetry, the left tended to create new genres that might be characterized as 'People's Modernism' (Thomas McGrath, Naomi Replanski, Norman Rosten, Muriel Rukeyser), 'Marxianized Romanticism' (Alfred Hayes, Aaron Kramer, Walter Lowenfels) and 'Collectivist Lyricism' (Joy Davidman, Eve Merriam, Edwin Rolfe). At the same time, Marxist literary theorists in the 1940s and 1950s sought to adapt the writings of Georg Lukács to the postwar era (Charles Humboldt), incorporate psychoanalytic methods (Harry Slochower) and extend Marxist critiques to neglected regions such as the US South (Barbara Giles).

In addition to a large number of women who were galvanized into radical activity when young in the 1930s and who blossomed in later decades (Olga Cabral, Martha Dodd, Janet Stevenson), there were pioneering Marxist Latinos (Alvaro Cardona-Hine, José Yglesias, Jesus Colon), Asian-Americans (Yoshio Abbe, Carlos Bulosan, H.T. Tsiang), Jewish-Americans (Ben Field, Yuri Suhl, Warren Miller, Helen Yglesias, Earl Conrad), Italian-Americans (Pietro DiDonato, John Fante, Vincent Ferrini, Frances Winwar) and other ethnic writers who remained or became associated with the literary left.

The African-American dimensions

However, the most dynamic, creative and, in many ways, the most influential trend within this Un-American Renaissance is the African-American component. This formed a crucial bridge between the old and new African-American lefts during the Cold War years. For quick and easy evidence of such an intimate trans-generational association, one only need look at the table of contents of the classic 1971 anthology *The Black Aesthetic*. Seven of the contributors were originally members or sympathizers of the US Communist Party: John O. Killens, Julian Mayfield, Loften Mitchell, Langston Hughes, Richard Wright, W.E.B. Du Bois and Alain Locke. Moreover, the quotation at the front of the volume is from Margaret Walker, also influenced by communism in the 1930s.[8]

One can also see clear marks of this cross-generational African-American radical tradition in recent writing such as the 1989 novel for young people, *Those Other People*. This is the last published work of Alice Childress (1921–94). Of course, true to the expectations of dealing with 'hidden history', the Putnam edition of the book nowhere identifies the author as African-American, as an important radical playwright and actress, or as the author of the extraordinary 'Conversations from a Domestic's Life' that originally appeared in Paul Robeson's newspaper *Freedom* during the witch-hunt years.[9] Yet every line of Childress's biography roots her firmly in the tradition of the African-American left. She was nourished in the soil of the Great Depression, steeled in the struggles of the witch-hunt and McCarthyism, and grew considerably through intimate association with the new rise of the Civil Rights movement in the late 1950s and the political struggles that afterwards ensued.

Born in Charleston, South Carolina, and coming of age in Harlem, Childress's first acting work was for the left-wing production *On Striver's Row*. This was a theatrical attack on the Black middle class in the E. Franklin Frazer vein, under the direction of Abram Hill, in whose American Negro Theater, a radical, largely pro-communist group in Harlem, Childress worked for the next 11 years. Her own first play, *Florence*, is a Black Marxist-feminist one-act drama, published in the October 1950 issue of the communist literary journal *Masses & Mainstream*. In 1950, Childress adapted Langston Hughes's *Simple Speaks His Mind* (1950) to the play *Just a Little Simple*, and, of course, her own 'Conversations with a Domestic' were modelled on the Simple stories. From then until her death, Childress issued a steady stream of plays and, later, novels, on Black feminist and liberation themes, such as *Gold through the Trees* (1952), *Trouble in Mind* (1955), *Wine in the Wilderness* (1969), *Mojo* (1970), *A Hero Ain't Nothin' But a Sandwich* (1973), *Wedding Band* (1973) and *A Short Walk* (1979).[10]

Childress's career is paradigmatic of the African-American literary left; in my view, it is a career far more typical than that of Richard Wright, the most famous canonical Black American literary communist. For example, the foundation in radical theatre of Childress's career is similar to that of Lorraine Hansberry, Julian Mayfield, Douglass Turner Ward, Theodore Ward, Loften Mitchell, Owen Dodson, Lonne Elder III, Ruby Dee, Ossie Davis, Paul Robeson, Maya Angelou and Shirley Graham.[11] Moreover, the large production of stories for children and young adults by Childress is similar to that of Arna Bontemps, Rosa Guy, Margaret Burroughs, Ann Petry, Shirley Graham, John O. Killens and Owen Dodson. Even the inexact information available about the political affiliations of Childress is quite characteristic of the witch-hunt and post-witch-hunt eras.

Indeed, Childress is nowhere on record as a public communist and may never have held membership, although strong sympathies are suggested by her associations. However, in the 1950s, if one were subject to being labelled an actual Communist Party member, one might face, at the least, vicious and simplified stereotyping and, more seriously, blacklisting and possible imprisonment if one were called before an investigating committee and refused to co-operate in naming names. Thus the politics of writers in that era are very hard to pin down, precisely because hardly anyone, least of all artists, wanted to be stamped with a Party label, for reasons of political self-protection and an understandable resistance to being simplistically tagged and relegated to a category.

Of course, some African-American leftists who came of literary age during the Un-American Renaissance, such as the novelists Julian Mayfield and Shirley Graham, left behind in interviews and other primary materials some record of communist affiliation.[12] Likewise, the politics of the outstanding playwright, Douglass Turner Ward, are readily available to the researcher in his 1950 pamphlet (under his original name, Roosevelt Ward), *Toward Bright Tomorrows*. It was published by the Labor Youth League (the Communist Party youth group of the time), of which Ward is identified as chair of the Harlem chapter and of which Audre Lorde was also a member.[13] Although novelist John O. Killens never said he was a member of the Communist Party, his complete endorsement of the communist perspective in his 13 page essay 'For National Freedom', in the summer 1949 issue of the communist journal, *New Foundations*, ought to make his politics unambiguous for all but those whose anti-communist cultural indoctrination simply will not allow them to believe that a brilliant novelist might also be a devoted communist.[14] The situation of playwright Lorraine Hansberry, novelist Shirley Graham, poet Lance Jeffers, and many others, appears to be similar.

Still, left-wing Cold War resistance must be recognized and theorized among writers whose connections were, and perhaps always had been, more distant, such as James Baldwin, whose communist sympathies occurred mainly in his high school years and who, by the 1950s, had passed through the right-wing social democracy of the *New Leader*. Chester Himes, who probably held a brief, but tumultuous, Party membership in Ohio or California, is another example of a writer somewhat removed from the communist-led movement but still influenced by it. He produced an agonizing testament of post-Stalinist communism in *The Lonely Crusade* (1947), before turning to his Harlem detective fiction. There is also Willard Motley, who has the distinction of politically collaborating with both communists and Trotskyists in the 1940s.

One writer of the 1940s and 1950s who has been revived is novelist Ann Petry. Petry was certainly influenced by Marxism and the communist movement during her journalistic period on the *People's Voice* in Harlem, where she was friends with communist Marvel Cooke.[15] Indeed, the politics behind Petry's 1946 novel *The Street* can hardly be understood without comparing the world of the protagonist, Lutie Johnson, to the activities and values documented in Ann Petry's left-wing newspaper reports of the time. It is the absences in Lutie's consciousness and experiences that point to the solutions necessary to redeem Harlem's working class: that is, the unions, the Black church as a site for progressive social action and the self-organization of women. Surprisingly, at the time of her 1953 anti-Cold-War novel *The Narrows*, Petry goes even further than she did in the 1940s, treating communism as simply a code word for anti-racist, anti-capitalist resistance.

No work, of course, has created more problems for understanding the African-American Cold War left than Harold Cruse's *The Crisis of the Negro Intellectual* (1967). The effectiveness of Cruse's book is due, at least in part, to the fact that it articulates some important truths about the need for African-American cultural autonomy, independence and self-determination. Moreover, Cruse's target, the US Communist Party, which he knew intimately, was certainly vitiated both politically and organizationally by tragic delusions about Joseph Stalin and the political system of the USSR. However, as Jerry Watts has recently pointed out in *Heroism and the Black Intellectual* (1994), the dichotomy posited by Cruse between integrationism and nationalism is an inaccurate description of the political choices and strategies of the time, or of now.[16] Indeed, rather than constituting what Cruse sees as the nadir of a progressively degraded African-American literary left tradition, characterized by an alleged toadying to crypto Jewish-nationalist 'Cultural Commissars' and capitulating to middle-class liberal integrationist yearnings, the politico-cultural thrust of the African-American dimensions of the Un-American Renaissance was founded on a basically sound understanding of Black nationalism and of national culture from a class perspective.[17]

Indeed, the authentic message of Killens, Hansberry, Mayfield, Lance Jeffers, Shirley Graham, Alice Childress and so many other African-American pro-communists who battled the reactionary 1950s on the cultural front is there before our eyes in poem after poem, play after play, novel after novel, if we can only get the current generation to read them. The essence is that the nationally oppressed need allies, but not allies on anyone's terms. And the left writers, certainly, who knew the whole history of racism and liberal betrayal in the United States, had no illusions that, in the final crunch, white workers and radicals would necessarily be by their side when it counted. Indeed, as Julian Mayfield put it so bluntly in his retort to Cruse in his oral history, 'You scratch a Black man in the Communist Party and you're going to find a Black man.'[18]

The bottom line, for the Black pro-communists in the Cold War, was not, it is true, an all-class Black nationalism; but it *was* national pride and integrity, or, as Du Bois put it in a passage frequently quoted by *Iron City* author Lloyd Brown, a 'pride of self so deep as to scorn injustice to other selves'.[19] Such a view, then, enabled one in many instances, despite hope for interracial unity, to go it alone. This is what happens in just about every African-American left-wing text, from the martyrdom of Richard Wright's Aunt Sue in *Uncle Tom's Children* (1940) to the concluding pledge of Lorraine Hansberry's Walter Younger in *A Raisin in the Sun* (1959).[20] For African-American leftists, the struggle must continue, whether or not the 'objectively necessary' allies are present. Moreover, the struggle is undertaken without self-pity, against overwhelming odds, and on behalf of a future time from which many of these Red Black writers would for ever be exiled. It may be that the slogan under which the authors of these texts were educated (often at the Party-led Jefferson School) was 'Black and White Unite and Fight'; but the melody of the song that bursts through the images, dramatizations and usually the climactic moments of the plot is almost always the blues, confirming Houston Baker, Jr's argument in *Blues, Ideology and Afro-American Literature* that the 'blues is the matrix'.[21]

Perhaps the story of the African-American dimensions of the Un-American Renaissance can be most accurately summed up by the climax to Frank London Brown's 1959 *Trumbull Park*. This is a factually based novel of a Black minority's resistance to a business-orchestrated white mob's violent campaign to drive them out of a Chicago public housing project in the early days of McCarthyism. The author, who died of cancer in his thirties, was a bona fide partisan of the literary left and an organizer for an interracial union to boot. However, as is almost always the case in these Black Cold War texts, his autobiographical persona in *Trumbull Park* finds himself at the crucial moment without the needed white allies, indeed, without much support from anyone. In the concluding passage, he has only the shield of cultural memory for solace and protection against the racists gathered to drive him and his family from the Trumbull Park public housing project:

> Oh, yes, the mob was still screaming; but now I heard singing – Big Joe Williams wailing:
>
> 'Every day, every day ... Well, it ain't nobody worried, and it ain't nobody cryin'!'
>
> And we walked with our chests stuck out, and our heads way up in the air – just like that big, dark, blues-shouting stud.
>
> And we took the long hip strides that Joe took as [the women and men screamed at us, 'Get out of here, you black jungle bunnies!']. So I started singing out loud, in the middle of cops, mobs, and everything else. Ol' Harry joined in, and I noticed a little water in his eyes. I felt a little choked up myself as we both sang loud and clear:
>
> *'every day, every day ... Well, it ain't nobody worried, and it ain't nobody crying.'*[22]

Legacy

Is it possible to indicate any predominating themes and characteristics in the literature of the overall left-wing cultural resistance to the Cold War? In my view, the 'Great Theme' of the US literary left in all decades has been anti-racism – for obvious reasons having to do with the history of this continent – and writers on the left during the McCarthy era continued that honourable tradition. Actually, throughout the entire 1940s and 1950s, the number of left-wing novels animated by a desire for racial unity through political struggle toward utopian ends are numerous and have rarely been studied. A list of just a few novels premised on the radical impulse for racial harmony might include: Benjamin Appel's *The Dark Stain* (1943), Howard Fast's *Freedom Road* (1944), Henrietta Buckmaster's *Deep River* (1944), Chester Himes's *The Lonely Crusade* (1947), David Alman's *The Hourglass* (1947) and *The Well of Compassion* (1948), Alexander Saxton's *The Great Midland* (1948), Lloyd Brown's *Iron City* (1951), Earl Conrad's *Rock Bottom* (1952) and *Gulf Stream North* (1954), Ann Petry's *The Narrows* (1953), John O. Killens's *Youngblood* (1954), Philip Stevenson's *Morning, Noon and Night* (1954), Mari Sandoz's *Cheyenne Autumn* (1953), Alfred Maund's *The Big Boxcar* (1956), W.E.B. Du Bois's 'The Black Flame Trilogy' (1957–61), Julian Mayfield's *The Hit* (1957) and *The Long Night* (1958), Robert Carse's *Drums of Empire* (1959) and Truman Nelson's *The Surveyor* (1960).

What characterizes these and most other left-wing works of fiction, starting with the more aggressively revolutionary anti-racist novels of the 1930s, is the implicit comparison of present realities to a utopian vision of a classless America in which racism, especially anti-Black racism, is felicitously dissolved through common struggle on a class basis. Often their vision is assembled from native US sources as they look back to slave revolts, abolitionism and reconstruction. At the same time, they take inspiration from radical utopian/dystopian classics by Nathaniel Hawthorne, Edward Bellamy and Jack London, incorporate folk cultures of resistance from the enslaved and indigenous populations, and refer to more twentieth-century events such as the inter racial Gastonia Strike, Gallup Strike and Scottsboro defence campaign.

The theme was pre-eminent in the mass and popular culture writings of the radicals, too. An instructive example is Howard Fast's *Tony and the Wonderful Door* (1952), a children's story which the doomed Ethel and Julius Rosenberg decided from prison to give their sons for Christmas.[23] Although the book has been reprinted under other titles, the original was published at the height of the Cold War by Fast's Blue Heron Press. In the story, Tony MacTavish Levy, an elementary school student, is the walking embodiment of multiculturalism. Because of his ancestry among Scotch, Haitian, Native American, Swedish, Italian, French, German, Jewish, Lithuanian and Polish relations, he refuses to answer his teacher's question about his 'national origin'. The book begins:

'Why,' asked Tony MacTavish Levy, 'do you keep calling them [Native Americans] wild? They are not wild. They are just nice, quiet people, like any other people.'

'I see,' said Miss Clatt [the bossy teacher], getting that look on her face. 'In other words, Tony, you know more about Indians than I do.'[24]

The plot concerns Tony's escape from his gloomy, urban, repressive world through a magic door to nature, right in his own back yard. He seeks to gain proof that there once existed – and therefore may exist again – a world where whites and indigenous people live harmoniously. Miss Clatt, the authority figure of the 'educational state apparatus', is eventually humbled.

Some of the left-wing mystery writers in the mass culture genre made detectives of colour a special theme: Chester Himes, in his Harlem crime novels; Len Zinberg, a Jewish communist who, under the pseudonym Ed Lacy, sold books in the millions and was credited with the creation of the first Black detective, Toussaint Marcus Moore; and Howard Fast who, under the pen-name E.V. Cunningham would in the 1970s write a series of detective mysteries based on Masao Masuto, a six-foot-tall Japanese-American Zen Buddhist police detective.

Since many left-wing writers in all categories are women, a gendered approach to left-wing mass culture in this era would possibly produce a set of semi-autonomous narrative typologies for the field, perhaps analogous to those proposed by Paula Rabinowitz in *Labor and Desire: Women's Revolutionary Fiction in Depression America* (1991). Among the characteristic trends to be theorized here would be the eruption of gender issues in the midst of anti-racist texts, such as in the tense relation that explodes between Simon and his wife in Henrietta Buckmaster's *Deep River*; the dilute and popularized 'feminism' in the young adult novels of Beth Meyers (better known on the left as Beth McHenry) in *The Steady Flame* (1952) and *The Doctor Is a Lady* (1954); and the cross-racial feminist radicalism revealed in 'internal' left-wing culture, in works such as Gerda Lerner and Eve Merriam's *Singing of Women: A Dramatic Review*.[25]

In the genre of the historical novel, the most prolific and influential Marxist of this era was, of course, Howard Fast, who produced *My Glorious Brothers* (1948), his vastly underappreciated *The Proud and the Free* (1950), *Spartacus* (1951) and *The Passion of Sacco and Vanzetti* (1953). Here it should be noted that *The Proud and the Free*, perhaps because of the excruciating political conditions under which it was written, not only anticipated but by far outdistanced the school of 'history-from-the-bottom-up' that would become a hallmark of 1960s New Left scholarship. Whereas these radical historians, most famously Jesse Lemisch, re-evaluated many episodes of early US history from the perspectives of working people, people of colour, women and the disenfranchised, none confronted the character of the revolutionary war itself as Fast did in his fictionalized history of the mutiny in the Continental Army. Cutting through the popular myth that the forces arraigned against the British were a 'classless' army with unified aims and objectives, *The Proud and the Free* breaks the military units into their class components of children of indentured servants and big landowners, free African-Americans and slave holders, and artisans and profiteers, to demonstrate the contradiction that the Pennsylvania line, which rebelled against its officers in January 1781, was trying to wage the battle for independence both under the leadership of the gentry and against it.

Beyond the examples of texts from the late 1940s and 1950s, Cold War literary resistance is not a literary theme or practice limited to the so-called McCarthy era itself. It is an ongoing one up to the present, as readers of Fast's *The Pledge* (1988) certainly know, or of other books such as E.L. Doctorow's *The Book of Daniel* (1971), K.B. Gildens's *Between the Hills and the Sea* (1971), Dorothy Doyle's *Journey through Jess* (1989), Mark Lapin's *Pledge of Allegiance* (1991), John Sanford's *A Walk in the Fire* (1991) and the very well-researched lesbian-feminist detective novel by Katherine Forrest, *The Beverly Malibu* (1989).

Finally, one might conclude by returning to the 'disappeared' literary career of Louisiana radical Barbara Giles to meditate a moment on the contours. She was born in 1906, raised in Bayou country on a sugar plantation where her father was bookkeeper for the refinery, graduated from high school at 15, attended state normal school for two years, and then graduated from Louisiana State University School of Journalism in 1925. Starting to write novels at the age of ten, under the influence of Honoré de Balzac and Victor Hugo, she pledged that one day she would do something analogous for the poor and racially oppressed of the South. After teaching at a high school for a while, Giles moved to Washington, DC, to work as a journalist, and from there to New York City, where she was employed as managing editor of the communist *New Masses*. Her literary speciality was Southern culture, especially William Faulkner, but she brought her lucid prose and biting wit to bear on a wide range of topics: political figures, mass culture, even an anti-communist novel by Hiram Hayden during the early Cold War that featured a female hack editor for the *New Masses* who seemd to be a caricature of herself.[26]

During the witch-hunt years, in contrast to the vast majority of her literary contemporaries, Giles acted courageously and without fear. Since there was no longer the possibility of public left-wing John Reed Clubs and American Writers Congresses, Giles became part of the brilliant Charles Humboldt circle that preserved the communist journal *Masses & Mainstream* after the Khrushchev revelations of 1956, until Humboldt was himself forced out and switched his allegiance over to the *National Guardian* just before his death.[27] Giles herself dropped away from the Party in 1966, considering it by then irrelevant, and threw herself into projects such as the Eugene McCarthy campaign until the death of her husband in 1971, after which she suffered a number of breakdowns. Long disowned by her Southern family, she died in New York City in obscurity on 19 April 1986, at the age of eighty-two.

However, when the new generation of Marxist-feminist and anti-racist activists and scholars generates its own history of the theory and practice of US literary resistance in the Cold War era, not only the still active and highly visible, Howard Fast but also the forgotten Barbara Giles, along with John Sanford, Philip Stevenson, John O. Killens, Martha Dodd, Lloyd Brown, Gordon Kahn and many, many others will all be very much *presente!*[28]

Notes

1 This description is based on Michael R. Belknap, *Cold War Political Justice: The Smith Act, the Communist Party, and American Civil Liberties* (Westport, Conn.: Greenwood, 1977), p. 153.
2 Jerome was born Jerome Isaac Romaine in Poland in 1896 and died in New York City in 1965.
3 See anon, 'Bail Posted for Communists', *New York Times*, 25 July 1951, p. 12.
4 See Jonathan Rosenbaum, 'Guilty by Omission', in Rosenbaum, *Placing Movies: The Practice of Film Criticism* (Berkeley: University of California Press, 1995), pp. 292–4.
5 Moreover, in the index of *Louisiana Women Writers* (1992), and in the introductory overviews and internal sub-chapters, neither Marxism nor communism nor a socialist left tradition exists as categories or even possible perspectives, even though revolutionary writers from that state from the 1930s to the 1950s include Arna Bontemps, Barbara Giles, Theodore Ward, Douglass Turner Ward, Alfred Maund and James Neugass.
6 Only recently was Flannery O'Connor reinscribed in her actual 1950s context in the stimulating new book by Jon Lance Bacon, *Flannery O'Connor and Cold War Culture* (1994).
7 Paul Lauter, ed., *The Heath Anthology of American Literature*, Vol. 2 (Lexington, MA: D.C. Heath and Co., 1990), pp. ix, xxvii.
8 Gayle Addison, Jr, *The Black Aesthetic* (New York: Anchor Books, 1971), epigraph.
9 These newspaper column 'conversations' are now available as the book *Like One of the Family*, republished after 30 years in 1986 in the Beacon series of Black Women Writers, edited by Deborah McDowell and introduced by Trudier Harris.
10 Childress's *Gold through the Trees* and *Just a Little Simple* remained unpublished.
11 Of course, famous pro-communists Richard Wright and Langston Hughes had important theatre connections as well.
12 See the unpublished oral history of Julian Mayfield at Howard University Library, Civil Rights Collection, and correspondence between Graham and Earl Browder in the Earl Browder Papers, Syracuse University Library.
13 See Lisa Duggan, 'Audre Lorde', in Mari Jo Buhle, Paul Buhle and Harvey J. Kaye, eds, *The American Radical* (London and New York: Routledge, 1994), pp. 353–60.
14 See Killens, 'For National Freedom', *New Foundations* (Summer 1949), pp. 245–58.
15 Interview with Marvel Cooke, New York City, October 1994.
16 Watts, *Heroism and the Black Intellectual: Ralph Ellison, Politics, and Afro-American Intellectual Life* (Chapel Hill: University of North Carolina Press, 1994), p. 8.
17 See my discussion of these policies in the chapter, 'Lloyd Brown and the African-American Literary Left', in Wald, *Writing from the Left: New Essays on Radical Culture and Politics* (London: Verso, 1994), pp. 212–32.

18 Oral History of Julian Mayfield, Howard University Library.
19 Quoted in Wald, *Writing from the Left*, p. 215.
20 Hansberry, *A Raisin in the Sun*, new edn (1959; New York: Signet, 1986), p. 148.
21 Baker, *Blues, Ideology and Afro-American Literature: A Vernacular Theory* (Chicago and London: University of Chicago Press, 1984), pp. 3–4.
22 Brown, *Trumbull Park* (Chicago: Regnery, 1959), p. 432.
23 See Julius and Ethel Rosenberg, *Death House Letters* (New York: Jero Publishing, 1952), p. 114.
24 Fast, *Tony and the Wonderful Door* (New York: Blue Heron, 1952), p. 5.
25 This is an early 1950s mimeographed bulletin published by the Council of the Arts, Sciences and Professions in New York City, featuring Sojourner Truth and Ella Mae Wiggins singing a cantata called 'Women are Dangerous'.
26 Interview with Jonathan Weil, New York City, October 1993.
27 Interview with Annette Rubinstein, New York City, October 1992.
28 It is a tradition in left-wing guerrilla movements in Central America for the names of deceased comrades to continue to be read during the roll call, with the remaining troops calling out '*presente!*' in unison as a tribute.

7 Poetry, politics and war
Representations of the American war in Vietnamese poetry

Dana Healy

> Afraid to die, they fight so they may live
> 'War' by Đông Hồ[1]

A mere glimpse at the history of modern literature in Vietnam reveals the extent to which its form, content and role in society have been dependent on political conditions. The turbulent history of the country during the twentieth century determined that literature became shaped by the needs of the anticolonial struggle, the national liberation movement, the revolution and wars of independence, and that creative endeavour was often, willingly or not, subordinated to higher goals. As in other South-East Asian countries previously dominated by colonialism, modern literature in Vietnam grew up hand in hand with nationalism; the growth of national sentiment in the early part of the twentieth century mobilized people across Vietnam, and literature gave expression to feelings of injustice and humiliation at the hands of foreign rulers and illustrated the desire for independence. At times when the whole nation was endangered and when patriotic sentiments were inflamed, writers were willing to forsake their creative freedom and devote their talent to the fulfilment of national aspirations, faithful to Hồ Chí Minh's teaching that 'there is nothing more precious than independence and freedom'.

Generations of Vietnamese people endured years of war, first against the French and later against the Americans, and consequently war literature constitutes a significant part of the modern Vietnamese literary canon. The American war[2] in Vietnam, the poetry of which is the focus of this chapter, was one of the most important conflicts of modern times, with a significance that reaches far beyond the dimensions of the military hostilities between the warring sides. It has become a symbol of the polarized ideological struggle of the Cold War and has generated many myths and great controversy. Given the war's impact on global history, and the wide-ranging and frequently studied spectrum of American literary responses to the war, the Vietnamese perspective is surprisingly under-explored in academic scholarship. As I aim to demonstrate, while American writing reflects a multiplicity of experiences, the primary role of Vietnamese propaganda was 'to paint the society as having a single will',[3] making the Vietnamese representation of the war more monolithic.

Literature as a weapon

To understand the literature written in the midst of the American war, one needs to understand the history of revolution, war and struggle which Vietnam went through and out of which the war literature grew. The onset of a postcolonial era in Vietnam was prompted by the August revolution in 1945. Hô Chí Minh's Declaration of Independence on 2 September 1945 and the formation of the Vietnamese Democratic Republic marked the beginning of a long process of decolonization, a process which, as Patricia Pelly asserts, went on well after the French withdrew from Vietnam in 1954, since 'many colonial norms and colonial representations remained in place, either as objects of unconscious assimilation or as negatives to be rooted out and eradicated'.[4] The Communist Party gradually emerged as the force which, under the banner of national liberation, unified various political factions and set out – with carefully thought out tactics – to secure its power even after independence had been achieved. The preparations for a transition from a colonial to a postcolonial state were being made in practical terms by the communists well before the deposing of the colonial regime.

Culture was to be an important tool with which to assert a new sense of authority outside the paradigms of colonialism and to reclaim a national identity bruised by years of foreign rule. Aware of the influence and the respect enjoyed by creative intellectuals within a society, and at the same time exploiting the patriotic sentiments of the artists themselves, Vietnamese officials were determined to bring this influence under their control. For them, defining the clear 'rules of the game' – that is, formulating cultural policies and outlining the role of the artist in society – was an important step in the enslavement of the culture. The year 1935 saw the beginning of a debate about the role of literature and the writer in Vietnamese society, as well as a polarization of that debate between those who advocated art for art's sake (*nghệ thuật vị nghệ thuật*) and those who supported art for life's sake (*nghệ thuật vị nhân sinh*). With the onset of the First Indochina War, the number of supporters of committed literature increased. If, during the 1920s and 1930s, Vietnamese literature freed itself from the constrictions of the traditional literary canon and became empowered by the development of a highly individualistic philosophy, by the late 1930s and early 1940s this individualism was being challenged by intensified nationalist feelings; many poets, seized by a sense of hopelessness and introspective melancholy, offered their pens to the service of the national liberation movement which provided them with a renewed sense of self-fulfilment. Poets who only a decade earlier had been fighting for the freedom of their poetic souls now abandoned their romantic idealism and, denouncing their previous selfishness, they declared themselves supporters of the Communist Party. Xuân Diệu, author of some of the most lyrical and intimate poetry, began rejecting his prerevolutionary work, labelling it 'presumptuous', and abandoned highly subjective and inward-looking poetry, and its themes of life, love and hope, for the new themes of revolution, party loyalty and the celebration of the working classes.

In their concerted effort to manage culture and 'legislate aesthetics', the Việt Minh took guidance in formulating cultural policies from the international communist movement, primarily the Soviet and Chinese, and initiated an ideological remoulding in the spirit of socialism. Inspired by Soviet writers, in particular by Maxim Gorky, Vietnamese leaders developed their cultural model in alignment with the principles of socialist realism, a programmatic style affirming socialism or communism as the only progressive social order, and suppressing individualism in favour of a collectivism with a strong tendency towards motivational optimism and didacticism.

The task of defining the fundamental policy on culture is associated with the name of Trường Chinh,[5] chief ideologue and Secretary General of the Communist Party between 1941 and 1956. He was a passionate follower of Marxism-Leninism and attempted to transform Vietnamese culture into a battleground on which the foundations of a new socialist Vietnam could be laid. His *Theses on Vietnamese Culture* from 1943 and *Marxism and the Issues of Vietnamese Culture* from 1948 set out the measures necessary to facilitate the moulding of culture into a tool of revolution and communism, and laid the foundations of a politicized aesthetics. Trường Chinh's fervent belief that 'To be a poet is to be true, pure, brave / Firm-willed, to have purpose and fire', and his appeal to poets to 'Seize the pen to cast down the world's tyrants / Make rhymes into bombs and from verse make grenades' so that 'your verse together with our workers' hands / shall plough the furrows of a splendid future',[6] were more prosaically articulated in the *Theses*. Creative intellectuals were assigned the role of a cultural cadre with the task of facilitating communication between the Party and the people. The 'pen as a weapon' and 'culture as a battleground' metaphors served to adjudicate in the dispute over the role of art and to ensure that everything which impeded the march towards socialism was eradicated. Adherence to socialist realism as the only acceptable method of creativity demanded that any work of art was created for the masses and served the cause of revolution. The ultimate arbiters of any creative work's worth were the masses who were, in Trường Chinh's words, 'the ultimate art connoisseur since they have many ears, eyes, intelligent brain, and a responsive collective sentiment [. . .]. What one does not ascertain, naturally another will.'[7]

The elevation of socialist realism into the only acceptable method of artistic creation posed numerous problems, both political and aesthetic. It curbed creativity and contributed to the emergence of a uniform art which was predictable and repetitive. Prose and poetry had to be realistic in form and socialist in content. While the critical realism of European writers was generally appreciated by the Vietnamese authorities for exposing social problems, it was deemed bourgeois, idealistic, decadent and unscientific since it did not propose class struggle, revolution and Marxism as solutions to such problems. It was also considered too pessimistic. By contrast, works of socialist realist prose and revolutionary poetry had to be imbued with optimism, motivating readers and painting a positive vision of the socialist future. Since works of socialist realism supplant the fate of the individual with collective duty, they did not offer complex psychological characterization. Stylistic considerations were unimportant: literary language and style were deliberately simple and unembellished, ensuring that the political message would be unambiguous and understood by everyone. Consequently, the primary impact of revolutionary writing is achieved through a loud and proclamative style, through boastful language filled with socialist rhetoric and political clichés, and through conventional and repetitive poetic metaphors. Socialist realism's claim to objectivity, however, was problematic. Trường Chinh urged writers to emphasise only truth useful to revolution. While it was possible to write about a defeat in battle, for example, it was necessary

> to make readers recognise how our soldiers courageously sacrificed themselves, why we lost, in that defeat which part was victorious, and, even if we were defeated, how our soldiers never hesitated because everyone was enthusiastically learning from the experience so as to prepare for victory in future battles.[8]

Kim N.B. Ninh points out that the *Theses* had little immediate impact.[9] However, the determination with which Hồ Chí Minh's government mounted its campaign to promote its cultural policies and the criticism and punishment aimed at those who opposed it, as well as the elimination of choice and political debate after the 1945 revolution, soon turned this pamphlet into the main 'manual' for cultural production.

The rise of the Cold War in the 1950s gradually transformed the dimensions of Vietnamese nationalism and subsumed it within the wider 'battleground' of the Cold War. Patriotism, the colonial legacy and the vision of socialist internationalism, together with the new dynamics of the Cold War, marked out the paradigms of the emerging postcolonial order in Vietnam. The victory at Điện Biên Phủ increased the prestige of the Việt Minh and radicalized both their leadership and their directives on art and literature. Their suppression of 'intellectual rebellion'[10] in the late 1950s intensified the ideological dictate over intellectual activities and tightened the organizational control of culture.

These trends continued during the Second Indochina War, which pushed aside the social, political and cultural aspects of decolonisation. American support and financial aid to the French (initiated during the Truman administration as a part of the policy of containment of communism) failed to prevent the demise of French colonial power at Điện Biên Phủ. The 1954

Geneva Conference formally ended the First Indochina War and temporarily partitioned Vietnam along the 17th Parallel, creating the communist-ruled Vietnamese Democratic Republic in the north and an independent Republic of Vietnam in the south. The American government stepped in to provide direct assistance to South Vietnam and helped to install the puppet regime of Ngo Dinh Diem. Financial, economic and military aid and the presence of a large number of advisers were supposed to prevent South Vietnam from falling into communist hands. In the North, the Việt Minh mounted a campaign to reunify Vietnam under their control and started infiltrating the South, establishing a support network and launching a propaganda campaign. From 1960 these activities were supported by the National Liberation Front which was formed in South Vietnam. The struggle for control over South Vietnam ultimately escalated into a full military conflict. Successive American administrations took turns to resolve the hostilities, although as the American war effort intensified so did the opposition to the war, both in the USA and internationally. On 27 January 1973 a ceasefire was agreed that paved the way for American withdrawal from Vietnam. The weakened South Vietnamese army could not stop the Việt Minh advance and, with the fall of Saigon on 30 April 1975, the nation was reunified under communist rule and the Vietnamese Socialist Republic was established.

The call for unity and commitment grew stronger during the war against America, as creative intellectuals, yet again, marched together to denounce the enemy. Literature became completely subsumed in the struggle for national liberation, moving away from anything which could be considered romantic, individualistic, egoistic or introspective in order to apply itself to motivating and providing revolutionary models for its readerships. Literary ideals such as aesthetics, entertainment or complex portrayals of reality were all suppressed in the name of these higher goals.

Poetry

Poetry is a much loved genre in Vietnam, occupying a privileged position in the hearts of its people and enjoying a prominent role in society. It encapsulates and embraces the lives of Vietnamese. This is true not only for folk poetry, springing from the soul of the people, but also for the scholarly poetic tradition, which acts as a testimony to the erudition of the individual and as evidence of intellectual and cultural attainment. The poet has long been deemed the voice of the nation's consciousness and poetry the nation's call-to-arms in time of crisis. As Nguyen Ba Chung observes,

> Poetry provided a means for articulating a sense of national identity, and for transmitting that identity to future generations. Ideas, feelings, images carried within Vietnamese poetry enabled the culture to recognise its deepest sense of self – to understand past suffering, and evoke an affirmative vision of future hopes.[11]

In this way, Vietnamese poetry from the war against America drew on a long tradition of poetic responses to foreign threats, which have left a deep mark on the genre. In times of war, poetry always returned to its patriotic roots by presenting images which stressed military prowess in defeating the enemy and what the politicians liked to call the 'fighting spirit' of the Vietnamese (*tinh thanh tranh dau*), reminding the Vietnamese people of the military achievements of such national heroes as Lý Thường Kiệt, Trần Hưng Đạo, Lê Lợi and Nguyễn Trãi and the Trưng sisters.[12] At the same time, war radicalized the sensitivities of Vietnamese poets, who were deeply affected by and personally involved in events. Mostly soldiers themselves, they wrote their poems as witness to the war, chronicling its origin, development and conduct. The poetic genre was much suited to the instability and hectic pace of the wartime period; only a scrap of paper on which to scribble a poem was needed, and just a few moments to read the lines. It was easy to copy or memorize a poem, and spontaneous poetry readings were organized for troops using often freshly written poems. Soldiers read poems for inspiration and comfort, while for the poets themselves the act of composition had a cathartic function and was part of a process of therapeutic unburdening. Their abundant political energies made neutrality an anathema, and since they saw the war as inevitable there exists little anti-war poetry or criticism of politicians. Strong political allegiances and the need to unite in the face of the enemy did not permit all aspects of the conflict to be reflected in wartime verse.

Nevertheless, there is some diversity in the poetry written during the American war. It varies from patriotic calls-to-arms in defence of the nation – morale-building, inspirational mobilisation verse, with its images of heroism, courage, dedication, sacrifice and endurance – to politically engaged, tendentious poetry which confirms and legitimizes the ideology of Marxism and which in its extreme form is no more than propaganda. It includes more sober poetry, which is 'a record of human struggle in the face of extremity, of love, life and death',[13] and poetry of compassion, articulating basic human concerns and, ultimately, the desire for peace. There is also a generational difference between the writers themselves. Some of the best-known war poets come from an older generation who burst on to the literary scene in the 1930s and who are usually more radical and politically explicit in their treatment of the conflict. These include Chế Lan Viên, Huy Cận, Xuân Diệu, Lưu Trọng Lư, Tố Hữu and Nguyễn Đình Thi, who differ from such younger poets as Phạm Tiến Duật, Nguyễn Duy, Xuân Quỳnh, Lâm Thị Mỹ Dạ, Nguyễn Đức Mậu, Hữu Thỉnh, Nguyễn Khoa Điềm, Trần Đăng Khoa and Phan Thị Thanh-Nhàn. As Nguyễn Đình Hoa points out, North Vietnamese revolutionary literature also had 'its southern branch' supported by the National Liberation Front, although its treatment of war mirrored that of its Northern counterpart.[14]

Themes in war poetry

Among the dominant themes in Vietnamese poetry from the war against America is the belief in the righteousness of the cause. The overwhelming support for the war and the absolute confidence in the justice of its objectives enabled Vietnamese poets to draw psychological strength from 'participation in meaningful group action'[15] and gave them a sense of mission, purpose and self-esteem. Their poetry is free from doubt, self-pity and guilt; unlike the Americans, the Vietnamese did not have to try to 'make sense of the war'. The invasion by foreign soldiers of Vietnamese soil made their participation inevitable and their struggle constituted a defence not only of the motherland but also of the very identity of Vietnam, a sentiment reflected in the Vietnamese way of referring to the war as the 'War of National Salvation against the Americans' (*chiến tranh chống Mỹ cứu nước*).

Poems written during the conflict pay tribute to this shared purpose. For example, 'Drivers of Lorries without Windscreens' (1965) by Phạm Tiến Duật captures the ethos of total dedication in its depiction of the lorry drivers who travel in the dark along the Hồ Chí Minh trail with supplies. Their ordeal is hard and dangerous and the poem is imbued with their devotion to duty, but at the same time is lightened by a palpable sense of determination to hold on to certain basic human emotions and to resist the numbing of feelings. As the poet puts it, as long as 'there's a heart in the truck, it's enough.'[16] A similar resoluteness and unity against the enemy can be found in Nguyễn Duy's 'The Bamboo of Vietnam'. The strength and resilience of bamboo is used as a metaphor for the Vietnamese people who, like the eponymous plant, 'don't seek cover in the shade' in the midst of hardship and who, because their 'hardy roots do not fear poor soil',[17] will rise again. As the poem goes on:

> In a storm one trunk will shield another,
> One branch pull, another push – so bind together,
> Because they love each other they do not stand alone,
> From that, dear friends, come forts and citadels.
> (lines 17–20)

The regenerative power of nature will guarantee that 'When old bamboo die, young ones rise right up' (line 30) in the same way as human tenacity will ensure that the fight will go on despite the sacrifices.

A more politically tinted representation of and appeal for total unity in the national struggle is articulated in Nguyễn Mỹ's poem 'The Red Farewell'. A soldier parting from his wife is symbolically linked to her and the whole nation by the ubiquitous red colour: the colour of heat, of the fire in the kitchen, of the woman's dress, of sunlight, of lips and of burning love. At the same time, the red colour is employed as a symbol of patriotism, ideological unity and dedication to duty:

Poetry, politics and war 121

> That redness in the flaming red
> Is like the fire red of the banana blossom,
> Like the redness of flames from the kitchen
> Of a distant village on cold, windy nights ...
> And the redness will follow
> As if there had been no farewell.[18]

Similarly, in the poem 'The Fire in the Lamps' (1967), Phạm Tiến Duật uses light penetrating through the darkness as a symbol of life and survival. When bombing loomed, life retreated to the darkness to hide from the enemy's aircraft and lamps allowed the children to go to school at night and young men to read their lovers' letters. The light from the lamps also symbolizes the desire for freedom. The enemy may extinguish the light but the people will always rekindle it just as they will always rise again in defence of their country:

> Still, night after night on our land
> The lamps are lit.
> They bring back the fire of a thousand years,
> from the time of our first struggling life,
> kept from generation to generation.[19]

The light here becomes a symbol of the future and of political will, of the five-pointed star of communism.

The bond between land and people is another theme of the genre, with many of these war poems being infused with a strong nationalistic sense of home and homeland. Kevin Bowen notes: 'The belief in the power of the land to sustain and transform the terms of struggle is pivotal to both poem and culture'.[20] Nguyễn Duy wrote some of the best verse expressing this deep love of country, a country of 'the maddening agony' where 'the honey comes from within'.[21] His 'Red Earth-Blue Water' (1971), while depicting the devastation caused by bombs, simultaneously resonates with lyrical images of 'bomb-raked funnels turned into rose water'[22] and heralds the survival of the land. The theme is particularly well demonstrated by a short poem 'Garden Fragrance' by Lâm Thị Mỹ Dạ, a poet from the South:

> Last night a bomb exploded on the veranda
> But sounds of birds sweeten the air this morning.
> I hear the fragrant trees, look in the garden,
> Find two silent clusters of ripe guavas.[23]

The opening line, pragmatic and unemotional, is contrasted with lyrical images of nature bursting with life. As with Nguyễn Duy's 'The Bamboo of Vietnam', nature is beyond the control of war, and does not succumb to it.

With effective brevity, the poem looks beyond and above the war and encapsulates a sense of hope and survival.

Numerous Vietnamese war poems derive much of their power from the tension implicit in the contrast between the peaceful tranquillity of the Vietnamese countryside (the familiar rural idyll of villages, rice paddies, ponds, rivers, mountains, buffaloes and children) and disturbing images of military devastation. One of the most powerful examples is a poem by Phô Đức entitled 'The Buffalo Boy on a Field of Corpses'. A young boy tending buffaloes is one of the symbols of rural Vietnam, an overused and strongly sentimental image. Juxtaposing it with a field of corpses, the poem communicates a profound sense of loss: loss of lives, loss of the beauty of the natural landscape and loss of the boy's childhood innocence when confronted by the horrors of which grown-ups are capable. This poem is unusually graphic in its description of death, with the mutilated bodies contaminating the peaceful, monotonous daily task of tending the buffaloes. The boy tries to understand what has happened and, more importantly, why. Yet to search for a rationale for war is beyond him, and his 'stupid brain'[24] cannot comprehend the absurdity of killing. For him the 'civilized' humans are worse than the animals:

> My buffaloes locked horns at times
> But cared for one another, lead by me.
> As humans, you were civilised, advanced –
> Why kill each other, strewing fields with flesh
> And watering soil with blood?
>
> (lines 25–9)

As suggested in the stanza, a major poetic theme is the omnipresence of war and its intrusion into every aspect of daily life. The demarcation line between the front and the rear was blurred, as was the distinction between soldier and civilian. The cruelty of war lay in its abrogation of people's right to their ordinary lives. The loss of life's trivialities and banalities is bemoaned in many war poems, and the community's perseverance in trying to hold on to some sense of normality during war is upheld. In 'Night Harvest' (1971) by Lâm Thị Mỹ Dạ, young girls harvest rice at night wearing conical hats, indifferent to the danger of unexploded bombs. They are 'not frightened by bullets and bombs in the air / Only by dew wetting our lime-scented hair',[25] and their 'rebellious' refusal to allow the war to hinder their lives helps to diminish its significance. Similarly, war does not free people from human desires, and many Vietnamese poems measure the cost of war in terms of emotional yearning. In 'Love Poems Written in the War', Nguyễn Khoa Điềm captures the agony of separation from a lover, describing the soul like 'a flame fiercely burning' with desire.[26] Amidst all the turmoil of war, it is the trauma of separation which tortures most, yet at the same time the strongest motivation to fight comes from 'hopes of our meeting' (line 106) and of being free to love. In a similar vein, Nguyễn Duy, in 'Longing' (1970), craves his love when 'climbing the high passes', 'crossing rivers' and 'holding fast to trenches'.[27]

Another common theme of the genre is the suffering of women and their contribution to the war effort: as one old Vietnamese saying has it, 'When war comes, even women must fight'. The social and cultural position of women in Vietnam is embedded with contradictions and tensions. Although Confucian morality placed them in a position of subordination to men, communist ideology assigned them equality and emancipation, creating a potential source of discord with the realities of Vietnamese society and family life. Intricate human relationships were further complicated by the war; the absence of men, who were off fighting in the jungle, demanded that women take on different roles, being expected not only to assume the responsibilities of the men but also to provide support for the front and to be direct participants in the conflict. Hue-Tam Ho Tai notes that while in Western literature war remains an overwhelmingly masculine experience, with combat considered the ultimate test of manhood, in Vietnam the guerrilla character of the war created an all-encompassing military space and necessitated the total involvement of even the female population. As Hue-Tam Ho Tai concludes, 'the representation of war as an exercise in patriotic self-defence makes possible its feminisation'.[28] Many Vietnamese poems relate the importance of women's contribution. Building the roads, filling the craters after bombing and keeping the Hồ Chí Minh trail free for the supply trucks were some of the duties left almost entirely to women. Hiding in the jungle, the girls and women waited for the bombs to be dropped and then filled in the craters and detonated any unexploded bombs. It was a life of immense hardship and danger: it was easy to die from shrapnel, exposure to chemicals or the unforgiving conditions in the jungle. Phạm Tiến Duật captures the life of such women in 'To the Young Women Volunteers' (1968), in which a soldier cherishes the memory of a chance encounter with a girl defusing bombs, recollecting her smile and the little taunts she exchanged with him and other passing soldiers. He is impressed by her unostentatious bravery and salutes the importance of her task:

> Next to the well a bomb has fallen;
> You sleep nearby, your feet dirty and unwashed.
> All day you defuse bombs,
> Cry out nights in your sleep.[29]

'Bomb-Crater Sky' by Lâm Thị Mỹ Dạ celebrates the heroism of a young girl who sacrificed her life in order to save others:

> They say that you, a road builder,
> Had such love for our country
> You rushed out and waved your torch

> To call the bombs down on yourself
> And save the road for the troops.[30]

Her selfless act remains the inspiration for others:

> By day I pass under the sky flooded with sun
> And it is your sky.
> And that anxious, wakeful disk:
> Is it the sun, or your heart
> Lighting my way
> As I walk down the long road?
>
> (lines 22–7)

Vietnamese poetry not only presents images of women's direct involvement in the war but also, perhaps more interestingly, images of women as the mothers of soldiers. Hue-Tam Ho Tai explains that in Vietnam, if a soldier died, the claim to his memory belonged above all to his mother. The grieving mother weeping over her lost child is a potent symbol of war and its horrors, and the suffering of mothers represents the suffering of the whole nation. Their courage is not that of the battlefield, but lies in their acceptance of the loss of their sons and husbands to war: a different type of heroism, more private and less ostentatious. Phạm Tiến Duật's poem 'The Mother at Nam Hoanh' (1968) poignantly depicts the courage of a mother whose 'husband had been killed by bombs while fishing', yet who nevertheless 'let her daughter enlist'.[31] In a village where bamboo trees still tremble from the bombing, she cares for passing soldiers, providing them with food and shelter. In spite of her personal loss, her parting words to the soldiers are defiant: 'Better to eat salt the rest of your life / than to live your life as a slave' (lines 18–19). As Chế Lan Viên states elsewhere, 'It's hard to be a mother in Vietnam'.[32] The war shifted the duties of a mother from teaching her child to recognize flowers and birds, to instructing him or her in recognizing the sound of approaching B52s and in seeking shelter. The mother's responsibilities toward her male offspring were particularly onerous. As 'The Mother at Nam Hoanh' continues:

> some days it is enough to teach
> our children to be men;
> yet these days we must do even more:
> make of them heroes every one –
> Such is the task of mothers in our land.
>
> (lines 12–16)

As the allusion to 'heroes' might suggest here, death is a potent symbol of conflict in Vietnamese war poetry, yet the genre is seldom brutally graphic in its description. More than death itself, it is the omnipresence of death, its proximity and permanent possibility, that conveys the traumas of war. Death is treated in a more abstract sense, as something which profoundly and persistently casts a shadow on life, as something waiting to happen. The immediacy of death is reflected not only through the constant fear of bombing and the need to be ready for evacuation but also by an approaching postman who may be bringing news of the death of a loved one.

The death of soldiers posed a number of culturally embedded dilemmas for the Vietnamese. As Shaun Kingsley Malarney points out, 'the dead soldier was one of the greatest threats to the legitimacy and authority of the Democratic Republic of Vietnam in the first three decades of its existence.'[33] It was an important part of the political agenda to ennoble death and guarantee that death would be seen as meaningful.[34] The glorification of death and its interpretation as the sacrifice of one's life for the nation and for the revolution prevented Vietnamese literature from treating the subject in a realistic and sober manner. In 'The Grave and the Sandalwood Tree' (1969), Nguyễn Đức Mậu celebrates the heroic death of a soldier 'killed – giving his life for his nation'.[35] Death is not treated by the poet as something tragic and traumatic, there is no mourning and no regrets; the death of a soldier is glorified and celebrated as the ultimate in bravery and devotion to duty:

> 'Killed – giving his life for his nation.' O, Hung!
> Your blood dyed the grass and a song flew into the earth.
> Your great sacrifice became a source of happiness.
> (lines 31–3)

To sacrifice one's life for the fatherland makes death meaningful and noble. The death is removed from the realm of private and personal into the realm of collective: it will inspire others and, like a sandalwood tree, will 'perfume the earth'.

> The sandalwood tree, beautiful as a soldier's life.
> It lives by simple faith. Its body grows and dies
> To perfume the earth, to perfume the earth and sky.
> (lines 61–3)

Killing is an everyday occurrence but this does not make it easy to come to terms with, as Nguyễn Duy suggests in his poem 'Stop' (1972).[36] Simpler but more effective is Phạm Tiến Duật's depiction of death in 'White Circles' (1972), which describes a village where most of the women and children wear white bands around their forehead, a sign of mourning. This poem is rather exceptional in that it avoids the glorification of death. Indeed, lines such as 'There is no loss greater than death' and 'the white mourning band takes the shape of a zero' were interpreted at the time as undermining the war effort.[37]

A theme that is naturally linked to self-glorification is the demonization of the enemy. With a few exceptions, the American soldier, and the American military more widely, is not individualized in poetry written during the war, but treated with the full force of Cold War rhetorical generalization: 'he is a murderer, a colonialist, an imperialist', rage the poets. Only occasionally is more specific reference made, as in Tố Hữu's accusal, in 'Emily Con' (1965), of Johnson and McNamara.[38] An exception is Nguyễn Duy's 'Stop', in which the enemy 'gains a face' and confrontation with the enemy is individualized. The otherwise anonymous enemy is a 'ranger with a face of a child';[39] in a soldier-to-soldier situation, killing is suddenly more difficult as the conflict is personalized.

At the same time, however, the poetry includes an important consideration of the conflict as civil war. The fighting placed the Vietnamese into opposing camps on either side of the 17th Parallel, dividing families, separating brothers, parents and children and turning them into enemies. The unity of the family is one of the pillars of Vietnamese society and the division of the family-nation was painful for many. The poetic treatment of this division makes use of the image of brothers separated from each other and of the metaphor of brother killing brother. Some poets called for the unification of the country, among others Lưu Trọng Lư, who in 'Pounding Waves at the Bay of Tung' (1958) weeps over the fact that Vietnamese soil cannot be reached by all Vietnamese. He dreams of 'a pair of arms that are wide and long / that can embrace all of the southern region':[40]

> O southern region of a thousand memories and a million of affections,
> Flesh of our flesh, blood of our blood,
> The flesh cannot be torn asunder,
> And your blood is still mingled with ours.
>
> (lines 63–6)

Similar sentiments are shared by Huy Cận, in 'Your Uncle's Child in the South is Eager to See His Father's Face' (1959),[41] and by Nguyễn Anh Dao, who sees the south of Vietnam as the mother, brothers and sisters who 'like arteries and veins of red blood are attached to the heart' and who longs for the unity of his country.[42]

In this way, Vietnamese war poets are anxious for a world without war and see peace as inevitable, although most have no specific vision of life after the war; peace is a dream of a 'country full of bloom', of houses 'filled with the fresh air of freedom / [where] sunlight reaches to find its way'.[43] For many, peace is identified with the hope of soldiers returning and families reuniting, while others have a more political vision of peace. In 'Lullaby for the Minority Children Growing Up on Their Mother's Backs' (1971), by Nguyễn Khoa Điềm, it is the promise of a freedom clearly associated with 'Uncle Ho' which is used to soothe and comfort a crying child.[44] For Tố Hữu 'the modest dreams all people share together' are 'peace, independence, warmth, eating your fill',[45] and there is no doubt in his mind that the peace is going to be socialist.

Beyond illusions: revisiting the past

The legacy of the American war in Vietnam was much more complex than the poetry and prose written during the war years would suggest. The political constraints at the time demanded total commitment and the poets themselves, convinced that the threat to their land had to be faced and fought, disciplined themselves to project messages of hope and inspiration. In November 1978, the literary journal *Văn Nghệ Quân Đội*, printed an essay entitled *Writing about the War*. Its author, Nguyễn Minh Châu, an accomplished writer and military veteran, launched a fierce criticism of Vietnamese literature from the war. While he acknowledged that many works written during the conflict aimed to 'contribute to the war efforts, along with the nation as a whole', they created, by suppressing everything which was not conducive to victory, a sanitized version of events, a 'dreamed reality' riddled with a dissonance between official accounts of war as a historical event and the personal memories of the participants.[46] Poets and writers had not been able to represent the pain, suffering, fear and deprivation of war; neither could they reflect the 'innumerable stories of individual fates' and 'all the facets of wartime life, dramatic and multifarious, just as it was'.[47] He urged them, now that the war was over, to go beyond 'the effervescent drama played on the outside' and to abandon the simplistic concept of a revolutionary hero as a superman and 'let the inner person rise and claim its right to life.'[48]

Nguyễn Minh Châu's criticism was ahead of its time; it took more than a decade for society to 'renovate' its attitudes towards the war and for a more complex picture to emerge. In 1986, altered political circumstances in Vietnam, conditioned by the changing international political climate and the gradual thawing of Cold War antagonism, had induced the Vietnamese government to adopt a programme of renovation (*đổi mới*), a Vietnamese version of Gorbachev's *perestroika* and *glasnost*.[49] The liberalized political environment meant a relaxation of control over creative activities and a greater freedom of expression, and enabled the relationship between writers and state to be renegotiated. The restrictive parameters of socialist realism were discarded, providing a catalyst for creativity. Poets, fiction writers, playwrights and critics began to capture the dilemmas of the Vietnamese present, yet at the same time felt an overpowering desire to retell the past. The discussion about the legacies of war contested its creative treatment as a conventional narrative of heroism and military accomplishment, renegotiating it as an individual human drama. De-glorification of the war allowed authors to go beyond the one-dimensional official portrayal of the Vietnam War as a triumphant victory by tackling taboo themes such as the devastating effects of the war, the agony, fear, cowardice and abuse of ideology.

While there is no doubt that political considerations significantly influenced the literary treatment of war, it would be short-sighted and simplistic to dismiss poetry from the war against America as nothing more than propaganda. The black and white vision of the world produced by Western Cold War rhetoric gave rise to many prejudices and stereotypes, and its treatment of the Vietnamese war was no exception. The Vietnamese were often portrayed as 'sadistic, heartless communist robots able to win through sheer cruelty and lack of respect for human life'.[50] Vietnamese poetry from the war can help to counteract such a simplistic view of Vietnamese society and to encourage a view of the Vietnamese, in Wayne Karlin's words, as 'human beings, their lives configured by the same passions, angers, love, hope and despair that marks all human lives'.[51]

Notes

1 Đông Hồ, 'War', *The Vietnam Review*, 4 (1998), p. 420, line 14.
2 In Vietnam, the full term used to designate the conflict is the 'War of National Salvation against the Americans'. I shall be using the 'American war', the appellation in common usage.
3 David Chanoff and Doan Van Toai, *Portrait of the Enemy* (New York: Random House, 1986), p. xv.
4 Pelly, *Postcolonial Vietnam: New Histories of National Past* (Durham, NC: Duke University Press, 2002), p. 5.
5 Trường Chinh (1907–88) wrote poetry under the name Sóng Hồng (Red Wave).
6 Trường Chinh, 'To Be a Poet', in Nguyen Khac Vien and Huu Ngoc, eds, *Vietnamese Literature: An Anthology*, trans. Nguyen Khac Vien, Huu Ngoc, *et al.* (Hanoi: Red River, n.d.), p. 570, lines 7, 8, 17, 18.
7 Quoted in Kim N.B. Ninh, *A World Transformed: The Politics of Culture in Revolutionary Vietnam, 1945–1965* (Ann Arbor: University of Michigan Press, 2002), p. 44.
8 Ibid., p. 44.
9 Ibid., p.44.
10 In the late 1950s some writers and intellectuals attempted to push for greater creative freedom. This activity was centred on two journals, *Nhân Văn* and *Giai Phẩm*. Its suppression and the harsh treatment of the participants silenced for decades any similar attempts at cultural liberalisation.
11 Nguyen Ba Chung, 'Imagining the Nation', *Boston Review*, 21: 1 (February/March 1996), http://www.boston review.net/BR21.1/chung.html (accessed 20 November 2004).
12 Two sisters, Trung Trac and Trung Nhi, were leaders of a successful uprising against the Chinese between 40 and 43 AD. Finally defeated in 43 AD, the sisters chose to commit suicide rather than surrender to the enemy.
13 Nguyen Ba Chung and Kevin Bowen, eds, *6 Vietnamese Poets*, trans. Martha Collins, Carolyn Forche, Linh Green, *et al.* (Williamtic: Curbstone Press, 2002), p. xviii.
14 Nguyễn Đình Hòa, *Vietnamese Literature: A Brief Survey* (San Diego: San Diego State University, 1994), p. 165. This chapter considers poetry from North Vietnam (the Vietnamese Democratic Republic) written during the American war. Only occasional reference is made to poets from South Vietnam.
15 Neil L. Jamieson, *Understanding Vietnam* (Berkeley and London: University of California Press, 1993), p. 267.
16 Phạm Tiến Duật, 'Drivers of Lorries without Windscreens', in Kevin Bowen

and Bruce Weigl, eds, *Writing between the Lines: An Anthology of War and Its Social Consequences* (Amherst: University of Massachusetts Press, 1997), p. 70, line 25.
17 Nguyễn Duy, 'The Bamboo of Vietnam', in Nguyễn Duy, *Distant Road*, trans. Kevin Bowen and Nguyen Ba Chung (Williamtic: Curbstone Press, 1999), p. 5, lines 16, 11.
18 Nguyễn Mỹ, 'The Red Farewell', in Kevin Bowen, Nguyen Ba Chung and Bruce Weigl, eds, *Mountain River: Vietnamese Poetry from the Wars, 1948–1993*, trans. Kevin Bowen, Nguyen Ba Chung, Bruce Weigl, *et al.* (Amherst: University of Massachusetts Press, 1998), p. 51, lines 31–6.
19 Phạm Tiến Duật, 'The Fire in the Lamps', in Nguyen Ba Chung and Bowen, eds, *6 Vietnamese Poets*, p. 219, lines 25–9.
20 Quoted in Fred Marchant, 'War Poets from Viet Nam', *Humanities*, 19: 2 (March–April 1998), http://www.neh.fed.us/news/humanities/1998-03/honey.html (accessed 24 November 2004).
21 Nguyễn Duy, 'Red Earth–Blue Water', in Nguyễn Duy, *Distant Road*, p. 11, line 19.
22 Ibid., p. 11, line 3.
23 Lâm Thị Mỹ Dạ, 'Garden Fragrance', in Nguyen Ba Chung and Bowen, eds, *6 Vietnamese Poets*, p. 95, lines 1–4.
24 Phổ Đức, 'The Buffalo Boy on a Field of Corpses', in Huỳnh Sanh Thông, ed., *An Anthology of Vietnamese Poems*, trans. Huỳnh Sanh Thông (New Haven and London: Yale University Press, 1996), p. 396, lines 25–9.
25 Lâm Thị Mỹ Dạ, 'Night Harvest', in Nguyen Ba Chung and Bowen, eds, *6 Vietnamese Poets*, p. 103, lines 13–14.
26 Nguyễn Khoa Điềm, 'Love Poems Written in the War', in Nguyen Ba Chung and Bowen, eds, *6 Vietnamese Poets*, p. 66, line 26.
27 Nguyễn Duy, 'Longing', in Nguyễn Duy, *Distant Road*, p. 3, lines 1, 3, 5.
28 Hue-Tam Ho Tai, 'Faces of Remembering and Forgetting', in Hue-Tam Ho Tai, ed., *The Country of Memory: Remaking the Past in Late Socialist Vietnam* (Berkeley and London: University of California Press, 2001), p. 173.
29 Phạm Tiến Duật, 'To the Young Women Volunteers', in Nguyen Ba Chung and Bowen, eds, *6 Vietnamese Poets*, p. 228, lines 40–3.
30 Lâm Thị Mỹ Dạ, 'Bomb-Crater Sky', in Nguyen Ba Chung and Bowen, eds, *6 Vietnamese Poets*, p. 99, lines 1–5.
31 Phạm Tiến Duật, 'The Mother at Nam Hoanh', in Nguyen Ba Chung and Bowen, eds, *6 Vietnamese Poets*, p. 213, lines 9, 10.
32 Chế Lan Viên, 'To Be Mother in Vietnam', in Nguyen Khac Vien and Huu Ngoc, eds, *Vietnamese Literature*, p. 714.
33 Malarney, 'The Fatherland Remembers Your Sacrifice', in Hue-Tam Ho Tai, ed., *Country of Memory*, p. 46.
34 Malarney points out that the death of a soldier at war bore several characteristics of what was culturally considered 'bad death'. For example, dying young, childless, violently and away from home, along with the impossibility of identifying the body and the inability of the soldier's family to bury the body or to perform funeral rites, were just some of the sources of great anxiety (see ibid., pp. 59–60).
35 Nguyễn Đức Mậu, 'The Grave and the Sandalwood Tree', in Nguyen Ba Chung and Bowen, eds, *6 Vietnamese Poets*, p. 132, line 30.
36 Nguyễn Duy, 'Stop', in Nguyễn Duy, *Distant Road*, pp. 83–5.
37 Phạm Tiến Duật, 'White Circles', in Nguyen Ba Chung and Bowen, eds, *6 Vietnamese Poets*, p. 233, lines 6, 7.
38 Tố Hữu, 'Emily Con', in Bowen, *et al.*, eds, *Mountain River*, pp. 61–5.

39 Nguyễn Duy, 'Stop', p. 83, line 4.
40 Lưu Trọng Lư, 'Pounding Waves at the Bay of Tung', in Jamieson, *Understanding Vietnam*, p. 272, lines 12–13.
41 Huy Cận, 'Your Uncle's Child in the South Is Eager to See His Father's Face', in Jamieson, *Understanding Vietnam*, p. 274.
42 Nguyễn Anh Dao, quoted in Jamieson, *Understanding Vietnam*, pp. 275–6.
43 Nguyễn Khoa Điềm, 'A Day of Celebration' (1975), in Nguyen Ba Chung and Bowen, eds, *6 Vietnamese Poets*, pp. 73–5, lines 12, 28–9.
44 Nguyễn Khoa Điềm, 'Lullaby for the Minority Children Growing Up on Their Mother's Backs', in Nguyen Ba Chung and Bowen, eds, *6 Vietnamese Poets*, pp. 45–7.
45 Tố Hữu, *Blood and Flower* (Hanoi: Foreign Languages Publishing House, 1978), p. 32.
46 Nguyễn Minh Châu, 'Writing about War', *The Vietnam Review*, 3 (1997), p. 440.
47 Ibid., p. 440.
48 Ibid., p. 441. Trần Dần, many years earlier, referred to this type of writing as 'smoke-and-fire literature', literature ostensibly describing soldiers but seeing only guns firing and fire raging.
49 The principles guiding the renovation of culture are defined in Resolution No. 5 of the Politburo of the Central Committee of the Vietnamese Communist Party, entitled *Renovating and Enhancing the Leadership and Management of Literature, Arts and Culture to a Higher Step of Development* and issued on 28 November 1987.
50 Wayne Karlin, quoted in Le Minh Khue, *The Stars, the Earth, the River* (Williamtic: Curbstone Press, 1997), p. xviii.
51 Ibid., p. xviii.

8 Remembering war and revolution on the Maoist stage

Xiaomei Chen

On 1 October 1949, at the founding of the People's Republic of China (PRC), Mao Zedong proudly declared in Tiananmen Square, 'We, the Chinese people, have now stood up.' This event marked the important moment in the history of the Cold War when socialist China became a strong ally of the Soviet Union against the capitalist West, headed by the United States. In the same year, a new patriotic play entitled *Growing Up in the Battlefield* (*Zhandou li chengzhang*), collectively written by Hu Peng and others, premiered. The play, discussed below, though it centred on the 'hot war' of the 1930s and 1940s, used the discourse of the Cold War era; at the same time it conveyed the classic image of a socialist nation encouraging the newly liberated Chinese people to fight bravely against the capitalist world – so unfairly divided between rich and poor – both in old China and in the rest of the world.

This chapter attempts to demonstrate the internal forces within Chinese society that led to a lasting discourse in which the 'hot war' before 1949 was remembered in order to justify a 'continued revolution' in socialist China. A military backdrop comprising the war of resistance against Japanese invaders and the civil war between the Kuomintang (KMT) Nationalist troops and those of the Chinese Communist Party (CCP) played an essential part in the construction of the revolutionary discourse of the PRC. That discourse skilfully exploited Cold War rhetoric on the Chinese stage so that the political agendas of the CCP might be carried out. It is my intention in this chapter to move beyond the bipolar view of the Cold War world, with the United States and the Soviet Union as its exclusive opposing poles. Instead, I focus on Chinese theatre as a dynamic stage on which Chinese constructions of the Cold War became integral to the formation of national identities via stories about home, family, motherhood, femininity, masculinity, collective identity and global revolution.

The ultimate goal of these Chinese stories was to justify and consolidate the political power of the CCP; they were also meant to provide the theoretical grounds for Mao Zedong's campaign to prevent socialist China from reverting to its pre-1949 semi-colonial and semi-feudal state. This is, of course, not to deny that the Chinese communist revolution had long been inspired by the Russian Revolution of 1917 and by its socialist ideology. Yet the Maoist socialist stage saw its function as the use of Cold War ideology to create a particular kind of Maoism by which China could be viewed as an important pillar of the socialist bloc. The Sino-Soviet split after the death of Stalin mandated that the CCP redefine itself as an emerging leader of the socialist bloc with its own unique vision, which consisted of a combination of Marxism, Leninism and 'Mao Zedong Thought'. And that vision was devoted to supporting the Third World independence movements of the 1960s in their rebellion against the domineering power of 'Soviet revisionists' and US imperialists. In a series of public speeches and printed statements from 1963 to 1964, for instance, Mao Zedong declared his unwavering support for the Panamanian people's 'just' and 'patriotic struggle' against US imperialism and its running dogs, for the people of the Congo's struggle against US intervention, and for the South Vietnamese people's resistance to the US–Diem authority, thus positioning himself as the spokesman and defender of the interests of the oppressed Third World.[1] Theatre productions such as *War Drums of the Equator* (*Chidao zhangu*), performed in various parts of the country from 1965 to 1966, dramatized the conflict between leftist Congolese forces under Patrice Lumumba and those supported by the UN and USA.[2] After a series of violent and murderous events, the emphasis on guerrilla war in the African jungle as the only way to defeat imperialist forces at the end of the play reinforced the global implications of Mao's theory that political power grew out of the barrel of a gun: 'without a people's army the people have nothing'.[3] Military stories therefore become indispensable for winning the Chinese revolution in the past and for the triumph of the world revolution in the present.

Contemporary Chinese politics was not the only inspiration for Cold War theatre. In order to celebrate Chinese nationalism, some well-made plays of the 1950s continued the Republican period's (1911–49) tradition of remembering the 'hot wars' imposed by imperialist powers on China and waged by the enemies of the Chinese people. Examples are the well-received plays of Tian Han, such as *The Song of Returning Spring* (*Hui chun zhi qu*), written in 1935.[4] Against the backdrop of the Japanese invasion of Manchuria in 1931, Tian Han's play revolves around the story of a patriotic soldier. Having lost his memory as the result of battlefield wounds, the soldier regains it three years later thanks to the care of his fiancée, who has returned from South-East Asia to nurse and marry him even though he fails to remember her. A left-wing dramatist committed by 1930 to a socialist vision of a new China, Tian Han reflected Chinese intellectuals' subscription to Cold War ideology and paved the way for the incorporation by the high-Maoist culture of the 1960s of facets of military history into revolutionary history. The perceived appeal of the Chinese revolutionary war to the oppressed peoples of the world did not reach its peak, however, until the height of the Chinese Cultural Revolution (1966–76), as typically expressed in its model theatre, which is the focus of the second part of this chapter.

The use of the military past to bolster the revolutionary present is best illustrated by *Growing Up in the Battlefield*, the key play of the period. Although little known outside dramatic circles, *Growing Up in the Battlefield* evokes the sufferings of the rural poor before 1949, an important theme in the literature of both the Republican period and the PRC. Set in a remote village in northern China, the play traces the fortunes of a family of three generations of peasants in the traumatic years from 1935 to 1945 and their trajectory from poverty-stricken country folk to class-conscious soldiers fighting to achieve equality, happiness and prosperity for poor peoples.

Act I begins with Zhao Laozhong's protest against an evil landlord, Yang Youde, who has fabricated a deed that allows him to claim ownership of Zhao's land. Zhao had delayed building family dwellings until he finished digging a well to irrigate his land, finally transforming it into fertile soil after many years of hard labour. To be sure, Zhao declares, it will not be easy to retain the land, since the well-connected Yang family can buy off local court officials. Nevertheless, Zhao believes that there must still be incorruptible officials at the provincial level; and in case that hope proves vain, surely they can be found in Beijing.[5] A dramatic suspense develops, however, with the homecoming of the son, Zhao Tiezhu, who informs all the family except his father of a court verdict in Yang's favour. Unaware of this ruling, Zhao Laozhong persists in his plan to travel to the Taiyuan Prefectural capital the next day to ensure his victory in court, and the more he insists on going, the more difficult it becomes for the son to tell him the truth. In the end, Zhao Tiezhu feels he has no choice but to break the news to his father that not only did the Yangs win the land, but that the Zhaos will have to pay Yang's legal expenses. In total despair, and intending to commit suicide, Zhao Laozhong turns to his innocent and loving grandson, Zhao Shitou, and asks him to fetch him a dose of poison, which the latter does without understanding what is happening. The plot here combines the traditional theatrical scene of *gu rou fen li*, or 'tearful separation between loved ones', with the effective dramatic technique of revealing a secret to the audience while keeping characters on stage in the dark.

Then, before Zhao Laozhong can breathe his last, he receives a visit from Yang Youde, who dares Zhao to sue him again. 'Our two families' feud will never be settled,' Zhao Laozhong vows. 'If we fail to win in this world, we will forever pursue justice in the devil's underworld' (11). Yang Youde declares in turn that he will keep Zhao company if the Zhaos appeal his case in the Supreme Court; if it comes to that, he will even take his case to Chiang Kai-shek, the generalissimo of the KMT, headquartered in Nanjing. Yang's proposed recourse to the KMT to back injustice provokes Zhao Tiezhu into burning down Yang's mansion and escaping from his home village to join the revolutionary army of the CCP. In this play, the personal grievances of one poor family foreshadow the irreconcilable class conflicts between the oppressed, poor peasants and the rich, privileged landlord, represented by the KMT.

Ten years have elapsed when the curtain rises on Act II, which is set in 1945 in a small town next to a major city in the north. Zhao Shitou, Zhao Tiezhu's son, has grown up with the help of the extended families of the poor people around him, and at this point he is almost eighteen years old. To escape persecution from the Yang family, his mother had taken him away from their home town ten years before and they lived under an assumed name. However, Yang Yaozu, Yang Youde's son, recognizes Zhao Shitou's mother and presses her for the whereabouts of her husband, who is still wanted for the arson that destroyed the Yangs' residence. Moreover, Yang Yaozu (whose name literally means 'glorifying ancestors') not only resolves to avenge his father but is also serving the KMT as a Japanese collaborator. The second generations, it seems, are as determined as the first to carry on their family feud on personal, national and ideological grounds. Seeing no other way open to them, Zhao Shitou's mother sends her son off to join the CCP-led Eight-Route Army so that he may fight against the Japanese and the KMT. Being close to his mother, and having been deprived of his father during his formative years, Zhao Shitou remains determined to look for his father and avenge his grandfather. Once again, the play connects a poor family's grievances with the issues of national salvation and the collective identities of the oppressed Chinese people.

Set in a liberated village in northern China three years later, in 1948, Act III begins with a bustling scene at a military headquarters; it is here that strategies are mapped out for a campaign against the KMT troops in the aftermath of the Japanese surrender in 1945. The words of the army's theme song, sung at the rise of the curtain, testify to the popularity of the 'people's army,' which – 'with guns tightly held' in their hands and with 'class hatred in their hearts' – represents 'the hope of the people'. Since the 'people' are their 'parents,' and 'unity' is their 'strength,' the people's army 'sees no obstacles' to conquering their enemies (27). It is in this 'new revolutionary family' that Zhao Shitou discovers his father, now a military commander. Even without knowing that the man is indeed his father, Shitou feels immediately drawn to this respected, gentle superior. The love and tender care with which a 'father' (or superior) looks after his 'son' (or recruit) is similar to the nurturing way the Communist Party wanted to care for its numerous 'children' in the big proletariat family. Equally oblivious to Shitou's true identity, Zhao Tiezhu educates him, treating him as a new recruit in a 'revolutionary family' composed of 'class' brothers with a shared hatred for the KMT. Now renamed Zhao Gang (which means 'Comrade Steel'), Zhao Tiezhu gently guides his soldiers toward achieving a heightened class consciousness. He convinces the new soldiers, who are eager to fight their way south to liberate their home villages from the KMT's rule, that revolution is not about settling personal grievances against one's own enemies. It is about liberating every single village in China in order to finally liberate humankind; this is the clear, overriding message that the new recruits must understand about what was later known as 'Cold War ideology', even while they are in the middle of the hot battles between the CCP and the KMT.

When urged by his new soldiers to talk about his own family, Zhao Tiezhu admits that he did have a family but lost contact with them 13 years ago. He does not plan to quit his military career or return home, he says, until all class enemies have been wiped off the face of the earth (31). Repeatedly the play juxtaposes Zhao's emphasis on the 'big family,' consisting of all the suffering peoples of the world, with his suppressed longings for his own family. Further questioned by Comrade Zhou, his political instructor and party representative, Zhao confesses that, no matter how hard he tried, he was never able to uncover any leads as to the whereabouts of his family. Still in love with his wife, he has never been tempted to approach any other woman and continues to hope that they will be reunited (33). In one scene, Zhao Tiezhu explains to his new recruits that he too harbours deep hatred for their class enemies and is intent on avenging his father, who was hounded to death by an evil landlord. Zhao Tiezhu's remarks are reinforced by those of his son: the son also seeks revenge against a hated oppressor, one who forced *his* father to flee from home and leave his family fatherless and facing hardships for most of the son's life (39). The audience members, of course, know the characters' true identities and are thus expected to be touched by the family's tragedy and to relate to it as if it were their own.

The plot device of unrecognized identities is taken further in Act III and Act IV. Zhao Tiezhu leads his soldiers to victory in the battle to liberate the village where his son and wife went to live after they had escaped from their home town. While Zhao Tiezhu remains in the dark as to the significance of this battle, his son becomes so impatient to obey orders to liberate his village and rescue his mother that Zhao Tiezhu feels compelled to remind him that liberating one's own family should not be the primary reason for joining the revolution. However, when Zhao Tiezhu and his unidentified son manage to save Zhao's wife, kill Yang Youde and arrest Yang Youde's son, it seems as if the commander has achieved a miracle: earlier on, he had promised his soldiers that the day when other oppressed peoples are liberated will be the day when the family of the soldiers will also be liberated. The logic of the play therefore dictates that the son should now tearfully bid his mother farewell and set out to avenge the wrongs done to his comrades' families just as they have done for him. Speaking from his broadened perspective, the father tells his wife that even though she has waited thirteen years for him, he cannot yet 'put down his gun', not before all class enemies have been wiped out. Had his father possessed a gun, he points out, the evil landlord could not have persecuted his father to death (74). This final scene seamlessly connects the family reunion with the teleological goals of socialist China. The traditional operatic scene of *da tuan yuan*, or 'great family reunion', illustrates the revolutionary theme that one's *xiao jia*, or 'small home,' cannot know happiness without looking out for the needs of *da jia*, or the 'big family', of all oppressed people.

A canonical play of the 1950s, *Growing Up in the Battlefield* served as a model for the subsequent war dramas of PRC theatre, which continued to centre on Cold War themes. This is seen, for example, in *Iron Transportation Troops* (*Gangtie yunshubing*), written by Huang Ti and premiered in Beijing in 1953.[6] On 14 February 1950, Stalin and Mao Zedong signed the first Sino-Soviet Treaty of Friendship, Alliance and Mutual Assistance in Moscow, an event which '[signalled] the opening of a second front in the Cold War in Asia' following the Berlin crisis of 1948, when the Soviet Union and the West defied each other for the first time since the Second World War.[7] As 'the first military confrontation of the Cold War', the Korean War of 1950 to 1953 threw China into direct conflict with the United States and its allies at the point when China sent millions of volunteer soldiers with Soviet equipment to the aid of socialist North Korea.[8] Set against this historical background, *Iron Transportation Troops* depicts the dangers and difficulties faced by a Chinese transportation unit as it struggles to keep the supply line open for Chinese and North Korean troops under the constant bombing of the US Air Force.

Among the lengthy, reportage-type dramatizations of the battle's twists and turns, one chief story makes the play work. At the beginning of Act I, on the eve of the PRC's October First National Day, the Chinese soldiers, touched by numerous gifts they have received from China and from other socialist countries such as Hungary, decide that the best way to celebrate the national day in Korea would be to win a major battle against the US imperialists. They keep the best gifts – a package of sugar from Hungary and a red scarf from the Chinese Young Pioneers – for their favorite Korean friend, six-year-old Xiao Yingzi, who loves to sing and dance for them. But to their great sorrow, they learn that Xiao Yingzi has been blinded after picking up a toy-like bomb dropped by the US Air Force. Later in the play, Xiao Yingzi's mother, the leader of a Korean road repair team in charge of keeping the bombed roads open for the Chinese transportation unit, challenges a captured US soldier to tell her why his country's soldiers cannot even spare innocent Korean children in their war of aggression. Her separation from her husband (who had left home to join the North Korean Army) and from her mother-in-law and her daughter, and her reunion with her husband following a major battle victory during the war, echoes the story line of *Growing Up in the Battlefield*. The distinction is that this play recounts the story of a Korean family, supported and appreciated by the 'big revolutionary family' of the Chinese transportation unit, which has taken up arms for the homeland of their socialist brothers and sisters. Injured children, separated spouses, sympathetic supporters and an idealistic longing for one's motherland all figure as chapters of the military history of the Cold War, rehearsed on the stage of 1950s China.

Contrasting with the solidarity of the socialist bloc dramatized by *Iron Transportation Troops*, a 1962 play entitled *The Second Spring* (*Di er ge chuntian*), written by Liu Chuan, levelled an indirect attack at the Soviet

Union. One of the very few experimental plays to employ Brecht's 'alienation effects', *The Second Spring* relates the great difficulties faced by Liu Zhiyin, a young woman naval engineer who must build the first speedboat for the Chinese navy without recourse to foreign technology. This theme of creating an independent, prosperous China without foreign assistance implicitly criticized Khrushchev's withdrawal of financial, technological and economic support from China. Two foreigners in the play are charged with highlighting this message. One is a businesswoman, apparently from a Western imperialist country, who visits Liu's father. As an overseas student thirty years before, Liu's father had made a scientific discovery that startled his classmates, and today the woman has come hoping to acquire his innovative technology to benefit her company. The second foreigner is the woman's male colleague and subordinate, a socialist exile who cannot return to his homeland in Latin America because it is now occupied by colonialists. He rejects his female boss's demand that he help her obtain Liu's technology, seeing the Lius as his genuine friends as opposed to 'those people in the world who merely talk about friendship and love while at heart always want to eat people alive'. 'They can only create war and hatred,' the exile declares. 'One has to rely on one's own strength by following the examples set up by people like you!'[9] For audiences familiar with the Sino-Soviet ideological debates of the early 1960s, these lines clearly referred to the Soviet Union's attempt to dominate its satellite countries by dictating the rules of their relations. Thus the implicit message of this play suggests a turning point in the depiction of military themes on the socialist stage, which now is heeding the CCP's call to be 'self-reliant' and 'independent,' and to renounce the illusion of Soviet support. These Cold War stories constitute the opening of a new front in China's ideological conflict with the Soviet Union, previously the leader in the Cold War against the capitalist West.

The anti-Soviet theme grew even more dominant in the high Maoist culture during the peak of the Chinese Cultural Revolution (1966–76). Partially provoked by what was then feared as the 'peaceful transformation' in the Soviet Union from a socialist country to a 'revisionist' and 'social-imperialist county,' the official press interpreted the initiation of the Cultural Revolution as ensuring that in China the 'red colours' of socialism would never change to the 'black colours' of capitalism. Consequently, the labouring people would never have to 'suffer for the second time'.[10] To combat the remaining feudalist, capitalist and revisionist cultures in the PRC, the official culture promoted 'revolutionary model theatre' devoted to Cold War themes that evoked the memory of revolutionary warfare in order to perpetuate the socialist revolution.[11] In the model theatre, not only did military commanders find their prototypes in the likes of Zhao Tiezhu, but female characters were also transformed from suffering, silent subalterns into revolutionary warriors and party leaders. No longer would Zhao's wife patiently wait for her father and son to return home. Indeed, in some plays, women warriors took their male counterparts' place as leaders, and for traditional roles associated with womanhood, motherhood and the intimacies of family life, they substituted a total dedication to revolutionary history.

Of the eight revolutionary model works officially promoted between the spring and summer of 1967, most were direct representations of the revolutionary war experience, dramatized in the three different artistic genres of Peking opera, ballet and symphonic music. The subject of the Peking opera *Shajiabang* is an armed struggle during the anti-Japanese war in which Guo Jianguang (a political instructor of the New Fourth Army) and seventeen wounded soldiers defeat Guomintang troops who collaborated with Japanese invaders.[12] The revolutionary modern ballet *The Red Detachment of Women* (*Hongse niangzijun*) tells the story of Wu Qinghua, a peasant girl who fled enslavement by a local tyrant on Hainan Island to join a women's detachment fighting KMT soldiers.[13] In the Peking opera *Taking Tiger Mountain by Strategy*, Yang Zirong, a People's Liberation Army scout, ventures into enemy headquarters disguised as a bandit to liberate the poor people from the north-east mountain area during the War of Liberation.[14] The Peking opera *Raid on the White Tiger Regiment* deals with the Korean War, during which Yan Weicai, leader of a scout platoon of the Chinese People's Volunteers, overthrows the invincible South Korean White Tiger Regiment that is supported by American military advisors.[15]

Following the success of the first eight revolutionary model works, another five were written which reinforced the Maoist blueprint for an ideal society. Almost all of them emphasized war experience and memory. The Peking opera *Azalea Mountain* features Ke Xiang, a female Communist Party secretary who turns a peasant army into a revolutionary unit as it struggles to overcome a local despot and nationalist troops. In this work, Ke Xiang, like Zhao Tiezhu of *Growing Up in the Battlefield*, is the military commander who persuades her soldiers that they must devote themselves to liberating all the poor people of the world before taking revenge on their personal foes. At the same time, Zhao Tiezhu's wife is the prototype for Mother Tu in *Azalea Mountain*, although, after having been captured by the enemy force, this suffering yet courageous woman encourages her godson and grandson to obey Ke Xiang's military orders instead of rushing recklessly into battle to rescue her and thereby putting the revolutionary army at risk.[16]

The Peking opera *Song of the Dragon River* (*Longjiang song*)[17] turns out to be the only one among the five pieces that depicts rural life of the 1960s. This was a time when the past sufferings of the local peasants before liberation were constantly invoked to justify their continuing sacrifices to the socialist state. Conveniently tracing the roots of peasants' suffering to the old society allowed the party to demand that the rural community sacrifice local interests to the global ambitions of the nation. The opera depicts the dilemma of peasants from a Dragon River Brigade who must abide by the decision of the county party committee to dam the Dragon River and flood their harvesting land in order to save a drought-ridden area. In rural China, where land is the peasant's lifeline, it has traditionally been almost impossible to convince peasants to give up their land. *Song of the Dragon River* has to take pains, therefore, to make the party's unusual demand credible; it does so by telling 'a bitterness story'[18] about the ruthless exploitation of the peasants at the hands of rich landowners of the old society, and contrasting this treatment with the caring government of socialist China. To heighten the local communities' sense of connectedness to oppressed peoples everywhere, Jiang Shuiying, the female Party leader, organizes a reading group to study Mao's essay 'In Memory of Norman Bethume', which celebrates the Canadian Communist Party member who supported Chinese soldiers in their war against Japan. This communist spirit that would impel a foreigner to selflessly adopt as his own the cause of the Chinese people's liberation helps the villagers to conceive of a sacrifice for their own compatriots as a natural and desirable impulse. In the war period before 1949, the historical figure of Dr Norman Bethume was respected as a model international communist. On the stage of the Cultural Revolution, however, he reappears to perform the same function as the male socialist exile in *The Second Spring*, who found in the CCP an inspirational guide in the world revolution against Soviet revisionists, the party's new enemies in the global war against capitalism and revisionism. Jiang Shuiying, indeed, explores her own vision of world revolution as she works to persuade a colleague to look beyond the nearby mountains that block his view and to recall the sufferings of the poor 'brothers and sisters' living in unemancipated Third World countries:

> In the world today
> How many slaves still in chains
> How many paupers suffer from starvation
> How many brothers take up arms
> How many sisters are exploited
> Let us strike hard at imperialism, revisionism and reactionaries
> All mankind will eventually be emancipated.[19]

In this way, *Song of the Dragon River* introduces to the Chinese stage the theme of anti-European colonialism in the Third World, and does so in order to justify the continuation of revolution in the Chinese countryside. Using similar tactics, the Peking opera *On the Docks* (*Haigang*), highlights a global discourse of world revolution as it portrays the working class in cosmopolitan Shanghai. Set in the Shanghai docks, where imperialists used to run their businesses, the opera spotlights Fang Haizhen, a female party secretary who was brutally exploited as a child labourer before the liberation of Shanghai in 1949. Her memory of a bitter past makes her keenly cognizant of the fact that people struggling to be free 'very much want the support of revolutionary people of the world'.[20] Fang Haizhen and her co-workers expose the hidden class enemy Qian Shouwei, who was attempting to flee abroad to his imperialist masters after abortive sabotage activities.

Their discovery enables the workers to complete the timely loading of a ship of rice seed destined for African people striving to develop their national economy and prise themselves loose from colonial exploitation (50). The shipment must arrive in time for sowing, and 'every sack will play a part in the African people's struggle' (57) against the imperialists who once predicted that rice could not grow in Africa and that Africans could solve their food problem only by importing grain (61). In the opera, the world powers' principal spheres of influence are symbolized by the opposite destinations of the Chinese oceangoing ships: Qian Shouwei's 'Scandinavian ship' goes to Europe, whereas the ship that Fang Haizhen protects from Qian's sabotage heads for Africa, the 'jungle' in the Third World where socialist China is respected as an inspirational leader. In the most popular lines of this scene, Fang Haizhen describes the port of Shanghai as having been linked 'with every / corner of our land, and support[ing] national / construction and the people the world over' (72). These lines form another instance of the campaign to persuade audiences of the necessity to continue the revolution in socialist China, in order to support the Third World's revolution against imperialism and colonialism.

Abetting model theatre's efforts, the official press in Cultural-Revolutionary China drove home the urgent need to transport 'Mao Zedong Thought' on to other stages around the world. For example, on 31 May 1967, the twenty-fifth anniversary of Mao's *Talks at the Yan'an Forum on Literature and Art*, a seminar on Mao's works was held by the Afro-Asian Writers' Bureau in Beijing, headquarters of China's great proletarian Cultural Revolution. Attended by more than 80 writers from over 34 countries, this gathering was described as a 'concrete manifestation of the fact that the whole world is entering a completely new era, an era in which Mao Tse-tung's thought is the great banner' and in which 'his revolutionary line and theory on literature and art are becoming a powerful ideological weapon for the revolutionary people of the world in their struggle against imperialism, revisionism and the reactionaries of all countries'.[21] As indicated by the official report from the Chinese press, the progressive writers of the Third World countries 'gazed with boundless respect at the huge portrait of Chairman Mao [...] and they read aloud the quotations from Chairman Mao's works written up in Chinese, Arabic, English and French'.[22] Besides reading poems by Chairman Mao, these writers also recited poems they had written 'in his praise, in praise of Mao Tse-tung's thought and of revolution'.[23]

Further proof that the dissemination of 'Mao Zedong Thought' was stimulating political and cultural change in Third World countries was marshalled in the form of frequent, vivid accounts in the Chinese press of theatrical performances by troupes from the Third World. For example, in July and August 1967 the press reported that the visiting Somali Artists' Delegation performed on a stage set in 'golden light [that] radiated from the backdrop showing a portrait of Chairman Mao, the red sun in the heart of the world's people'.[24] With surging emotion, the Somali artists, 'holding copies of *Quotations from Chairman Mao Tse-tung* and standing before Chairman Mao's portrait', sang the Somali song, 'Sing the Praise of Chairman Mao', and the Chinese song, 'The East Is Red', both of which were met by 'stormy applause from the audience'.[25] The international Mao cult acquired additional credence when the Chinese press claimed that, in 1967 alone, 33 different kinds of portrait of Mao were distributed all over Asia, Africa and Latin America. As of June 1969, there were more than 1,100 editions of Chairman Mao's works published in 70 different languages in 60 countries and regions, including 52 editions of the *Selected Works of Mao Tsetung* translated and published in 32 languages in 35 countries.[26] It seems that the official press's construction of a worldwide Maoist community in real life rendered even more credible model theatre's construction of an imagined international community on stage.

The effects of the global theatre of the Maoist Cultural Revolution, with its promotion of world revolution, penetrated beyond Africa, as demonstrated by the frequent performances of visiting fellow socialist countries, such as Albania and Romania. For example, the Tirana amateur troupe's 'With Pick in One Hand and Rifle in the Other', staged in Beijing in 1967, was taken to be proof of Mao's revolutionary victory as reflected in the literature and art of China, and likewise proof of 'Comrade Enver Hoxha's wise leadership' in the process of further revolutionizing the entire life of Albania.[27] When the giant portraits of the two great leaders appeared on stage, with 'the brilliant red flags of our two countries wav[ing] side by side',[28] it symbolized the challenge posed by the two self-proclaimed leaders of the Third World countries to the imperialism of the West and to the 'social imperialism' of the Soviet Union. Similarly, the performance in August 1971 by the Doena Art Troupe of the Armed Forces of Romania was acclaimed in the Chinese press for demonstrating the revolutionary friendship and militant unity of the two countries as well as the two parties' socialist construction and their 'common struggle against imperialism and its lackeys'.[29]

The Chinese stage also attracted Maoist factions of a pro-Moscow Communist Party in the capitalist world. In July 1967, the Japanese Haguruma Theatre, overcoming 'the many obstacles put in their way by the US and Japanese reactionaries and the revisionist clique of the Japanese Communist Party, finally reached Beijing, where Chairman Mao lives and where the world-shaking great Cultural Revolution was born'.[30] With 'boundless love for our great leader', they performed, in August, a play entitled *Advancing through the Storm*, an account of the struggle waged by the workers of the Iwaguni Bus Company, under the leadership of the left wing of the Japanese Communist party, against American imperialism, Japanese monopoly capital and the Miyamoto revisionist clique.[31] To Chinese audiences, this event offered yet another illustration of socialist China's impact on the world, resulting in the great red banner of 'Mao Zedong Thought' being seen 'flying high [even] in the heart of revolutionary people of Japan!'[32] In the troupe's other work, the five-act play *Prairie Fire*, the peasant leader,

Mosuke, who leads an uprising in the Chichibu mountain area of Japan in 1884, 'comes to see more clearly the necessity of organizing the people to take up arms and fight for political power' in his struggle against Shokichi, a landowner and capitalist.[33] A Chinese critic pointed out that these Japanese plays demonstrated the universality of Maoist 'truth', since the comrades of the Haguruma Theatre, who hailed from a foreign country, had 'analyzed and portrayed this uprising in the light of Marxism-Leninism and Mao Zedong's thought'.[34] As in many Chinese model plays, these Japanese plays evoked the past to certify the 'truth' of the present: 'Through the fight put up by Mosuke and other members of the Party of the Poor, *Prairie Fire* expresses the great concept of the seizure of political power by force.'[35]

This imagined international Mao cult may sound naive and remote three decades after the heyday of the Cultural Revolution. Yet the Cold War themes it employed in memory of revolutionary war and its constant warnings against peaceful transformation from a socialist China to a capitalist and revisionist China still give pause to those who resent the increasing gap between the rich and the poor in contemporary China. Economic progress and rising living standards aside, the exploitation of the rural migrant workers as cheap labour and the constant loss of agricultural land to urban development make one reconsider whether Mao had a point after all in campaigning for 'continued revolution' in socialist China.

No wonder, therefore, that in April 2000 a play entitled *Che Guevara* (*Qie Gewala*) was such a great smash, primarily for its call to arms.[36] The play depicts Che Guevara as a military hero of the Cuban revolution at the height of the Cold War period when he has sacrificed everything to bring justice and equality to the poor peoples in other countries of the Third World. In contemporary China, where many people are victimized by party corruption and by exploitation from the new rich, *Che Guevara*'s call for a new revolution through military war directed at liberating the disadvantaged and poor peoples once again touched a deep chord. In highly poetic language, the cast asks the audience a number of questions. Forty-years ago, Che Guevara gave up his career as a medical doctor to join the Cuban revolution; had he known that the socialist revolution for which he eventually died would '[change] its colors' by the end of the twentieth century, would he have had any regrets? What would Che Guevara say about the increasing gap between rich and poor in contemporary, capitalist China, for instance? Had he known about the eventual collapse of the socialist bloc, would he have sacrificed his personal happiness for the noble cause of the Cold War? The cast on stage answered these questions eloquently and without any hesitation: Che would have had no regrets, since he had always believed in a society that was equal and free from oppression and Western imperialist domination. Had he to do it all over again, he would still have pursued a military career in order to liberate all the poor peoples in the world. Between the play and the pop cultural fetishes, such as the Che-brand merchandise (T-shirts, biographies, souvenirs and the like), Che became a new role model, one with real values that overlapped the 'old-fashioned' values of a socialist China. Indeed, the Che play embodies a harsh critique of the materialist culture of post-Maoist society — its agendas of globalization and capitalization — and a sharp mockery of the intelligentsia's collaboration with the government in betraying the poor. Paradoxically, however, the Che military play also met the requirements of the status quo: in spite of its attacks on party corruption, it could also be received as supporting the party's own campaign to combat corruption and its much-touted desire to help the majority of poor Chinese to eventually 'get rich', after 'a small number of people got rich first'.

Just as Che declares on stage that, as long as oppression and exploitation persist, he will never put down his gun in the struggle for equality and liberation, so one might conclude that as long as the dream of equality persists, both inside and outside China, military heroes, heroines and plays on the Chinese stage will continue to remind us of that dream. This is likely to be the case despite the fact that the rapid changes in China are making them far scarcer. All in all, it consoles this particular author that, in DVD and VCD form and as gift items, model theatre survives and still sells well in the contemporary Chinese market, serving to recall the idealist dreams of Maoist China, a complex era whose memory of 'hot wars' and history of Cold War have come down to the Chinese people as both a remarkable heritage and a burden.

Notes

1 Mao Tsetung, *Quotations from Chairman Mao Tsetung* (Beijing: Foreign Languages Press, 1972), pp. 78, 82, 86.
2 Li Huang, *et al.*, *War Drums on the Equator*, trans. Gladys Yang, *Chinese Literature*, 7 (1965), pp. 3–72.
3 Mao Tsetung, *Quotations*, p. 99.
4 Tian Han, *Hui chun zhi qu*, in Tian Han, *Tian Han quan ji* [Collected Works of Tian Han], Vol. 3, eds Dong Jian, *et al.* (Shijiazhuang: Huashan wenyi chubanshe, 2000), pp. 109–51.
5 Hu Peng, *et al.*, *Zhandou li chengzhang*, in Li Moran, *et al.*, eds, *Zhongguo huaju wushi nian ju zuo xuan: 1949.10–1999.10 (An Anthology of Chinese Spoken Drama in Fifty Years: 1949.10–1999.10)*, Vol. 1 (Beijing: Zhongguo xiju chubanshe, 2000), pp. 6–7. Subsequent page numbers are given in the text.
6 The drama script of *Gangtie yunshubing*, written by Huang Ti, was first published in *Juben (Drama Script)*, 10 (1953), pp. 28–75. It was premiered by the China Youth Art Theatre in 1953.
7 Jeremy Isaacs and Taylor Downing, *Cold War: For 45 Years the World Held Its Breath* (London: Bantam Press, 1998), p. 86.
8 Ibid., p. 90.
9 Liu Chuan, *Die er ge chuntian*, in Li Moran, *et al.*, eds, *Zhongguo huaju wushi nian ju zuo xuan*, Vol. 3, p. 229.
10 The phrases in quotation marks are sayings that frequently appeared in the official press and in the unofficial publications of the Red Guard familiar to people who lived through that era.
11 For more information on model theatre see Xiaomei Chen, *Acting the Right Part: Political Theater and Popular Drama in Contemporary China* (Honolulu: University of Hawaii Press, 2002), pp. 73–158.

12 The model play version of *Shajiabang*, revised collectively by the Peking Opera Troupe of Beijing, was first published in *Hongqi (Red Flag)*, 6 (1970), pp. 8–39. An English version, from an anonymous translator, was published in *Chinese Literature*, 11 (1970), pp. 3–62.
13 The Chinese script of *Hongse niangzijun*, revised collectively by the China Ballet Troupe, was first published in *Hongqi*, 7 (1970), pp. 35–65. An English version, from an anonymous translator, was published in *Chinese Literature*, 1 (1971), pp. 2–80.
14 The Chinese script of *Zhiqu Weihungshan*, collectively revised by the Taking Tiger Mountain by Strategy Group of the Shanghai Peking Opera Troupe, can be found in Anon., ed., *Geming yangbanxi juben huibian (The Collection of Revolutionary Model Plays)*, Vol. 1 (Beijing: Remin chubanshe, 1974), pp. 7–73. An English version, from an anonymous translator, was published in *Chinese Literature*, 8 (1967), pp. 129–81.
15 The model play version of *Qixi Baihutuan* by the Shandong Provincial Peking Opera Troupe was first published in *Hongqi*, 11 (1972), pp. 26–54. An English version, from an anonymous translator, was published in *Chinese Literature*, 3 (1973), pp. 3–48.
16 Wang Shuyuan, *et al.*, *Dujuanshan*, *Hongqi*, 10 (1973), pp. 46–83. An English version of *Azalea Mountain*, by an anonymous translator, was published in *Chinese Literature*, 1 (1974), pp. 3–69.
17 *Song of the Dragon River* was collectively revised by the Song of the Dragon River Group of Shanghai, and an English version, from an anonymous translator, is found in *Chinese Literature*, 7 (1972), pp. 3–52. The Chinese script of *Longjiang song* was first published in *Hongqi*, 3 (1972), pp. 36–62.
18 Known as *yi ku si tian*, to tell a 'bitterness story' about one's hardship before 1949 in order to appreciate the sweet, new life after the founding of the PRC was a common practice in the 1960s for validating the political power of the CCP.
19 Song of the Dragon River Group of Shanghai, *Longjiang song*, *Hongqi*, 3 (1972), p. 60. The translation is mine. The forth and fifth lines were repeated once as a singing effect, but I have deleted this from my translation.
20 On the Docks Group of the Peking Opera Troupe of Shanghai, *On the Docks*, trans. anon., *Chinese Literature*, 5 (1972), p. 70. Subsequent page numbers are given in the text. For the original Chinese script see *Haigang*, *Hongqi*, 2 (1972), pp. 22–48.
21 Anon., 'Seminar Sponsored by the Afro-Asian Writers' Bureau to Commemorate the 25th Anniversary of Chairman Mao's "Talks"', *Chinese Literature*, 9 (1967), p. 49.
22 Ibid., p. 49.
23 Ibid., p. 49.
24 Anon., 'Performance by Somali Artists' Delegation', *Chinese Literature*, 11 (1967), p. 137
25 Ibid., p. 137.
26 Anon., 'The World's Revolutionary People Enthusiastically Translate and Publish Chairman Mao's Works', *Chinese Literature*, 11–12 (1969), p. 154.
27 Anon., 'Revolutionary Songs and Dances, Militant Friendship', *Chinese Literature*, 12 (1967), p. 103.
28 Hu Wen, 'Militant Songs and Dances from Romania', *Chinese Literature*, 1 (1972), p. 92.
29 Ibid., p. 92.
30 Hsiang-tung Chou, 'Let the Flames of Revolution Burn More Fiercely!', *Chinese Literature*, 12 (1967), p. 107.
31 Ibid., p. 107.

32 Ibid., p. 111.
33 Ibid., p. 111.
34 Ibid., p. 108.
35 Ibid., p. 109.
36 Huang Jisu, *et al.*, *Qie Gewala*, in Liu Zhifeng, ed., *Qie Gewala: fanying yu zhengming* (*Che Guevara: Reception and Debate*) (Beijing: Zhangguo shehui kexue chubanshe, 2001), pp. 13–69.

9 Revolution and rejuvenation
Imagining communist Cuba

Hazel A. Pierre

A cycle of revolution and rejuvenation has characterized the imagining of Cuban nationhood since its independence from Spain in 1902. Its shifting approach to nationalism and decolonization has been punctuated by a neo-colonialist phase from 1902, the communist period that followed the 1959 revolution and the current phase that was inaugurated by the end of the Cold War in 1989. However, although the post-Cold-War period has heralded the adoption of a more pragmatic foreign policy, it has not diminished the island's ideological adherence to socialist principles as the foundation of Cuban nationalism. Given the peculiar circumstances of Cuba's history of colonization and slavery and its more than 40 decades of socialism, this chapter argues for a very specific approach to analysing the notion of Cuban nationhood. While acknowledging the many virtues that recommend two of the more influential theories of nation – namely, the imagined community and the narrated nation, as advanced by Benedict Anderson and Homi K. Bhabha respectively[1] – it is proposed here that auto/biography,[2] as appropriated by Cuban, Latin American and other minority writers and artists, offers an alternative conceptual tool by which nation can be understood and theorized. With a focus on the communist phase of Cuban nationhood, I shall be pursuing a comparative analysis of two texts, Fidel Castro Ruz's 'History Will Absolve Me' and Cristina García's auto/biographical novel *Dreaming in Cuban*. Taken together, the texts facilitate an examination of the nature and range of auto/biographical practice, illustrating its complicity in the imagining of nation (and identity) in the specific context of communist Cuba. Contrasting in perspective, date of publication and historical context, they also illustrate the diversity of that imagining. After surveying some of the advantages of auto/biography for the study of national construction over the theories of Anderson and Bhabha, this chapter will explore the competing and changing imaginings of the communist Cuban nation from the perspective of its main architect, as well as its enthusiastic participants and dissidents.

Over the past two decades, Anderson and Bhabha have revolutionized the theorization of nation. In particular, their theories have been widely applied in the social sciences and humanities for clarifying the concept of nationhood in the so-called postcolonial world. Although the two theorists differ in approach – with Anderson's work being underpinned by Marxism and Bhabha's by post-structuralism – they both agree that it is in the realm of culture that nation-ness derives its legitimacy. Anderson and Bhabha have privileged the cultural and linguistic components of the nation by founding their theorisations in the multiple significations produced through such cultural artefacts as the newspaper and the novel, which validate the idea of nation by making it viable across geographical spaces and in the minds of the peoples in whose name it is invoked. None the less, in spite of their innovations, criticism has been made of their work. The two most prevalent critiques have been of the universalising tendencies implicit in Anderson's claims for the 'profoundly modular character' of non-Western nations,[3] and of the ahistoricity of Bhabha's methodology, which succeeds in dispelling the deep-seated socio-political issues that underpin the emergence of nations, especially after the Second World War.[4] In each instance, the criticism has some validity. Anderson's claims for modularity are particularly curious, since he reveals a sensitivity to the coincidence of the rise of capitalism with the emergence of the modern concept of nation, and also accurately affirms that 'communities are to be distinguished, not by their falsity/ genuineness, but by the style in which they are imagined'.[5] This suggests recognition of the specific historical contexts from which nations emerge and which effectively influence their individual characters. For former colonies such as Cuba, the significance of history cannot be overstated with regard to the ongoing process of re-imagining nation. Yet the confluence of events that facilitated the success of the 1959 revolution and the island's movement towards communism, such as the widespread dissatisfaction with the corrupt dictatorships of General Gerado Machado and Fulgencio Batista, the unequal distribution of wealth, the vehement opposition of the United States and the ready embrace of the Soviet Union, cannot be easily encapsulated in the promulgations of these theoretical paradigms. Furthermore, the dependency on post-structuralist linguistic formulations, as postulated in Bhabha's narrated nation, results in a denial of agency that clearly opposes the resistance, revolution and rejuvenation that have exemplified the evolution of nations in Cuba and Latin America. Thus, as Robert Young has observed, 'What those in the West call "third world nationalism" has never been successfully analysed by theorists of nationalism because it never operated according to a general model or even ideology'.[6]

However, in pointing to culture as the arena in which nation acquires its legitimacy as a concept, Anderson and Bhabha provide an interesting lead towards an alternative interpretative tool for the Cuban context. Through careful examination of the specific historical and cultural evolution of Cuba, what is revealed is a remarkable propensity for and tradition of auto/ biographical practice, particularly the *testimonio*, which reaches as far back as slave narratives – such as that by Esteban Montejo – and which remains popular in contemporary times, notably amongst male, nationalist thinkers and artists such as Cirilo Villaverde, Nicolás Guillén and Alejo Carpentier. The post-Boom[7] period following the 1959 revolution saw the emergence of several women writers, such as Nancy Morejón and Excilia Saldaña, who also produced work in this genre. Indeed, the revolution heralded a further escalation in the popularity of the auto/biographical tradition, not because it privileged individualism, which would be an anathema in communist Cuba, but rather because it facilitated witness to experiences that were of historical and national importance. As Doris Sommer explains, the *testimonio* 'is juridical and broadly political, because a speaker "testifies" against abuses by a class or community'.[8] Since 1970, the *testimonio* has been the preferred mode of auto/biography in Cuba and has been bestowed with added political status by its establishment as a category for the prestigious Casa de las Américas literary prize. The parameters that shape contemporary Cuban auto/biography were thus largely established by the seminal texts of these early writers.

As envisaged by Cuban and Latin American intellectuals and artists, auto/biography in all its forms underpins much of the region's cultural production and has been an integral component in the development of these new nation-states, marking a genre in which perhaps the most credible resistance has been mounted against colonizing and imperialist enterprises. As such, auto/biography has not only contested the inherited knowledges of history and self but has been a site for the re-inscription of recuperated histories, for the imagining of new nation spaces and for the insertion of self and agency. In other words, auto/biography has been instrumental to decolonization projects, participating in the 'interrogation, unmasking, and the establishment and ratification of a disidentified colonial self, not entirely free of its European pre-texts perhaps, but aware, actively resistant, and independently creative'.[9] In this context, auto/biographical practice is situated at the centre of the fight for national culture in the region, and, as Frantz Fanon has pointed out, this fight has been effectively bound up with the movement for national liberation and cultural development.[10]

Although sharing many commonalities with its Western antecedent, Cuban auto/biography is interdisciplinary in nature, encompassing fields such as history, philosophy, biography and literature. The genre also varies both in mode, ranging through the slave narrative, *testimonio*, confession and narratives of childhood and 'coming of age' (the *Bildungsroman*), and in form, including the essay, diary, travelogue, prose narrative, poetry, short story, filmic texts and oral histories which have been transposed. Often, as in García's *Dreaming*, different modes and forms are synthesized in the single auto/biographical composition. The fluidity of the genre, as conceived by minority artists and intellectuals, sometimes defies easy definition and detection; as Sylvia Molloy contends, auto/biography demands a particular attitude to reading as much as writing.[11]

The inherently retrospective and introspective posture of the genre also suits it to the task of history writing and the recuperation of cultural memory, so crucial for the national projects both of Cuba specifically and of Latin America and the Caribbean more generally. Central to this task is the question of how to remember (and forget) the trauma of history that prescribed the beginnings of these nations, not only the unspeakable atrocities but also the brutal suppression of cultural heritage, religious practices and languages. For Cuba and Latin America, this trauma has been repeated through the intermittent revolutions that have been fought against US imperialism. For this reason, trauma has been a crucial determining factor in the choice of what literary strategies to deploy for telling the stories of self and nation. Giving voice to such trauma tests the boundaries of memory and the competence of language to communicate or testify to historical experiences. Writers and artists have experimented continuously with inherited languages, often aspiring to a syncretic merger of the inherited with remnants of the ancestral tongues in order to arrive at what Edward Kamau Brathwaite refers to as 'nation languages'.[12] The process of mastering the 'nation language' is synonymous with that of transcending trauma and with the beginnings of healing. In other words, the very act of enunciating trauma is at the same time painful and cathartic.

Moreover, because trauma has circumscribed so much of Cuban, Latin American and Caribbean experience, the conventional address of the *testimonio* and auto/biography is invariably communal rather than individual. Use of the subject pronoun 'I', therefore, does not refer exclusively to the first-person narrator but rather gestures to the 'we' of the community from within which it emanates. As Sandra Pouchet Paquet asserts, 'The individual predicament of the writer as autobiographical subject illuminates the collective predicament of an island community. The autobiographical act emerges as a means to an end rather than an end in itself.'[13] From their representative vantage point, auto/biographers engage in an examination of self that not only questions the validity and commitment of their enterprise as intellectuals or artists within their communities but also evaluates the problems, and possible solutions to the problems, of the evolving nations. Elaborating on the complexity involved in the auto/biographical act in the Caribbean, Pouchet-Paquet explains how the process of self-enquiry is tied to cultural assessment:

> [T]here is a clearly defined tension between the autobiographical self as a singular personality with the psychological integrity and the self as a way into the social and political complexities of the region [. . .]. Self-revelation becomes a way of laying claim to the landscape that is at once geographical, historical, and cultural [. . .]. In the process, the autobiographical self as subject is transformed into a cultural archetype, and autobiography becomes both the lived historical reality and the myth created out of that experience. Personal experience and historical events alike are transformed into autobiographical myth.[14]

In auto/biographical writing, evidently, myths of self merge with myths of historical and cultural beginnings, with the project of recuperating lost cultural histories being related to that of enunciating histories of self in the construction of identity. Trauma, coupled with the genre's instinctual fluidity, facilitates multiple subject addresses as well as the varied creative, social and political objectives that inform auto/biographical practice in the region.

However, the enunciation of the communal 'I', with its implied representativeness, raises some problems. Even as it accommodates the democratic inclusion of multiple voices – through the biographical references and sketches that inhere in the recounting of a life – questions of authenticity arise about the extent to which one individual may qualify above another to speak on behalf of the group. In other words, on what basis is either Fidel Castro or Cristina García qualified to speak on behalf of 'the people' of Cuba? Although this does not diminish the claim of the auto/biographical voice to enunciate a collective 'I', it does highlight the difficulties that persist in accessing the subaltern voice. This is perhaps exemplified in the transcription of slave narratives. While some advance the view that slave narratives – along with other testimonial forms which insist on the individual's witness of life experiences as archetypical of the group – are evidence of the entrance of 'the people' into the wider discourses of nationhood, such narratives are invariably mediated. As Miguel Barnet illustrates in his introduction to Montejo's *The Autobiography of a Runaway Slave*, his own particular interests as the interviewer and amanuensis of Montejo's testimony dictated the questions asked, the 'facts' gleaned and, as such, the story told.[15] At the same time, Barnet's admission of the 'need to check the facts' against the historical record and against other personal testimonies gestures to the other problematic facet of bearing witness: the tensions between truth and fiction, born of the selective remembering of the facts, which co-exist in the act of speaking as an individual on behalf of many. However, the necessity for a verification of details does not only arise with regard to non-fictional texts such as Montejo's *Autobiography* and Castro's 'History' but also bears upon fictional auto/biographical texts such as García's *Dreaming in Cuban*. Moreover, although the representativeness of Cuban auto/biography is problematic, it is paradoxically key to the act of imagining nation, as Leigh Gilmore argues:

> Autobiography's investment in the representative person allies it to the project of lending substance to the national fantasy of belonging [. . .]. The nation prompts fantasies of citizens, rendered real, embodied, and whole through incorporation into the national.[16]

In their respective constructions of the Cuban nation, both Castro and García deploy differing strategies and voices in their auto/biographical narratives, albeit to varying degrees of success. Castro's 'History' also contrasts sharply with García's *Dreaming* in authorial intention and point of view.

Unlike *Dreaming*, 'History' is patently non-fictional, constituting the transcription of Castro's orally delivered legal defence of his leadership role in the Moncada revolution in 1953. In this regard, the text is more accurately *testimonio* in its form and purpose, but is also imbued with other auto/biographical attributes, since it details some of Castro's preoccupations and ideological concerns during that early segment of his revolutionary life, and, more obviously, bears witness to the atrocities suffered by him and his *compañeros* while imprisoned. In what is a wide-ranging, defiant testimonial, 'History' documents that particular historical moment, while also rhetorically constructing a post-revolutionary Cuban nation that is devoid of the corruption, poverty and oppression that characterized its neo-colonialist period.

The privilege of representing the citizenry of the nation, which the *testimonio* and wider auto/biographical practice claim, is problematized by the judicial context in which Castro's text was delivered. Yet his testimony is mediated not only by the institutional circumstances in which he found himself but also by wider, ideological criteria for the establishment of truth. Castro repeatedly reminds his audience that, as the revolution's leader, he is mandated to speak truthfully of the events that transpired for reasons that transcend his judicial context. According to him, his unswerving commitment to justice and to the homeland and the shared belief of his *compañeros* that theirs was a just struggle, have emboldened him to 'speak [...] with words that are the blood of the heart and the essence of truth'.[17] Castro's assumption of the dual roles of defendant and counsel ensures that he mounts a defence that is at once personal and communal, with greater emphasis being placed on the enunciation of a political rather than cultural vision. Framed within these parameters, Castro espouses a vision of post-revolutionary Cuba that is idealistic, utopian and predominantly masculinist in scope. This is evidenced especially in the explication of the five revolutionary laws that are deployed as the cornerstone of the revolution's political manifesto. These laws were aimed primarily at instituting greater equality in the distribution of the island's wealth and resources and at the reclamation of sovereignty that had been proclaimed in the Constitution of 1940. The transformed nation would have recognized the equality of all through the institution of democratic elections and representation, the pursuit of social and agricultural reform, the elimination of class prejudices and the bolstering of an education system that was seen as key to liberation and decolonization. Curiously, this utopian vision, with its drastic political and constitutional changes, does not appear to anticipate the opposition of external interests such as the USA.

Central to Castro's idealized imagining of nation are 'the unredeemed masses', defined in part as those 'to whom everything is offered but nothing is given except deceit and betrayal', and with whom and on whose behalf the struggle is identified.[18] Yet, although differentiated by race, class and employment classifications, 'the people' are homogenized in Castro's monologic testimony. His Cuba, for example, remains largely un-gendered, thereby tacitly evoking a predominantly masculinist perspective. Indeed, the very landscape is masculinized as 'the fatherland', and a list comprising male revolutionaries – from Carlos Manuel de Céspedes to Antonio Maceo to José Martí – is invoked as the only one worthy of association with the noble revolutionary ideals. As a corollary of this, minimal space is allocated for the discussion of female experience, with women being tangential to Castro's idealist vision despite their willing participation as combatants in the struggle. At one point, mention is made of how, along with their male counterparts, they are deserving of higher wages for their jobs as teachers, which implies a role in the cultural reproduction of the nation's cultural values and ideals. Yet while mention is made, for instance, of two imprisoned females,[19] and of others who were 'at the point of producing a rebellion at Camp Columbia',[20] no larger roles are suggested for them in the future utopian nation. That 'History' conforms to the masculinist perspectives that dominated *testimonio* and auto/biographical practice at the historical moment of its first enunciation might be partly attributed to the still embryonic nature of the feminist movement, even in the USA and Europe. However, it is because 'History' adheres to this perspective that the nation imagined by Castro in 1953 is limited in scope and does not attempt to envision real transformation, one that would necessarily have needed to engage with the taboo subjects of race, ethnicity, gender and religion.

By enjoining his own vision to the long historical tradition of male revolutionaries, Castro suggests associations in leadership goals and objectives. In so doing, a symbolic transference of the mantle of 'El Líder' is achieved by which Castro also comes to embody the continuity of the Cuban struggle for independence. However, such associations have further implications for the definition of Cuban nation and identity. Within this historical framework, Castro boldly advocates a single, unswerving ideal of Cubanness that is predicated on a continual duty to fight for freedom and, moreover, to sacrifice one's life for the fatherland, since 'to live in chains is to live in disgrace and abject submission, and that to die for the fatherland is to live'.[21] Understood in these terms, Cuban nationhood is thus more accurately defined by the preferred term *patriotismo* than that of *nacionalismo*.[22] By offering himself as the living embodiment of *patriotismo*, Castro invites the Cuban people to invest in his personal brand of charismatic leadership and sacrificial love of nation. Interestingly, while there are no hints of Castro's philosophical leanings toward socialism, there are some fundamental similarities between his definition of Cubanness and his future political commitments.

Whereas Castro deploys a utopian, masculinist imagining of a post-revolutionary Cuba, García's *Dreaming* admits multiple, predominantly female voices that offer competing versions of the communist nation. Published in 1992, some three years after the end of the Cold War, García's is a retrospective lens that assesses the span of Cuban history from the years preceding the 1959 revolution to the 1980s. Like her auto/biographical persona,

Pilar Puente, García was born in Cuba but migrated to the USA in 1961 after the revolution, and her auto/biographical project was undertaken during residence in the USA. Yet her portrait of the nation does not necessarily suffer as a result. Perhaps because she came of age in cosmopolitan New York, García seeks to understand the complexity of the Cuban experience, presenting a multidimensional, more objective perspective of communist Cuba that contrasts with the usual anti-Castro stance appearing in the works of exiled writers and artists domiciled in Miami. Admitting in an interview that she 'grew up in a very black-and-white situation',[23] in which her parents were 'virulently anti-Communist' while her 'relatives in Cuba were tremendous supporters of Communism',[24] García pledges allegiance to neither side. Although this simultaneously includes her within and alienates her from these camps, as García demonstrates in her novel, it is part of the ongoing experience of Cuban exiles of succeeding generations to come to terms with an increasingly problematized cultural identity.

The novel, which García acknowledges is 'emotionally [...] very autobiographical'[25] even though the details are not factual, chronicles the impact of the 1959 revolution on the already fractious relationships among three generations of the del Pino family. As the characters testify to their experiences of the revolution, they inevitably engage with issues – such as gender, race, class and religious practices – that Castro failed to address in any depth in 'History'. However, what becomes evident in each of the characters' narratives is a nostalgia either for the prerevolutionary Cuba or for the achievement of the democratic freedoms and equality envisioned in Castro's 'History' that once appeared possible, if only momentarily. The manner in which these freedoms were eroded after 1959 is exemplified by the position of writers themselves. García, like most of Cuba's women writers, emerged after the Boom, when literacy and education programmes were established and publication incentives for intellectuals and artists were initiated. The formation of the Union of Writers of Cuba provided a community among Cuban artists in which discussion of issues affecting the new society could be pursued. Yet although several writers and artists emerged as a result of these initiatives, counterrevolutionary opinions were censored, and even as Castro sought to allay fears of censorship he asserted that creativity should be geared towards bolstering the revolution: 'within the revolution, everything; against the revolution, nothing.'[26] Although benefiting from the interest and opportunities for women writers created within Cuba, exiled or dissident authors such as García found publishers for their works primarily in the USA or Spain.

On the issues of freedom and censorship, as on so many features of communist Cuba, 'History' and *Dreaming* radically disagree, an outcome of their emergence from very different historical moments. There are certainly ways in which García's novel can be seen to converge with Castro's 'History': not only does *Dreaming* begin its narrative with the 1959 revolution, but it also fictionally represents Castro as the same charismatic, seductive (albeit loathsome tyrant to some) El Líder who in 'History' embodies the revolution, its aspirations and failings. Each of the characters, however, who are representative of the varying factions of opinion about the revolution, implicitly interrogates Castro's vision of Cuba and his bold declaration: 'Condemn me, it does not matter. History will absolve me!'[27] With the advantage of the retrospective stance that auto/biography allows, the characters find their voice by retelling their personal histories, questioning Castro's historical legacy while also attempting some kind of reconciliation with the ironic reality that became manifest after the revolution.

The del Pino family, which has been dispersed between Cuba and the USA, can be seen as a microcosm of the Cuban nation and diaspora. The political thrust of the revolution has divided the loyalties of the del Pinos as it had in other Cuban families. Luz Villaverde, one of the granddaughters who stays in Cuba, correctly advises her brother, Ivanito, who is ambivalent about the revolution, that 'families are essentially political and that he'll have to choose sides'.[28] Thus, the matriarch, Abuela Celia, represents those who champion the revolution. Discontented with the injustices and inequalities of Batista's Cuba, and enticed by the prospect of positive change, Celia gives her full allegiance to El Líder. Her husband, Jorge, on the other hand, who was passionate about his job as a salesman for an American company selling electric brooms and portable fans before the revolution, is equally intolerant of the ensuing hostilities with the USA and the drastic changes which it portends for the island.

Of their three offspring, the two girls, Lourdes and Felicia, like their father, are opposed to the revolution, while Javier, the only male child, shares his mother's fervour. The political affiliations between fathers and daughters, mothers and sons, reflect the fractures in relationships between mother/daughter and father/son that have resulted from past misunderstandings, suppressed information and broken lines of communication. Daughters and sons feel rejected by mothers and fathers respectively, a feeling exemplified in the relationship between Lourdes and Celia. Lourdes, unaware of her parents' marital tensions that led to her mother's negative response to her birth, instead builds a close relationship with her father. Early memories of her mother are overwhelmed by a sense of rejection and abandonment, encapsulated in Celia's words as she entered the asylum, 'I will not remember her name' (74). The revolution initiated a lasting separation from her mother, as Lourdes, her husband, Rufino, and daughter, Pilar, flee Cuba for the USA after their dairy farm is confiscated. Jorge too follows for specialist medical treatment that was presumably unavailable in Cuba.

Ironically, this pattern of affiliations is repeated in the third generation of the del Pino family. Felicia, who stays in Cuba, is at first indifferent, then openly opposed, to the revolution after the fiasco of the Missile Crisis. She steadfastly refuses to conform to the values of the 'New Socialist Woman', even after arduous military training intended to transform 'malcontents' and 'social misfits' into 'would-be guerrillas' (105–7). Whereas her daughters,

Luz and Milagro, both born after the revolution, gravitate to their father, Hugo Villaverde, Felicia's only son, Ivanito, remains loyal to his mother despite her crazed attempt on his life. He fears his father and prefers estrangement from him even as his sisters seek to re-establish ties with Hugo. The pattern diverges, however, since the granddaughters, Luz, Milagro and Pilar, who themselves have difficult relationships with their mothers, are the ones who embrace and sustain strong links with the revolutionary Abuela Celia, a link which is critical to their coming to terms with their personal and family histories and with their Cubanness. Critics such as William Luis have suggested that the cross-generational alliances between the granddaughters and their grandmother (and with their fathers) might have been aimed at exacting revenge against their mothers for the pain of rejection and abandonment. Luis has further suggested that this pattern of generational conflict echoes Cuban society, in so far as the younger generation, for whom the spectre of Batista's Cuba is alien, are destined to rebel against the older generation which has been responsible for instituting the desolation and hardship which they associate with the communist nation.[29]

García deploys a complex set of narrative strategies in *Dreaming* that facilitate a multiplicity of voices and perspectives. The combination of prose and epistolary styles, multiple subject addresses and personal and communal stories that inevitably intersect, results in a heterogeneous definition of communist Cuba and Cubanness. Thus, although female perspectives are privileged, they share space with male voices. Moreover, as the male and female characters engage with their experiences of the revolution, what becomes apparent are the instances of stasis, change and continuity that together have shaped the imagining of Cuba, past and present. Through elements of magical realism, García also equips her auto/biographical persona for the role of recounting the personal and national histories of family members. Thus Pilar, like many of the other female characters, can communicate telepathically through dreams, even with the dead, and has an infallible memory that reaches back as early as two years old. Pilar learns about the various versions of the family and communal stories, however, from her conversations with her grandmother, and has an important source of information in her grandmother's un-mailed letters to her Spanish lover. With Lourdes, Pilar also makes an important return journey to Cuba during which she is able to arrive at her own conclusions, in spite of the various stories to which she has become privy. As she observes, 'Even though I've been living in Brooklyn all my life, it doesn't feel like home to me. I'm not sure Cuba is, but I want to find out. If I could only see Abuela Celia again, I'd know where I belonged' (58). Pilar's journey to a sense of self and belonging that incorporates her Cuban heritage and her American present is deemed impossible without access to this vital source.

Interspersed with the personal histories are accounts of recorded historical incidents that defined Cuba in the postrevolutionary period, such as the Bay of Pigs invasion, the Missile Crisis, the Angolan War, the Peruvian Embassy escape and the Mariel boatlifts (in which thousands of Cuban dissidents fled the island). Pilar is ably poised as an omniscient, first-person narrator to inscribe these stories, but also shares this responsibility with other third-generation family members: Luz, Milagro and Ivanito, as well as Herminia Delgado, Tía Felicia's best friend. These first-person narratives are critical for arriving at a holistic perspective on the testimonies and, by extension, on the changing imaginings of communist Cuba. Whereas the first two generations hold stringently positive or negative positions on the revolution, these third generation and Afro-Cuban narratives often contradict these positions. This is evident, for instance, in the stories told about Felicia's first husband, Hugo. While Felicia, Celia and Ivanito concur with respect to Hugo's harshness and abusiveness, his daughters proffer an alternative version that illustrates his softer, more caring side, a side to which Ivanito is never privy despite his sisters' best-laid plans to dispel his impressions. Similarly, Pilar is positioned to reveal the individual experiences that have coloured the characters' divergent views of the revolution: Lourdes's rape, Celia's abandonment by her parents and then by her husband that precipitated her marriage to the revolution, Felicia's inability to cope in the oppressive environment that culminates in her madness and death, and Ivanito's escape to Peru. These versions of history, told from the differing viewpoints of the characters, call into question not only the veracity of each version but also the silencing of others. As Pilar muses, 'Who chooses what we know or what's important? I know I have to decide these things for myself. Most of what I've learnt that's important I've learnt on my own, or from my grandmother' (28). Herminia's story raises similar concerns about dominant historical accounts, and explicitly explores the hidden or silenced issues of race and religion that have affected Afro-Cubans. Invested with the family history passed on by her father, Herminia is able to contrast their experience before the revolution with her current situation. Compared to the abuse and gruesome deaths suffered by her grandfather and uncles during the Little War of 1912, which was fuelled by fear of Afro-Cubans, after the revolution 'things have gotten better' (185). That fear had also caused the stereotyping of and discrimination against her family because her father was a *babalawo*, or high priest of santería, the Afro-Cuban religion which was banned after the revolution. Predictably, Herminia does not point to race as a pervasive problem in communist Cuba, which is perhaps indicative of the revolution's greater emphasis on Cubanness as opposed to race.[30] Alternatively, Herminia suggests that the empowerment of women, in what remains a patriarchal society, will require much more time. Moreover, Herminia reflects on the fact that Afro-Cuban history is consigned to 'a footnote in our history books' (185) and then, like Pilar, goes on to question the veracity and completeness of empirical historical accounts as opposed to the oral history that she inherits from her father. She concludes, 'I trust only what I see, what I know with my heart, nothing more' (185).

The necessity of finding a language by which characters can testify to their lives and traumatic experiences becomes another hurdle in the task of re-establishing communication lines within and across generations. While Lourdes welcomes how immigration and the acquisition of a new language makes her reinvention possible, it also alienates her from her homeland, where she speaks 'another idiom' (221) unintelligible to resident Cubans. However, Pilar must surmount this language barrier in order to do justice to the histories she recounts. Existing between two nations and languages, Pilar initially resorts to painting as an alternative symbolic system, musing that 'Painting is its own language ... Translations just confuse it, dilute it, like words going from Spanish to English' (59). Yet when Pilar's experimental punk painting of the Statue of Liberty, conceived to celebrate the opening of Lourdes's second bakery, provokes a violent reaction from guests, she is forced to ponder the meaning of freedom in Western democracies, which is so often opposed to what prevails in a communist dictatorship. In Cuba, however, Abuela Celia's suggestion that freedom is 'nothing more than the right to a decent life' (233) is deemed too simple a definition.

Pilar's adoption in New York of *botánica*, an equivalent of the Cuban santería, is the key that unlocks the cultural and linguistic codes that enables her to reconcile her Cuban and American heritage. Subsequent to her induction, Pilar gains access into people's thoughts and can 'glimpse scraps of the future' (216). Returning to Cuba, not only does Pilar confirm her heritage as a daughter of Changó, like Tía Felicia and Herminia Delgado, but she is also freed from the fetters of her grandmother's and mother's opposing perspectives. For the first time, she can dream in Spanish, as if blending the symbolic systems of painting and language in the syntax of her dreams, an indication of an irrevocable acceptance of her dual heritage. It is only from this position that Pilar can assert an independent, though representative, 'I' on behalf of the third and succeeding generations of Cubans, perhaps evinced in her facilitating Ivanito's escape to Peru. Most of all, Pilar fulfils her grandmother's wishes by remembering and inscribing the important narratives of family and nation. Through this act, one critic suggests, the matrilineal lines are reconnected.[31]

The *testimonio* – and the wider practice of Cuban auto/biography – accomplishes the imagining of nation because it facilitates the interrogation of inherited history and the re-inscription of alternative histories and subjectivities, both of which are critical determinants to the style in which nation is imagined in former colonies. Together, Castro's 'History' and García's *Dreaming* assemble multiple but related versions of Cuban communist history in the Cold War period. Whereas characters like Pilar and Herminia question the privileging of dominant empirical history over the oral transferences of stories between generations, the appropriation of the auto/biographical genre actually surmounts this problem. For auto/biographical practice also intrinsically enjoins what Sommer has called empirical knowledge and emotional knowing as it interrogates the dominant discourses of history.[32] In this way, neither form of knowledge is elevated over the other;

the two co-exist within the auto/biographical framework, making possible the recall of multiple versions of histories and, by extension, providing insight into the imaginings of Cuba and Cubanness.

Notes

1 See Anderson, *Imagined Communities: Reflections on the Origin and Spread of Nationalism* (1983), and Bhabha, 'DissemiNation: Time, Narrative, and the Margins of the Modern Nation', in Bhabha, ed., *Nation and Narration* (London and New York: Routledge, 1990), pp. 291–322.
2 The slash in auto/biography is used to differentiate its appropriated forms and modes in the literatures of Latin America, the Caribbean and other minority groupings. Similar connotations are associated with critics such as Liz Stanley, *The Auto/biographical I: The Theory and Practice of Feminist Auto/biography* (Manchester and New York: Manchester University Press, 1992), pp. 2–19. Like its Western counterpart, auto/biography is not easily defined. As Stanley suggests, in its appropriated sense, the genre posits 'all [the] ways of writing a life and also the ontological and epistemological links between them' (ibid., p. 3). Fundamental to these multiple ways of remembering and writing lives is the displacement of individual introspection (which characterized traditional autobiography) by the communal.
3 See, for example, Ania Loomba, *Colonialism/Postcolonialism* (London and New York: Routledge, 1990), pp. 184–210, and Partha Chatterjee, *The Nation and Its Fragments: Colonial and Postcolonial Histories* (Princeton: Princeton University Press, 1993), pp. 3–13. Loomba argues that in this respect Anderson's argument conflates with previous thinking on nationalism in non-Western countries and succeeds in reducing it to a 'derivate discourse'. Similarly, Chatterjee points to the implicit contradiction in Anderson's thesis since such modularity would virtually eliminate the need for any 'imagining' or 'creation' by other nations. It should be noted that Neil Lazarus offers counter-arguments against what he calls Chatterjee's 'tendentious' reading of Anderson. See Lazarus, 'Disavowing Decolonisation: Nationalism, Intellectuals, and the Question of Representation in Postcolonial Theory', in Lazarus, *Nationalism and Cultural Practice in the Postcolonial World* (Cambridge: Cambridge University Press, 1999), pp. 68–143.
4 See, for example, Alex Callinicos, 'Wonders Taken for Signs: Homi Bhabha's Postcolonialism', in Teresa L. Ebert and Donald Morton, eds, *Post-ality: Marxism and Postcolonialism* (Washington: Maisonneuve Press, 1995), pp. 98–112, and Benita Parry, 'Signs of Our Times: Discussion of Homi Bhabha's *Location of Culture*', *Third Text*, 28/29 (1994), pp. 5–24.
5 Anderson, *Imagined Communities: Reflections on the Origin and Spread of Nationalism*, rev. edn (1983; London and New York: Verso, 1991), p. 6.
6 Young, *Postcolonialism: An Historical Introduction* (Oxford: Blackwell, 2001), p. 172.
7 The period from around 1965 to 1969, when there was a renaissance of the Cuban novel, is commonly referred to as 'the Boom'. This was largely the result of the education and publication incentives implemented by Castro's communist administration on its accession to power. The Boom was dominated by male writers. Cuban women writers generally emerged after this period and worked primarily in poetry.
8 Sommer, *Proceed with Caution, When Engaged by Minority Writing in the Americas* (Cambridge, MA, and London: Harvard University Press, 1999), p. 117.
9 Helen M. Tiffin, 'Rites of Resistance: Counter-Discourse and West Indian Biography', *Journal of West Indian Literature*, 3: 1 (1989), p. 30.

10 Fanon, *Wretched of the Earth*, new edn, trans. Constance Farrington (1961; London: Penguin, 1967), pp. 166–99.
11 Molloy, *At Face Value: Autobiographical Writing in Spanish America* (Cambridge: Cambridge University Press, 1991), p. 2.
12 Brathwaite, *History of the Voice: The Development of Nation Language in Anglophone Caribbean Poetry* (London and Port of Spain: New Beacon Books, 1984), p. 5.
13 Pouchet-Paquet, 'West Indian Autobiography', in William Andrews, ed., *African American Autobiography: A Collection of Critical Essays* (New Jersey: Prentice Hall, 1993), p.197.
14 Ibid., pp. 197–8.
15 Barnet, 'Introduction' to Esteban Montejo, *The Autobiography of a Runaway Slave*, new edn, ed. Alistair Hennessy (1968; London: Warwick/Macmillan Caribbean, 1993), pp. 27–31.
16 Gilmore, *The Limits of Autobiography: Trauma and Testimony* (Ithaca and London: Cornell University Press, 2001), p. 12.
17 Castro, 'History Will Absolve Me', in Castro, *Revolutionary Struggle 1947–1958: Volume 1 of the Selected Works of Fidel Castro*, eds Rolando E. Bonachea and Nelson P. Valdés (Cambridge, MA, and London: MIT Press, 1972), p. 165.
18 Ibid., p. 183.
19 Ibid., p. 166.
20 Ibid., p. 178.
21 Ibid., p. 220.
22 Antoni Kapcia, *Cuba: Island of Dreams* (Oxford and New York: Berg, 2000), p. 22.
23 García, quoted in William Luis, 'Reading the Master Codes of Cuban Culture in Cristina García's *Dreaming in Cuban*', *Cuban Studies*, 26 (1996), p. 204.
24 García, quoted in ibid., p. 204.
25 García, quoted in Rocío G. Davis, 'Back to the Future: Mothers, Languages, and Homes in Cristina García's *Dreaming in Cuban*', *World Literature Today*, 74: 1 (2000), p. 62.
26 Castro, 'Address to Intellectuals', in Julio García Luis, ed., *Cuban Revolution Reader: A Documentary History of 40 Key Moments of the Cuban Revolution* (Melbourne and New York: Ocean Press, 2001), p. 81.
27 Castro, 'History', p. 221.
28 García, *Dreaming in Cuban* (New York: Ballantine Books, 1992), p. 86. Further references to *Dreaming* will be given in the text.
29 Luis, 'Reading the Master Codes', p. 212.
30 Ibid., pp. 214–15. Luis points to criticism of Castro's revolution that illustrates that 'blacks have not fared well under the Revolution. They have not been given the opportunity to promote their own culture, but instead are encouraged to become culturally whiter. Afro-Cubans have been given the mechanism with which to abandon their religious and cultural past' (212).
31 Davis, 'Back to the Future', p. 67.
32 Sommer, *Proceed with Caution*, p. 162.

10 An anxious triangulation

Cold War, nationalism and regional resistance in East-Central European literatures

Marcel Cornis-Pope

The recent history of East-Central European literatures is framed by two forceful interventions: one immediately after the communist takeover in the mid-1940s, when large numbers of writers were executed, imprisoned, forced into exile or into conformity; the other after 1989, when these literatures were again submitted to a radical re-evaluation that removed old hierarchies and canons, calling into question even some of the dissident writers under communism. In particular, the cultures of the Baltic region and the Balkans lapsed into forms of nationalism or ethnocentrism that undercut their traditional multiculturality, converting them into 'nationalizing spaces'. The nationalizing state, Rogers Brubaker explains, is

> the state of and for a particular ethnocultural 'core nation', whose language, culture, demographic position, economic welfare, and political hegemony must be protected and promoted by the state. The key elements here are 1) the sense of ownership of the state by a particular ethnocultural nation that is conceived as distinct from the citizenry or permanent resident population as a whole; and 2) the 'remedial' or 'compensatory' project of using state power to promote the core nation's specific (and heretofore inadequately served) interests.[1]

The Soviet strategy of submerging the pre-socialist national-ethnic identities of East-Central Europe, while at the same time encouraging ethnic interests whenever they served the Soviet policy of division and control, made the post-communist transition especially difficult. The newly liberated states were confronted with a doubly unsolved legacy, having been nationalistic before the Second World War, and communist after.

According to Vladislav Todorov, there is an insidious likeness between these two legacies. Both gave rise to totalitarian regimes – one emphasizing class, the other ethnicity or race – and 'both [...] worked out their own technologies and ideologies for the liquidation of possible political agents, who, by definition, represent non-party interests'.[2] But for Todorov there are also important distinctions. The racial-party regime predicates its power on the alleged 'organic unity of "blood and soil" as a genetic source of national purity and the historical mission of the race'.³ The class-party's power is self-reproductive and to a great extent 'illegitimate', 'representing' the party *nomenclature*, not the proletariat, whose power is liquidated (together with that of other classes) because it 'subverts and competes with the [party's] political representativeness'.⁴

Though Todorov's distinctions between the two forms of totalitarian liquidation make fascism appear theoretically more feasible (though not more defensible) than communism, they can be used to explain the drift of both national communism and post-communism towards the ethnic model. For example, Ceauşescu's 'dynastic' communism grafted an ethnocentric approach on to an 'unreconstructed Stalinism',⁵ hoping to legitimize the authoritarianism of the latter through the exaltation of nationalism in the former. The emphasis on national specificity, used initially to justify a more or less token de-Stalinization of Romania, provided the basis for Ceauşescu's later xenophobic form of socialism. Built on an assortment of left-wing and right-wing nationalisms ('class-party' turned into 'race-party'), Ceauşescu's nationalist communism provided a theoretical model for post-communist nationalism in various guises, from the cultural intolerance of ultra-nationalistic publications to the ethnic terror in former Yugoslavia.

It is evident today that the communist regimes, far from resolving the oft-toted nationality question, only complicated it, advocating alternatively a crude 'internationalist' levelling of cultures and an even cruder form of xenophobic communism. Both tendencies subordinated the definitions of national culture to self-serving political goals that undermined the local interests and traditions of each country. With the collapse of 'universalist' communism, one more aspect of the 'totalitarian claim to all-inclusiveness'⁶ was demystified. But the 1989 movements did not bring instantaneous democracy. As they emerged from Soviet domination, the East-Central European cultures were confronted by the resilient 'communist political customs – all the habits, mentalities, attitudes, symbols, and values that had permeated social life for decades' – as well as by the 'resentful myths and atavistic phobias' of an ethnic kind,⁷ kept dormant by four decades of forced national amnesia.

The establishment of democratic states throughout the region depends on a successful re-examination of the conflictive notion of difference inherent in East-Central European ideas of ethnicity and nationhood. This process should not lead to a simplistic disregard of ethno-cultural differentiations (something like the cultural 'levelling' pursued by the former totalitarian societies), but rather to the development of a transactive socio-cultural space that would allow each ethnic group to contribute its own interests and traditions. Clearly, this task cannot be accomplished by adepts of either the class-party or race-party systems, nor can it be achieved through purely political means. For this reason, it may be useful to seek models for a nonconflictive definition of national identity in the region's literary cultures. Literature here has always operated both within and outside the national narrative, 'employing different signifying practices' than those of nationalism to explore the 'civic Imaginary'.[8] East-Central European literatures have often seized upon the play of cultural differences within the relatively homogeneous nation-space, proposing more flexible models of intercultural and interethnic exchange.

Nationalism itself has played a complex role in the region's communist and post-communist literary cultures. During the Second World War, nationalism fed the resistance against Nazi and Soviet occupation, but also encouraged an anti-minority, anti-Semitic and xenophobic fervour. After the communist takeover of East-Central Europe, nationalism functioned – however discreetly – as a form of resistance against Soviet-imposed 'internationalism' (a code word for ideological homogenization). Inspired by Stalin's culture tsar, Andrei Zhdanov, local versions of socialist realism sprouted all around the region, disrupting national traditions and redefining culture as a tendentious political activity that served communist (Soviet) agendas. In the first phase of the cultural revolution, initiated in the late 1940s, the 'enemy' was national or international modernism. This phase was followed by the aggressive promotion of class-oriented art that exacerbated social and political polarization. As part of an ongoing 'cleansing of the past', writers with 'bourgeois' or 'nationalist' affinities were forced into exile or were sentenced to prison. Kazys Boruta, Antanas Miskinis, Viktoras Katilius and other Lithuanian writers were deported to Siberia between 1946 and 1951. The Bulgarian camp in Lovech, the Romanian camps in Pitești and on the Danube Canal and the Yugoslav camp on Goli Otok (Goli Island, which targeted Soviet 'sympathizers' with similarly ruthless methods) competed with the Soviet gulag in their effective extermination of 'dissenters'. Those who survived the communist gulags – the Moldavians Nicolae Costenco and Alexei Marinat, the Ukrainian Vasyl' Barka or the Romanians Ion Caraion and Paul Goma, among others – continued to be repressed and could publish works inspired by their dramatic experiences only in exile or after 1989.

The Cold War confrontation with the West, set in motion by the Yalta Agreement that divided Europe into 'spheres of influence', brought additional pressures to bear on writers. At the height of Stalinism, poets across the region assisted the Soviet 'peace' propaganda, attacking Western militarism and representing Soviet expansionism as an 'emancipatory' force. Eugen Jebeleanu's collage poem *Surâsul Hiroșimei* (*The Smile of Hiroshima*, 1958), for example, takes us on a journey through a nuclear inferno, rehearsing dialogues and reactions preceding and following the nuclear detonation. While the book avoids direct moralizing, the suffering it records amounts to an indictment of American imperialism. Similarly, Hungarian poets such as László Zelk dutifully sang hymns to Stalin, the Red Army and the Hungarian leader Mátyás Rákosi for liberating the country.

The body of narrative writing churned out in the late 1940s and 1950s pursued similar Stalinistic themes. The most talented Romanian novelist of the period, Petru Dumitriu, tried to justify the existence of a communist gulag (on the Danube canal) in *Pasărea furtunii* (*Bird of Storm*, 1954). A decade later, however, after his defection to France, he published a strong denunciation of the communist dictatorship in *Incognito* (1964). Laurenţiu Fulga's *Oameni fără glorie* (*Men without Glory*, 1956), which focused on the Romanian army's retreat after its defeat on the Don River bend, describes the suffering of the soldiers and of the population behind the front line, while praising the heroism of the Red Army. The second novel of his projected Second World War trilogy, *Steaua bunei speranţe* (*The Star of Good Hope*, 1963), is set in a prison camp, where officers undergo a process of self-examination, debating past mistakes and dreaming of a better future that is linked, once more, to communism. The topics of Fulga's two volumes roughly correspond to István Örkény's *Lágerek népe* (People of the Camps, 1947), but in the latter the interpretative perspective follows more closely the official communist one.

As the Cold War confrontation between East and West sharpened, all official literature became a weapon of class struggle. Critic George Călinescu's 1948 warning that 'a literary weapon is not helpful unless it remains literary, unless it stirs emotions in the soul of the reader and moves him through the force of believable artistic images',[9] remained largely unheeded. When the official literature ran out of past enemies (the defunct bourgeoisie, the kulaks), the party ideologues invented new enemies such as the 'counter-revolutionaries', regarded as far more dangerous than the traditional ones.

In the West, the Cold War gave rise to what Alan Nadel has described as a 'containment culture'.[10] America's policy of deterrence against the Soviet bloc was matched by narratives of containment at home, emphasizing conformity 'to some idea of religion, to "middle-class" values, to distinct gender roles and rigid courtship rituals'.[11] Common to both external and internal versions of containment was the effort to retain well-defined boundaries between 'Other and Same', whether the other was the Soviet Union or heretics at home. Across the ideological divide, the Soviet Union produced powerful counter-narratives of containment, from Joseph Stalin's defensive cordon of satellite countries and stabilization of power through brutal purgings, to Leonid Brezhnev's quashing of labour and national movements in Eastern Europe and co-option of Third World countries into the Soviet sphere of influence. At home, this narrative emphasized bureaucratic rationalization and terror against the internal 'enemy' who refused conversion to *homo Sovieticus*.

Not surprisingly, the proliferation of conflicting narratives of containment caused in time an ideological implosion, with these narratives disabling each other. In the United States, the failure of containment as a foreign policy triggered the Vietnam drama, while the failure of containment as a discursive practice marked the beginnings of American postmodernism,[12] a theoretical and artistic movement that called into question the containment paradigm itself. In communist Eastern Europe, an ideological system regarded as stable and all-pervasive created in much the same way conditions for its own dispersal. By turning 'language and discourse [into] the ultimate means of production',[13] communism colonized the political imagination of its people but also generated a surplus: more symbolic work than the ideological system could control. This excess favoured to some extent the system's opponents, allowing them to articulate 'kinds of social consciousness other than the authoritarian ones'.[14]

The resistance to orthodoxy took various forms, from the development of Aesopian narratives, whose double-coded meanings undermined the totalitarian demands for a uniform imagination, to national(istic) narratives that opposed Soviet domination more directly. While the onslaught of conformist literature was the prevailing phenomenon between 1948 and 1954, this period also witnessed the gradual emergence of credible works that offered fewer concessions to the official ideology. The process of readjustment was painfully slow, illustrated in the subtle changes that the same work underwent in subsequent editions. Milovan Đilas rewrote his autobiographical *Članci* (*Essays*, 1947) in *Conversation with Stalin* (1962), the latter portraying some of the same events, people and judgements – for example, his first meeting with Stalin – but from the perspective of a disillusioned socialist. The critique of Stalinism, begun timidly after Stalin's death in 1953, was continued more boldly after 1956 by reform-minded communist writers (Tibor Déry, Gyula Háy, Ludvik Vaculík, Adam Ważyk) and by the Hungarian Petőfi Circle, composed of young writers who moved from a critique of Stalinism to a questioning of the ideology that made its excesses possible. As censorship relaxed, a new generation of writers shifted away from the precepts of socialist realism, returning to more complex models of representation. Albania's break with the Soviet Union in 1961, for instance, encouraged a number of younger writers (Ismail Kadare, Dritëro Agolli, Fatos Arapi)[15] to search cautiously for 'something new' in both poetry and fiction. However, certain types of literature (prison documentaries, anti-communist memoirs) that challenged communism's very essence continued to be censored. While Ion C. Ciobanu's fiction, which portrayed the Stalinist deportations more obliquely, was published in Soviet Moldova over several decades,[16] his colleague Alexei Marinat's account of internment in the Stalinist prisons could not appear before 1989.[17] Likewise Ion D. Sârbu's *Jurnalul unui jurnalist fără jurnal* (*The Journal of a Journalist without a Journal*, 1991–3), which turned an autobiographical drama (which included seven years of prison and labour camp) into a meditation on the paradoxical fate of a traditional socialist persecuted both by the Nazis and by the communists, was published only in the early 1990s, several decades after it was written.

By the end of the 1960s, most of the new literature showed a strong revisionist vocation that went beyond aesthetic matters. The poetry of Zbigniew Herbert, Ana Blandiana, Sándor Weöres, and others, dramatized the speaker's own fragmentary existence in a style that was often ironic, reflecting the limitations of both perception and representational language. The novelists also became aware of the prohibitive boundaries set up by the communist power around 'truth' and of their need to challenge them, a need which they proceeded to fulfil in a variety of ways. First, on the model of Mikhail Bulgakov, they introduced a strong element of subjectivity and mythopoiesis into the prescriptive realism of the fifties (as seen in such writers as Géza Ottlik, Marin Preda, Josef Škvorecký and Ismail Kadare). Second, writers sharpened their political focus in the anti-Stalinistic fiction of the following two decades (most obviously, Aleksandr Solzhenitsyn, but also Bohumil Hrabal, Miklós Mészöly, Milan Kundera, György Konrád, Jurek Becker and Augustin Buzura). Finally, they questioned the very foundation of communist reality in bolder experimental fiction (Alexandr Zinoviev, Christa Wolf, Danilo Kiš, Peter Nádas, Gabriela Adameşteanu, Péter Esterházy). Much of this literature reflected a disillusionment with the socialist utopia, a conflict of generations and a thwarted hope for change. Ludvík Vaculík's novel, *Sekyra* (*The Axe*, 1966), highlighted the tragic rift between the older Stalinist generation and their disaffected children, as well as the author's own disaffection with the Communist Party. The fiction published by Vladimír Páral in the 1960s presented an equally disenchanted view of communist Czech society, with its citizens channelling their frustrated energies into consumerism and extramarital affairs.[18] Gothic allegory replaced the festive realism of the earlier decade. In *Vdekja më vjen prej syve të tillë* (*Death Comes from Such Eyes*, 1974), by the Albanian Rexhep Qosja, a social utopia dissolves in a frightening web of political intrigue and secret police interrogation. The genre of film included similar themes. In Živojin Pavlović's *Zaseda* (*The Ambush*, 1968), an idealistic Dalmatian communist, on a mission to Serbia after the war, witnesses chilling examples of deterioration: people are liquidated on casual denunciations, partisan commanders invent victories and hide dismal mistakes, theft and debauchery are rampant.

Much of this literature encouraged a reading between the lines, as was the case with *Fuvarosok* (*Transporters*, 1983), a short story by Péter Esterházy in which the first-person narration of a raped young girl could also be interpreted as an allegory of the Soviet occupation of Hungary. Analysts of postwar East-Central European literature have often argued that metaphoric indirection was a poor substitute for political action, and that even 'dissident' writers tended to accommodate the power structures through their indirection.[19] It is clear that, prior to 1989, most East-Central European writers were committed to an *aesthetics of resistance* rather than one of open opposition, proudly maintaining their separation from the party controlled domain of the political. But that did not make pre-1989 literature necessarily apolitical. The metaphoric explorations and symbolic disguises of this literature often upset the official dogmas in significant ways. Therefore, it should not come as a surprise that, while a number of Slovenian and Serbian documentary novels on the Goli Otok camp were accepted, Danilo Kiš's seven dark tales about the communist revolution and Stalinistic terror, *Grob-*

nica za Borisa Davidoviča (*A Tomb for Boris Davidovich*, 1975), caused controversy precisely because of its recourse to a historical metafiction that could raise larger ideological issues than a documentary work.

The specific post-Stalinistic context in which East-Central European writers worked was framed by the contradictory drives of socialism, nationalism, Soviet hegemony and experimentalism. The suppression in 1968 of the Czechoslovak attempt to establish 'communism with a human face' exacerbated the conflict between Soviet hegemony and alternative models of (national) communism. The countries that had refused to participate in the Prague invasion (Romania and Yugoslavia) developed a form of defensive (anti-Soviet) nationalism that in time became offensive xenophobia, contributing to – instead of opposing – Cold War polarization. For example, Dumitru Radu Popescu's *Vînătoarea regală* (*The Royal Hunt*, 1973) suggested, however allegorically, that communism was a foreign import, a 'plague' that distorted the national spirit. The novel's title episode opens with a simulacrum of a 'royal hunt' organized by the new masters of a southern Romanian village led by communist official Galatioan. This event disrupts the archaic laws of the village and mocks traditional powers, with the villagers enjoying momentary control over dogs named Caesar, Napoleon, Peter, Franz Joseph, Hitler and Joseph (Stalin). But this hunting scene is followed by a mysterious outbreak of rabies, shrewdly manipulated by Galatioan and his confederates. At their instigation, the village lapses into forms of social cannibalism and sacrifices dissenters like Dănilă, the village doctor and amateur investigator of party abuses. The narrator, illustrating the line of adolescent observers in the fiction of Leon Borowski, Josef Škvorecký, Bohumil Hrabal and Imre Kertész, who retain a healthy detachment from the 'official' world, asks a pointed question at the end of the episode:

> Oh, God, how come the dogs went mad in our village while in other places around they went about their own business without foaming mouths, or had been taken for shots at the right time and had their mouths looked at, why us? And then I asked myself: but what if [Dănilă] wasn't rabid? What if it was they, they who were trying to destroy him? And they urged on the dogs against him and were driving him to the grave, guiltless.[20]

As in Eugène Ionesco's *Rhinoceros*, the plague comes from outside, contaminating an archaic Romanian culture that loses the capacity to defend itself against foreign bodies (biological and ideological). This allegorical idea was echoed in other novels published in Romania during the 1970s, but readers did not miss the irony that the 'foreign' infiltration during the Stalinistic period had in the meantime been replaced by autochthonous forms of dictatorship led by Gheorghe Gheorghiu-Dej and Nicolae Ceauşescu.

That irony was lost, on the other hand, on writers such as Eugen Barbu,

An anxious triangulation 167

who fed Ceauşescu's growing nationalist xenophobia. His chronicle of eighteenth-century Wallachia, *Principele* (*The Prince*, 1969), pitted an idealized local scholar, Ion Valahul (Ion the Romanian), against the corrupt Greek princes which ruled the country for the Turks. Barbu's vision of a region fallen prey to foreign rulers and their corrupt practices could easily be read as a xenophobic allegory of Romania's postwar history. Even the subtler *Hazarski rečnik* (*Dictionary of the Khazars*, 1984), by the Serbian Milorad Pavić, which challenged the communist doctrine of history by fusing historical periods and by mixing races and cultures, still reinforced an ethnic-national narrative through its association of the Serbs with the fictive empire of the Khazars.

Romanian, Yugoslav, Czech and, to some extent, Hungarian nationalism deftly exploited the work of writers such as Popescu, Kundera, Pavić and Esterházy, who had opposed Stalinism (or communism more generally) in the name of local or regional interests. Still, as soon as nationalism became an important part of the revamped official ideology, it was submitted to questioning by writers who regarded with distrust any kind of grand narrative. The narrator of the Slovenian Marjan Tomšič's short story 'Anita'[21] makes clear that the title character feels no attraction either for 'il Duce' (Benito Mussolini) in Italy or for the communist partisans in Yugoslavia. Like other of Tomšič's characters, she resists the divisions promoted either by fascist or by socialist governments. The language of Tomšič's fiction also shows a preference for the local Istrian idiom – a blend of 'Slovene', 'Croat' and 'Italian' expressions – over a specific national language. Even structurally his work is hybrid, combining realism and fantasy, archaic localism and Europeanism, in a way that recalls the 'magic realism' of the Latin America writers.

Echoing some of the same models, Ștefan Bănulescu questions Romanian culture's aspiration towards grand legitimizing narratives. His novel *Cartea de la Metopolis* (*The Book of Metopolis*, 1977), illustrates this disposition to the point of parody. In the Danubian city of Metopolis (a transparent guise for Bucharest), imperial Byzantium functions as a legitimizing myth for Romanian culture. But the play *O feerie bizantină* (*A Byzantine Masquerade*), ordered by the city's new ruler, Bazacopol, is an ironic reminder of the degradation of Byzantine archetypes into nationalistic clichés. Bazacopol's grandiose plans for restructuring threaten the traditionalist world of Metopolis, contributing – together with 'those interested in snatching the riches from under it' – to the 'cutting off and submerging' of the great city.[22] Few Romanian readers missed the allusion to the fate of historical Bucharest that Ceauşescu set out to demolish in the late 1970s. But the novel also offered a counter-model to Bazacopol: the imaginative tailor, Polydor, who works miracles with his scissors. He functions as a symbol for the recreative writer who uses the materials of the past in imaginative ways to recast them as new garments.

This type of imaginative recasting is at the centre of much pre-1989

East-Central European literature. The difficult subjects of postwar East-Central European history – the destruction of traditional communities in the war and the Holocaust (Kiš, György Konrád, Sorin Titel), the horrors of the communist gulag (Kiš, Marinat, Vasyl' Barka, Paul Goma, Karol Štajner), the loss of identity through exile (Witold Gombrowicz and Emil Cioran) or the alienated experiences of common folk under communism (Kundera, Hrabal, Esterházy, Bănulescu, Páral, Qosja) – required such a complex strategy. Štajner begins an account of his detention in the Soviet Gulag, *7000 dana u Sibiru* (*Seven Thousand Days in Siberia*, 1971), by wondering if his experiences will be regarded as 'unlikely and tendentious'.[23] The events of his detention both demanded and undermined the documentary character of the writing. Kiš's stories in *A Tomb* are likewise problematic, adopting a documentary style but not being strictly speaking autobiographical or factual. The genre and approach of Konrád's *Kerti mulatság* (*A Feast in the Garden*, 1985), first circulated in samizdat, is equally mixed. The character-author, David Kobra, is both an extension of and a counterpart to Konrád, with his narrative partly covering the latter's story from his childhood persecution as a Jew to his experiences in 1956, and also including characters from Konrád's own life in a way that breaches the boundary between reality and fiction. The work hesitates between novel, essay and autobiographical diary.[24] According to Beatrice Tötössy, much Hungarian literature in the 1960s and 1970s resorted to similarly unstable, hybrid structures. In their desire to free themselves from the impositions of a socialism 'that had produced infinite rules and bonds for Hungarian culture and civilization', and from the 'state of ritual immobility', writers such as Zoltán Endreffy, Ernő Kulcsár Szabó and Béla Bacsó advocated a return to a discourse of 'doubt' and to ironic modes of articulation.[25] Other writers such as Esterházy, Endre Kukorelly and Miklós Erdély[26] took rearticulation even further, pursuing a new linguistic-rhetorical 'authenticity' liberated from the monologic discourse of power.

There are a number of starting points associated with the new modes of literature in East-Central Europe, with periodization varying greatly from country to country. Nevertheless, most critics would include in the 'canon' of experimental literature Kundera's Czech novels beginning with *Žert* (*The Joke*, 1967); Esterházy's prolific writings, culminating with his monumental *Bevezetés a szépirodalomba* (*Introduction to Belles Lettres*, 1986), a montage of thematic and narrative experiments, mixing fiction, autobiography and history; the fiction of Kiš and Pavić in Serbia; and the theatre of Sławomir Mrożek, Tadeusz Różewicz and Tadeusz Kantor in Poland. Other works usually mentioned are *Éleslövészet* (*Shooting with Live Ammunition*, 1981), by the Hungarian-Slovak Lajos Grendel, *Štefica Cvek u raljama Života* (*Štefica Cvek in the Jaws of Life*, 1981), by the Croat Dubravka Ugrešić, and *Lumea în două zile* (*The World in Two Days*, 1975), by the Romanian George Bălăiţă. All dramatize the struggle of a writer, narrator or community to gain a truthful vision of life in an age dominated by ideological and cultural clichés. The focus on the ideological clichés and myths of Eastern Europe is central also to another, unusual type of fiction. These are the 'dictionary novels' of Ferenc Temesi (*Por/Dust*, 1986–7), Pavić (*Dictionary of the Khazars*) and Mircea Horia Simionescu (*Ingeniosul bine temperat/Well-Tempered Ingenuity*, 1969–83), which catalogue, parody and reinvent the features of a native town, national culture or regional identity. For example, Simionescu's narrative cycle, composed of a pseudo-'onomastic dictionary', a 'general bibliography' of themes and myths, a 'breviary' of the century's real or imagined catastrophes and an autobiographical 'toxicology' (to quote the titles of the four volumes that constitute Simionescu's narrative cycle),[27] subverts almost every procedure in the realistic repertory, while simultaneously exposing the author's culture as a world sick with inertia and stereotypy.

Some of this literature called into question the official theories about the unfolding of the 'socialist revolution' and even the efforts to reform or change the system from inside. Josef Škvorecký, who emigrated to Canada in the early 1970s, treated the Prague Spring satirically in *Mirákl* (*The Miracle Game*, 1972), drawing a parallel between the political 'miracle' of 1968 and a fraudulent miracle manufactured by the Catholic Church in a small Czechoslovak town in 1948 (the year of the communist takeover). This analogy mocked the naïve idealism of the Prague Spring, while also pointing to the ideological continuum between established religion and communism. Václav Havel, who remained in Czechoslovakia after the violent repression of the Prague Spring, continued to write plays and essays that indicted the political compromise underwriting the 'normalization' of the 1970s and early 1980s.[28]

The work published by a new generation of writers emerging in the 1980s, just before the collapse of communism, was even more disruptive, attacking the official representations more directly, and exposing the contradictory ideological drives of state socialism, nationalism and anti-Sovietism. For example, Mircea Nedelciu's novel *Zmeura de cîmpie* (*Wild Berries*, 1984), dramatized the difficulties of extricating the culture's 'soul of facts' from official fictions that masqueraded as truths. Similar concerns can be found in the fiction of Ryszard Kapuściński and Miško Kranjec,[29] who mix reportage, document and quasi-document with historical interpretation, problematizing official representations. It can be found also in the work of feminist writers such as Gabriela Adameșteanu, Krystyna Kofta and Liudmila Petrushevskaia who break down grand traditional narratives (those of nationalism included) to accommodate a more honest representation of female experience. Alternating between an objectified style of narration and first person-interior monologue, historical narrative and oral recounting, Adameșteanu's *Dimineața pierdută* (*Wasted Morning*, 1983) recovers areas of reality overlooked by the official historical discourse. This recovery is to a great extent 'female', attentive to the minutest details of life and emphasizing techniques of oral narration, diary and subjective monologue. Adameșteanu's intricately constructed novel responds to the deterioration of

Romanian social life and discourse under Ceauşescu with a complex interplay of perspectives that promises to return some sense of coherence to the familial and national narrative.

The 'yearning for the real' was present not only in the fiction of the 1980s but also in its poetry and visual art, replacing the 'yearning for style'. The young artists emerging in the 1980s resorted to the most incongruous codes and representational strategies to suggest – in direct antithesis to communist totalitarianism – a 'heterogeneous, fragmentary, and plural world'.[30] Literary criticism also played an important role in the process of re-evaluation. Equipped with the interpretative strategies of structuralist poetics, post-structuralism, semiotics and post-Marxist sociology, a new generation of critics proceeded to reconstruct genres, styles and forms, encouraging innovation and norm-breaking. A revisionistic-experimental concept of representation emerged gradually, rooted in the self-questioning perspective of a character-focalizer, as against the classic 'representational' perspective rooted in an omniscient narrator. The rethinking of realism became part of a broader critique of the constitutive ideas of Eastern European cultures, which also included the questions of national specificity, the socializing role of literature and aesthetic autonomy.

At the same time, we need to remember that for every victorious discourse in pre-1989 East-Central Europe there were others that never managed to break through and gain recognition. Even if censorship was more relaxed in the post-Stalinist era, its effects were no less pernicious, writers turning the terror of institutional censorship into the 'enlightened despotism' of internalized checks.[31] New literary trends would emerge only after older ones weakened or broke up. The experimental-satirical work of Kundera and Miloš Forman found only a brief window of opportunity in pre-1968 Czechoslovakia. Similarly, Kiš's innovative fiction could emerge only when the 'specific Yugo-hybrid of socialist realist doctrines' receded, and even then it continued to struggle with a xenophobic Serbian culture that 'rejected foreign literary influences as unauthentic', preferring instead 'realism with a specific national flavour'.[32] As a further complication, the postmodern privileging of the local over the 'universal' was exploited by nationalist regimes such as those of Yugoslavia and Romania. Tomislav Longinović offers the example of the short-lived but influential group of postmodern theorists that rallied around the Belgrade journal *Vidici*,[33] whose intention was to expose the ethnic and nationalist parochialism of Yugoslav culture but whose open-ended, paradoxical philosophies anticipated the ideological indeterminacies of postcommunist Yugoslavia. In the Baltic countries, the relationship between postmodernism, socialism and nationalism was even more complex, with the three terms interacting in unpredictable ways. As Epp Annus and Robert Hughes argue,

> *Nationalism* would seem to be a modern project, something essentially unifying and teleological, and on that account quite remote from postmodern thinking. *Socialism*, in turn, not only strives to overcome

national thinking, but also explicitly expresses its disdain towards the postmodern. Yet, in our view, conditions in the period of late socialism in the Baltic States — and very likely in socialist countries more generally — provoked a complex interconnection between the three ideologies.[34]

On the surface, postmodern experimentation challenged the grand narratives of both socialism and Soviet hegemony, serving the movement of national resistance. But nationalism is a teleological project, moving the nation towards an ideal, perfect future, so that in combating one grand narrative (that of socialism), resistant literature retrieved another (that of modern progress). In this sense, postmodernism functioned both as an alternative to, and as one of the catalysts of, post-Soviet nationalism. Even the more experimental writers who challenged the modernist project (whether socialist or nationalist) still promoted a type of 'double discourse' that expressed a nostalgic 'longing for the perfect past' while at the same time acknowledging 'that this harmonious past is but a myth and has never existed as reality'.[35] Such work complicated the relationship between past and present, history and fiction, socialism and nationalism, without resolving it.

This partly explains why, immediately after 1989, the East-Central European cultures underwent an identity crisis. The postcommunist landscape appeared for a while strikingly incoherent: an Enlightenment rhetoric of cultural emancipation co-existed with some form or other of nationalism; a nineteenth-century notion of market capitalism overlapped with a distrust of mass consumerism; and over-politicized modes of cultural production competed with aestheticism and cheap entertainment. And yet there is enough evidence that an alternative, more democratic model of political and literary culture is finally taking root in the region. The post-1989 transition has encouraged a critical rethinking of key concepts such as that of 'national culture' or of 'natural order' based on ethnic commonality. In the 1990s, several literary and cultural magazines in Romania devoted issues to the imbrications between ethnocentrism, nationalism and racial and social hatred. They also touched on some of the culture's sore spots, such as the streak of messianic nationalism in major Romanian writers of the nineteenth and twentieth centuries, or the contribution of certain postwar writers to the red version of nationalism. Similar debates took place in Poland and the Baltic countries, leading to a cautious rediscovery of multicultural borderlands and multinational traditions at the centre of what had for some time been perceived as monocultures. Once the multiple linguistic and communitarian roots of East-Central European populations are recognized, national identity can no longer be viewed as monologic but rather as dialogic, a form of 'multiple cultural identity'.[36] As Victor Neumann argues, this view of national identity allows us simultaneously to recognize the 'similitude of human values, their common origin', and to 'assume pluralism by claiming participation in more cultural identities'.[37]

Neumann's notion of multicultural identity echoes the emphasis on hybridity and on a politics of inclusion to be found in postcolonial theory. By reframing discussions of present-day East-Central Europe through the Western concept of postcoloniality, recent theoretical interventions, such as those in the volume from which I have quoted Neumann, have helped reposition literature, emphasizing its role in promoting multiple identity and multicultural or transcultural communication. The postcolonial framework is helpful to East-Central European cultures, located as they are at the intersection of three imperial systems (Ottoman, Habsburg and Tsarist/Soviet), at least in a metaphoric sense. It helps them understand the postcommunist phase as a 'decolonization', an attempt at liberating their traditions not only from the domination of the Soviet paradigm but also from older colonial vestiges (such as the Ottoman or Austro-Hungarian). A process of 'decolonization' has been pursued vigorously after 1990, not only in the Baltic region but also in Bulgaria, Slovakia, Moldova and the Ukraine, where contemporary literature continues to reflect a psycho-political trauma of identity endemic to the area. To be sure, the postcolonial framework needs to be applied guardedly, with a nuanced understanding of the East-Central European context. With few exceptions, most countries in the region did not consider themselves 'colonies' of the Soviet Union, but benefited from a certain 'autonomy' that allowed them to articulate their own brands of national communism. Still, the majority of these countries remained within the ideological sphere of Soviet influence, many of them underwent a process of Russification at one time or another, and their cultural and economic production was strictly controlled from Moscow. Even without a Soviet military occupation, the countries of East-Central Europe shared a subaltern position, being deprived of true initiative or independence. In that sense at least the status of a 'semi-colony' applies to them.[38]

The best literature published in the region after 1989 has challenged both the grand narrative of Marxist-Leninism and the patriarchal retreat into nationalism. The grand narrative of communism has been easier to deflate. For example, based on documents indicating that his father, a member of an old aristocratic family, was forced to work for the communists as an agent from 1957 to 1980, Esterházy's *Javított kiadás* (*Emended Edition*, 2002) deconstructs both the collective narrative and the writer's family story under communism. This work adopts the form of a diary that Esterházy kept while reading what his father had written for the political authorities, including reports at the time the leaders of the 1956 revolution were executed. Ádám Bodor's *Szinisztra körzet: egy regény fejezetei* (*Sinistra District: Chapters of a Novel*, 1992) is more heavily allegorical, presenting a suffocating territory somewhere in the Carpathian Mountains that annihilates all those who stumble into it (readers did not miss the allusion to the totalitarian space created by Ceauşescu's regime).

Other literature published since 1989 has broached the more difficult questions of national identity, gender and race. In Estonia, while critics called for a new national literature after 1989, writers offered ambiguous products that mocked the narrative of national celebration: one novel focused on Tarzan's activities in Estonia during the nationalist celebrations of independence,[39] another on the return to Tallinn of national poet Lydia Koidula's husband in the role of a contemporary Dracula who promises to use blood banks instead of live prey during trying national times.[40] The problematization of national and ethnic identity has gone even further in the work of 'hybrid' minority writers: the German–Romanian Herta Müller, the Hungarian–Slovak Lajos Grendel and the Jewish Serbian–Hungarian Danilo Kiš. Together with other multiculturally minded writers, they have reclaimed an inclusive and borderless notion of East-Central Europe, remapping the region as a continuum that cuts across former Cold War East–West divisions. *Viena, Banat* (1998), by Richard Wagner, former member of the German–Romanian Aktionsgruppe Banat, tries to create a similarly inclusive map as a response to the protagonist's fractured life, part of it spent in communist Romania as a marginalized German ethnic, the other part in Germany where he is at best a 'Swabian from the Banat'; that is, a member of a vanishing breed who speaks German 'like a foreigner'.[41] Realizing that his topographic distinctions have been to a great extent artificial – his 'West was an illusion, created against the crushing banality of life in the Banat'[42] – the protagonist tries to draw his own map that might reconcile the two halves and geographies of his life. This map includes the names of East European localities in several languages, restoring the multicultural world of his youth and saving the protagonist from the 'feeling of ultimate loss';[43] it also gives the protagonist and those throngs of East-Central European immigrants that in 1989 converged on the open Austrian border some sense of belonging.

As Mircea Cărtărescu admits, 'nothing will be as before: the system has become unrecognizable, making impossible the reference to the same literary paradigm. A chaotic diversification and dissipation of texts, a hybridization of media, [...] an increasing virtualization of "possible worlds" will turn literature into a form of generalized mind game.'[44] There is an anxious awareness of radical change in such statements, but also the knowledge of new expanded opportunities. The present literary map of East-Central Europe is not only more diverse, but also more richly layered, emphasizing transitional, multicultural and cross-genre forms.

Notes

1 Brubaker, *Nationalisms Reframed: Nationhood and the National Question in the New Europe* (Cambridge: Cambridge University Press, 1996), pp. 103–4.
2 Todorov, 'Introduction to the Political Aesthetics of Communism', in Alexander Kiossev, ed., *Post-Theory, Games, and Discursive Resistance: The Bulgarian Case* (Albany: State University of New York Press, 1995), p. 94.
3 Ibid., p. 89.
4 Ibid., pp. 90, 92.

5 Vladimir Tismaneanu, *Reinventing Politics: Eastern Europe from Stalin to Havel* (New York: The Free Press/Macmillan, 1992), p. 226.
6 Karl Friedrich and Zbigniew Brzezinski, *Totalitarian Dictatorship and Autocracy* (Cambridge, MA: Harvard University Press, 1965), p. 27.
7 Tismaneanu, *Reinventing Politics*, p. 249.
8 Simon During, 'Literature – Nationalism's Other? The Case for Revision', in Homi Bhabha, ed., *Nation and Narration* (London and New York: Routledge, 1990), pp. 138, 144.
9 Călinescu, quoted in Ana Selejan, *România în timpul primului război cultural 1944–1948: Vol. 2, Reeducare și prigoană* (Sibiu: Thausib, 1993), p. 86.
10 Nadel, *Containment Culture: American Narratives, Postmodernism, and the Atomic Age* (Durham: Duke University Press, 1995), p. 3.
11 Ibid., p. 4.
12 Ibid., p. 67.
13 Katherine Verdery, *National Ideology under Socialism: Identity and Cultural Politics in Ceaușescu's Romania* (Berkeley: University of California Press, 1991), p. 91.
14 Edith W. Clowes, *Russian Experimental Fiction: Resisting Ideology after Utopia* (Princeton: Princeton University Press, 1993), pp. 4, 5.
15 See Kadare, *Shekulli im (My Century*; Poems) (Tirana: Naim Frashëri, 1961); Kadare, *Gjenerali i ushtrisë së vdekur (The General of the Dead Army*) (Tirana: Naim Frashëri, 1963); Agolli, *Hapat e mija në asfalt (My Steps on the Pavement*; Poems) (Tirana: Naim Frashëri, 1961); and Arapi, *Shtigje Poetik (Poetic Paths*) (Tirana: Naim Frashëri, 1962).
16 Ciobanu, *Codrii (The Woods*), 2 Vols, new edn (1954, 1957; Moskva: Izvestia, 1969); Ciobanu, *Podgorenii (The Mountain People*) (Chișinău/Kishinev: Lit-ra artistike, 1982).
17 See Marinat, *Eu și lumea: proză documentară (Me and the World: Documentary Prose*), new edn (1989; Chișinău: Uniunii Scriitorilor, 1999).
18 See especially Páral, *Veletrh splněných přání (A Tradefair of Fulfilled Desires*) (Prague: Mladá fronta, 1964) and *Milenci & vrazi: Magazín ukájeni před rokem 2000 (Lovers and Murderers: A Story of Gratification before the Year 2000*) (Prague: Mladá fronta, 1969).
19 See, for example, Miklós Haraszti, *L'Artist d'Etat* (Paris: Librairie Arthème Fayarde, 1983); Timothy Garton Ash, 'The Hungarian Lesson', *New York Times Book Review*, 5 (December 1985), p. 5.
20 Popescu, *The Royal Hunt*, trans. J.E. Cottrell and M. Bogdan (1973; Columbus: Ohio State University Press, 1985), p. 173.
21 Tomšič, 'Anita', in Tomšič, *Kažuni* (Ljubljana: Kmečki glas, 1990), pp. 42–58.
22 Bănulescu, *The Book of Metopolis* (1977), fragments trans. Alina Carac, *Romanian Review*, 2 (1986), p. 17.
23 Štajner, *7000 dana u Sibiru* (Zagreb: Globus, 1971), p. 7.
24 See Guido Snel, 'Gardens of the Mind: Fictionalized Autobiography in East-Central Europe', in Marcel Cornis-Pope and John Neubauer, eds, *History of the Literary Cultures of East-Central Europe*, Vol. 1 (Philadelphia: John Benjamins Publishing Company, 2004), pp. 395–6.
25 Tötössy, *Scrivere postmoderno in Ungheria* (Rome: ARLEM, 1995), pp. 29–30.
26 See Kukorelly, *A valóság édessége (The Sweetness of the Reality*; Poems) (Budapest: Magvető, 1984); Kukorelly, *A Memória-part (The Memory Shore*) (Budapest: Magvető, 1990); Kukorelly, *Rom: A szovjetónió története (Ruin: The Story of the Sovietonion*) (Budapest: Jelenkor, 2000). The work of Miklós Erdély, filmmaker, conceptual artist, writer and painter, is too diverse to be cited here. For Esterházy see below.
27 Simionescu, *Ingeniosul bine temperat (Well-Tempered Ingenuity*): Vol. 1, *Dicționar*

onomastic (Bucharest: EPL, 1969); Vol. 2, *Bibliografie generală* (Bucharest: Eminescu, 1970); Vol. 3, *Breviar* (Bucharest: Cartea Românească, 1980); and Vol. 4, *Toxicologie* (Bucharest: Cartea Românească, 1983).

28 Havel, 'Český úděl?' (*The Czech Lot?*), *Tvář*, 4: 2 (February 1969), pp. 30–3; Havel, 'Na téma opozice' (*On the Theme of an Opposition*), *Literární listy*, 1: 4 (April 1968), pp. 11–21; Havel, *Selected Plays 1963–1983*, trans. Vera Blackwell, George Theiner and Jan Novak (London: Faber and Faber, 1992); and Havel, *The Power of the Powerless: Citizen against the State in Central-Eastern Europe*, ed. J. Keane (London: Hutchinson, 1985).

29 See Kapuściński, *Busz po polsku* (*Bush in Polish*), new edn (1962; Warsaw: Czytelnik, 1990); Kapuściński, *Chrystus z karabinem na ramieniu* (*The Rifle Carrying Christ*) (Warsaw: Czytelnik, 1975); Kranjec, *Rdeči gardist* (*The Red Guard*), 3 Vols (Murska Sobota: Pomurska založba, 1964–7).

30 Magda Cârneci, *Art of the 1980s in Eastern Europe: Texts on Postmodernism* (Bucharest: Paralela 45, 1999), p. 41.

31 Miklós Haraszti, *The Velvet Prison: Artists under State Socialism*, trans. Katalin and Stephen Landesmann (New York: New Republic/Basic Books, 1987), p. 77.

32 Tomislav Z. Longinović, *Borderline Culture: The Politics of Identity in Four Twentieth Century Slavic Novels* (Fayetteville: University of Arkansas Press, 1993), pp. 109–10.

33 Longinović, 'Postmodernity and the Technology of Power: Legacy of the *Vidici* Group in Serbia', *College Literature*, 21: 1 (1994), p. 121.

34 Annus and Hughes, 'Reversals of the Postmodern and the Late Soviet Simulacrum in the Baltic Countries', in Cornis-Pope and Neubauer, eds, *History*, pp. 54–65.

35 Ibid., p. 63.

36 Victor Neumann, 'Perspective comparative asupra filozofiei multiculturale' ('Comparative Perspectives on Multicultural Philosophy'), in *Postcolonialism & Postcomunism: Caietele Echinox* (*The Echinox Notebooks*), Vol. 1 (Cluj-Napoca: Dacia, 2001), p. 66.

37 Ibid., p. 68.

38 Ion Bogdan Lefter, 'Poate fi considerat postcomunismul un post-colonialism?' ('Can Postcommunism Be Considered a Post-Colonialism?'), in *Postcolonialism & Postcomunism*, pp. 118–19.

39 Toomas Raudam and Edgar Rice Burroughs [Toomas Raudam], *Tarzani seiklused Tallinnas* (*Tarzan's Adventures in Tallinn*) (Tallinn: Fööniks, 1991).

40 Mati Unt, *Doonori meelespea* (*Donor's Guidelines*) (Tallinn: Kupar, 1990).

41 Wagner, *Viena, Banat*, trans. Wolfgang Schaller (Bucharest: Univers, 1998), pp. 19, 34.

42 Ibid., p. 113.

43 Ibid., p. 122.

44 Cărtărescu, *Postmodernismul românesc* (Bucharest: Humanitas, 1999), p. 462.

11 'Lifting each other off our knees'

South African women's poetry of resistance, 1980–1989

Mary K. DeShazer

Scholars of the Cold War have traditionally emphasized ideological and military conflicts between the democratic West and the communist East.[1] Yet such conflicts occurred on a global scale between 1945 and 1989, in part because of the Western-sanctioned spread of extreme nationalist, anti-communist states. During this period right-wing governments strove to suppress movements for freedom and self-determination by oppressed people in such countries or areas as Argentina, Chile, Cuba, El Salvador, Guatemala, Nicaragua, Mozambique, Zimbabwe, South Africa, Lebanon and the West Bank. Among these sites of contestation South Africa stands unique in its government's blend of virulent racism and ultra-conservative Afrikaner nationalism; the triumph of this ideology led to the political victory of the Nationalist Party in 1948 and the subsequent passage of legislation and policies instituting the notorious system of apartheid, forced racial segregation and hierarchy. The apartheid era in South Africa lasted until 1994 and generated a widespread resistance movement, as the African National Congress (ANC), the South African Communist Party and other left-leaning political organizations challenged the racist domination of indigenous African people, who comprised 87 per cent of the population, by descendants of European colonial settlers, who comprised 13 per cent.[2]

Although internal resistance to apartheid grew during each decade, the 1980s deserve particular scrutiny given the degree of governmental repression that occurred. First, however, some historical contextualization is necessary. During the 1950s the ANC launched a widespread Defiance Campaign that led to non-violent demonstrations throughout the country, including the famous 1956 women's march to Pretoria to protest against laws requiring black Africans to carry identification books known as 'passes'. The 1960s took a violent turn, as government forces gunned down 69 unarmed protesters in what became known as the Sharpeville massacre; in 1961 Nelson Mandela and other ANC leaders were arrested for treason and sentenced to life imprisonment, and the ANC developed its own militant wing. The 1970s witnessed a major uprising in the black township of Soweto in 1976, as children protested against 'Bantu' (segregated and inferior) education in demonstrations that quickly spread to other townships.[3] During the 1980s both governmental repression and anti-apartheid activism intensified, as President P.W. Botha continued the Nationalist Party's policy of forcing Africans to relocate to remote 'homelands'; these relocations produced massive migration, as poor blacks sought work in the cities or in the gold and diamond mines. The increasing economic stagnation of both rural areas and urban townships, coupled with a disabling recession and high unemployment rates, magnified the discontent of the black population. Having promised face-saving reform to white South African business leaders and the international community in an effort to challenge his country's growing status as a pariah nation, Botha unsuccessfully attempted to downplay unrest by signing a non-aggression pact with the postcolonial government of Mozambique and by embarking on a European public-relations tour in 1984. Yet as indigenous people protested against outrageous rental prices and demanded educational reform, Botha unleashed the South African Defense Force to fire on unarmed crowds, to conduct house-to-house raids at dawn and to teargas, imprison or kill protesters. In March 1985, as demonstrations swelled, Botha used his 'state of emergency' declaration, the first since 1960, to ban public gatherings and detain protesters indefinitely. By September of 1985 the government had arrested ten thousand activists and the death toll from that year's unrest surpassed seven hundred.[4] Still the people defied the bans and gathered on street corners, at funerals, in union halls and stadiums; and where they gathered, they recited poems.

Poetry thus emerged as a vital arena of struggle: a means of representing history from the perspective of the dispossessed; of chronicling dead or imprisoned heroes; of refusing any notion of literature as objective or dispassionate. In discussing protest poetry of the 1960s and 1970s, Nadine Gordimer claims that black South Africans were forced, for survival's sake, to be cryptic rather than explicit; hence they turned to poetry, an indirect form of resistance.[5] Piniel Viriri Shava argues, however, that during the 1980s radical poetry changed: it directly challenged the racist hegemony by accusing, warning and exhorting; and it rejuvenated an audience of activists.[6] By tapping into this audience's anger and by providing solidarity in struggle, poetry contributed to a collective resistant consciousness.

Black women's contributions to the battle against apartheid are well known, their poetic contributions less so. Their political activism has been documented in academic studies, oral histories and chants such as this one from the 1956 march to Pretoria: 'You have tampered with the women; / you have struck a rock! / You have dislodged a boulder; / you will be crushed.'[7] To be sure, the most prominent anti-apartheid activists were black men: Nelson Mandela, Walter Sisulu, Govan Mbeki and Oliver Tambo, among others. Yet African women such as Lillian Ngoyi, Dorothy Nyembe and Winnie Mandela, along with Indian women such as Fatima Meer and Ela Ramgobin and white women such as Helen Joseph and Ruth First, organized protests against pass laws, established non-racial women's resistance leagues and experienced detention. In the 1980s women's leadership continued, as seasoned activists and township mothers protested against rising costs, supported educational demands and demanded living wages. Despite widespread recognition of women activists' achievements, however, a misconception has flourished that black women did not contribute significantly as poets until the end of the 1980s, when academic and grassroots organizations started publicly to lament their absence. In fact, many black women wrote resistance poetry during the 1970s and 1980s, and some published their writing. The result is a substantial body of gendered revolutionary poetry that has been largely overlooked.

Motivated by the belief that 'culture is a weapon of struggle', these revolutionary poets addressed in polemical terms such themes as colonization, land seizures, forced relocations and state-sponsored violence.[8] During the past decade, however, certain politically engaged critics have interrogated anti-apartheid poems for their 'ungainly platitudes' and 'narrow range of themes', even as they have critiqued the sterile aestheticism of a rigidly Eurocentric poetic tradition.[9] In her essay 'Standing in the Doorway' poet Ingrid de Kok argues for the necessity of a 'postnationalist' imaginary that would foreground post-apartheid literary representations yet also reassess anti-apartheid texts, as part of a project to 'unwrite, retell, and organize the nature of the record'.[10] Gender would figure prominently in this imaginary, since women's voices have emerged as an important source of postcolonial agency. I have argued elsewhere that dissident women poets developed a distinctive poetics of resistance to challenge the crimes of the apartheid state.[11] In this chapter I want to accept de Kok's invitation to 'resist cultural amnesia' by re-examining, from the standpoint of a white US feminist critic, the political and literary efficacy of black women's anti-apartheid poetry of the 1980s. From today's vantage point, ten years after the ANC established the nation's first democratic government and 20 years after the Nationalist Party declared a 'state of emergency' in response to activists' success in making the country ungovernable, it seems useful to reconsider what this body of poetry has contributed to its historical moment, to the burgeoning women's movement in South Africa, to the complex field of South African literary studies and to shifting definitions of Cold War literature.

Four anthologies that feature black women's poetry offer exemplary resistant texts and contexts: *Malibongwe – ANC Women: Poetry Is Also Their Weapon* (1982), *Black Mamba Rising: South African Worker Poets in Struggle* (1986), *Izinsingizi: Loudhailer Lives* (1988) and *Buang Basadi / Khulumani Makhosikazi / Women Speak* (1989). The militant poets of *Malibongwe*, members of the ANC's radical wing, Umkhonto we Sizwe (Spear of the Nation), lived in exile; their topics ranged from childbirth to struggle and genocide. The worker poets of *Black Mamba Rising* and *Izinsingizi* addressed economic exploitation; although most poets were men, two women, Nise Malange and Sana Naidoo, celebrated workers' rights through a gendered lens. The poets of *Buang Basadi* explored women's struggles and challenged patriarchy; their poems were presented at a 1988 conference on women and writing, sponsored by the Congress of South African Writers (COSAW). These poets' depictions of black women's activism and their 'double shift' at home and on the job presaged the development of a South African feminism that would confront sexism along with apartheid. Black women's resistance poems deserve retrospective analysis because they contributed to a collective, militant ideology and to a concomitant poetics, as well as documenting the gendered subjectivities of the writers. Also important to an analysis of these poetic interventions is an understanding of differing critical views on the contradictions and political urgencies of realist representation itself.

The important volume of poetry-in-arms, *Malibongwe* (*In Praise of Women*), was published in Sweden in 1982 as part of the banned ANC's celebration of the Year of the Woman. This collection reveals in its subtitle, *ANC Women: Poetry Is Also Their Weapon*, the secondary status of women and their writing, even within the anti-apartheid movement, as well as the ANC's belief in the power of poetry to construct counter-hegemonic knowledge. In emphasizing the struggle for national liberation, most poets downplayed women's emancipation. Some poems in *Malibongwe* offer no overtly gendered perspective: for example, those poems warning the oppressors that justice will prevail or celebrating the founding of the ANC. Yet other poems reveal the poets' sense of themselves as women, through their tributes to female activists, their use of childbirth imagery, their exploration of militant motherhood and their portrayal of South Africa as a maternal figure. The anthology's editor, Sono Molefe, emphasizes the exiled writers' collective voice:

> Who are these women? [...] There are those who battled police, their dogs and bullets on the streets of their country in 1976. There are students and former school-teachers. There are trained soldiers, daughters of workers; militant patriots fully engaged in the continuous act of liberation, one and all, struggle is their chosen path.[12]

The editor also addresses the vexed question of a revolutionary aesthetic, making no apology for the poems' polemical nature; their themes are justice and its aberrations, their technique 'thrillingly new: nerve-filled and public.'[13]

Molefe's revolutionary discourse typifies that of black cultural critics during the 1980s in endorsing poetry as a tool of struggle and employing a political litmus test to evaluate it. Oswald Mtshali, for example, claimed that poets 'have not got the time to embellish this urgent message with unnecessary and cumbersome ornaments like rhyme, iambic pentameter, abstract figures of speech and an ornate and lofty style. We will indulge in these luxuries which we can ill-afford at the moment when we are free people.'[14] Es'kia Mphahlele argued similarly that the black writer 'tends to document minute-to-minute experience. There is a specifically African drama in the ghettos that the writer cannot ignore [...]. He [*sic*] must simply come to terms with the tyranny of place or grapple with it [...] because his writing depends on his commitment to territory.'[15] Although other black scholars decried this stenographic element of black writing – Lewis Nkosi, for example, protested against 'journalistic fact parading outrageously as imaginative literature'[16] – Molefe embraces the dominant perspective of poetry as documentary:

> There is no romance here, though all attest a love deeply rooted in their usurped land. No academic optimism where illusory easy victories are spun out of pseudo-revolutionary theories! No unwarranted pessimism in the context of international and continental struggles. Only pounding reality, now unpalatable – now lifting, but always moving towards the known to-be-known success of the African Revolution.[17]

Molefe's trope of 'pounding reality' supports Louise Bethlehem's claim that a 'rhetoric of urgency' underlies anti-apartheid writing, one that privileges realism over literary experimentation and documentation over aesthetic considerations. Although Bethlehem criticizes apartheid-era writers' unthinking shift from 'the trope-of-truth to the trope-as-truth', she acknowledges the strategic value of an 'instrumentalist approach' to language.[18]

An urgent rhetoric and linguistic instrumentalism can be seen in the poems of *Malibongwe*, along with an exilic consciousness and performative dimensions. Exile produces in these poets both outrage at their lack of self-determination and longing for a reclaimed homeland; as Molefe notes, 'without South Africa's present political aberrations of justice and equality none of the voices in this collection would have opted for exile'.[19] Many poems were broadcast over the ANC's underground Radio Freedom, while others were recited at international youth festivals in Cuba. Marxist ideology influenced these poets' discourse, since the ANC was aligned with the South African Communist Party and with Cuba, hence the rhetoric of 'comrades', 'militant patriots' and the 'path of revolution'. Yet allusions to indigenous African culture also appear, particularly in the imagery of spears and shields, the ritual praise of tribal chiefs and the repeated naming, often in African languages, of historically important places.

Lindiwe Mabuza's narrative poem 'Manguang' illustrates these strategies. Having translated the title as 'the meeting place of leopards',[20] the poet celebrates this site as the birthplace of the ANC in 1912. The speaker, a personification of the dissident group itself, contrasts the Xhosa name 'Manguang' with its counterpart in Afrikaans, 'Bloemfontein', an area that 'today, the enemy calls my cradle'. The apartheid state, that is, has co-opted this site, renamed it oppressively and condemned its radical history. Three rhetorical techniques employed by Mabuza – strategic repetition, capitalization for emphasis and linguistic code-switching – further enhance the poem's 'polemical historicity'.[21] Activists arrived *en masse* in 1912, as the waters of the nearby Tukela River ensured safe passage and river creatures greeted travellers,

> Spirited by the call of
> MANGUANG
> And bubbled
> Deep in their water-home
> Ndlelanhle!
> Just to let the freedom riders pass!
> (lines 113–18)

A blend of epic journey and creation myth, Mabuza's narrative enshrines the ANC's birthplace but also lambastes the apartheid state: 'Today, / The enemy tramples / On the burial place / Of our umbilical cord / With iron boots, tanks / And bullet-belts' (lines 199–204). As the umbilical imagery reveals, 'Manguang' features recurring, if mixed, metaphors of pregnancy, childbirth, midwifery and militant parenthood. 'Unconquerable custodians of justice', the freedom riders, whom the speaker calls 'parents', are destined to engender 'a pregnant idea' (lines 90–3). The personified ANC acknowledges the pain and triumph of its birth:

> But I'm an extraordinary spirit
> A power, a force, a home
> A shield, a spear, a child
> Born with stubborn leopard spots
> Of racism
> But born nonetheless
> Breathing, kicking, stretching
> Into the future [. . .].
> (lines 181–8)

If African leaders birthed the ANC, its workers served as 'true midwives of our wealth' (line 249). The poem ends with a rhetorical question – 'And / What's my name?' – followed by the speaker's emphatic declaration: 'THE AFRICAN NATIONAL CONGRESS.' An ironic twist occurs as the ANC records the arrival of its own radical offspring: 'I gave birth to UMKHONTO / WE SIZWE on the 16th December / 1961' (lines 258–65). Thus Mabuza offers a political literacy narrative, chronicling ANC history for fellow activists.

Other poems manifest characteristics of *izibongo*, Zulu praise poems traditionally recited to celebrate tribal chiefs but modified to honour movement leaders. As Elizabeth Gunner has demonstrated, although *izibongo* were conventionally associated with war and the male authority of the *izimbongi* (bard), women also composed praise poems but performed them in private ceremonies to explore gender identity and familial problems.[22] *Malibongwe* features poems that combine 'male' militancy with 'female' exploration of gender and place. While many *Malibongwe* poets pay homage to famous men, others recount the heroism of dissident women. Alice Ntsongo's 'Women Arise', for example, references two historical periods in which women's resistance thwarted the apartheid state: 1913 and 1956, the years of the most vehement opposition to the government's attempts to force black women to carry passes. Just as women in 1913 marched into the ironically named 'Orange Free State', 'forcing the final cowards / to burn that violent law / their special restrictive permits of paper / that arrested human movement', so in 1956 did 'warrior-women' converge defiantly on the 'contaminated steps of Pretoria's Union Buildings'.[23] Again a historical polemic appears but with a gendered focus, as the poet offers a litany of exemplary women: 'Lillian [Ngoyi] and Helen [Joseph] / who followed Charlotte Maxeke / leading our women to the apex' (lines 20–2). As participants in the March to Pretoria long recounted the story, Prime Minister Strydom feigned absence rather than confront twenty thousand chanting women carrying petitions. Ntsongo creates her own version of this triumphant moment:

Strydom rewhitened
looked, then preferred to hide . . .
taught his secretary lies . . . 'Out on business!'
                              (lines 31–3)

Subverting the sobriety of the ritual praisesong, the poet coins the racially coded verb 'rewhitened' to dramatize the Minister's shock, uses ellipses ironically to mark his prevarications and employs the idiomatic expression 'out on business' as a metonym for the banality and smokescreens that characterized the apartheid state. This poem reminds women of the 1980s that their foremothers' burdens now belong to them: 'Mothers can march to battle! WOMEN OF AFRICA, ARISE!' (lines 40–1). Again the imagery of militant parenting is prevalent but with a shift: the elision of motherhood and womanhood, an essentialist gesture that recurs throughout *Malibongwe*. Ntsongo's poem and others like it use a gendered perspective to present South Africa's history of dissent, to exalt women as mothers and thereby to mobilize their audience.

Contemporary worker poetry originated in KwaZulu/Natal, spearheaded by members of a vibrant democratic trade union movement that established cultural centres. The editor of *Black Mamba Rising*, Ari Sitas, notes that this anthology and its counterpart, *Izinsingizi*, contain poems 'composed for performance at mass-meetings, trade union and community gatherings, for festive and somber occasions'.[24] Although these anthologies are male-dominated – they feature seven men and two women poets – the women's voices are distinctive. Poems by the best-known female worker poet, Nise Malange, probe themes of unemployment and union activism, as well as of women's collaborative struggles. 'First May 1985' begins its tribute to South African workers on International Labor Day with a rhetorical question – 'Who among the oppressed workers can fail to imagine this day?' – and follows with a call to resistance:

> Millions of workers are out of employment
> Millions of workers are facing retrenchment
> Millions of people are dying of hunger.
>
> This is the day that workers must reorganize themselves,
> This is the day for unification of the working class, [. . .]
> This is the day that worker organisations must unite and pass
> A resolution[25]

Features of performance poetry are evident in this poem's 'additive, aggregative, formulaic, and copious' rhetoric, such as strategic repetition to keep the *izimbongi* on track, an aggregation of the text of the resolution that Malange proposes and the predictable revolutionary tropes of retrenchment and collectivity.[26] The poem ends by praising 'the underprivileged, the unemployed, the oppressed, / those languishing in jails and in exile', and by 'salut[ing] the day of the workers' (lines 31–5). As Sitas points out, such poems lose much of their oral power on the printed page, where there is little sense of 'the songs, the chants, the ululating, their improvisatory nature and of course, the popular responses that accompany their oration'.[27] Initially performed at a union rally, 'First May 1985' represents a hybrid form of *izibongo* that intervenes discursively against apartheid.

Malange's 'Nightshift Mother', which addresses women's double shift, is typical of female worker poetry in its gendered revolutionary subjectivity and its kinetic quality. Its poignancy comes from the anxious speaker's voice, while its energy lies in its dancing rhythms and celebration of collective resistance:

> Left with a double load
>   at home
>   my children left uncared
>
> Anxiety
>   at work
>   my boss insists we should
>   be grateful for the opportunities
>   he gives women to be exploited
>
> Anxiety
> And I am stranded with these loads,
> This 'nightshift job' which brings home pittance[28]

With no training and no childcare, this single mother minds her children by day and cleans offices at night, where she is 'lost in these vast buildings / forgotten and neglected / exploited as you sleep' (lines 21–3). The pronoun 'you' reveals the speaker's intended audience: the exploiter himself. This angry worker speaks for other women, 'unmarried mothers, widows, / elder women, migrants, but always / mothers' (lines 25–7). As the poem ends, Malange documents black women's solidarity:

> We are
> cleaning and cleaning
> lifting each other off our knees
> and fighting our exploitation
>   (lines 28–31)

A more elegiac representation of women's resilience occurs in Sana Naidoo's 'I Remember', which pays homage to a prototypical rural woman

> Walking barefooted . . . calloused . . .
> Along the dusty, winding roads,
> Struggling through thorn-studded fields,
> [. . .]. Her baby bobbing on her back.[29]

When this woman reaches her makeshift home, she is too tired to sleep, yet 'sleep she must', to face 'the agony, the pain which / afresh the new day will surely bring' (lines 25–6). Empathizing with rural women, Naidoo pays tribute to women's domestic labour alongside factory and office work.

Both Malange and Naidoo have indicated that gender is as important a part of their creative identity as race and class. 'We are always attacked as women, in any kind of work that we do,' claimed Malange in 1990, 'and we need to be brave in order to succeed.'[30] At a writers' forum that same year, Naidoo asserted that

> I write as a woman, for women. I try to deal honestly with my own experiences, the inequalities I've endured as a woman, the traditions I've dared to break away from. I write about my survival in a male-dominated society – above all about the positive changes I've made in my life, and what I still want to do. It's a call to women to aspire likewise.[31]

In their dual emphasis on racial solidarity and gender empowerment, these worker poets anticipated the rise of South African feminism during the transition to democracy.

A conference on women's literature sponsored by COSAW in 1988 attested to the prevalence of emerging feminist voices. The conference anthology, *Buang Basadi / Khulumani Makhosikazi / Women Speak*, emphasizes women's writing in indigenous languages, as indicated by the title being in Xhosa, Zulu and English. Featured are poems and proceedings from panels on worker poetry, literacy movements and images of women in South African literature. In 'Breaking the Silence', a dialogue among black women poets, Boitumelo Mofokeng expressed dismay that so few women from the Soweto era were still writing. Citing as inhibiting factors the absence of a writers' network and a lack of support for women by *Staffrider*, the national COSAW journal, Mofokeng challenged male critics for their sexism. Such forthrightness was typical of *Buang Basadi*, since writers sought to raise awareness among their female peers and to educate sympathetic men. Mofokeng called women to action, urging them to write about their experiences of discrimination. Black women suffer because of race, gender and legal status as minors under customary law, she noted; they are economically abused, along with men, and are sexually abused by men: 'A literature from these women, or about their experiences, would provide an important social documentation of their lives.'[32] Mofokeng's own poems emphasize freedom and healing grace:

> Liberate my soul
> From the shackles
> Of bondage
> Liberate my soul
> From the shackles
> Of sexual oppression
> Liberate my mind
> Liberate my heart[33]

Her identification of sexual oppression as a problem stands in dramatic contrast to a *Malibongwe* poet's earlier disparagement of 'distorted women's lib'.[34] Indeed, Mofokeng offered conference participants a feminist manifesto:

> Let us remove the barriers! Let us break the silence. Let us stand up and speak our minds before the men do it for us. Let us fight the social and political obstacles that prevent us from occupying our rightful place in society [...]. Let us find more ways to explain our stand and why we want to be part of the whole society. Let us not wait, to be a disgrace to our children and grandchildren. We owe it to them. The future is theirs.[35]

Unlike the poets of *Malibongwe*, Mofokeng confronted patriarchy directly and employed a rhetoric of militant motherhood in the service of women's liberation.

Although Roseline Naapo's rhetoric is less militant, her poetry likewise serves the cause of feminism by documenting the difficult lives of domestic workers who live alone in cubicles outside of white homes. Here they are allowed no visitors, are grossly undercompensated, are forced to care for white children, while rarely seeing their own, and are dismissed in old age:

> Madam,
> remember when I was young and happy,
> remember when I used to perform
> your choruses in time [. . .]
> Today I'm old [. . .]
> Madam,
> did you ever consider
> that today I need you
> as you needed me
> in the sixteen years
> I worked for you?[36]

Naapo's direct address exposes the error of any nostalgic view of interracial sisterhood, given many white employers' exploitation of black women, yet in confronting the 'madam' she leaves open the possibility of a transformed relational dynamic. At the COSAW conference Naapo encouraged illiterate domestic workers to tell their stories: 'Say whatever you can say without knowing how to write. The next person will write it down for you, and it can be compiled into a book.'[37] Like Mofokeng and Naapo, Nise Malange urged grassroots organizations to counter sexism and black women to write actively:

> The struggle to change patriarchal attitudes, share the double shift and achieve higher wages and better working conditions, is being forced onto the agendas of organizations. As long as culture is not part of the same agenda, women miss one of the most powerful tools for bringing about cultural transformation.[38]

It is difficult to gauge whether anthologies such as *Malibongwe*, *Black Mamba Rising*, *Izinsingizi* and *Buang Basadi* had significant impact on women who lacked literacy in English. Yet these publications offered welcome opportunities for educated black women to explore issues of race, militancy, class and gender in poetry.

To assess the importance of black women's poems to this historical era, it is again useful to recall their socio-political context, this time through the lens of activist Jeremy Cronin, whose essays from the 1980s remain insightful on the role of 'insurgent' poetry. Cronin argues that this verse constitutes a counter-hegemonic form of orature:

> It can only be understood and analysed in its relation to a range of tradi-

tional and contemporary oral and verbal practices: songs, chants, slogans, funeral orations, political speeches, sermons, and graffiti. It can be understood only in terms of its major mode of presentation and reception. [...] We must contextualize it within the rolling wave of semi-insurrectionary uprisings, mass stayaways, political strikes, consumer boycotts, huge political funerals (involving anything up to seventy thousand mourners at a time), factory occupations, rent boycotts, school and university boycotts, mass rallies and physical confrontation over barricades with security forces.[39]

Cronin investigates such verbal devices as phonic exaggeration and lengthened final syllables (for example, 'cuppa-ta-lismmmmma' for 'capitalism'), strategies that 'give the English a pronounced, indeed, an exaggerated African texture'.[40] He also explores the ways in which these poetic techniques strike audiences as both indigenous and subversive: '"Capitalism," the signifier, is taken over, smacked about on the lips, and transformed.'[41] Although the poems that Cronin analyses were performed by black male artists, his insights apply as well to the poetry of women insurgents. *Malibongwe* poets such as Mabuza and Ntsongo mocked the architects of apartheid and rallied the masses via radio, while worker poets such as Malange and Naidoo inspired activists at May Day celebrations and mourned the plight of rural women before urban audiences. Resistance poetry thus served 'to mobilize and unite large groups of people. It transform[ed] them into a collective that is capable of facing down a viciously oppressive and well-equipped police and army [...]. It forc[ed] open space [...] for people to govern themselves in this land of their birth.'[42] Cronin may overreach in his claims; no literature of resistance protected black citizens from police brutality or defeated apartheid; but it energized dissidents and contributed to political transformation.

The issue of resistance poetry's reception in post-apartheid South Africa is a thorny one. In a collaborative essay written in 1990, members of Durban's Culture and Working Life Project raised a plaintive query: 'Will these times we are living through be *remembered* through our work?'[43] Throughout history revolutionary artists have risked, if they are polemical, their art being disparaged or forgotten once the crisis has passed. Indeed, the increasingly hegemonic emphasis on struggle poetry as the only appropriate type of writing produced a backlash around 1989, best illustrated in ANC activist Albie Sachs's call for a five-year moratorium on the claim that 'culture is a weapon of struggle' in order to free artists 'still trapped in the multiple ghettoes of the apartheid imagination' and to 'shake off the gravity of their anguish'.[44] Although fierce debates ensued among activists and scholars, the majority endorsed Sachs's position that literary critics should develop 'broad parameters rather than narrow ones' – with 'the criterion being pro- or anti-apartheid' – and that artists should 'write better poems and make better films and compose better music'.[45] On the face of it these creative goals seemed reasonable, and Sachs acknowledged the contributions of anti-apartheid art. Cultural critic Njabulo Ndebele shared Sachs's concern about the dominance of struggle art: 'How do we free ourselves from notions of culture that are tied to the ethos of oppression?'[46] Yet as a partial result of these debates, poetry-in-arms receded from the literary limelight, and militant poets suffered from a 'crisis of position' in the emergent culture.[47] In an ironic gender reversal, male poets arguably were marginalized to a greater extent than women, in part because the latter's themes signified a 'new South Africa' that was embracing racial and gender equality.

Critical examination of black women's literature increased dramatically during the early 1990s, as feminism gained influence through the prominence of the Women's National Coalition (WNC), a 560-member umbrella organization of women's groups from across the political spectrum that initiated further dialogue about gender rights and the new constitution. Led by Frene Ginwala, ANC Research Director (now Speaker of the South African Parliament), the WNC developed a Women's Charter to accompany the nation's new Bill of Rights. Furthermore, the WNC challenged apartheid *and* patriarchy. Inspired by the WNC and the Rural Women's Movement, which offered literacy training to village women, a Black South African feminism developed around three assumptions: that women's identities are shaped by interlocking race, class and gender oppression; that feminist struggle must encompass the struggle for freedom from a 'brutal white state'; and that women must 'challenge and transform Black patriarchies even though Black men have been our allies in the fight for national liberation'.[48]

In the academy, feminists extended scholarly attention to militant, worker and anti-sexist poetry. Some analyses provoked controversy: for example, Cecily Lockett's claim that white scholars should 'develop a more sympathetic womanist discourse' for analysing black women's writing, whose value she considered 'primarily socio-historical'.[49] Other white feminists proved more insightful: Lynda Gilfillan rightly argued that the *Malibongwe* poems were important to the ANC's historical development, and Dorothy Driver reasoned thoughtfully that many black women in the 1990s found in writing a place 'to locate or create new selves away from the "camouflage of coherence," the political order which stereotypes them in another's eyes'.[50] US critic Anthony O'Brien devoted a chapter of his study of South African literature to Malange's poems and praised feminist and worker poetry as 'the beginning of the radical impulses that matter most in the transformation of South African culture beyond its normalization in the image of Western capitalism'.[51] Black feminists scrutinized the writers of *Buang Basadi* in a 1990 issue of the journal *Current Writing* devoted to feminist criticism. Zoe Wicomb praised Mofokeng and Malange for their decision 'not to protect patriarchy' in analysing barriers to women's writing.[52] Malange's claim that 'you do not have to be [...] specially gifted to be able to tell or write a story' evoked criticism from Sisi Maqagi, who viewed it as 'symptomatic of the successful way in which black women have, in spite of their conscious resistance, imperceptibly absorbed devalued images of themselves'.[53] Wicomb expressed concern over black writers' naivety, as revealed in Naapo's assertion that illiterate women should seek scribes:

> Far from offering a new paradigm for art and writing (who would recommend illiteracy for the writer?), it tells us something about the conditions of textual production, about naïve attitudes towards the mediated text and points to an area of enquiry where the voices in texts struggle for dominance. Our culture boasts of a number of such ambiguous biographies-autobiographies of illiterate servants written by white women whose voices cannot be effaced.[54]

In advocating attention to how textual meaning is produced as well as to content, academics such as Maqagi and Wicomb seemed to some grassroots writers overly theoretical, to others incisive.

In addition to evaluating the feminist reception of black women's poetry of the 1980s, it is important to consider what this body of writing has contributed to the shifting field of South African literary studies. From my point of view, this poetry offers three key contributions: new insights regarding textual hybridity, fresh metaphors of geography and place and a distinctive role in the reevaluation of oral literature. Regarding issues of hybridity, a widely accepted critical axiom purports that the contemporary signifier 'South African literature' can be characterized either as ruptured or as re-emerging. One proponent of the former view, Leon de Kock, claims that any concept of a unitary national literature conceals a 'referential fracture' because of the various languages, cultures and forms represented by oral bushmen's song, the Dutch epic of colonial occupation, the transnational English lyric and the modern poem in Afrikaans, all examples of the 'thoroughly polyglot South African scene'.[55] As a result of the history of colonialism and apartheid, English-language publication remains the most visible body of literature, yet it represents only a small portion of the poetry available. Because of this vexed hybridity, South African literature cannot be considered an integrated field. Rather, it exists in a 'poetics of the seam' where 'difference and sameness are hitched together' and a discursive 'shadow of doubleness' lurks.[56]

Ingrid de Kok, in contrast, promulgates a view of South African literature as healthily hybrid, enhanced by vibrant postnationalist reassessment and reinvention. While a dualistic view of South African literature as troubled by the 'harsh landscape of the past' and a 'hazy vista of the future' is tempting, de Kok prefers to explore this literature's 'connective tissue'.[57] Although she acknowledges that the body of written and oral texts designated South African contains rough edges and lacunae, she finds its hybridity exciting: 'South African literature interacts in a global market, and the "interfluences" within the country are further enriched by exchanges with a variety of international forms and practices.'[58] While a 'shadow of doubleness' appears in the racially polarized discourse of certain *Malibongwe* poems, feminist and worker poetry moves away from dichotomous language to provide the 'connective tissue' of which de Kok speaks. Furthermore, the *Buang Basadi* poets and their critics from *Current Writing* interact vigorously with a global literary market. Both Mofokeng and Wicomb have acknowledged the 'interfluence' of African, Afro-British and African-American women writers upon their work, especially Bessie Head, Miriam Tlali, Hazel Carby, Toni Morrison and Alice Walker.[59] Finally, the healthy hybridity of militant, worker and feminist poetry appears in its fluid blending of English and indigenous languages.

With regard to the second contribution to South African literary studies, new geographical metaphors, black women's poetry offers distinctive perspectives on a familiar theme. In South Africa, landscape, contours, ridges and vistas figure prominently as critical and poetic tropes. For example, the white dissident novelist Breyten Breytenbach has chronicled both colonialism and postcolonialism in gendered, hybrid and environmental metaphors:

> What I want to write about is the penetration, expansion, skirmishing, coupling, mixing, separation, regrouping of people and cultures – the glorious bastardization of men and women mutually shaped by sky and rain and wind and soil.[60]

Similarly, critic Stephen Gray has analysed South African literature as a form of 'boundary crossing', a trading across linguistic, racial, gender and socio-economic barriers.[61] Land-based metaphors and gendered boundary crossings abound in the poetry of *Malibongwe*, *Black Mamba Rising*, *Izinsingizi* and *Buang Basadi*. Recall, for example, Mabuza's celebration of Manguang for both its indigenous identity as 'the meeting place of leopards' and its modern identity as a site of contestation. Or consider Malange's poetic representation of her peripatetic childhood in geographic terms, as her family moved from a squatters' shack in Vrygrond to 'standard housing' without electricity in Nyanga East township, and then to a different life in the bundu of the Transkei, 'collecting cowdung [...] / and wandering in the forests to bring wood to light the fires'.[62] As Rita Barnard has noted, in its 'cataloguing of all strategic sites of struggle', anti-apartheid poetry offered a valuable form of 'cognitive mapping' through which 'places of exclusion' became 'places of empowerment'.[63] Black women's poetry participated in such cognitive mapping by illuminating how sites of racial and gender exclusion could become sites of resistance and remembering.

Regarding the third contribution to South African literary studies, an emphasis on orality, black women's poetry of the 1980s anticipated the efforts of recent literary scholars to reevaluate the cultural significance of oral poetry as South Africa has attempted to remake its government and its art.

Especially prominent have been debates as to whether oral forms represent a quintessential, precolonial African genre or whether these forms have been problematically hybridized. As scholar Masizi Kunene explains, 'to Africans, written literature violated one of the most important literary tenets by privatizing literature', since its traditional value accrued by 'being disseminated in communally organized contexts'.[64] By associating writing negatively with privatization and orality positively with communalism, Kunene seems to endorse the perspective of oral forms as 'purely' African. Yet black women's anti-apartheid poetry defies such categorization, as does 1980s struggle poetry more generally, because it was usually written and published in English yet also disseminated orally and communally. Another scholar, Isabel Hofmeyr, celebrates oral literature's hybridity, claiming that its study belongs 'not in some "traditional" space, but in a contemporary globalized world in which oral forms compete with, circulate alongside, and mutate with other cultural forms'.[65] Women's militant and worker poems reveal the subversive potential of such mutations, since they disrupt the gendered assumptions of *izibongo* by featuring women *izimbongi* who praise publicly their female counterparts.

Although South African resistance literature has not traditionally been considered in a Cold War context, such recontextualization seems vital. After all, anti-apartheid writing intensified during the 1980s because of support for the apartheid regime by US President Ronald Reagan, who deplored the resistance movement's communist ties and sympathized with the Nationalist Party. Defying the will of Congress and heeding the calls of conservative multinational corporate leaders, Reagan adopted a policy of 'constructive engagement' with the apartheid government, which he shockingly praised for having 'eliminated the segregation that we once had in our own country'.[66] In contrast, the economic sanctions and cultural boycott that progressive European nations and certain US cities and artists imposed on South Africa in the 1980s arguably hastened the National Party's disintegration, the negotiated release from prison of Nelson Mandela and the success of the newly constituted, democratic ANC.[67] Black women's poetry contributed to an international body of Cold War literature by exposing the apartheid state's atrocities, by praising resistant workers and militants and by insisting that gender take centre stage in the ANC's political agenda. By extending the boundaries of historical memory, this poetry continues to work against forgetting.

Notes

1 See, for example, Richard M. Freed, *The Russians Are Coming! The Russians Are Coming!: Pageantry and Patriotism in Cold-War America* (1998); Ron Robin, *The Making of the Cold War Enemy: Culture and Politics in the Military-Intellectual Complex* (2001); and Stephen J. Whitfield, *The Culture of the Cold War* (1991).
2 For useful background into the origins and politics of apartheid see Nigel Worden, *The Making of Modern South Africa: Conquest, Segregation, and Apartheid* (1994).

3 For a detailed account of these forms of resistance see A. Marx, *Lessons of Struggle: South African Internal Opposition, 1960–1990* (1992).
4 Barney Mthombothi, 'Introduction', in Fatima Meer, ed., *Resistance in the Townships* (Durban: Madiba Publications, 1989), pp. 2–8.
5 Gordimer, 'Writers in South Africa: The New Black Poets', in Rowland Smith, ed., *Exile and Tradition* (London: Longman and Dalhousie University Press, 1976), p. 134.
6 Shava, *A People's Voice: Black South African Writing in the Twentieth Century* (London: Zed Books, 1989), pp. 3–9.
7 For details on South African women's history see the video *You Have Struck a Rock: Women and Struggle in South Africa* (Berkeley: South Africa Media Project, 1986); and Judy Kimble and Elaine Unterhalter, '"We Opened the Road for You, You Must Go Forward": ANC Women's Struggles, 1912–1982', *Feminist Review*, 12 (1982), pp. 11–35.
8 Albie Sachs, 'Preparing Ourselves for Freedom', in Ingrid de Kok and Karen Press, eds, *Spring Is Rebellious: Arguments about Cultural Freedom* (Cape Town: Buchu Books, 1990), p. 19.
9 Stacey Stent, 'The Wrong Ripple', in de Kok and Press, eds, *Spring Is Rebellious*, p. 74; Sachs, 'Preparing Ourselves', p. 20.
10 De Kok, 'Standing in the Doorway: A Preface', *World Literature Today*, 70: 1 (1996), pp. 4–8.
11 DeShazer, *A Poetics of Resistance: Women Writing in El Salvador, South Africa, and the United States* (Ann Arbor: University of Michigan Press, 1994), pp. 133–231.
12 Molefe, ed., 'Foreword' to Molefe, *Malibongwe – ANC Women: Poetry Is Also Their Struggle* (Stockholm: ANC, 1982), p. 4.
13 Ibid., p. 4.
14 Mtshali, 'Black Poetry in South Africa', in Christopher Heywood, ed., *Aspects of South African Literature* (London: Heinemann, 1976), p. 127.
15 Mphahlele, 'The Tyranny of Place and Aesthetics: The South African Case', in Charles Malan, ed., *Race and Literature* (Pinetown, SA: Owen Burgess Publishers, 1987), p. 54.
16 Nkosi, 'Fiction by Black South Africans', in G. D. Killam, ed., *African Writers on African Writing* (London: Heinemann, 1973), p. 110.
17 Molefe, 'Foreword', p. 4.
18 Bethlehem, '"A Primary Need as Strong as Hunger": The Rhetoric of Urgency in South African Literary Culture under Apartheid', *Poetics Today*, 22: 2 (2001), pp. 366–72, 381–3.
19 Molefe, 'Foreword', p. 4.
20 Mabuza, 'Manguang', in Molefe, ed., *Malibongwe*, p. 9, line 8.
21 The phrase 'polemical historicity' appears in Barbara Harlow, *Resistance Literature* (New York: Methuen, 1987), p. 37.
22 Gunner, 'Songs of Innocence and Experience: Women as Composers and Performers of *Izibongo*, Zulu Praise Poetry', in Cherry Clayton, ed., *Women and Writing in Southern Africa: A Critical Anthology* (London: Heinemann, 1989), pp. 11–12.
23 Ntsongo, 'Women Arise', in Molefe, ed., *Malibongwe*, pp. 49–50, lines 1–29.
24 Sitas, 'Introduction' to Sitas, ed., *Black Mamba Rising: South African Worker Poets in Struggle* (Durban: Culture and Working Life Publications, 1986), p. 1.
25 Malange, 'First May 1985', in Sitas, ed., *Black Mamba Rising*, p. 53, lines 17–24.
26 Jeremy Cronin, '"Even Under the Rine of Terror . . .": Insurgent South African Poetry,' *Research in African Literatures*, 19 (1988), p. 19.
27 Sitas, 'Introduction', pp. 1–2.
28 Malange, 'Nightshift Mother', in Gill Evill, ed., *Izinsingizi – Loudhailer Lives:*

South African Poetry from Natal (Durban: Culture and Working Life Publications, 1988), pp. 15–16, lines 1–11.
29 Naidoo, 'I Remember', in Evill, ed., *Izinsingizi*, p. 27, lines 3–5, 11.
30 Malange, speaking in COSAW, ed., *Buang Basadi / Khulumani Makhosikazi / Women Speak: Conference on Women and Writing* (Johannesburg: COSAW Publications, 1989), p. 12.
31 Naidoo, speaking in M.J. Daymond and Margaret Lenta, 'Workshop on Black Women's Writing and Reading', *Current Writing: Text and Reception in Southern Africa*, 2: 1 (1990), p. 74.
32 Mofokeng, speaking in COSAW, ed., *Buang Basadi*, p. 8.
33 Mofokeng, 'Liberate My Soul', in COSAW, ed., *Buang Basadi*, p. 18, lines 4–11.
34 Gloria Mtungwa, 'Militant Beauty', in Molefe, ed., *Malibongwe*, p. 51.
35 Mofokeng, speaking in COSAW, ed., *Buang Basadi*, p. 8.
36 Naapo, 'Madam', in COSAW, ed., *Buang Basadi*, p. 18, lines 1–4, 7, 13–18.
37 Naapo, speaking in COSAW, ed., *Buang Basadi*, p. 10.
38 Malange, speaking in COSAW, ed., *Buang Basadi*, p. 12.
39 Cronin, 'Under the Rine of Terror', p. 12.
40 Ibid., p. 14.
41 Ibid., p. 14.
42 Ibid., p. 22.
43 Culture and Working Life Project, 'Albie Sachs Must Not Worry', in de Kok and Press, eds, *Spring Is Rebellious*, p. 102.
44 Sachs, 'Preparing Ourselves', p. 21.
45 Ibid., p. 28.
46 Ndebele, *South African Literature and Culture: Rediscovery of the Ordinary* (Manchester: Manchester University Press, 1994), p. 124.
47 Rita Barnard attributes this phrase to Mark Devenney. See Barnard, 'Speaking Places: Prison, Poetry, and the South African Nation', *Research in African Literatures*, 32: 3 (2001), http://muse.jhu.edu/journals/research_in _african_literatures (accessed September 2004).
48 Amanda Kemp, Nozizwe Madlala, Asha Moodley and Elaine Salo, 'The Dawn of a New Day: Redefining South African Feminism', in Amrita Basu, ed., *The Challenge of Local Feminisms: Women's Movements in Global Perspective* (Boulder: Westview Press, 1995), pp. 133, 144–54.
49 Lockett, 'Feminism(s) and Writing in English in South Africa', *Current Writing: Text and Reception in Southern Africa*, 2: 1 (1990), pp. 17–19.
50 Gilfillan, 'Black Women Poets in Exile: The Weapon of Words', *Tulsa Studies in Women's Literature*, 11: 1 (1992), pp. 79–80; Driver, 'Transformation through Art: Writing, Representation, and Subjectivity in Recent South African Fiction', *World Literature Today*, 70: 1 (1996), p. 46. Driver attributes the phrase 'camouflage of coherence' to Zoe Wicomb.
51 O'Brien, *Against Normalization: Writing Radical Democracy in South Africa* (Durham, NC: Duke University Press, 2001), p. 2.
52 Wicomb, 'To Hear the Variety of Discourses', *Current Writing: Text and Reception in Southern Africa*, 2: 1 (1990), p. 39.
53 Maqagi, 'Who Theorizes?', *Current Writing: Text and Reception in Southern Africa*, 2: 1 (1990), p. 24.
54 Wicomb, 'To Hear the Variety of Discourses', p. 40.
55 De Kock, 'South Africa in the Global Imaginary: An Introduction', *Poetics Today*, 22: 2 (2001), p. 264.
56 Ibid., pp. 282–6.
57 De Kock, 'Standing in the Doorway', p. 6.
58 Ibid., p. 7.

59 Daymond and Lenta, 'Workshop', p. 85; Wicomb, 'To Hear the Variety of Discourses', pp. 35–44.
60 Breytenbach, *Dog Heart: A Travel Memoir* (Cape Town: Human and Rousseau, 1998), p. 41.
61 Gray, 'Some Problems of Writing Historiography in Southern Africa', *Literator*, 10: 2 (1989), p. 21.
62 Malange, 'A Time of Madness', in Evill, ed., *Izinsingizi*, pp. 12–13, lines 33–6.
63 Barnard, 'Speaking Places', pp. 10–11.
64 Kunene, 'Some Aspects of South African Literature', *World Literature Today*, 70: 1 (1996), p. 16.
65 Hofmeyr, 'Not the Magic Talisman: Rethinking Oral Literature in South Africa', *World Literature Today*, 70: 1 (1996), p. 90.
66 David Corn, 'Reagan's Bloody Legacy', *TomPaine.Common Sense*, http://www.tompaine.com (accessed 6 September 2004); see also Christopher Coker, *The United States and South Africa, 1968–1985: Constructive Engagement and Its Critics* (1986).
67 On this point see Stephen Anzovin, *South Africa: Apartheid and Divestiture* (1987).

12 Outwitting the politburo
Politics and poetry behind the Iron Curtain

Piotr Kuhiwczak

In her poem 'The End and the Beginning', written only four years after the end of communism in Eastern Europe, Wisława Szymborska contemplated our ability to relegate even the most traumatic events to the realm of history, implying that forgetting the past is both natural and inevitable. What is more, she appeared to suggest that, once the conflict is over, it is neither defeat nor victory that matters, but the practical issues that the onset of peace forces us to confront. The first line of the poem boldly declares that 'After every war someone has to tidy up'.[1] The process of cleaning up takes countless forms and is neither morally heroic nor visually dramatic: there are 'no sound bites, no photo opportunities, / and it takes years. / All the cameras have gone / to other wars' (lines 18–21). Szymborska ends the poem with a reflection on the onset of total amnesia:

> From time to time someone still must
> dig up a rusted argument
> from underneath a bush
> and haul it off to the dump.
>
> Those who knew what this was all about
> must make way for those
> who know little.
> And less than that.
> And at last nothing less than nothing.
> (lines 33–41)

When the poem came out, commentators linked it to the Yugoslav wars rather than to the end of communism, which implies that even in the early 1990s the end of communism was beginning to be eclipsed by other more topical events. It would be pointless to debate which specific event inspired Szymborska to write this poem because its mastery depends precisely on the fact that we do not know which conflict she had in mind when she put pen to paper. For those who had the misfortune to live many years in the shadow of the Cold War and who still remember the gruesome realities of the eastern side of the Iron Curtain, the poem is perhaps a painfully sobering but nevertheless effective antidote to what the Yugoslavs aptly call *yugonostalgia*: a longing for the idealized world of a socialist state with secure jobs, crèches, paid holidays, dissidents, secret police and street demonstrations.[2] Even more sobering is a discovery that for contemporary students such concepts as 'the Soviet Union', 'détente' and *'perestroika'* are as alien as the terminology relating to the Reformation or the French Revolution.[3] For a while the newly opened archives in Eastern Europe and Russia gave employment to historians, but on the whole the discourse about the Cold War has been replaced by discourse about 'restitution', 'transition', 'return to Europe' and eventually about EU membership. An earlier interest in Eastern European literatures and languages waned just after 1989, and Nobel Prizes for Czesław Miłosz, Wisława Szymborska and more recently Imre Kertész have not reversed this general trend.[4]

It may just be the case that every momentous historical event needs to be forgotten in order to be rediscovered and studied decades later by means of scholarly diligence and objective distance. Perhaps only at the point when we know 'less than nothing', as Szymborska says, we can get interested again in long-forgotten events. The success of Norman Davies's books on the city of Breslau/Wrocław and most recently on the Warsaw Uprising show that this delayed response to history has its advantages.[5] But if history has got clear linear characteristics and is firmly embedded in time, it would be difficult to view literature in the same way. Although some literary works have a limited lease of life and are very much products of a particular *Zeitgeist*, on the whole we do not read poems or novels for their historical value. Literature can transcend not only historical but also cultural and linguistic boundaries. Its value is primarily aesthetic, and the fact that we have no problem discussing William Shakespeare in the context of Greek tragedy illustrates literature's unusual ability to liberate us from the constraints of temporal boundaries.[6]

If this is the case, can we say that literature, and more generally art, is at present the most useful and functional remnant of the Cold War period? With the possible exception of a realist novel, it is certainly not the aim of literature to depict or represent reality faithfully, and it would be wrong to treat literary works solely as a source of knowledge about life behind the Iron Curtain. However, while all Eastern European writing is in some sense representational, its relation during the Cold War to a climate of repression and censorship is revealing, and perhaps its greatest inherent value is the ability to tell us what it means to live and write under pressure. This aspect of Eastern European writing has not been lost on critics in the West. As early as 1965, in his aptly titled book *Under Pressure*, A. Alvarez wrote:

> the whole movement of *avant-garde* Western art during the last half-century has been one of a steady internal migration. Even our most politically minded writers seem to recreate society in terms of their own selves, from the outside in, as though their environment were a wide-

screen projection of their inner tensions. In Poland, despite its Western bias in artistic styles and preoccupations, precisely the reverse happens: the artists recreate themselves in terms of the public world; social facts become the equivalent of psychic phenomena, with the same inwardly reverberating power and inescapability. If there is a radical difference between the arts on either side of the Iron Curtain it is less in the kinds of pressure which impel the artists than in the directions in which those pressures force them.[7]

The value of this observation lies in the fact that Alvarez sees the art on either side of the political divide as complementary. Artists in Western and Eastern Europe belonged to the same tradition, but divergent political systems forced them to respond differently to external pressures. It was very unusual of a Western critic to take such a holistic view. On the whole, during the period of Soviet domination, Eastern European writers were perceived in the West as political creatures, as either dissidents or collaborators. Additionally, these simplistic attitudes were strongly coloured by domestic politics. Even as the Berlin Wall was crumbling, Euro-communists and some of their socialist allies were hoping that Soviet communism could be transformed into 'socialism with a human face'. In contrast, the right often saw literature from behind the Iron Curtain as yet one more form of protest against communist rule.[8] The tendency to politicize the literature affected even such distinguished writers as Stephen Spender. In the introduction to a volume of Polish poetry published as late as 1980, after having listed countless misfortunes that fell on Poland over several hundred years, he wrote:

> These are realities with which poets and poetry in our part of the world do not have to deal. Not having to do so must make a poet from the West who reads the work by Polish dissidents in the present volume ask himself [*sic*] how he uses his freedom for the purposes of writing his poetry. By contrast with this tremendous burden of suffering, oppression, torment and injustice, he feels that many of our preoccupations as poets in the West are trivial. The poets writing in this volume may not be free: but the very lack of freedom becomes their tremendous subject matter. At the same time it is a terrible demonstration of the lack of freedom that they seem condemned by it to write variations on themes of oppression. The totalitarian state chooses the themes that poets write about just because they are in bitter opposition to totalitarianism.[9]

The choice of poem Spender was asked to reflect upon could be counted a mitigating circumstance here. Additionally, he admitted that accessibility through translation was a difficulty bound to influence critical judgement. Nevertheless, statements like this one were influential and contributed substantially to the general view of what it meant to write under political pressure.

It is important then that we remind ourselves that literature behind the Iron Curtain was not political in the way that politics was understood on the Western side of the divide. Because of imperial domination, some countries in Eastern Europe developed literary traditions centred on what one Polish critic calls the 'romantic paradigm'.[10] The Hungarian and Polish uprisings of the early and mid nineteenth century generated both 'national' poets, such as Adam Mickiewicz and Sandor Pötöfi, and a wealth of secondary literature deeply immersed in the politics of the day. The paradigm weakened briefly after the First World War, when countries such as Poland, Hungary and Czechoslovakia gained independence, but the Nazi and Soviet occupations revived politically conditioned writing. However, post-Second-World-War realities were not as conducive to the fuelling of the 'romantic paradigm' as the earlier dominations. The sophistication of state control in the Soviet empire required from writers the deployment of a more advanced survival strategy. In *The Captive Mind* (1953), Czesław Miłosz analysed how the new empire set to dominate the minds of its citizens not only by means of brutal coercion but also through a combination of seduction and political pressure. In the countries that found themselves in the Soviet sphere of influence, cultural policy was based on a system of total governmental control modelled on the Soviet prototype, which in turn drew on systems that had been developed in tsarist Russia.[11] The main element of this system was so-called preventive censorship, which meant that every manuscript had to be submitted to censors before the publication could go into print. The censors had clearly defined lists of topics that were not supposed to be mentioned publicly, but they were also looking for allusions and potential interpretation of innocuous phrases. One could say that a well-trained censor was supposed to know what the reception studies scholars in Germany call the readers' 'horizon of expectations'.[12] In the countries that were incorporated into the Soviet Union this basic model worked until the end of the empire. In the satellite states of Eastern Europe the censorship arrangements gradually evolved into a more subtle but also more dangerous system, and in the 'late' phase of the empire – that is, from approximately the 1970s onwards – the combination of coercion and seduction outlined by Miłosz was getting more pervasive. In 1987, a Hungarian intellectual, Miklós Haraszti, called this totalitarian phenomenon a 'velvet prison', which gives us a good sense of how Miłosz's 'captive mind' had evolved over a period of just a few decades:

> Censorship is no longer a matter of simple state intervention. A new aesthetic culture has emerged in which censors and artists alike are entangled in a mutual embrace. Nor is it as distasteful as traditional critics of censorship imagine. The state is able to domesticate the artist because the artist has already made the state his home.[13]

Thus totalitarianism creates more than one trap for art. Tacit collaboration is one option, but hard resistance to totalitarian power may easily create its own totalitarian response. So poets who wrote overtly oppositional poetry found themselves in the same position as pamphleteers before them. Their writing was topical, and popular with the readers, but short-lived and not always of a good literary standard.[14] Nevertheless, it would be a falsification of history to say that the Soviet empire alone altered Eastern Europe's traditional 'romantic paradigm'. Many writers who survived the war in German-occupied Europe found it hard to continue as if nothing had happened. How to write in the postwar period was a difficult issue for all Europeans, but Theodor Adorno's bold statement that it was impossible to write poetry after Auschwitz had a cathartic value only for the West. For the East, as it was defined by the Yalta agreement, the war did not end in 1945, and, for all its horrific significance, Auschwitz did not stand for the end of civilization. On the contrary, the experience of Auschwitz proved that although culture was fragile, it had an immense capacity for survival, very often at a cost in human life.

It was not an accident that poetry turned out to be the best asylum for cultural values. Its resilience had already been proved in prewar Stalinist Russia, where Osip Mandelshtam's and Anna Akhmatova's poetry survived only because it was possible to memorize it. After the Stalinist terror came to an end, poetry became even more useful as a form of social communication. Poems are short, they can be easily written down, passed on in multiple carbon copies, written on scraps of paper, circulated among a small group of friends and smuggled in and out of prisons and internment camps. Their language is highly metaphoric and often enigmatic, and their meanings can be shared only by those who understand the codes, subtexts and veiled allusions. For all these reasons, poetry in Eastern Europe had a much wider appeal than in the West. In countries where capitalist social structures were not allowed to develop, poetry readers constituted a distinct social class. What Nadezhda Mandelshtam says in *Hope against Hope* about the Russian intelligentsia applies to some extent to the whole of Eastern and Central Europe:

> Poetry does indeed have a very special place in this country. It arouses people and shapes their minds. No wonder the birth of our new intelligentsia is accompanied by a craving for poetry never seen before – it is the golden treasury in which our values are preserved; it brings people back to life, awakens their conscience and stirs them to thought. Why this should happen I do not know, but it is a fact.[15]

But it is not only the question of social class which is interesting here. What this quotation also touches upon is the formal clash between long-standing traditions and a new doctrine. The tenets of Soviet cultural policy were developed early on by Lenin, but their practical implications began to be felt strongly in the early 1930s just after the First All-Union Congress of Soviet Writers held in 1934. It was at this congress that the Communist Party declared 'socialist realism' to be the only method of depicting reality in a work of art. But depicting alone was not sufficient: an artist had to use art actively for re-shaping the world and establishing a new proletarian social order. After 1945 this method was transplanted wholesale to Eastern Europe, where the unions of writers, modelled on the Union of Soviet Writers, had to adopt socialist realism as the dominant artistic convention. Unsurprisingly, prose became a preferred genre under the new regime, and Maxim Gorky became a classic of the genre, translated into all languages used in the region. But poetry was more problematic, not being a genre that comfortably co-exists with a realist approach. Realist poetry, even if written without political pressure, quickly degenerates into pamphlet-style propaganda,[16] which is why some poets, who did not want to compromise their art or produce obligatory hymns praising the wisdom of Stalin, withdrew from the active artistic life and confined themselves to internal emigration.

A few years after Stalin's death, when the political terror eased, the 'silenced' poets began to ask themselves whether it was now possible to write freely in a socialist state. What they needed to consider were the style, the subject matter and the poetic strategies that might allow them to preserve freedom of expression under circumstances in which freedom was not tolerated. The choices were limited because the state held a total monopoly on publishing. The monopoly was eventually broken in the 1970s with the rise of clandestine publishing, or 'samizdat', which flourished at first in Poland and then to some extent in other Eastern bloc countries. The emergence of the independent presses was obviously of particular importance for poetry, which, as mentioned, could be easily passed from hand to hand on single sheets of paper. Eventually, by the mid-1980s, many poets published more in the underground presses than in the state-run publishing houses. This dual system meant that the same poet was able to publish freely in clandestine publications and more cautiously in the state publishing houses, where, because the censor's eye was trained to identify allusions even when they were not intended, censorship was unpredictable. The tug of war between the poet and the censor was often described as a 'cat and mouse' game. The allusions and the symbolic language were becoming more esoteric, while the censors' suspicion was sharpened with each new version of the poem they were asked to scrutinize. The absurdity of the system in Poland is perhaps best illustrated by the case of translated poetry by John Donne and George Herbert being censored because the translator was considered politically suspect.[17] But it is not only writing that was affected by censorship. The schizophrenia of this dual publishing was mirrored in a schizophrenia of dual reading. The clandestine publications, although obtained with difficulty and a degree of risk, allowed for free and independent reading, while the censored texts required from the reader critical skill of a higher order, a particularly close reading that attempted a reconstruction of what the text *might* have contained before it was censored. Some of the strategies were analysed in detail before and just after the collapse of the

Berlin Wall,[18] but today, long after the momentous events, we can clearly see that a lot of writing that was considered then as topical and representative has not survived well as literature. This concerns in equal measure overtly political poetry published by the clandestine presses, and allusive poetry touched by the deadly red pencil of the censor. The first kind of writing was too close to political events of the day, and like all political poetry it ceases to interest a reader of poetry and becomes relevant only to a literary historian. The overtly allusive poetry loses its value when censorship no longer exists and when the reader's eye is no longer capable of decoding deletions that might have taken place in the process of censorship. As the memory of oppression recedes into the distant past, one contemporary critic looks at Eastern European poetry without seeing it as a 'special case':

> Aha! Let us remove this bushel of oppression, and substitute the dazzling neon of re-nascent capitalism. Fifty years inveighing against the Capitalist, and now you must worship the entrepreneur (who sees no duty to keep you alive). What does this do to poetry?[19]

Obviously, the question refers to poetry written today, but we may extend its scope and ask how the change of circumstances alters the reading of poetry that was written before the 'dazzling neon' was switched on. Which strategies have survived and why?

On re-reading poetry from behind the Iron Curtain, we can identify two criteria that determine which writing has survived well and which has not. The first is an ability to contextualize immediate historical circumstances and to relate them to other places and literary traditions, often to old empires and to the classical world. The second is an attempt to place communist *homo politicus* against a whole range of human and animal behaviours in order to test its self-proclaimed superiority over all previous types of social formations. Both approaches required a great deal of emotional detachment from the grim realities of the communist world, as well as a good dose of scientific scepticism towards all social systems we generate as human beings. They also proved useful in deflecting the censor's attention from what might be perceived as applicable to the immediate circumstances. If a poem appeared to be about ancient Greeks, or the animal world, then it was hard to strike it out as anti-socialist commentary. After all, state-sponsored publications had to be filled with something, and not every censor was highly trained in close reading of the poetic language.

The first factor is particularly conspicuous in Polish poetry, and it was used as an effective artistic device mainly because the inclusion of Poland within the Soviet empire was seen by the Poles as a relegation to the peripheries of the known world. In his volume of essays, *Witness of Poetry*, Miłosz stated that he was born on the border between Rome and Byzantium, an area of Europe that was perceived by Western Europe as a culturally blank space, one that Miłosz termed *Ubi leones*.[20] Paradoxically, this geographical and political marginalization contrasted strongly with the wide-ranging significance of the ideological experiments that were taking place on the borders of the old and new empires. What was to become a poetic metaphor originated in actual experience. Another Polish poet, Zbigniew Herbert, before becoming a citizen of the People's Republic, also experienced the clash of civilizations under the rule of four other regimes: Polish, Soviet, German and Ukrainian. The countries of this region have always been dominated by competing empires, religions and ideologies, and as a result the pull of Western tradition has always been felt much more strongly than in countries situated further West.

The poetic device that emerged from this configuration was based on a contrast between the world of the Soviet empire and that of the West, which was epitomized as a classical and Mediterranean civilization. As a result the poetry written in the distant east is teeming with classical motifs, and Greek and Latin gods populate these brief but cogent poems. Artur Miedzyrzecki's poem 'End of the Game' gives a good idea of the complexity of the situation. It turns on the death of the Polish princess, Wanda, who refuses the marriage to a German duke required of her by the Polish state.

> Instead of becoming the empress of joined kingdoms
> As suggested by her father's counsellors
> Instead of renouncing her vain delusions
> In favour of the great-four-poster of history where in full view of the world
> Foetuses of dynasties are conceived
> And even the earliest embryo can be assured of the profoundest happiness
> Which his reign will secure for his future subjects
>
> Instead of living up to these basic obligations of sovereigns
> Which time and again were called to her mind by her father the king
> Princess Wanda rejects the marriage offer of a mighty duke
> And plunges into the Vistula
>
> The game is therefore interrupted
> The dark century begins
> And there isn't even a chronicler to record with care
> The dialogue of Polish Creon and Polish Antigone
>
> We all come from her
> On this land of suicidal leaps
> Where so often there was no other way out
> And there are always so many gaps in documents.[21]

This example is a good one to show how the meanings of Greek culture were reactivated in the 'barbaric' East. One did not need to have much classical education to make sense of the poem. I remember myself that *Antigone* was a set text in my grammar school, and the curriculum required the teachers to organize a debate called 'The Choice of Antigone'. It is still not clear to me why the authorities did not foresee that the seemingly 'dead' Greek text would have such subversive force in the context of a neo-totalitarian system, but miracles used to happen even in atheist states. Although we were only 14, we realized that what the Greeks understood by the state was not exactly what we could see around us, and that under communism the family bond was indeed the only bond which remained outside its corrupting influence. As a result, our hearts went out to Antigone because she ignored the law of the state and buried her kin. It was only many years later, with the rise of Solidarity and a clandestine civil society, that my generation came to the conclusion that, in fact, Antigone's choice was a regression, and that a civil society can develop only when it is possible to construct a state which is not based on the principle of kinship. What is more the last four lines, where the past and the present tenses are cleverly interposed, suggest that the dilemma has not been resolved, and that essentially the socialist state is only another phase leading to more 'suicidal leaps'.

In this context, I hope it is easier to see why the lessons we could learn from classical culture became so important, and why the Greek and Roman gods migrated north in such large numbers. Once the classical world was re-evoked by poets, readers could grasp the truth that their predicament was by no means unique. Similar dilemmas had been encountered before, and useful parallels could be drawn between the follies of the past and the present, as they are by Herbert in a delightful poem entitled 'Damastes (Also Known As Procrustes) Speaks':

> My movable empire between Athens and Megara
> I ruled alone over forests ravines precipices
> without the advice of old men foolish insignia with a simple club
> dressed only in a shadow of a wolf
> and terror caused by the sound of the word Damastes
>
> I lacked subjects that is I had them briefly
> They didn't live as long as dawn however it is slander
> To say I was a bandit as the falsifiers of history claim
>
> In reality I was a scholar and social reformer
> My real passion was anthropometry
>
> I invented a bed with the measurements of a perfect man
> I compared the travelers I caught with this bed
> It was hard to avoid – I admit – stretching limbs cutting legs
> The patients died but the more there were who perished
> The more I was certain my research was right
> The goal was noble progress demands victims

I longed to abolish the difference between the high and the low
I wanted to give a single form to disgustingly varied humanity
I never stopped in my efforts to make people equal

My life was taken by Theseus the murderer of the innocent Minotaur
The one who went through the labyrinth with a woman's ball of yarn
An impostor full of tricks without principles or a vision of the future
    I have the well-grounded hope others will continue my labor
    And bring the task so boldly begun to its end.[22]

There has been no tyrant in ancient or modern history who has not somewhat resembled Damastes. All of them have had some good ideas and many have wanted humanity to be happy, but that happiness was always to be organized along clearly prescribed lines, never spontaneous. Unfortunately, humanity is 'disgustingly varied' (line 18) and something must be done to improve these irregularities. Unlike similar-sounding characters in Robert Browning's monologues, Damastes is neither mad nor emotionally disturbed. He carries out his project in a perfectly rational manner until Theseus, an ordinary man 'without principles or a vision of the future' (line 22), puts a stop to this experiment in human perfectibility that is costing so much blood. Perhaps one does not need to be a trained censor to see the allusions to communist doctrine here. The fifth stanza talks about equality, and cleverly puts this ideal in a critical light. Damastes and a communist commissar would agree that human variety needs to be curtailed with utmost determination in order to 'bring the task so boldly begun to its end' (line 24).

Although the poems I have quoted so far have serious implications, it is noticeable that they have a good deal of subtle irony too. And this is perhaps another thing which has been translated from Greece. This time, however, it is not Ancient Greece that I have in mind. If I were asked which European poet has exerted the strongest influence on Eastern Europe, I would say, without hesitation, C.P. Cavafy. Subtle irony, detachment, a muted voice and an oblique way of looking at the history of his own country have all earned him a firm place in the pantheon. Herbert's prose poem, 'From Mythology', shows the nature of the relationship between Cavafy and modern Eastern European poetry:

First there was a god of night and tempest, a black idol without eyes, before whom they leapt, naked and smeared with blood. Later on, in the times of the republic, there were many gods with wives, children, creaking beds, and harmlessly exploding thunderbolts. At the end only superstitious neurotics carried in their pockets little statues of salt, representing the god of irony. There was no greater god at that time.

Then came the barbarians. They too valued highly the little god of irony. They would crush it under their heels and add it to their dishes.[23]

Unlike in Cavafy's poem, 'Waiting for the Barbarians',[24] here the barbarians actually arrive and destroy the little god of irony. In his *Art of the Novel*, Milan Kundera quotes Rabelais, who invented the word *agelaste*, which comes from the Greek and describes a man with no sense of humour. Then Kundera writes:

> Never having heard God's laughter, the *agelastes* are convinced that the truth is obvious, that all men necessarily think the same thing, and that they themselves are exactly what they think they are. But it is precisely in losing the certainty of truth and the unanimous agreement of others that man becomes individual.[25]

It is irony and an ability to look at things from a distance which distinguishes culture from barbarism and real writers from pretend ones. Cavafy was a master of both distance and irony. Looking at Greek culture from afar, he saw what usually escaped others. In his poem about the fall of Constantinople he did not mourn the city, but pondered the predicament of the demotic culture of the Pontic Greeks. On a closer look one sees that Cavafy's version of Greek history is not the unconditional triumph of civilization we might like to think. Cavafy reveals this history through his carefully drawn portraits of ambiguous characters. Folly and blindness appear here next to courage and dignity, and misfortunes are brought about not by gods but by mortals (for instance, in the poems 'In a Large Greek Colony, 200 B.C., Trojans').[26] It is these features of Cavafy's poetry that helped Eastern European poets to take a broader view of their predicament and escape self-pity and narrow provincialism. Cavafy helped the Poles and Czechs to realize that communism was only one of the many manifestations of human folly, and probably not the worst. What communism had in common with other follies was an absolute lack of distance and an absence of humour. The image of *agelastes* crushing the little god of irony is perhaps the most appropriate image one needs to bear in mind while reading the best of Eastern European poetry. In the relentlessly committed discourse of communism, irony, humour and paradox had no place, since they suggested that there were no absolute truths or unquestionable values. But by being universal in themselves, irony and humour could be applied to any context, helping to lift the local concerns to the level of global importance.

Looking at two poems by Mirosław Holub and Wisława Szymborska, we can see how this interplay between the local and general was arranged to the point that the vigilant authorities had difficulties in pinning down the subversive thoughts with which the poems are spiked. A good example of this strategy is Holub's 'Žito the Magician', where the court magician, Žito, manages to fulfil even the most impossible wishes of the current ruler.

> To amuse his Royal Majesty he will change water into wine.
> Frogs into footmen. Beetles into bailiffs. And make a Minister
> out of a rat. He bows, and daisies grow from his finger-tips.
> And talking bird sits on his shoulder.[27]

Žito is what Eastern Europeans called a 'courtly artist', an epitome of what Haraszti described as the 'symbiotic relationship between artists and the modern socialist state.'[28] The relationship is almost a voluntary one, because coercion has been replaced with incentives, systems of privilege, prizes and free access to the media. Žito is not like the Poets Laureate, who once they accept the honour must remain loyal to the crown as part of their contract. He is free, but the nature of the relationship corrupts him, and he begins to lose any sense of the real and forgets that his magic power has limitations. The reminder comes from unexpected quarters:

> Then along comes a student and asks: Think up sine alpha
> greater than one.
>
> And Žito grows pale and sad: Terribly sorry. Sine is
> between plus one and minus one. Nothing you can do about that.
> And he leaves the great royal empire, quietly weaves his way
> Through the throng of courtiers, to his home in a nutshell.
>
> (lines 11–17)

So it is science, and not art, which brings both the artist and the Royal Majesty down to earth. Scientific laws are just laws. Not only do they show that there is a natural end to every mystification, but they also prove that, unlike human beings, nature is incorruptible. There is no doubt that the poem arises directly from Holub's experience as a scientist, as a figure who works and lives within a state system that is utterly corrupt and who thrives on applying the rules in an arbitrary fashion. Being a scientist and an artist, Holub can clearly see that the collaboration of the artist with power is beset with moral ambiguities, and yet it is the responsibility of the artist to recognize the point beyond which collaboration with the state is damaging. Holub's success in this poem depends on an unusual mix of parable with scientific knowledge. On the surface Holub states what the communist regimes liked to hear – that it is objective science, and not some kind of black magic, that matters – and yet these regimes used science to support a variety of ideologically utopian visions from social engineering to grandiose, environmentally damaging projects. In a subtle and humorous way, Holub shows that, if truly respected, science can effectively unmask ideological mystifications.

Szymborska has no scientific training behind her, and yet science is often a subject of her poetry. Like Holub, she has managed to escape the label of dissident poet. In fact, she was so successful in deflecting public attention that her receipt of the Noble Prize astonished many Western commentators, as the immediate press comments reflected.[29] In her acceptance speech she said that her writing was fuelled by the fact that she could not stop being amazed by what she saw around her: 'In the language of poetry, where each word counts, nothing is ordinary and nothing – no stone, no cloud above, no day, no night, and most of all, no life on earth – is normal.'[30] To achieve this attitude means to cast doubt on everything, including one's own ability to comprehend. If Szymborska achieved this only at a linguistic level we could place her conveniently within the Russian formalist tradition. But *ostranenie* in the strictly formalist and technical sense has never been her aim, although she is capable of stretching Polish to the limits in a way that few other Polish poets have managed.[31] Szymborska's doubt is total and multilayered, and it was the totality of her scepticism that put her on a collision course with the totalitarian system.

All these qualities can be found in 'Psalm' from her collection, *A Large Number*, published in 1976. A psalm, in essence a prayer expressing a lament, regret or thanksgiving, is used here to communicate the poet's thoughts on the strange ways of the world. But the tone of Szymborska's poem contrasts with the subject matter, because the regret and lament are about the imperfect state of borders, which is not exactly a topic we normally associate with the psalm form. The poem opens with the unusual lament, 'Oh, the leaky boundaries of man-made states!'[32] But as we move to the next line we already see that Szymborska's aim is not to mourn but to highlight a paradoxical contrast between nature and man-made structures. Borders, often heavily guarded, are significant only in the human universe. Nature simply ignores them and shows no respect.

> Need I mention every single bird that flies in the face of frontiers
> or alights on the roadblock at the border?
> A humble robin – still, its tail resides abroad
> while his leaky beak stays home. If that weren't enough, it won't stop bobbing.
>
> (lines 6–10)

But having established a contrast between the human and the natural worlds, Szymborska immediately proceeds to destroy this binary opposition, which is based on the illusion of a natural order.

> And how can we talk of order overall
> when the very placement of the stars
> leaves us doubting just what shines for whom?
>
> Not to speak of the fog's reprehensible drifting!
> And dust blowing all over the steppes
> as if they hadn't been partitioned!
> And the voices coasting on obliging airways,
> that conspiratorial squeaking, those indecipherable mutters!
>
> Only what is human can be truly foreign.
> The rest is mixed vegetation, subversive moles, and winds.
>
> (lines 22–31)

What has become clear towards the end is that the separation of the human world, which was the opening position in the poem, is yet another illusion and another construct of a human mind. From the point of view of the universe – if universe has a point of view – it is the human world that is 'foreign'. Our separation from nature is not an objective phenomenon but a construct based on deeply subjective perception. This radical, and yet deeply ironic, examination of reality contains the essence of Szymborska's approach. On the one hand, the poem could be seen as a clever play on the theme of dichotomy between nature and culture, except that there is no trace of philosophical discourse here. The poetic discourse originates in the radical examination of what we often see as 'normal', and in the playful scrutiny of our mental habits.

In its historical context, the poem was doubly subversive. The restriction of movement was one of the chief weapons of the communist states, and the Berlin Wall became the symbol of the abusive nature of the Soviet empire. To show that frontiers were merely peculiar figments of the human imagination was a daring thought in itself, but to claim that it was chaos and not order that was the essence of being meant a denial of a Marxist doctrine based on a principle of historical inevitability. Even single words and phrases – such as 'foreign soil', 'roadblock', 'chaos', 'smuggling', 'territorial waters', 'conspiratorial' and 'subversive' – belonged to the vocabulary reserved in public discourse for the description of everything that was alien or hostile to the socialist state. And yet it is difficult to point to any line in the poem and say that it refers to particular circumstances in the communist world.

In 1991, just after the 'Eastern bloc' countries made a daring leap to freedom, Poland's literary scene was somewhat shaken by a short poem written by Zbigniew Machej, then a relatively unknown poet. The poem, entitled 'An Old Prophecy', presents an ambiguous vision of literature in a world where political power no longer limits artistic freedom. For an artist trained to recognize the pitfalls and meanderings of cultural politics in a socialist state, this newly gained freedom may prove difficult to navigate. Machej's prophecy was brutal in its directness:

> The hands that tore off thorns
> shall cleanse themselves before clasping hands that wove
> whips. Dignity and desire shall find refuge under the same
> roof, and the wolf shall lie down with the black sheep
> and the ugly duckling. Dreams of a wholesale business
> selling exotic fruits shall eclipse the longing for pure art.[33]

The poem does not present the dawn of freedom idealistically, but as a confused time of compromise in which the wolf, the black sheep and the ugly duckling have to learn how to live peacefully under the same roof. Indeed, the political developments in Eastern Europe since 1992 have proved Machej's prophecy accurate. For literature, censorship and political oppression have gone away, but the rules of the market have imposed a different order of constraints.

The immediate response to the change was a call for new poetic language and a conviction that literature written behind the Iron Curtain needed to be relegated to history. Younger poets, wishing to forge a clean break from the past, began to view poets such as Herbert, Szymborska and Miłosz as an obstacle on the way to a new but not very clearly conceived renewal of literary tradition. One can understand that for a budding artistic talent the poetic strategies that emerged in Eastern Europe between 1945 and 1989 may be an asset and a burden simultaneously. Surveying Cold War poetry, however, it would be simplistic to view political circumstances as the sole factor stimulating its growth and development. After all, no oppressive government can turn a political activist into a distinguished poet if that activist is not a poet in the first place. There is no doubt that the political, or more widely existential, constraints imposed on a writer called for an artistic response, but the fact that the response had to be expressed under the constraint of censorship led to the development of a very specific poetics whereby each word had its weight and whereby a poet and a reader entered a conspiratorial pact of mutual understanding.

It would be unrealistic to expect this tradition to survive intact in contemporary times, when dominant ideologies take little interest in artistic expression, and often turn an artist into a producer that must compete for both funding and public attention. However, there is no doubt that the best poets of the Cold War era not only managed to outwit the agents of the politburo but also created a poetry that stands a chance of remaining permanently in what Seamus Heaney called 'the atlas of civilization'.[34]

Notes

1 Szymborska, 'The End and the Beginning', in Szymborska, *View with a Grain of Sand: Selected Poems*, trans. Stanisław Barańczak and Clare Cavanagh (New York: Harcourt Brace and Company, 1995), pp. 178–9, line 1.
2 Two Yugoslav writers, Dubravka Ugrešić and Slavenka Drakulić, have written extensively on the subject in their essays. See Ugrešić, *The Culture of Lies* (1995) and Drakulić, *How We Survived Communism and Even Laughed* (1988).
3 I owe this observation to several colleagues who teach literature and history both at secondary and tertiary level in the UK as well as in the former 'Eastern bloc' countries.
4 This observation is based on my work for the Arts Council's Literary Translation Advisory Board in the late 1990s.
5 See Davies, *Microcosm: A Portrait of a Central European* City (2002) and *Rising '44* (2003).
6 Italo Calvino in *Why Read the Classics* (1991) and Zbigniew Herbert in his poem 'Why the Classics' (in Herbert, *Selected Poems*, trans. P.D. Scott and Czesław Miłosz (Manchester: Carcanet, 1985), pp. 137–8) discuss the issue of literature's universal appeal.
7 Alvarez, *Under Pressure. The Writer in Society: Eastern Europe and the USA* (Harmondsworth: Penguin, 1965), pp. 23–4.

8 I wrote more extensively about these issues in my essay 'Before and After *The Burning Forest*: Modern Polish Poetry in Britain', *The Polish Review*, 1 (1989), 57–71.
9 Spender, 'Introduction' to Anthony Graham, ed., *Witness Out of Silence: Polish Poetry Fighting for Freedom* (London: Poets and Painters Press, 1980), p. 9.
10 Interviews with Maria Janion, in Katarzyna Janowska, *Rozmowy na nowy wiek* (2001) and Maria Janion, *Do Europy – tak, ale razem z naszymi umarłymi* (2000).
11 The Research Institute for Languages of Finland is currently carrying out an extensive comparative research project on the Russian censorship in nineteenth-century Finland. Detailed analysis of censorship in Poland with original censorship documentation can be found in Jane Leftwitch Curry, ed., *The Black Book of Polish Censorship* (1984).
12 See Hans Robert Jauss, *Towards an Aesthetic of Literary Reception* (1977).
13 Haraszti, *The Velvet Prison: Artists under State Socialism*, trans. Katalin and Stephen Landesmann (1987; New York: The Noonday Press, 1987), p. 5.
14 Michael March's anthology *Child of Europe* (1990) contains many examples of this kind of writing.
15 Mandelshtam, *Hope against Hope*, trans. Max Hayward (1970; London: Penguin, 1976), p. 400.
16 Vladimir Mayakovskii's is perhaps the most instructive example of what happens when the socialist realist doctrine is applied to poetry.
17 Stanisław Barańczak, *Breathing under Water and Other East European Essays* (Cambridge, MA: Harvard University Press, 1990), pp. 61–95.
18 See Stanisław Barańczak, *A Fugitive from Utopia: The Poetry of Zbigniew Herbert* (1987), Barańczak, *Breathing under Water and Other East European Essays* (1990), Seamus Heaney, *The Government of the Tongue* (1988).
19 Chris Miller, 'On Not Writing the East European Poem', *PN Review*, 30: 5 (2004), p. 69.
20 See Miłosz, *Witness of Poetry* (1983). It is also worth noting that one of the most important poems by a Russian poet, Josip Brodsky, is entitled 'A Flight from Byzantium'. See Brodsky, 'A Flight from Byzantium', in Brodsky, *Collected Poems in English*, ed. Ann Kjellberg, trans. Anthony Hecht, *et al.* (2000; Manchester: Carcanet, 2001), p. 12.
21 Miedzyrzecki, 'End of the Game', in Daniel Weissbort, ed., *The Poetry of Survival: Post-War Poets of Central and Eastern Europe* (London: Anvil Press, 1991), p. 193, lines 1–22.
22 Herbert, 'Damastes (Also Known As Procrustes) Speaks', in Herbert, *Report from the Besieged City and Other Poems*, trans. John and Bogdana Carpenter (1983; New York: The Ecco Press, 1985), p. 44, lines 1–24.
23 Herbert, 'From Mythology', in Herbert, *Selected Poems*, p. 93.
24 Cavafy, 'Waiting for the Barbarians', in Cavafy, *Selected Poems*, trans. Edmund Keeley and Philip Sherrard (London: Hogarth Press, 1975), p. 14.
25 Kundera, *The Art of the Novel*, trans. Linda Asher (1986; London: Faber and Faber, 1988), p. 159.
26 Cavafy, 'In a Large Greek Colony, 200 B.C., Trojans', in Cavafy, *Selected Poems*, p. 112.
27 Holub, 'Žito the Magician', in Holub, *The Fly*, trans. Ewald Osers, George Theiner and Ian and Jarmila Milner (Newcastle-Upon-Tyne: Bloodaxe Books, 1987), p. 51, lines 1–4.
28 Haraszti, *Velvet Prison*, p. 8.
29 See Julian Isherwood, 'Obscure Polish Poetess Is Awarded Nobel Prize', *Daily Telegraph*, 4 October 1996, p. 18, and Marianne McDonad, 'Poetry's Mozart Is Nobel Winner', *Independent*, 4 October 1996, p. 7. For genuine poetry connoisseurs, Szymborska's achievement was no surprise. Her poetry was published in

English by *PN Review* in 1982 and *The Modern Poetry in Translation* as early as 1975. *The Cambridge Quarterly* reviewed her work in 1987. She was widely translated into German and Scandinavian languages.
30 Szymborska, *Poeta i Świat* (Stockholm: The Nobel Foundation, 1996), unpaginated. My translation.
31 There is a fine tradition in Polish poetry of pushing the limits of standard languages from Bolesław Leśmian (1877–1937) to Ewa Lipska (born 1945).
32 Szymborska, 'Psalm', in Szymborska, *View with a Grain of Sand*, pp. 95–6, line 1.
33 Machej, 'An Old Prophecy', in Donald Pirie, ed., *Young Poets of a New Poland*, trans. Donald Pirie (London: Forest Books, 1993), p. 150, lines 9–14.
34 Heaney, *The Government of the Tongue* (London: Faber and Faber, 1988), pp. 54–71.

13 The anti-American
Graham Greene and the Cold War in the 1950s

Brian Diemert

In *Another Life* (1999), Michael Korda, an editor at Simon and Schuster, remembers Graham Greene as obsessed with his difficult relationship with the United States. Because he had as an Oxford undergraduate briefly joined the Communist Party, Greene was once denied entry into the United States and often had trouble acquiring a visa. Convinced 'the FBI [...] had a dossier on him, and were adding to it at every opportunity', Greene 'had no doubt that his telephone calls and mail were being monitored'.[1] Finally obtained through freedom of information, the dossier, in Korda's account (324), was 'a slim envelope' containing a few clippings and a report on Greene's attendance at a 1948 'International Congress of Intellectuals' held in Warsaw.[2] Greene 'brooded darkly on the possibility that the FBI file was a fake, that somewhere they had concealed the *real* file' (325), of which Korda found no evidence. The extent to which the matter preoccupied Greene 'as if it were the Holy Grail' (323) reveals a number of things about the author in the Cold War period. Obviously, he considered himself antagonistic to the United States, but, as an examination of his Cold War writing shows, his hostility to the United States and its foreign interventions did not make him a Soviet supporter. Indeed, Greene found the Cold War's insistent and pervasive binarism particularly disturbing. Stalinism and Soviet tyranny were abhorrent, but so was a Western 'freedom' that documented an individual's activities in secret files. In this context, Greene struggled to find a middle ground.

To speak of the Cold War era is to speak of both a historically datable era (from the end of the Second World War to the collapse of the Eastern bloc during 1989 and 1990) and a particularly charged period extending from the late 1940s to, perhaps, the October 1962 missile crisis. Afterwards, coexistence seemed increasingly normal, as is evident in such agreements as the 1963 Nuclear Test Ban Treaty, while communism's developing polycentrism meant that it could no longer be perceived as a monolithic threat. None the less, for nearly 20 years after the Second World War, US and Soviet relations were frighteningly hostile. In this context, the thoughtful person was often at odds with the prevailing ethos; indeed, in the United States, as we well know, many writers, artists and intellectuals were blacklisted: unable to work in their fields or, worse, imprisoned for contempt of Congress. In Britain, security concerns were also intense, but those who challenged Cold War attitudes were not the pariahs they would have been in the United States: there was no equivalent to Joe McCarthy in Britain.[3] For British writers such as Greene, then, to propound a vehemently anti-American position did not mean one was unpatriotic. Indeed, such difference might be regarded as just the opposite.

British writers responded in several ways to the immediate postwar period. Usually critics recognize an inward turn in fiction and poetry,[4] with domestic issues prevailing in plays such as *Look Back in Anger* (1957) and in novels as diverse as *Lucky Jim* (1954) and *Room at the Top* (1957). But there was another side of British fiction – and Greene is exemplary here – that exploited international concerns. Spy fiction, for example, became increasingly popular and tended to affirm readers' beliefs in a secret world existing beneath ordinary reality. Ian Fleming's enormously popular James Bond stories evinced the triumph of the West and of commodity over numerous totalitarian demagogues representing such well-concealed but pervasive enemy organizations as SPECTRE and SMERSH. The sense of a shadow world was pervasive in the period, for, unlike the Second World War, the Cold War was largely invisible to Western populations, appearing only in proxy wars, as in Korea or Vietnam, and in public discourse. Consequently, for many observers, such as LynnDianne Beene, 'Cold War fiction' means espionage fiction,[5] and, indeed, spies and spying appear in the work of writers (for instance, Elizabeth Bowen in *The Heat of the Day* (1949) or C.P. Snow in *The New Men* (1954)) who are not usually regarded as authors of spy fiction.

Still, when we speak of the Cold War's effects on literature, we have to wonder what we mean. Is Cold War fiction any fiction published during the Cold War? Is it fiction about Cold War issues or, more specifically, the conflict between superpowers? Or is it fiction that evinces particular aesthetic effects in terms of both narrative and diegesis? Is there, in fact, a Cold War discourse? Similar questions are implicit in any discussion of periodization, but for our present purposes it may be better to consider them in relation to one author, Graham Greene, while recognizing the Cold War's pervasive effects on society and literature: the fear of nuclear annihilation, the dampening of political debate, the Manichean global vision, the paranoia and the widespread sense of crisis and helplessness among nations, and certainly among citizens, under the sway of either of the two superpowers. After the Second World War, Greene's fiction turned towards these geo-political concerns. It is interesting, then, that Robert Hewison should continue to see Greene's work as rooted in 'the old ambiguous world' of the 1930s.[6] For Hewison, 'Greene avoided the provincialism of most English novelists by setting his stories abroad, often in locations that were about to become politically highly charged [. . .] but the warring political interests and the suffering they cause in the real world are projections of the eternal struggle of the principles of good and evil, resolved, though only temporarily, by the working of grace achieved through suffering'.[7] Such a remark can be offered only through a willed blindness to the manifest content of Greene's books, yet as we shall see it echoes a typical response to Greene's political work. Certainly, it is true that a novel such as *The Quiet American* (1955) is both thematically and stylistically linked to Greene's earlier work, yet it is surely reductive to argue that 'contemporary reference' in *The Quiet American* is 'a mask for the perennial nature of [Greene's] themes', and that the book is an act of 'revenge' against the United States for refusing him entry.[8] Instead, this novel constitutes one of the most explicit critiques of American Cold War policy that we can find in British fiction from the 1950s. Along with *The Third Man* (1950) and *Our Man in Havana* (1958), *The Quiet American* shows us Greene's acute sense of the period's political tensions.[9]

As a British citizen often travelling abroad, Greene was doubly outside the frame of the main Cold War combatants, the United States and the USSR. Although several of his protagonists – D. in *The Confidential Agent* (1939), Rowe in *The Ministry of Fear* (1943) or Fowler in *The Quiet American* – learn that they must eventually choose a side, Greene found this notoriously difficult to do and always strove to avoid ideological labelling (in the 1930s, for example, he refused to 'take sides' on the Spanish Civil War). Instead, he shares E.M. Forster's position in 'What I Believe' (1938), which places personal loyalties and affection ahead of political or national causes: blind devotion to large, abstract notions of virtue, nationhood or ideology is fundamentally destructive of all that is human.[10] In *The Ministry of Fear*, Tolstoy is quoted on the theme: 'Remembering all the evil I have done, suffered and seen, resulting from the enmity of nations, it is clear to me that the cause of it all lay in the gross fraud called patriotism and love of one's country';[11] significantly, Dr Forester, a Nazi fifth-columnist, had once scored this passage and later erased his markings.

The Third Man, a work perhaps better known as a film than a book,[12] also explores such issues as personal loyalty and belief in the face of emerging Cold War divisions. More detective than spy story, it details the experiences of Rollo Martins who has been invited to Vienna by Harry Lime, an old friend who, Martins slowly discovers, is using the occupied city as a base for racketeering. The novella presents postwar Vienna as a city of sectors and frontiers that imagistically reflects Cold War realities and, for Greene, looks back to the 1930s when the image of 'the frontier [was] an insistent element' in British literature.[13] This image had immense appeal for Greene, whose 'Letter to a West German Friend' opens with a nostalgic appreciation for the frontier,[14] an entity which, in Germany, offered a clear division between East and West that obviously appealed to him. *The Third Man* does not focus on the East/West conflict, but difficulties with the Soviets are never far from the book's centre. The Russian sector is home to most of those involved in Lime's racket (a '"racket works very like a totalitarian party"', as the narrator says),[15] and frequent kidnappings in the city's

British, French and American zones speak to the ever present danger of Soviet penetration of Western spheres of influence. Equally significant is Greene's use of the sewer system, which points up the porous nature of the 'frontiers', of the sectional division of Vienna and, by extension, of all Cold War boundaries.

A curious but not irrelevant aspect of *The Third Man* is that it quickly became associated with espionage and scandal. The film's popularity is probably to blame, but after the defections of Guy Burgess and Donald Maclean, who were assumed to have had help with their defections, 'the third man' became 'the magic phrase'.[16] A.A. DeVitis notes that Greene was echoing T.S. Eliot's *The Waste Land* ('Who is the third who walks always beside you?') in his title, and using, as Eliot had, 'the third' to refer to the moment on the road to Emmaus when the risen Christ walks unrecognized among his disciples.[17] The return of Harry Lime thus becomes an allegory of profane resurrection. Yet the ties to espionage are not easily dismissed: Lime does have an agreement with the Russians,[18] and the media's 'third man' in the aftermath of the Burgess and Maclean defections turned out to be Greene's friend and one-time supervisor Kim Philby, who had, in fact, used the sewers to help rescue rebels during the ill-fated Vienna uprising in 1934. (Newspapers had implied the third man was Philby long before his defection.)[19] Greene's loyalty to Philby is amply expressed in his introduction to Philby's *My Silent War* (1968), although Greene's sudden resignation from the SIS (Secret Intelligence Service) in 1944 may have been precipitated by the knowledge that Philby was working for the Soviets.[20] (Greene always denied he even suspected this.) In light of these points, it is interesting to imagine *The Third Man*, as Shelden seems to do,[21] as revealing Philby's identity to those who have eyes to see it. Certainly, if one thinks of Martins as a figure for Greene (Martins claims his next book is called *The Third Man*),[22] then Lime, an old friend with a secret life, can easily be read as Philby. However, while Greene remained loyal to Philby, Greene's fictional counterpart does dispatch Lime.

As this development suggests, Greene's position in the Cold War was ambiguously at odds with the tendency of Cold War rhetoric to reduce political nuances to simple binaries centred on support for either the United States or the Soviet Union. As Bertrand Russell noted, this structure eliminated dissent by identifying it 'in the popular mind with support for the "enemy", the "devil", the inconceivably wicked Russians. The nice thing about this was that it also became impossible to question the power-struggle itself.'[23] Increasingly sympathetic to communism, Greene was no Stalinist,[24] yet he was disgusted with America's anti-communist measures and its callow foreign policy. To an extent, he found a middle ground in the Church, especially when, as in Poland, it so obviously stood in opposition to tyranny;[25] yet the Church's support for the Catholic McCarthy, reflected in statements by Bishop Fulton Sheen and Cardinal Spellmann, was abhorrent to Greene.[26] Faced with this division in his allegiance, he travelled to developing nations where socialism and communism were evolving along lines distinct from the Soviet or the Chinese models. Consequently, especially after his visits to Vietnam, he increasingly championed both the interests of smaller, Third World countries and their leaders, such as Ho Chi Minh, Castro, Allende or Torrijos, in their struggles with the United States.

In the 1950s Greene's journalism demonstrates as well as his fiction does his perspective on the Cold War. Among the many essays Greene wrote touching on Cold War affairs, two of the most significant are his 'The Return of Charlie Chaplin: An Open Letter' from 1952 and the 'Letter to a West German Friend' from 1963. In the latter, Greene aligns Catholicism with communism as a belief system.[27] Western capitalism, on the other hand, offers consumerism and so remains spiritually vacuous: 'In a commercial world of profit and loss man is hungry often for the irrational. [. . .] Capitalism is not a belief, and so it is not a magnet.'[28] One can take the point that communism was regarded as an equivalent faith, but behind Greene's praise of communism in all its varieties lies a mixture of idealism and an iconoclastic desire to prick dominant Western beliefs about the ideology. For example, in the 'Letter to a West German Friend' he writes: 'The West is inclined to attach heroic motives to all those who escape across or through the wall. Courage they certainly have, but how many are "choosing freedom" for romantic motives, love of a girl, of a family, or a way of life, and how many are merely tempted by a standard which includes transistor radio-sets, American blue jeans and leather jackets?'[29]

The letter to Chaplin, 'one of the great liberals of our day',[30] contains some of Greene's most critical statements on Cold War issues. Although anxious in the post-Nuremburg world to separate the citizenry from its government,[31] Greene sees a paradoxical hysteria in the United States. He imagines Chaplin's films being presented as evidence of 'un-American' activities because they challenge authority,[32] a point that touches the very core of the American dilemma in the 1950s, for in its literature and politics America celebrates the individual's unfettered freedom. Hence, the literature is filled with rebellious characters who refuse to be contained: from Natty Bumpo and Huck Finn, to Edna Pontellier and Holden Caulfield, America's literary heroes are the children of Jefferson, Emerson and Thoreau. Yet the Cold War's political and artistic culture offered a very narrow band of the permissive. Greene's reflections on Chaplin take pride in Britain's refusal to join the American-led crusade to root out domestic communism: 'lying rather closer to danger, [Britain] is free from the ugly manifestations of fear'.[33] Coming so soon after the defections of Maclean and Burgess, Greene's comments clearly express his commitment to liberal democracy, and he implies, through an allusion to Titus Oates, that Britain learned the lessons of McCarthyism long ago.[34] None the less, Greene concludes, 'the disgrace of an ally is our disgrace, and in attacking you [Chaplin] the witch-hunters have emphasized that this is no national matter. Intolerance in any country wounds freedom throughout the world'.[35]

In many respects, Greene's condemnation of American domestic policy fits his increasing antipathy towards the United States that is most obviously manifest in *The Quiet American*, a novel whose prescience can still amaze, despite not being one of his best. Set in the years just before the 1954 Geneva Conference that partitioned Vietnam, *The Quiet American* is narrated by Thomas Fowler, a veteran *Times* correspondent posted in Saigon during the communist uprising against French rule, and details the Briton's relationship with Alden Pyle, an American operative who, before he is murdered, covertly directs aid to an anti-communist 'third force'. The novel thus touches on the moment when French colonial power was about to be exchanged for American power. As if to underscore the transition, the book opens and closes with Fowler telling us that he was watching American bombers being unloaded when Pyle was killed; the point is repeated, but there are significant differences in language usage that help emphasize the increasing intensity of American involvement. On the first occasion, Fowler says, 'I could see lamps burning where they had disembarked the new American planes'; on the second, the language is sharper and more explicit: 'I [...] stood awhile watching the unloading of the American bombers. The sun had gone down and they worked by the light of arc-lamps.'[36] 'Planes' has become 'bombers', 'lamps' are now 'arc-lamps', the passive 'had disembarked' is now expressed in the participle 'unloading'. Within the time of the narrative, the moment is nearly the same, but Fowler's heightened description underscores the growing American presence.

Greene visited Vietnam four times in the early 1950s and reported on the situation there in articles for *Paris Match*, *Sunday Times* and other publications.[37] Written when Korea dominated the news, the essays offer both intelligent appraisal of the war and an exceptional presentation of a particular milieu; indeed, several of Greene's descriptions, such as those of the landscape around Phat Diem and of the experience of vertical bombing, appear almost wholly unaltered in *The Quiet American*. As does the novel, Greene's journalism clearly expresses his disquiet with the American presence in Vietnam and with the containment policy.[38] In his first account, 'Indo-China: France's Crown of Thorns' (1952), he wrote, 'Western slogans and all that talk the politicians retail about the necessity of containing Communism seem here to apply only to a very small part of the picture'.[39] Two years later, the Americans get his attention: '"*the bar tonight was loud with innocent American voices and that was the worst disquiet. There weren't so many Americans in 1951 and 1952.*" They were there, one couldn't help being aware, to protect an investment, but couldn't the investment have been avoided?' (Greene's emphasis).[40] Greene recognized that the war was far more complicated than simple Cold War rhetoric suggested. He astutely anticipated the course of American involvement and knew the situation could only be resolved by the Vietnamese themselves: 'Vietnam cannot be held without the Vietnamese, and the Vietnamese army [...] cannot, except here and there stiffened by French officers, stand up against their fellow country men trained by Giap since 1945'.[41]

Generally, in the late 1940s and 1950s, the United States treated communism as monolithic, with Moscow assumed as its malevolent ideological and governing centre. Greene quickly realized that this was not the case in Vietnam and that the Viet Minh evinced an idealism that was far from Stalinist.[42] Indeed, Greene thought the West's preoccupation with communism simplified the Vietnam conflict because it effaced nationalism from a consideration of the problem;[43] yet nationalism, as the Americans later realized, was precisely the difficulty. The problem Greene saw was that the American tendency to read indigenous, nationalist movements as communist virtually guaranteed they would become so.

Greene was never committed to communism but his experience in Vietnam and his meeting with Ho Chi Minh convinced him that communism could exist free of Stalinism and of the Soviet influence.[44] To some extent, the novel reflects this position through Fowler's comments, but the book does little to affirm communism as a viable future for Vietnam. Instead, the thrust is, as it is in the journalism, towards the liberal goal of self-determination. When Pyle suggests the Vietnamese "'don't want Communism'", Fowler responds: "'They want enough rice [. . .]. They don't want to be shot at. [. . .] They don't want our white skins around telling them what they want'" (94). Speaking as a representative of an old colonial power that has "'learned not to play with matches'" (157), Fowler argues for the withdrawal of Western influence from Vietnam and the establishment of an independent state (96). The position is analogous to Conrad's anti-imperialist stance in *Heart of Darkness* (1902). In both cases, the colonized nation and people are poorly understood, but the departure of foreign influence is essential if there is to be a way forward. As Fowler says, "'We've no business here. It's their country'" (107); earlier, in a passage highly reminiscent of Conrad, he reflected: 'This was a land of rebellious barons. It was like Europe in the Middle Ages. But what were the Americans doing here? Columbus had not yet discovered their country' (37).

When we look at *The Quiet American* in its context we see Greene's acute critique of American Cold War politics manifesting itself in large and small ways. On the one hand, Fowler quips that "'Bright, young American'" children are "'ready to testify'" (133), and wonders, when noticing that Pyle's shirt 'was comparatively restrained in colour and design', whether he had 'been accused of un-American activities' (73). But in a broader sense we also see a novel that uses the language and tropes at hand to represent a situation that fundamentally stood outside the Cold War's dualistic vision, with Greene viewing Vietnam, even more than postwar Vienna, as exposing the porous nature of dualistic thinking. The means by which he could represent the situation, however, were limited by the period. For instance, the question of political engagement is framed in the language of postwar French existentialism – Fowler even using the French term *engagé* (96, 97, 138–9, and elsewhere) – and the problem of choosing sides is presented through allusions to Pascal (16, 138). Vigot, for example, the French officer investigating Pyle's murder, quotes: '"Let us weigh the gain and loss [...] in wagering that God is, let us estimate these two chances. If you gain, you gain all; if you lose you lose nothing'"; to which Fowler offers another quotation, '"Both he who chooses the heads and he who chooses tails are equally at fault. They are both in the wrong. True course is not to wager at all'" (138). Fowler, of course, cannot remain uninvolved, and so becomes complicit in Pyle's death. Yet the inability to retain neutrality is also a feature of Greene's earlier work, most notably *The Confidential Agent*, where the problem of choosing sides is said to be not 'so much a question of morality as a question of simply existing'.[45] Such an observation is remarkably close to Monsieur Heng's comment in *The Quiet American*, '"Sooner or later [...] one has to take sides. If one is to remain human'" (174).

Also limiting Greene's account is his tendency, derived from his devotion to Conrad and juvenile imperial fiction, to engage the orient in terms inflected with more than a century of imperialist discourse. His Vietnam, for example, is in many ways symbolized in the character of Phoung, the Vietnamese mistress that Fowler and Pyle compete for and that Fowler connects intrinsically to the country ('I had seen the flowers on her dress beside the canals in the north, she was indigenous like a herb' (14)). In this way, not only is the competition between American and Englishman a struggle between two different visions of Vietnam, but also an orientalist dichotomy is established between the West (active, masculine and rational) and the feminized East (silent, passive and mystical). Typically for male orientalists, Fowler and Pyle speak for Phoung (who lacks 'the gift of expression' (134)) and for the silenced colonial subjects. For example, Fowler says that '"These people don't suffer from obsessions'" (133) and at one point Pyle remarks, '"These people aren't complicated'", to which Fowler responds, '"Is that what you've learned in a few months? You'll be calling them childlike next'" (176). In this case, Fowler criticizes Pyle's objectifying language, but Fowler is equally objectifying, referring to the Vietnamese as '"childish'" himself (104).

The themes, milieux, situations and characters of Greene's earlier work supply many of the other tropes he uses in *The Quiet American*. For instance, the love triangle of Fowler, Phoung and Pyle is a feature of *The End of the Affair* (1951), while a preoccupation with guilt and betrayal are evident in *The End of the Affair*, *The Heart of the Matter* (1948) and *The Ministry of Fear*. Of course, we have to move cautiously in attributing claims in *The Quiet American* to Greene because, as critics have long recognized, the temptation is to identify Fowler with Greene, despite Fowler's obvious unreliability. Fowler's relationship with Phoung colours all his dealings with Pyle, who, as Brian Thomas points out, functions as Fowler's shadowy double.[46] None the less, Greene's general tone evinces deep scepticism of crassly materialistic and unresponsive American values: as he says through Fowler, 'I was angry; I was tired of the whole pack of them with their private stores of Coca-Cola and their portable hospitals and their too wide cars and their not quite latest guns', concluding that Pyle "'had no more notion than [the French] what the whole affair's about'" (31).

One senses in *The Quiet American* a pervasive fatalism, though how much of this can be attributed to retrospective vision is hard to say. To be sure, Fowler's world-weary attitude contrasts strongly with Pyle's callow 'innocence'. As in Henry James's fiction, much admired by Greene, an old trope is at work: new-world innocence is crushed by old-world complexity and indigenous practice.[47] Many American reviewers in the 1950s were bothered by Greene's anti-Americanism, and to read some of their comments today is to recognize the extent to which political climate can affect literary response. Several complained that Greene misrepresented the American case, that he blamed the United States for terrorist atrocities and failed to offer a genuine anti-communist voice in the novel. Robert Gorham Davis's review in *The New York Times* saw the book's Americans as 'caricatures [. . .] often as crude and trite as those of Jean Paul Sartre'.[48] While Davis's review is not without validity – Pyle, to say nothing of Phoung, is a rather wooden figure, though this could be considered Fowler's and not Greene's doing – we can now see that much of the negative comment, especially in the United States, was motivated by two factors stemming from Cold War culture. The first is the obvious hostility to anything that was potentially critical of American policy and of the United States generally. As Stephen J. Whitfield shows, even mild dissenting voices were condemned as communist dupes, agitators or spies.[49]

The second factor is the more general influence of New Criticism on literary critics. At the height of its influence in the 1950s, the New Critical method, as Sinfield notes,[50] complimented Cold War interests, because it discouraged discussion of a work's political content in favour of formal concerns and of comment on the human condition. In this respect, criticism tended to dismiss Greene's political content or not see it as integral to the work. Instead, the book was discussed in relation to existentialism[51] or, as Hewison did, to religious themes.[52] As Davis suggests in his review, *The Quiet American* 'can be seen to be more profoundly related to Greene's earlier religious novels than its polemic character at first suggested. In those novels God is reached only through anguish because religion is always paradoxical in its demand.'[53] Religious concerns have always been a useful way into Greene's fiction, but especially in the 1950s and 1960s a critical emphasis on these issues gave Greene a kind of *gravitas* and critics a chance to sidestep the possible dangers of political expression.[54] This is not to suggest they are misguided in their considerations of Greene's work or of *The Quiet American*. Indeed, one of the best and most detailed close readings of the novel is by Brian Thomas, whose consideration of Greene's use of the romance idiom is none the less largely silent on the book's political or historical arguments.[55] Similarly, there is some truth, however mockingly presented, in A.J. Liebling's link between Fowler and Bogart:[56] beyond the novel's exploitation of the eternal triangle – Fowler, Phoung and Pyle – the book reminds one of

Casablanca in Fowler's repeated insistence that, like Rick Blaine, he is not involved, only to find himself unable to remain detached after seeing the devastation caused by Pyle's misguided attempts to work with General Thé, and, more importantly, by Pyle's indifference to the suffering he has caused. '"When he saw a dead body'", Fowler says, '"he couldn't even see the wounds'", seeing instead '"A Red menace, a soldier of democracy'" (32). Pyle's determination to defeat communism through ethically dubious means is, of course, the novel's most telling aspect. Greene saw the Western powers increasingly adopting methods they condemned in their adversary, finding, for example, 'moral judgements [...] singularly out of place in espionage'.[57] In this, Greene repeated John le Carré's heartfelt question: 'how long can we defend ourselves [...] by methods of this kind, and still remain the kind of society that is worth defending?'[58] Consequently, it is pointless to quarrel about Greene's representation of Americans like Pyle or to argue about points of emphasis, such as the role of General Thé, that history later ignored.

The problem to be focused upon, rather, is Greene's awareness of the all-encompassing quality of Cold War binarism. With the USSR and communism needing to be contained in the Cold War period, the metaphor of the boundary insisted that the contained was embodied in finite space, thus being conceived as a 'closed' society; but the entity that contains was boundless: it is all that is outside the contained and is, consequently, 'open' and free. Deconstruction, though, as Jacques Derrida taught us,[59] recognizes that the contained and the container cannot exist independently, nor can the observer – a Greene or a Fowler – conceptually stand outside the frame. Container and contained are firmly tied both in deconstructive reasoning and in Greene's texts. As Beatrice says in *Our Man in Havana*, '"You taught us that [there is something greater than one's country] with your League of Nations and your Atlantic Pact, NATO and UNO and SEATO. But they don't mean any more to most of us than all the other letters, U.S.A. and U.S.S.R. And we don't believe you anymore when you say you want peace and justice and freedom. What kind of freedom?"'[60] The point is Nietzschean: 'He who fights monsters should look to it that he himself does not become a monster. And when you gaze long into an abyss the abyss also gazes into you.'[61]

Greene's difficulty is that any attempt to break away from the East/West binary repeatedly fails and, instead of bringing synthesis, reconstructs the original structure. In *The Quiet American*, Greene anticipates this move in so far as Pyle's search for a third option in Vietnam reconstructs the binary with America as the new power. At one point, Domingues, Fowler's Asian assistant, explains to Fowler:

> 'He [Pyle] was talking about the old colonial powers – England and France, and how you two couldn't expect to win the confidence of the Asiatics. That was where America came in now with clean hands.'

'Hawaii, Puerto Rico,' I said, 'New Mexico.'

'Then someone asked him some stock question about the chances of the Government here ever beating the Vietminh and he said a Third Force could do it. There was always a Third Force to be found free from Communism and the taint of colonialism – national democracy he called it . . .'

'It's all in York Harding,' I said. 'He read it before he came out here. He talked about it his first week and he's learned nothing.' (124)

Fowler's disdain for 'York Harding', a composite of several American thinkers on foreign policy, points to a naivety in American attitudes that were routinely reinforced in school textbooks of the 1950s.[62] Yet the notion of a 'third force' is another attempt to escape either/or thinking. Inevitably, however, the attempt fails because it remains bound by Cold War choices: that is, the 'third force' would be an arm of the Americans, so the East/West, communist/capitalist construction is unhindered. The only way out of the dilemma, then, may be the one Pascal prescribes, which is not to choose at all. It is the position Sartre took as well: 'The point is that all is lost if we want to *choose* between the powers which are preparing for war. [. . .] The historical agent is almost always the man who in the face of a dilemma suddenly causes a third term to appear, one which up to that time had been invisible.'[63] For Sartre, the third term was, in 1947, still to be invented. Greene's own search for a way out of binaries is a consistent feature of his career, and in this sense, his struggle is also Pyle's and America's. The problem, which may help explain *The Quiet American*'s weaknesses, is the impossible one of finding a way to step outside the conceptual structure and outside the rhetoric by which one is contained.

By the early 1960s, the Cold War had moved into a new phase, as it became increasingly 'difficult to foresee a future in which Soviet Communism would be radically dislodged, overthrown, or transformed'.[64] Greene's later fiction anticipates and reflects the changed mood after the earnestness of *The Quiet American*, but he remained deeply suspicious of American aims. Variously he invoked the Church, liberalism, Third World communism or some combination of liberation theology in a continued search for communism's human face.[65] Characters such as Dr Magiot (*The Comedians* (1966)), Leon Rivas (*The Honorary Consul* (1973)) or Maurice Castle (*The Human Factor* (1978)), in their differing conceptions of communism, show Greene's persistent attempts to imagine a future outside the Cold War's binarism. In this sense, much of Greene's postwar fiction is Cold War fiction in so far as his narratives respond to circumstances largely affected if not dictated by the Cold War. Looking at Greene, one often feels the social, political and cultural milieus that the Cold War generated were ideal for his temperament and thematic preoccupations. Always secretive, Greene seemed born to a world of division and betrayal: at least, that is how he presents his life in *A Sort of Life* (1971) and *Ways of Escape* (1981). Both books, however, are products of the Cold War era, which leaves us to wonder at the extent to which Greene internalized the Cold War's legacy of suspicion and read it back into his own past. With the Cold War over, Greene's work can be reassessed both for what it said then and for what it says to us now.

Notes

1. Korda, *Another Life: A Memoir of Other People* (New York: Random House, 1999), p. 314. Further references to Korda's memoir are to this edition and page numbers are included in the text.
2. Greene describes the file quite differently. See Greene, '"Freedom of Information"' in Greene, *Reflections*, ed. Judith Adamson (Toronto: Lester and Orpen Dennys, 1990), pp. 303–5.
3. Churchill refused in April 1954 to establish a British equivalent of the House Un-American Activities Committee.
4. See, for example, Bernard Bergonzi, *Wartime and Aftermath: English Literature and Its Background 1939–1960* (Oxford: Oxford University Press, 1993), pp. 84, 101, 139.
5. Beene, *John le Carré* (New York: Twayne, 1992), pp. 77–87.
6. Hewison, *In Anger: British Culture in the Cold War, 1945–1960* (Oxford: Oxford University Press, 1981), p. 76.
7. Ibid., p. 76.
8. Ibid., p. 76.
9. Although Greene denied a continued connection with British Intelligence agencies (see, for example, Greene, *Ways of Escape*, new edn (1980; Harmondsworth: Penguin, 1981), p. 126), his appearance in dangerous places – Prague, Kenya, Vietnam – on the eve of profound change led commentators and biographers to speculate that he maintained contact with MI6 (see Paul Fussell, for instance, in 'Can Graham Greene Write English?', in Fussell, *The Boy Scout Handbook and Other Observations* (Oxford and New York: Oxford University Press, 1982), p. 97).
10. Forster, 'What I Believe', in Forster, *Two Cheers for Democracy*, new edn (1951; London: Edward Arnold, 1972), pp. 65–73.
11. Greene, *The Ministry of Fear*, new edn (1943; Harmondsworth: Penguin, 1982), p. 131.
12. Greene considered the book as 'the raw material' for the film: Greene, 'Preface' to Greene, *The Third Man and The Fallen Idol*, new edn (1950; Harmondsworth: Penguin, 1973), p. 10.
13. Bernard Bergonzi, *Reading the Thirties: Texts and Contexts* (London: Macmillan, 1978), p. 66.
14. Greene, 'Letter to a West German Friend' (1963), in Greene, *Reflections*, p. 207.
15. Greene, *Third Man*, p. 80.
16. Bruce Page, David Leitch and Phillip Knightley, *The Philby Conspiracy* (New York: Ballantine, 1981), p. 259.
17. Eliot, 'The Waste Land' (1922), in Eliot, *Selected Poems*, new edn (1954; Faber and Faber, 1961), p. 65, line 359; De Vitis, *Graham Greene*, rev. edn (1964; Boston: Twayne, 1986), p. 43.
18. Greene, *Third Man*, p. 105.
19. Page, *et al.*, *Philby Conspiracy*, pp. 261–3.
20. Michael Sheldon, *Graham Greene: The Man Within* (London: Heinemann, 1995), pp. 308, 316, 323. Norman Sherry is non-committal on the matter (see Sherry, *The Life of Graham Greene, Vol. 2: 1939–1955* (New York: Viking, 1995), p. 183).

21 Sheldon, *Graham Greene*, pp. 317, 321.
22 Greene, *Third Man*, p. 70.
23 Quoted in Alan Sinfield, *Literature, Politics and Culture in Postwar Britain* (Oxford: Basil Blackwood, 1989), p. 96.
24 Marie-Françoise Allain, *The Other Man: Conversations with Graham Greene by Marie-Françoise Allain*, trans. Guido Walman (1981; London, Sydney, Toronto: Bodley Head, 1983), p. 95.
25 Greene, 'Catholic Temper in Poland' (1956), in Greene, *Reflections*, p. 193.
26 Greene, 'The Return of Charlie Chaplin: An Open Letter' (1952), in Greene, *Reflections*, p. 149.
27 Greene, 'Letter', p. 212.
28 Ibid., p. 209.
29 Ibid., p. 211.
30 Greene, 'Return of Charlie Chaplin', p. 148.
31 Ibid., p. 148.
32 The joke is that Chaplin is un-American because he is British: see ibid., p. 149.
33 Ibid., p. 149.
34 Ibid., p. 148.
35 Ibid., p. 150.
36 Greene, *The Quiet American*, new edn, ed. John Clark Pratt (1955; New York: Penguin, 1996), pp. 11, 181. All further references to *The Quiet American* are to this edition and page numbers are included in the text.
37 These pieces are now found in Greene, *Collected Essays* (1969) and Greene, *Reflections* (1990).
38 'Containment' is a kind of shorthand for a complex array of American foreign policies that were to prevent the spread of communism. Although not alone in theorizing the concept, George F. Kennan is usually seen as the policy's chief architect: 'it is clear,' Kennan writes in 'The Sources of Soviet Conduct', 'that the main element of any United States policy toward the Soviet Union must be that of a long term, patient but firm and vigilant containment of Russian expansive tendencies' (in Kennan, *American Diplomacy 1900–1950* (Chicago: University of Chicago Press, 1951), p. 119).
39 Greene, 'Indo-China: France's Crown of Thorns', in Greene, *Reflections*, p. 130.
40 Greene, 'Return to Indo-China' (1954) in Greene, *Reflections*, p.161.
41 Ibid., p. 164.
42 Greene, 'Indo-China', p. 134.
43 Ibid., p. 134.
44 Judith Adamson, *Graham Greene: The Dangerous Edge – Where Art and Politics Meet* (London: Macmillan, 1990), p. 133. See Greene's discussion of Ho Chi Minh in 'The Man as Pure as Lucifer' (1955), in Greene, *Collected Essays*, new edn (1969; Harmondsworth: Penguin, 1981), pp. 301–3.
45 Greene, *The Confidential Agent*, new edn (1939; Harmondsworth: Penguin, 1980), p. 32.
46 Thomas, *An Underground Fate: The Idiom and Romance in the Later Novels of Graham Greene* (Athens and London: University of Georgia Press, 1988), pp. 42–3.
47 On the new world/old world trope and the novel's link to Henry James's fiction see John Cassidy, 'America and Innocence: Henry James and Graham Greene', in Greene, *Quiet American*, pp. 469–78.
48 Davis, 'In Our Time No Man Is a Neutral', review of *The Quiet American* in *The New York Times* (11 March 1956), http://www.nytimes.comn/books/00/02/20/specials/greene-quiet.html (accessed 4 May 2004).
49 Whitfield, *The Culture of the Cold War*, 2nd edn (1991; Baltimore and London: Johns Hopkins University Press, 1996), pp. 20–1, 179.

50 Sinfield, *Literature, Politics and Culture*, pp. 104–5.
51 See, for example, De Vitis, *Graham Greene*, pp. 109–13; or Miriam Allott, 'The Moral Situation in *The Quiet American*', in Robert O. Evans, ed., *Graham Greene: Some Critical Considerations*, new edn (1963; Lexington: University of Kentucky Press, 1967), pp. 188–206.
52 For some fine comment on the religious aspects of Greene's work see R.W.B. Lewis, 'Graham Greene: The Religious Affair', in Lewis, *The Picaresque Saint: Representative Figures in Contemporary Fiction* (Philadelphia and New York: Lippincott, 1959), pp. 220–74; Francis L. Kunkel, *The Labyrinthian Ways of Graham Greene* (1960); and Philip Stratford, *Faith and Fiction: Creative Process in Greene and Mauriac* (1964).
53 Again, Whitfield is particularly good at demonstrating how 1950s America framed religious devotion as a distinguishing feature of the United States as opposed to the officially atheist world of communism (Whitfield, *Culture of the Cold War*, pp. 77–100).
54 Davis, 'In Our Time'. Interestingly, Robert Gorham Davis was summoned before HUAC on 25 February 1953. Realizing the committee knew about his Marxist past, Davis co-operated. In such circumstances, we can understand his defence of American interests in his review (see Vicky C. Hallett, 'Red Square: A Scrutiny', in *The Harvard Crimson Online*, http://www.thecrimson.com/fmarchives/fm_02_15_20001/article2A.html (accessed 7 July 2004). There are fine studies of Greene's political themes. I especially recommend Maria Couto's *Graham Greene: On the Frontier – Politics and Religion in the Novels* (1988); Judith Adamson's *Graham Greene: The Dangerous Edge – Where Art and Politics Meet* (1990), and, more modestly, my own *Graham Greene's Thrillers and the 1930s* (1996).
55 See Thomas, *An Underground Fate* (1988).
56 See Liebling, 'A Talkative Something-or-Other', in Greene, *Quiet American*, pp. 349–50.
57 Greene, 'The Spy' (1968), in Greene, *Collected Essays*, p. 311.
58 Quoted in Whitfield, *Culture of the Cold War*, p. 208.
59 Derrida often discusses the way in which borders and edges disappear, but one of the most applicable discussions here is Derrida, 'Living On: Border Lines', trans. James Hulbert, in Harold Bloom, *et al.*, *Deconstruction and Criticism*, new edn (1979; New York: Continuum, 1986), pp. 75–176.
60 Greene, *Our Man in Havana*, new edn (1958; Harmondsworth: Penguin, 1977), p. 217.
61 Friedrich Nietzsche, *Beyond Good and Evil*, new edn, trans. R.J. Hollingdale (1886; Harmondsworth: Penguin, 1975), aphorism 146, p. 84.
62 See Whitfield, *Culture of the Cold War*, p. 57.
63 Jean-Paul Sartre, *What Is Literature?* new edn, trans. Bernard Frechtman (1948; London: Methuen, 1981), pp. 217–18.
64 Whitfield, *Culture of the Cold War*, p. 205.
65 Allain, *Other Man*, p. 95.

14 The excluded middle
Intellectuals and the 'Cold War' in Latin America

Jean Franco

The 'Cold War' is hardly an adequate term for a period in which hot wars were fought by the Soviet Union against dissident satellites and by the US against 'communism'. The armed truce between the great powers was not extended to the entire world which was, nevertheless, caught up in the bipolar confrontational logic. In Latin America, the period from the Second World War to the 1990s was marked by US intervention in Guatemala, the Dominican Republic and Grenada, by the Bay of Pigs debacle, by covert operations and eventually by the intellectual and political defeat of the left accelerated by military governments that came to power under the aegis of the United States. Given this scenario, it is easy to lose sight of the fact that it was also a period of innovation, experiment and belief in liberation from political and economic dependency, a period in which there was a convergence between politics and culture. The Cold War in Latin America was not just about the great powers and their influence but about this other story that was eventually stifled, one in which the literary intelligentsia played a crucial role. This role can be understood only in relation to what Pascale Casanova terms 'the world republic of letters'[1] and the claim for universality made from the centre, most notably from Paris, which was the magnet that had drawn generations of Latin American writers and the standard according to which they would be evaluated. The Cold War altered this relationship. Paris remained a magnet, but the 1945–89 period was one in which the USA and the Soviet Union also vied for cultural supremacy, pitting freedom against peace. While a few Latin American writers were drawn in by one side or the other, the majority attempted to find a third space, one that corresponded both to the political aspiration of a uniquely Latin American form of progress and to the cultural aspiration of liberating its literature from mere imitation and copying. Originality was to define both its political and its literary solutions: the third space between the Cold War extremes. Although these aspirations foundered politically they helped to launch the 'boom' of Latin American literature in the 1960s and early 1970s.

Even before the Cold War got under way, Latin America had been subjected to that mixture of propaganda and conviction that went by the name of 'American values'. During the Second World War, an impressive propaganda machine was put together by Nelson Rockefeller's Office of Hemispheric Affairs that poured money into all kinds of Latin American ventures – from radio stations and movies to art exhibitions and publications – in order to influence the hearts and minds of Latin Americans in support of the Allied cause.[2] After the war, both the Soviet Union and the United States focused attention on Europe, although the Congress for Cultural Freedom, founded to counter Soviet influence and to recruit intellectuals to the US cause, also had outposts in several Latin American cities and published a journal, *Cuadernos*. Edited by the Spanish ex-Trotskyist Julián Gorkín, *Cuadernos* was, from the first, out of touch with younger writers, many of whom were concerned with issues such as underdevelopment and corruption rather than the abstract cosmopolitanism promoted by the journal that, consistently with US policy, showed a distrust of independent national projects. But the USA had far more effective weapons for its policies in the Hollywood films, radio and television programmes and popular US magazines published in Spanish, *Reader's Digest* being the most egregious example of a journal that reflected the American way of life without resorting to overt propaganda.[3]

It was inevitable that both sides would try to court intellectuals. The Soviet Union gave the poet Pablo Neruda and the novelist Jorge Amado a prominent European presence through their peace congresses, while the USA attempted to woo intellectuals by its defence of the freedom of the writer. Latin American intellectuals had traditionally fulfilled a pedagogical role, but what distinguished the writers of the 1960s was that they taught their public not through moralizing anecdotes but through critical reading. In most European countries and in the United States, pedagogy fell to the academy or cultural journalism; in Latin America, writers were public intellectuals who commanded a substantial power base in journals and newspapers and used it effectively. Jorge Luis Borges, Carlos Fuentes, Octavio Paz, José Lezama Lima, Gabriel García Márquez, Mario Vargas Llosa, Julio Cortázar, Augusto Roa Bastos and José Maria Arguedas – the list could be longer – introduced theories of reading and understanding to elucidate not only their own work but also that of their forerunners and contemporaries. They created canons and a corpus of criticism, revamping literary genealogies even while maintaining the autonomy of literature and its independence from reality. Vargas Llosa's spirited reading of the fifteenth-century novel of chivalry *Tirant lo Blanc* was an implied criticism of pedestrian realism. Borges's entire work is an allegory of reading. Cortázar inserted theories of reading and creation into his novel *Hopscotch*. In his book *Don Quixote or the Critique of Reading*, Fuentes drew parallels between Cervantes's time and his own. '[A]s if he foresaw all the dirty tricks of servile literary naturalism,' Fuentes argued, 'Cervantes destroys the illusion of literature as a mere copy of reality and creates a literary reality far more powerful and difficult to grapple with: the reality of a novel in its existence at all levels as a critique of reading.'[4] During the entire decade of the 1960s, writers became arbiters of taste, especially for the young generation of students and critics. Indeed, the presence of young people at readings, in conferences and mass meetings at which writers pronounced on politics, revolution and literature, was a striking testimony to the continuing power of the 'lettered city'. An ideology of the aesthetic supported these writers in their claims that literature was a free zone. Like Flaubert, who according to Nathalie Sarraute had once envisaged 'a book with no attachments to the outside world, which would be self-sustaining thanks to the internal force of its style, as the earth holds itself in the void being supported',[5] the so-called 'boom' generation of the 1960s saw literature as a free-standing model, and one that could serve as an example for politics. Fuentes, for one, believed that 'the creative recreation' already practised in literature could also be realized politically in Mexico: 'A country like ours, a country of simultaneity and historic coexistence can construct a generous and revolutionary Utopia starting from these cultural realizations, from this effort of selection that really separates the dead and oppressive weights from living and emancipating realities.'[6]

But the independent position that writers traditionally claimed and their status as secular prophets was now assailed from both sides. On the one hand, their status as trendsetters was challenged by the guerrilla, and on the other their national concerns were confronted by the different demands of an international market. Nevertheless, for a brief period in the 1960s some of them believed that politics and culture had happily converged in Cuba.

The Cuban Revolution of 1959, as the self-proclaimed 'first liberated territory' of the Americas, represented a serious challenge to US domination in the region. It was, above all, a *national* liberation that claimed to be a model for other Latin American and Third World countries. On the cultural front, its literary prizes, its journal, *Casa de las Américas*, its defiance of its northern neighbour, its successful literacy campaign, its embrace of the Third World, attracted a host of sympathizers among writers and intellectuals. It was primarily to counter this influence that the USA in 1965 began covertly funding a new journal, *Mundo Nuevo*, which was specifically directed towards a generation of writers (known as the boom generation) who were beginning to attract international attention. Published in Paris and edited by a respected Uruguayan academic, Emir Rodríguez Monegal, *Mundo Nuevo* focused on contemporary literature while carefully abstaining from overt support of US policies. Indeed, but for the revelation of CIA funding that discredited the journal and led to its closure, its defence of the freedom of the artist and the autonomy of art and literature might have been a winning card, especially when Cuba began demanding unconditional allegiance to its cause.

The Cuban revolution was the catalyst of the culture wars of the 1960s and early 1970s, that pitted critics against defenders, the engaged versus the disengaged. Unlike the Soviet Union, which had promoted a dreary brand of realism amongst its supporters, Cuba appeared, at first, less dogmatic, more innovative in its cultural practices, more concerned with breaking out of the elitism of the lettered. In the early years, Cuba seemed able to embrace both the political vanguard and the avant-garde, although very soon the ante for the engaged intellectual was raised when 'commitment' came to mean participation in revolutionary warfare.

To represent the Cold War period simply as a stand-off between the USA and the Soviet Union is to overlook these wars of national liberation in which Cuba played an active part, sending troops to the Congo, Luanda and Angola. Such activities underscore the fact that from the point of view of the Third World this was a period of liberation and revolution. As Jorge Castañeda points out, Che Guevara embodied this *Zeitgeist* in his confidence that vast changes were about to occur and that revolutionary action would accelerate fundamental change. Castañeda's judgment is harsh as he alleges that Guevara's book on such action, entitled *Guerrilla Warfare* (1961), 'helped mobilize the youth of Latin America on behalf of just causes' yet 'must also be held responsible for the wasted blood and lives that decimated those generations'.[7] Whether Guevara can be held responsible or not, it is undoubtedly true that he had no tolerance for those intellectuals who stood on the sidelines at a time when revolution appeared imminent in Africa and Latin America. Indeed, several poets and writers died in the struggle, among them the Peruvian poet Javier Heraud, the Argentine poet Francisco Urondo, the journalist and writer Rodolfo Walsh, and, most tragically, Roque Dalton, who was killed by members of his own guerrilla group.[8]

The insistence by Che Guevara and other radical leaders that the time had come to join the revolution divided writers between the martyrs and those on the sidelines, but also undermined 'the lettered city' itself: that is, the long-standing hegemony of the humanist intellectual. Meanwhile, Cuba's status as intellectual leader was severely damaged by the flight of dissident intellectuals such as Guillermo Cabrera Infante and by the reports of the persecution of homosexuals and critics of the regime.[9] But it was the public censure of the poet Heberto Padilla for writing poetry 'against the Revolution' in 1969 and his brief imprisonment and confession of guilt in 1971 that broke what had seemed like a united front of writers. Vargas Llosa immediately resigned from the editorial board of *Casa de las Américas* and became an implacable critic. Along with a group of European and Latin American intellectuals, he signed a protest letter that compared the event to Stalinist tactics and expressed the wish that the Cuban revolution should return to that moment when it was a considered 'a model of socialism'. Among those who did not sign the letter were García Márquez and Cortázar.[10]

What is often lost sight of is that the USA also castigated its critics. The fate of Angel Rama, the Uruguayan intellectual who coined the term 'lettered city' to describe the historical relationship of the intellectual to power, exemplifies the polarized cultural politics of the 1960s and 1970s in which no nuanced position could be granted space. Like many of his contemporaries, Rama viewed Latin American culture (as well as its economy and politics) as a work in progress but one in which literature was deeply engaged. He argued that, from the conquest, the lettered had enjoyed a unique position of privilege that removed them from *realpolitik* and led to a propensity for idealized projects that they then tried to put into practice. As he pointed out, the grid designs of the cities of the New World illustrated this attempt to give material form to an abstract design. A deep culture division, Rama believed, came to separate the lettered from the unlettered, cultivated language from popular language, the high from the low, a division that would persist until well into the twentieth century. Nevertheless, he also argued that modernization opened the way for a democratic culture emancipated from dependency on the metropolis. Theatre, the press and popular literature offered ways of acquiring knowledge that did not necessarily pass through the elite institutions of the university.[11]

As literary editor of the influential left-leaning *Marcha*, Rama reviewed contemporary writers, and wrote on Cuban cultural policy and occasionally on politics. He commented on the CIA funding of *Mundo Nuevo* and engaged in a vigorous polemic with his fellow countryman and its editor Emir Rodríguez Monegal.[12] He became critical of Cuba's policy towards its writers and nevertheless was fiercely attacked as a Castro supporter by the exiled Cuban writer Reinaldo Arenas.[13] When *Marcha* was banned by the military government in 1973, he lived as a Latin American exile, first in Caracas and then in the United States where he took up a position at the University of Maryland. It was here he learned what it was like, as he said, to live 'in the belly of the monster'.[14] Under what *The Nation* would term the 'tawdry provision of the McCarron act', the Immigration and Naturalization Service decreed his deportation.[15] Why this happened is not at all clear, although it is possible that the Uruguayan military government through its embassy was showing off its resolute participation in the war on communism by helping to expose sympathizers, even though Rama had always maintained an independent position. The absurdity of the charges was exposed by Rama himself in a preface to *The Lettered City*. Among the charges against him was that he had been the literary editor of *Marcha*, described erroneously as an organ of the Communist Party, and that he had helped found the Biblioteca Ayacucho that was said to frequently publish the work of communist writers. In fact, the Biblioteca Ayacucho, which Rama launched when living in Caracas, published editions of major contributions to Latin American culture, including pre-Columbian poetry and writings from the colonial period and the nineteenth century. Among the many modern writers included in the collection were two outstanding poets, Neruda and César Vallejo, both of whom had been members of the Communist Party but who could not possibly have been omitted from such a collection.[16] Rama's case was taken up by the PEN American Center, the Authors League of America, the Latin American Studies Association, the editors of the International Comparative Association and many human rights organizations, but in vain. The irony of it was that, before his deportation, he was working in the Library of Congress on 'an essay that explores the relation of the intelligentsia to power and argues for the broad democratization of intellectual functions'.[17] His book *The Lettered City* was published posthumously after he died in a plane crash in 1983.

The significance of Rama's expulsion transcends the anecdotal details. Imagine a Raymond Williams who, instead of becoming Professor of Drama at Cambridge University, had been ignominiously hounded from his post; or a Stuart Hall unable to collaborate in the thrilling experiment of an Open University. The difference speaks volumes. Yet Rama fulfilled a role that was not unlike theirs. He was an independent intellectual who never earned a doctorate, and whose criticism like that of Williams is engaged with 'culture' in the widest sense as 'a constitutive social process creating specific and different "ways of life"'.[18] In Latin America, as Rama had demonstrated, intellectuals played a far more active role in constituting the idea of 'America' and later of nationhood.

Rama introduced two important concepts into the study of the intelligentsia – the mask and transculturation – to account for the way writers negotiated commodification, on the one hand, and the popular classes on the other. The mask – an image borrowed from Nietzsche[19] – describes the use of the past in order to disguise the commodified aspects of the present, a strategy used in late nineteenth-century and early twentieth-century modernist writing. Transculturation – a much discussed term in Latin American criticism – accounts for the way that a dominated culture 'is able to register or transcribe itself into the dominant,'[20] a process which Rama explored through the writing of José María Arguedas, who registered the rhythms and sensibilities of Quechua in Spanish. What I want to stress here is Rama's investment in the democratization of culture and in the emancipation (another key word in his vocabulary) from a colonized sensibility. Though criticized by some scholars for offering a cultural rather than a political solution to Latin American problems, Rama was firmly embedded in the Latin American traditions of the humanist public intellectual and of the independent critic that were embraced by many of his contemporaries.[21]

When Cuban communism proved to be flawed, many placed their hopes of emancipation on Salvador Allende's 'Chilean Road to Socialism' and, after his overthrow in 1973, on Nicaragua's Sandinista Revolution. What else did Che Guevara hope to achieve in Bolivia or the Colombian guerrilla in Marquetaria but a liberated territory? The Zapatista autonomous municipalities and *caracoles* are more recent manifestations of a similar ideal that, despite defeat of most of the guerrilla movements, has not wholly disappeared.[22] There was, however, a sinister side to the liberated territory. During the Sendero Luminoso's attempt to control southern Peru, 70,000 people were killed by the Sendero or the army. In Colombia the liberated territory of the guerrilla was turned over to coca production.

Behind most of these projects was the idea that Latin American countries must find their own path to modernity. Yet even as novelists publicly endorsed this aspiration, in their novels the *topos* of the liberated territory served to explore both emancipation and its historical failures. I am speaking of novels of the 1960s that helped to launch Latin American literature into global culture, and which identified magic realism and eccentricity with the region's originality. As they draw on the past, they remind us of the long history of liberated territories in Latin America, from the conquest onwards. Literature and politics come together in the fantasy of a just society founded in a space cleaned of all prior failures, a fantasy, moreover, that could claim historical antecedents. The Spanish conquerors were lured by such dreams. In the sixteenth century, Lope Aguirre made a futile attempt to found a free community independent of the Spanish Empire. Bartolomé de las Casas founded the Christian community of Vera Paz, and the Jesuits missionaries who had abandoned the sinful luxury of Europe founded missions in the area that now belongs to Paraguay, Brazil and Argentina, where the indigenous lived communal lives of work and prayer. In the nineteenth and early twentieth centuries, the continent attracted Tolstoyan and anarchist communities. The alternative community was imagined as the pure antithesis to the miseries of the real nation – of market-driven capitalism and bureaucratic communism alike – and was often envisaged as a return to pre-capitalist relations. This too had historical antecedents in Catholic anti-capitalism. The 'non-material incentives' that Che Guevara advocated when he was Minister of Economy in Cuba, as well as the anti-materialism of the militant vanguard, especially the Tupamarus of Uruguay, were reminiscent of older condemnations of usury. Yet the distrust of money was not confined to the Latin American vanguard: conceptual artists threw money into the Seine and cast dollar bills into the Stock Exchange. 'Money is the alienated ability of mankind,' Marx had written, and distrust of the money economy linked politics to art, surfaced in literary texts, art happening, among hippies and in political movements, and even re-emerges from time to time today, although neither the idealized austerity of the guerrilla nor the idealized simplicity of the peasant could be easily sustained in the era of rapid globalization, a lesson that in the 1960s and the early 1970s still had to be learned.[23] As Félix Guattari would point out, such fantasies raised the question of 'whether or not it is possible to stop seeing use value and exchange value as mutually opposed. The alternative of rejecting all complex forms of producing and demanding a return to nature merely reproduces the split between different forms of producing-desiring production and production of recognized social utility.'[24]

In situating their novels in the past, writers explored these alternative communities fully conscious of their historical failure. In *The War of the End of the World*, Vargas Llosa writes of the nineteenth-century attempt by followers of Antonio Conselheiro to found a religious community in north-east Brazil independent of the republican state.[25] In response, the secular state sent an army against the rebels who were wiped out to the last man. In *I the*

Supreme, Augusto Roa Bastos describes post-independence Paraguay that under Dr Francia cut itself off from trade and contact with other nations in an attempt to keep out foreign influences. The novel details Dr Francia's impossible struggle to 'dictate' his own place in history while protecting the Paraguayan population from contamination from Europe. He is defeated not by an invading army but by his own mortality.[26] In García Márquez's *The Autumn of the Patriarch*, the absolute ruler, who recalls the Dominican Republic's President Trujillo and the Venezuelan president, Vicente Gómez, is eventually forced to sell his country's ocean to foreign powers.[27] The project of national or regional autonomy outlined in these novels identifies specificity with eccentricity. The eccentricities of Dr Francia or García Márquez's patriarch represent a certain kind of originality but they cannot halt the global forces of capitalist modernization. What seems to have preoccupied the authors is an ethical problem discussed by Gillian Rose in her book *Mourning Becomes the Law*, in which she shows the flaws in the extremes of communitarianism and liberalism. As Rose argues, while communitarianism is indifferent to individual liberties (hence the threat of totalitarianism exposed by the boom novelists), libertarianism calls for 'reinforcement of the police function to contain the consequences of inequality', a consequence that would be amply demonstrated when the military regimes came to power in the 1970s.[28] In a rather different version of the liberated territory, García Márquez's *One Hundred Years of Solitude*, which enthralled an entire generation and continues to do so, depicts Macondo as a territory that aspires to be outside history but that becomes history's victim, destroyed by its isolation and the incest on which it was founded, condemning it to return to nature. Like other novels based on historical precedents, Macondo's 'originality' is inseparable from an isolation that globalization was already threatening.

Novelistic representations of liberated territories not only transcribe historic failures but also reflect on literature itself. The secular and humanistic project of the intelligentsia had been to create a thinking population capable of reading and understanding at a sophisticated level, a project that was thwarted by the information society that was the offspring of modernization and by the displacement of the literary intelligentsia by experts whose style of rationality did not admit fantasy. This is why many novelists drew on 'traditions' and magic, on the remnants of the very past that the intelligentsia was supposedly anxious to shed. Even Vargas Llosa, a rationalist if ever there was one, ends his novel *The War of the End of the World* with the words of an old woman who, after the extermination of the rebels, declares that she has seen a dead rebel leader join the archangels in heaven. While literature had sought to displace religion and challenge God, the ending of Vargas Llosa's novel seems to suggest that it had not completely displaced myth and the sacred. Latin American literature, while bound to the secular project of modernity, repeatedly conjures spectres of the past that confound rationality.

Alongside myth, religion was an element that would also enter the political and intellectual arena in the late 1960s. The theology of liberation and the commitment to the poor made by the bishops at the Medellin conference of 1968 disrupted the secular tradition embraced by the intelligentsia and attracted a different kind of intellectual: that is, the priests who organized base communities to discuss not only religion but politics, who encouraged literacy and who believed that the poor would inherit the earth. In the revolutionary climate of the 1960s and 1970s, it was not unusual for these priests to be drawn into the revolutionary cause. Camillo Torres of Colombia (who was greatly admired by the poet Ernesto Cardenal) took the ultimate step and was killed fighting in the ranks of the guerrilla army. Several Jesuit priests were active in the Sandinista cause in Nicaragua and, after the overthrow of President Somoza, became members of the government. Ernesto Cardenal served for a time as Minister of Education, and founded poetry workshops in which peasants, soldiers and housewives participated.[29]

While training for the priesthood in Colombia, Cardenal had visited indigenous communities whose belief systems were antithetical to capitalism. His collection of poems *Homage to the Indians of America* (1969) constitutes a collage of citations of native texts that allows us, in Gordon Brotherston's words, to 'appreciate the cadences and etymologies, script forms, and even material substance of the prior texts as well as the literary and cultural traditions to which they belong'.[30] Already influenced by Ezra Pound, one of whose cantos describes 'usura' as a 'sin against nature' ('with usura, sin against nature, / is thy bread ever more of stale rags / is thy bread dry as paper'),[31] he was drawn to indigenous groups who maintained communitarian values. In Colombia he had visited a community that kept out traders because 'they create inequality': 'Money does not circulate, but they have many coins: in necklaces along with the teeth of monkeys and alligators.'[32] In his poems, he commemorated those cities, now in ruins, that had 'no leaders, no administrations, no dynasties, no governing families, no political parties'[33] and celebrated the ancient Inca civilization of Tahuantinsuyu because its people had 'no MONEY / and because they had no money / there was no prostitution or theft / they left the doors of their houses open'.[34]

Towards the end of his training for the priesthood and acting on a suggestion of Thomas Merton, Cardenal announced his decision to found a contemplative community in Solentiname on the San Juan river in Nicaragua. He announced this in a letter he wrote to the bilingual journal *El Corno Emplumado / The Plumed Horn*, edited by Margaret Randall and Sergio Mondragon, a journal that brought together US and Latin American poets. Planned at first as a contemplative community in a Nicaragua that was still governed by Anastasio Somoza, Solentiname gradually turned into a showcase, a place where art was integrated into everyday life, and where sermons reflected an idiosyncratic mixture of Marxism (nurtured by Cardenal's visits to Cuba) and liberation theology that reconciled Marxism with belief in God.

The secular intelligentsia of the lettered city had, for the most part, been removed from the poverty and ignominy of life at the lowest level, whereas many parish priests were daily faced with the problems of the poor. When the Medellin congress of bishops in 1968 had announced a commitment to the poor, members of the priesthood sympathetic to liberation theology became active in forming 'comunidades de base', group meetings which raised consciousness through discussions of the Gospels and which encouraged literacy.[35] In Solentiname, the daily meetings to discuss the Bible were transcribed and elaborated by Cardenal in his book *El Evangelio en Solentiname*. These discussions often stressed the moral superiority of the poor and the need for revolution in order to effect change. But they also celebrated the beauty of life in idyllic natural surroundings and re-imagined the city as a community bonded by love. Solentiname attracted not only the radical wing of the Catholic Church but also writers and intellectuals drawn to a community in which peasants were painters and craftspeople and which seemed to fulfil the long-standing project of sectors of the avant-garde who believed that the aesthetic was the model for unalienated labour. In 1977, after Cardinal and other members of the community began to support and participate in the Sandinista cause, Somoza bombed the community out of existence just before he himself was overthrown.

One of the visitors to Solentiname had been Julio Cortázar, the Argentine novelist resident in Paris who was attempting to reconcile his distance from Latin America with engagement in its politics. His story 'Apocalypse in Solentiname' is something of a requiem for the communitarian ideal and paradoxically for the lettered city that had protected the literary from the intrusion of political reality. Told in the first person, the story begins with the narrator's description of a visit to Solentiname written in an irritatingly patronizing tone. Writers and others are referred to familiarly by their first names as Ernesto (Cardenal) and Sergio (Ramírez). Cortázar, who was not lacking in sophistication and who had travelled the world as a translator, explores a character who reverts to a naive primitivism when confronted with the peasant painters of Solentiname. Here was 'once again the first vision of the world', the 'clean look of someone who describes his surroundings as a hymn of praise'.[36] The narrator's primitivism, however, underscores his polarized view of the world, divided between innocence and evil. Back in Paris, viewing the slides of the still photographs he had taken of the Solentiname paintings, he finds that, far from being congealed in the idyllic past, they now register the violence of the present. Instead of naive paintings, all the horrors of disappearance and death that are the daily realities of the continent appear before his eyes: a bomb exploding in Buenos Aires, the execution of the poet Roque Dalton by members of his own party. Using a sexist division of labour to drive home his point, Cortázar has the French girlfriend, Claudine, represent the pedestrian viewpoint of one who can see only the obvious (in other words, cannot see anything beyond the idyllic still photographs frozen in the past), whereas the Latin American first-person narrator miraculously sees the coming horror. The conviction that art and literature could not adequately deal with horror was deepened by US politics in Central America. As Cortázar wrote to one of his correspondents, 'Every day it becomes more difficult for me to read literature as I used to do, letting myself be carried away by each book as if someone were speaking to me from behind my shoulder; at each moment the sense of menace returns and sometimes I spend more time listening to shortwave radio in search of news than reading or listening to records.'[37] By this time, he was active in exile organizations and gave evidence before the Russell Tribunal on Torture. In 1975, looking back on *Hopscotch*, an experimental novel that caused a sensation when it was first published in 1963, he wrote, 'It all seems different, distant, absurd.'[38]

Under the rubric of 'revolution', culture and politics converged, an outcome that had long interested sectors of the avant-garde in both Europe and the Americas.[39] The 'happenings' of the 1960s, the conceptual art movement, the hippies, all set out to disrupt the normal and the routine as a way of challenging the status quo. Their tactics were adopted also by militant vanguards, notably by the Tupamaros, the guerrilla movement of Uruguay that staged spectacular actions that included robbing banks and distributing money to the poor. Artists learned to use the public stage to organize dissent. Even under military regimes such as that of Pinochet in Chile, where opposition was silenced, avant-garde artists were able to stage a number of actions.[40]

Nevertheless, the Cold War placed icy paws on such projects. The bombing of Solentiname and Rama's expulsion from the USA as a communist were but two indications that the rubric under which people could be labelled enemies of the state embraced an ever larger sector of the population. The military governments of the Southern Cone indiscriminately rounded up middle-of-the-road socialists, students, radicals and even their families as enemies to be exterminated. The abstract universal, 'freedom', became a vicious irony at a time when civil wars were being fought between the contras and the Sandinistas in Nicaragua and between the government of El Salvador and a liberation army. Guerrilla movements, over-hasty in pronouncing a revolutionary situation, were hardly able to compete with state terror.[41] Death, disappearance and exile would eliminate utopian hopes, and commodification under neoliberalism encouraged a collective amnesia about the recent past.[42] Even Mexico, which had a civilian president, tallied up a record of disappearances. In Guatemala, during the 1980s, there were an estimated 200,000 violent deaths, many of them among the indigenous population. In the Southern Cone, the violence of the shift from projects of national autonomy to censorship and silence, and then from the silence of the dictatorships to the traumatized transitions to democracy, discouraged any revival of a utopian project. For the military governments not only won the war on communism but also laid the foundation for a new kind of state that ushered in neoliberal restructuring as well as an information economy. The agents of change were first of all the military, for whom information was to be extracted by torture and repression but who also recognized the possibilities of television for the control of information, and second a professional intelligentsia whose education was pragmatic rather than classical and humanistic. The secular project initiated by the Enlightenment was transformed into a grim parody in the disenchanted world of these technologically advanced, repressive states. Worse, when people found themselves looking for unmarked graves and attempting to identify their children or parents from piles of bones, they lost for ever that dream of the liberated territory.

The liberated territory had served as the allegory for a nation that could be imagined as independent and self-sustaining. It was rendered obsolete when, in the 1990s, the very concept of nationhood changed, with the state becoming the facilitator of globalization, and the idea of national autonomy seeming nonsensical given that national borders were now porous. When Mexico, a country with a strong nationalist ideology, signed the Free Trade Agreement with Canada and the United States, it signalled this epochal change in the role of the state.

The epitaph of the lettered city was written at the onset of the era of violence by Rodolfo Walsh, an Argentine novelist, short-story writer and investigative journalist who had worked in Cuba in the early years of the Revolution. In 1972, he wrote a letter to Roberto Fernández Retamar, the editor of the Cuban journal *Casa de las Américas*, that described the climate of surveillance and repression in Argentina that foreshadowed the takeover of the military in 1976.

> You will understand that the only things about which one could or would want to write are exactly those that cannot be written or mentioned; the only possible heroes, the revolutionaries, need silence; the only ingenious things are those that the enemy still doesn't know: the possible discoveries need a well in which to hide; all truth happens below, as does hope; the one who knows does not tell; the one who tells something, does not know; the result of the best intellectual endeavors are daily burned and next day they are reconstructed and again burned. This painful change is nevertheless extraordinary. For some, life is now full of meaning, although literature cannot exist. The silence of intellectuals, the collapse of the literary boom, the end of the salon is the most formidable testimony that those who cannot yet bring themselves to participate in the ongoing though slow-moving popular revolution – still cannot be the accomplices of the oppressor culture nor accept privilege without feeling guilt, nor detach themselves from the suffering and struggle of the people which, as always, is seen to be the principal protagonist of history.[43]

'Literature cannot exist', wrote Walsh, who was one of a group of Argentine writers – among them Juan Gelman and Paco Urondo – who had joined the Montoneros, a nationalist and militant wing of the Peronist movement. Their lives were subsequently tragic. Urondo killed himself when ambushed by the army. Gelman, who was sent to Rome by the movement, suffered a bitter loss when his son and his pregnant daughter-in-law were captured by the army; the son was executed, the daughter-in-law was taken to Uruguay where she gave birth to a child and was then killed. The child was put out for adoption, as were many of the children born to political prisoners. Gelman spent nearly three decades trying to trace this child, and finally successfully appealed to the President of Uruguay to release information that led to its discovery. Unlike Walsh, Gelman never thought that literature was impossible. In his poetry he wrote of torture and defeat, admonishing his fellow poets for their obsession with their own personal death[44] and asking what supports people whose hopes have been ruined: 'It's strange / remnants of human ideas are piled up on the corner of the neighbourhood / where they had fallen in the time of the unpassion [despasion].'[45] Not only does his poetry capture the inadequacy of language now called on to bear witness to horror, but it also draws on mysticism of Juan de la Cruz and Santa Teresa for a language to express the unexpressible: the sound of silence. Many of Gelman's poems written in the late 1970s thus run counter to the unsustainable macho appeal of the guerrilla movements by evoking a feminine domain of domesticity, family love and the surrender of the self. It was, indeed, the figure of the woman as mourner who would assume centre stage in the person of the Mothers of the Plaza de Mayo, to whom Gelman dedicated an oratorio.[46]

Walsh's fate was, if anything, even more tragic. He had been a member of various militant groups before joining the Montoneros in 1976, when the military government came to power. In September of that year, his daughter Maria Victoria, a member of the Montoneros, was killed in an army attack on her hide-out. In an act of desperation, Walsh then wrote and distributed an open letter to the military government detailing their crimes: the thousands of disappearances, the death camps, the use of torture, and the indiscriminate seizure and murder of civilians who were not members of guerrilla organizations. He also wrote that these crimes were not the worst. It was the economic policies that explained not only the crimes but also the planned poverty that had now been visited on Argentina, a policy dictated by the International Monetary Fund. In the last lines of the letter, he acknowledges that he wrote it 'without hope of being heard, with the certainty of being persecuted, but firm in the engagement [*compromiso*] that I assumed of bearing witness in difficult times.'[47] Days later he was shot and killed in downtown Buenos Aires and his body disappeared.

In his discussion of the discourse of the end of utopia in his book *Twilight Memories*, Andreas Huyssen suggests that in Germany, a country with its own traumatic past, rather than disappearing, the utopian acquired a different temporality in 'the shift from anticipation and the future to memory and the past'.[48] This is strikingly true of much recent Latin American fiction and poetry as writers try to piece together the fragments of broken aspirations. The Mexican writer Carmen Boullosa has written a series of 'historical' novels that again and again re-imagine historic failures: the Egypt that succumbed to the Roman empire in *Cleopatra Dismounts*, the free pirate communities of the Caribbean, the indigenous at the time of the conquest.[49] In *Por la patria*, Diamela Eltit transcribes the fragmented language and communities that no longer add up to a nation.[50] Memory had been compromised when post-dictatorial governments attempted to repackage the past in ways that erased the experience of the families of the disappeared and other victims, and in many countries it was women (largely absent from the lettered city) who took a prominent role in recovering memory and in taking account of the poverty of language and of narrative in the new era. And it is this emergence of new actors on to the scene – not only women but also the indigenous population and Afro-Americans – that now vitalizes Latin American post-Cold-War culture.

Notes

1 See Casanova, *La République mondiale des lettres* (1999).
2 I cover this in greater detail in my book *The Decline and Fall of the Lettered City: Latin America in the Cold War* (Cambridge, MA, and London: Harvard University Press, 2002). See especially Chapter 1, pp. 21–56.
3 Joanne P. Sharp, *Condensing the Cold War: Reader's Digest and American Identity* (2000). During the Allende regime, Ariel Dorfman and Armand Mattelart analysed Disney comics for their subliminal message, in *How to Read Donald Duck: Imperialist Ideology in the Disney Comic* (1975).
4 Fuentes, *Don Quixote or the Critique of Reading* (Austin: University of Texas Press, 1976), p. 49.
5 Sarraute's article on Flaubert was discussed by Mario Vargas Llosa in his book *The Perpetual Orgy: Flaubert and Madame Bovary*, trans. Helen Lane (1975; New York: Farrar, Straus and Giroux, 1987), p. 39.
6 Fuentes, 'Kierkegard en la Zona Rosa', in Fuentes, *Tiempo Mexicano* (Mexico: Joaquin Mortiz, 1971), p. 40.
7 Castañeda, *Compañero: The Life and Death of Che Guevara* (New York: Alfred Knopf, 1998), pp. 193–4.
8 On the Argentine writers see Donald C. Hodges, *Argentina's 'Dirty War': An Intellectual Biography* (1991). On Roque Dalton's death see Jorge Castañeda, *Utopia Unarmed: The Latin American Left after the Cold War* (New York: Alfred A. Knopf, 1993), pp. 130–1.
9 I discuss aspects of Cuban cultural policy in Chapter 3 of *The Decline and Fall of the Lettered City*, pp. 86–117.
10 Vargas Llosa, *Contra viento y marea* (Barcelona: Seix Barral, 1983), pp. 166–8.
11 See Rama, *La ciudad letrada* (Hanover: Ediciones del Norte, 1984), especially Chapter 6, 'La ciudad revolucionaria', pp. 154–61.
12 The polemic was carried on in issues 1302 to 1306 of *Marcha* that appeared in May and June of 1966.
13 In his diary, he writes of having distanced himself from Cuba after the Padilla affair: Rama, *Diario, 1974-1983* (Montevideo: Trilce, 2001), p. 130. But he also maintained an acute interest in cultural politics there. Reinaldo Arenas's unjust

attack on Rama for supporting Castro is explicable only in the light of the exacerbated polarities of the Cold War during which 'Castro supporter' and 'CIA agent' were common accusations.
14 Ibid., p. 167.
15 Rama, *La ciudad letrada*, p. xviii. This same act had kept the novelist, Carlos Fuentes, out of the US for many years and was responsible for turning back the Guatemala writer, Tito Monteroso, when on his way to a conference in Chicago.
16 Ibid., p. xviii.
17 Ibid., p. xix.
18 Williams, *Marxism and Literature* (Oxford and New York: Oxford University Press, 1977), p. 19.
19 Friedrich Nietzsche, *Beyond Good and Evil*, new edn, trans. R. J. Hollingdale (1886; Harmondsworth: Penguin, 1973), pp. 223, 133. Rama's posthumously published book on Spanish-American modernism has the title *Las máscaras democráticas del Modernism* (Montevideo: Arca, 1994).
20 Alberto Moreiras, *The Exhaustion of Difference: The Politics of Latin American Cultural Studies* (Durham: Duke University Press, 2001), p. 188.
21 John Beverley, *Subalternity and Representation: Arguments in Cultural Theory* (Durham: Duke University Press, 1999), p. 45.
22 On the Zapatistas see June Nash, *Mayan Visions: The Quest for Autonomy in an Age of Globalization* (2001).
23 For instance, during the recent economic crisis in Argentina, the conceptualist artist Roberto Jacobi and the journal *Ramona* put paper bills they called the 'Venus' into circulation through exchanges on the Internet.
24 Guattari, *Molecular Revolution: Psychiatry and Politics*, trans. Rosemary Sheed (1977; London: Penguin, 1984), p. 64.
25 See Vargas Llosa, *The War of the End of the World* (1981). The extermination of this community was recounted in a Brazilian classic by Euclides da Cunha, *Os Sertoes* (1902), translated into English as *Rebellion in the Backlands* (1944).
26 See Roa Bastos, *I the Supreme*, trans. Helen Lane (1974).
27 See García Márquez, *The Autumn of the Patriarch* (1975).
28 Rose, *Mourning Becomes the Law: Philosophy and Representation* (Cambridge: Cambridge University Press, 1997), p. 5.
29 See Mayra Jiménez, ed., *Poesia campesina de Solentiname* (1983).
30 Brotherston, *Book of the Fourth World: Reading the Native Americas through their Literature* (Cambridge: Cambridge University Press: 1992), p. 342.
31 Pound, 'Canto XLV', in Pound, *Selected Cantos of Ezra Pound* (London: Faber, 1967), p. 67, lines 13–15.
32 Cardenal, *Las ínsulas extrañas, Memorias II* (Mexico: Fondo de cultura económica, 2003), p. 45.
33 Cardenal, 'Las ciudades perdidas', in Cardenal, *Homenaje a los indios americanos* (Buenos Aires: Carlos Lohlé, 1972), pp. 15–17, lines 21–3. My translation.
34 Cardenal, 'Economía de Tahuantinsuyu', in ibid., p. 38, lines 22–5. My translation.
35 Liberation theology is complex and varied. Among its distinguished theologians were the Peruvian Gutierrez and the Brazilian Leonard Boff. While weakened by the Vatican censure of liberation theology, the influence persists in certain areas. See Denis Lynn Daly Heyck, *Surviving Globalization in Three Latin American Communities* (2002), which reveals the ongoing influence of the practices initiated by liberation theology.
36 Cortázar, 'Apocalípsis en Solentiname', in Cortázar, *Alguien que anda por ahí* (Mexico: Hermes, 1977), pp. 79–89. The quotation is on page 82 and the translation is mine.
37 Letter to Saúl Sosnowski, 9 November 1981: Cortázar, *Cartas 1969-1983*, ed. Aurora Bernárdez (Barcelona: Alfaguara, 2000), p. 1750.

38 Letter to Jean L. Andreu, 21 April, 1975: in ibid., p. 1569.
39 See Peter Bürger, *Theory of the Avant-Garde* (1981).
40 Richard, 'Una cita limítrofe entre neovanguardia y postvanguardia', in Richard, *La Insubordinación de los Signos: Cambio político, transformaciones culturales y poéticas de la crisis* (Santiago: Cuarto Propio, 1994), pp. 37–54.
41 For an in-depth examination of the Argentine guerrilla see Donald C. Hodges, *Argentina's 'Dirty War': An Intellectual Biography* (1991).
42 Idelber Avelar, *The Untimely Present: Postdictatorial Latin American Fiction and the Task of Mourning* (Durham: Duke University Press, 1999).
43 The letter is cited at http://www.literature.org/Walsh/rwcarta.html (accessed 11 January 2005).
44 See Gelman, 'Bellezas' (from the collection *Relaciones*), in Gelman, *Pesar Todo: Antología* (Mexico: Fondo de Cultura Económica, 2001), pp. 120–1.
45 Gelman, 'Now', in Gelman, *Pesar Todo*, p. 384, lines 10–11. My translation.
46 See Gelman, *La Junta Luz: Oratorio a las Madres de Plaza de Mayo* (1985).
47 Walsh, 'Carta abierta de Rodolfo Walsh a la Junta Militar (1977)', *El latinoamericano*, http://www. ellatinoamericano.cjb.net (accessed 27 November 2004).
48 Huyssen, *Twilight Memories: Marking Time in the Culture of Amnesia* (New York: Routledge, 1995), p. 95.
49 See Boullosa, *Cleopatra Dismounts* (1992) and *They're Cows, We're Pigs* (1991).
50 See Eltit, *Por la patria* (1986). For a discussion of women writers during the period of transition see Francine Masiello, 'Gender Traffic on the North/South Horizon', in Masiello, *The Art of Transition: Latin American Culture and Neoliberal Crisis* (Durham: Duke University Press, 2000), pp. 107–39.

Bibliography

Aaron, Daniel, *Writers on the Left: Episodes in American Literary Communism* (New York: Harcourt, Brace and World, 1961).
Achebe, Chinua, *Things Fall Apart*, new edn (1958; Oxford: Heinemann, 1986).
——, *Morning Yet on Creation Day* (London: Heinemann, 1975).
——, *Anthills of the Savannah*, new edn (1987; London: Pan Books, 1988).
Adameşteanu, Gabriela, *Dimineaţa pierdută* (Bucharest: Cartea Românească, 1983).
Adamson, Judith, *Graham Greene: The Dangerous Edge – Where Art and Politics Meet* (London: Macmillan, 1990).
Addison, Jr, Gayle, *The Black Aesthetic* (New York: Anchor Books, 1971).
Agolli, Dritëro, *Hapat e mija në asfalt* (Tirana: Naim Frashëri, 1961).
Ahmad, Aijaz, *In Theory: Classes, Nations, Literatures* (Delhi: Oxford University Press, 1994).
Aksenov, V., *V poiskakh grustnogo bebi: Kniga ob Amerike* (New York: Liberty, 1987).
——, 'Kruglye sutki non-stop', *Novyi mir*, 8, 1976, 51–122.
Ali, Tariq, and Howard Brenton, *Moscow Gold* (London: Nick Hern Books, 1990).
Allain, Marie-Françoise, *The Other Man: Conversations with Graham Greene by Marie-Françoise Allain*, trans. Guido Walman (1981; London: Bodley Head, 1983).
Allott, Miriam, 'The Moral Situation in *The Quiet American*', in Robert O. Evans, ed., *Graham Greene: Some Critical Considerations*, new edn (1963; Lexington: University of Kentucky Press, 1967).
Alman, David, *The Hourglass* (New York: Simon and Schuster, 1947).
——, *The Well of Compassion* (New York: Simon and Schuster, 1948).
Alvarez, A., *Under Pressure. The Writer in Society: Eastern Europe and the USA* (Harmondsworth: Penguin, 1965).
Amadi, Elechi, *Estrangement* (London: Heinemann, 1986).
Amis, Kingsley, *Lucky Jim* (London: Victor Gollancz, 1954).
Amis, Martin, *Einstein's Monsters*, new edn (1987; London: Vintage, 2003).
Anderson, Benedict, *Imagined Communities: Reflections on the Origin and Spread of Nationalism*, rev. edn (1983; London and New York: Verso, 1991).
Anderson, Raymond H., 'Soviet Reply to Trial Critics', *The Times*, 4 March 1968, 8.
Andreev, Iu., 'O romane Vsevoloda Kochetova *Chego zhe ty khochesh'?*', *Literaturnaia Gazeta*, 7 (1970), 4.
Anisfield, Nancy, ed., *The Nightmare Considered: Critical Essays on Nuclear War Literature* (Ohio: Bowling Green State University Popular Press, 1991).
Anon., 'Bail Posted for Communists', *New York Times*, 25 July 1951, 12.
——, 'N.N. Shpanov', *Literaturnaia Gazeta*, 5 October 1961, 4.

——, 'Seminar Sponsored by the Afro-Asian Writers' Bureau to Commemorate the 25th Anniversary of Chairman Mao's "Talks"', *Chinese Literature*, 9 (1967), 48–56.
——, 'Performance by Somali Artists' Delegation', *Chinese Literature*, 11 (1967), 137.
——, 'Revolutionary Songs and Dances, Militant Friendship', *Chinese Literature*, 12 (1967), 102–6.
——, 'The World's Revolutionary People Enthusiastically Translate and Publish Chairman Mao's Works', *Chinese Literature*, 11–12 (1969), 154–6.
Anzovin, Stephen, *South Africa: Apartheid and Divestiture* (New York: H.W. Wilson, 1987).
Appel, Benjamin, *The Dark Stain* (New York: The Dial Press, 1943).
Arapi, Fatos, *Shtigje Poetike* (Tirana: Naim Frashëri, 1962).
Armah, Ayi Kwei, *The Beautyful Ones Are Not Yet Born* (London: Heinemann, 1969).
——, *Two Thousand Seasons*, new edn (1973; London Heinemann, 1979).
Ash, Timothy Garton, 'The Hungarian Lesson', *New York Times Book Review*, 5 (December 1985), 5.
Aston, Elaine, *Caryl Churchill*, 2nd edn (1997; Tavistock: Northcote House, 2001).
Auster, Paul, *In the Country of Last Things*, new edn (1987; London: Faber, 1989).
Avelar, Idelber, *The Untimely Present: Postdictatorial Latin American Fiction and the Task of Mourning* (Durham: Duke University Press, 1999).
Bacon, Jon Lance, *Flannery O'Connor and Cold War Culture* (Cambridge: Cambridge University Press, 1994).
Baker, Houston A., *Blues, Ideology and Afro-American Literature: A Vernacular Theory* (Chicago and London: University of Chicago Press, 1984).
Bălăiță, George, *Lumea în două zile* (Bucharest: Editura Eminescu, 1975).
Bănulescu, Ștefan, *The Book of Metopolis* (1977), fragments trans. Alina Carac, *Romanian Review*, 2 (1986), 10–34.
Barabash, Yuri, *Aesthetics and Politics*, trans. anon. (1968; Moscow: Progress Publishers, 1977).
Barańczak, Stanisław, *A Fugitive from Utopia: The Poetry of Zbigniew Herbert* (Cambridge: Harvard University Press, 1987).
——, *Breathing under Water and Other East European Essays* (Cambridge, MA: Harvard University Press, 1990).
Barbu, Eugen, *Principele* (Bucharest: Editura tineretului, 1969).
Barker, Howard, *The Hang of the Gaol and Heaven* (London: John Calder, 1982).
——, *Two Plays for the Right: The Loud Boy's Life and Birth on a Hard Shoulder* (London: John Calder, 1982).
——, *A Passion in Six Days and Downchild* (London: John Calder, 1985).
——, *The Power of the Dog* (London: John Calder, 1985).
——, 'Oppression, Resistance and the Writer's Testament', interviewed by Finlay Donesky, *New Theatre Quarterly*, 11: 8 (November 1986), 336–44.
——, *Arguments for a Theatre*, 3rd edn (1989; Manchester: Manchester University Press, 1997).
——, *Collected Plays: Volume One* (London: John Calder, 1990).
Barnard, Rita, 'Speaking Places: Prison, Poetry, and the South African Nation', *Research in African Literatures*, 32: 3 (2001), http://muse.jhu.edu/journals/research_in_african_ literatures (accessed 6 September 2004).
Barton Johnson, D., 'Aksenov as Travel Writer: *Round the Clock, Non-Stop*', in

Edward Możejko, ed., *Vasiliy Pavlovich Aksenov: A Writer in Quest of Himself* (Columbus, OH: Slavica, 1984), 181–92.

Baudrillard, Jean, *Jean Baudrillard: Selected Writings*, ed. Mark Poster, trans. Jacques Mourrain (Cambridge: Polity Press, 1988).

Bauer, Raymond A., 'Brainwashing: Psychology or Demonology?' *Journal of Social Issues*, 13: 3 (1957), 41–7.

Beene, LynnDianne, *John le Carré* (New York: Twayne, 1992).

Beliaev, Albert, *The Ideological Struggle and Literature: A Critical Analysis of the Writings of U.S. Sovietologists*, new edn (1975; Moscow: Progress Publishers, 1978).

Belknap, Michael R., *Cold War Political Justice: The Smith Act, the Communist Party, and American Civil Liberties* (Westport, CT: Greenwood, 1977).

Bercovitch, Sacvan, ed., *Reconstructing American Literary History* (Cambridge, MA, and London: Harvard University Press, 1986).

Bergonzi, Bernard, *Reading the Thirties: Texts and Contexts* (London: Macmillan, 1978).

——, *Wartime and Aftermath: English Literature and Its Background 1939–1960* (Oxford: Oxford University Press, 1993).

Berkoff, Steven, *Sink the Belgrano! and Massage* (London: Faber, 1987).

Bethlehem, Louise, '"A Primary Need as Strong as Hunger": The Rhetoric of Urgency in South African Literary Culture under Apartheid', *Poetics Today*, 22: 2 (2001), 365- 89.

Beverley, John, *Subalternity and Representation: Arguments in Cultural Theory* (Durham: Duke University Press, 1999).

Bhabha, Homi K., ed., *Nation and Narration* (London and New York: Routledge, 1990).

Bleik, Patritsiia, 'Vstrechi s sovetskimi pisateliami', *Nashi Dni*, 33 (1964), 102–22.

Blekher, L.I., and G. Iu. Liubarskii, *Glavnyi russkii spor: Ot zapadnikov i slavianofilov do globalizma i novogo srednevekov'ia* (Moscow: Akademicheskii proekt, 2003).

Blish, James, *Black Easter and The Day after Judgement*, new edn (1968; London: Arrow Books, 1981).

Block, Alan A., *Anonymous Toil: Re-Evaluation of the American Radical Novel in the Twentieth Century* (Lanham: University Press of America, 1992).

Bodor, Ádám, *Sinisztra körzet: egy regény fejezetei* (Budapest: Magvető, 1992).

Booker, M. Keith, *Colonial Power, Colonial Texts: India in the Modern British Novel* (Ann Arbor: University of Michigan Press, 1997).

——, 'The Historical Novel in Ayi Kwei Armah and David Caute: African Literature, Socialist Literature, and the Bourgeois Cultural Tradition', *Critique*, 38: 3 (1997), 235–48.

Booker, M. Keith, and Dubravka Juraga, *Bakhtin, Stalin, and Modern Russian Fiction: Carnival, Dialogism, and History* (Westport, CT: Greenwood Press, 1995).

Borowski, Tadeusz, *This Way for the Gas, Ladies and Gentlemen*, trans. Michael Kandel (1946; London: Penguin, 1976).

Boullosa, Carmen, *They're Cows, We're Pigs*, trans. Leland H. Chambers (1991; New York: Grove Press, 1997).

——, *Cleopatra Dismounts*, trans. Geoff Hargreaves (1992; New York: Grove Press, 2003).

Bowart, Walter, *Operation Mind Control* (London: Fontana/Collins, 1978).

Bowen, Elizabeth, *The Heat of the Day*, new edn (1949; London: Vintage, 1998).

Bowen, Kevin, and Bruce Weigl, eds, *Writing between the Lines: An Anthology of War and Its Social Consequences* (Amherst: University of Massachusetts Press, 1997).

Bowen, Kevin, Nguyen Ba Chung and Bruce Weigl, eds, *Mountain River: Vietnamese Poetry from the Wars, 1948–1993*, trans. Kevin Bowen, Nguyen Ba Chung, Bruce Weigl, *et al.* (Amherst: University of Massachusetts Press, 1998).

Bowker, Mike, and Robin Brown, eds, *From Cold War to Collapse: Theory and World Politics in the 1980s* (Cambridge: Cambridge University Press, 1993).

Boyer, Paul, *By the Bomb's Early Light: American Thought and Culture at the Dawn of the Atomic Age*, 2nd edn (1985; London: University of North Carolina Press, 1994).

Braine, John, *Room at the Top* (London: Eyre and Spottiswoode, 1957).

Brathwaite, Edward Kamau, *History of the Voice: The Development of Nation Language in Anglophone Caribbean Poetry* (London and Port of Spain: New Beacon Books, 1984).

Brenton, Howard, *Plays: Two* (London: Methuen, 1989).

——, *Berlin Bertie* (London: Nick Hern Books, 1992).

Breytenbach, Breyten, *Dog Heart: A Travel Memoir* (Cape Town: Human and Rousseau, 1998).

Brians, Paul, 'Nuclear Family/Nuclear War', *Papers on Language and Literature: A Journal for Scholars and Critics of Language and Literature*, 26: 1 (1990), 134–42.

——, *Nuclear Holocausts: Atomic War in Fiction 1895–1984* (Kent, Ohio: Kent State University Press, 1987).

Brodsky, Josip, *Collected Poems in English*, ed. Ann Kjellberg, trans. Anthony Hecht, *et al.* (2000; Manchester: Manchester University Press, 2001).

Brotherston, Gordon, *Book of the Fourth World: Reading the Native Americas through their Literature* (Cambridge: Cambridge University Press, 1992).

Brown, Dorothy H., and Barbara C. Ewell, eds, *Louisiana Women Writers: New Essays and a Comprehensive Bibliography* (Baton Rouge: Louisiana State University Press, 1992).

Brown, Frank London, *Trumbull Park* (Chicago: Regnery, 1959).

Brown, Lloyd L., *Iron City*, new edn (1951; Boston: Northeastern University Press, 1994).

Brubaker, Rogers, *Nationalisms Reframed: Nationhood and the National Question in the New Europe* (Cambridge: Cambridge University Press, 1996).

Bucher, Lloyd M., with Mark Rascovich, *Bucher: My Story* (Garden City, New York: Doubleday, 1970).

Buhle, Mari Jo, Paul Buhle and Harvey J. Kaye, eds, *The American Radical* (London and New York: Routledge, 1994).

Buckmaster, Henrietta, *Deep River* (New York: Harcourt, Brace and Co., 1944).

Bulychev, Kir, *Kak stat' fantastom* (Moscow: Drofa, 2003).

Bürger, Peter, *Theory of the Avant-Garde*, trans. Michael Shaw (1981; Minneapolis: University of Minnesota Press, 1984).

Burroughs, William, *Exterminator!* (London: Calder and Boyars, 1974).

Callinicos, Alex, 'Wonders Taken for Signs: Homi Bhabha's Postcolonialism', in Teresa L. Ebert and Donald Morton, eds, *Post-ality: Marxism and Postcolonialism* (Washington: Maisonneuve Press, 1995), 98–112.

Calvino, Italo, *Why Read the Classics*, trans. Martin McLaughlin (1991; London: Jonathan Cape, 1999).

Canfield, Roger, *Stealth Invasion: Red Chinese Operations in North America* (Fairfax, VA: United States Intelligence Council, 2002).

Cardenal, Ernesto, *Homenaje a los indios americanos* (Buenos Aires: Carlos Lohlé, 1972).

——, *El evangelio en Solentiname* (Caracas: Signo Contemporáneo, 1976).
——, *Las ínsulas extrañas, Memorias II* (Mexico: Fondo de cultura económica, 2003).
Cârneci, Magda, *Art of the 1980s in Eastern Europe: Texts on Postmodernism* (Bucharest: Paralela 45, 1999).
Carruthers, Susan L., '*The Manchurian Candidate* (1962) and the Cold War Brainwashing Scare', *Historical Journal of Film, Radio and Television*, 18: 1 (1998), 75–94.
Carse, Robert, *Drums of Empire*, new edn (1959; London: World Distributors, 1960).
Cărtărescu, Mircea, *Postmodernismul românesc* (Bucharest: Humanitas, 1999).
Casanova, Pascale, *La République mondiale des lettres* (Paris: Seuil, 1999).
Castañeda, Jorge, *Utopia Unarmed: The Latin American Left after the Cold War* (New York: Alfred A. Knopf, 1993).
——, *Compañero: The Life and Death of Che Guevara* (New York: Alfred Knopf, 1998).
Castro, Fidel, 'History Will Absolve Me', in Castro, *Revolutionary Struggle 1947–1958: Volume 1 of the Selected Works of Fidel Castro*, eds, Rolando E. Bonachea and Nelson P. Valdés (Cambridge, MA, and London: MIT Press, 1972), 164–221.
Cavafy, C.P., *Selected Poems*, trans. Edmund Keeley and Philip Sherrard (London: Hogarth Press, 1975).
Chanoff, David and Doan Van Toai, *Portrait of the Enemy* (New York: Random House, 1986).
Chatterjee, Partha, *The Nation and Its Fragments: Colonial and Postcolonial Histories* (Princeton: Princeton University Press, 1993).
Chen, Xiaomei, *Acting the Right Part: Political Theater and Popular Drama in Contemporary China* (Honolulu: University of Hawaii Press, 2002).
Childress, Alice, *Florence*, printed in *Masses & Mainstream*, 3 (October 1950), 34–47.
——, *Like One of the Family: Conversations from a Domestic's Life* (New York: Independence, 1956).
——, *Wine in the Wilderness* (1969), in Elizabeth Brown-Guillory, ed., *Wine in the Wilderness: Plays by African American Women from the Harlam Renaissance to the Present* (New York and London: Greenwood Press, 1990).
——, *Mojo*, printed in *Black World*, 20 (April 1971), 54–82.
——, *Trouble in Mind*, in Lindsay Patterson, ed., *Black Theatre* (New York: Dodd, Mead, 1971).
——, *A Hero Ain't Nothing But a Sandwich* (New York: Coward, McCann and Geoghegan, 1973).
——, *Wedding Band* (New York: French, 1973).
——, *A Short Walk* (New York: Coward, McCann and Geoghegan, 1979).
——, *Those Other People* (New York: Putnam, 1989).
China Ballet Troupe, *Hongse niangzijun*, *Hongqi*, 7 (1970), 35–65.
Chinodya, Shimmer, *Harvest of Thorns*, new edn (1989; London: Heinemann, 1992).
Chinweizu, Onwuchekwa Jemie and Ihechukwu Madubuike, *Toward the Decolonization of African Literature: African Fiction and Poetry and Their Critics* (Washington, DC: Howard University Press, 1983).
Chomsky, Noam, *Towards a New Cold War: Essays on the Current Crisis and How We Got There* (London: Sinclair Browne, 1982).
——, *World Orders, Old and New* (London: Pluto Press, 1997).
Churchill, Caryl, *Mad Forest* (London: Nick Hern Books, 1990).

——, *Plays: Two* (London: Methuen, 1990).
——, *Far Away* (London: Nick Hern Books, 2000).
Ciobanu, Ion C., *Codrii*, 2 Vols, new edn (1954, 1957; Moscow: Izvestia, 1969).
——, *Podgorenii* (Chişinău/Kishinev: Lit-ra artistike, 1982).
Clark, Katerina, *The Soviet Novel: History as Ritual* (Chicago: University of Chicago Press, 1981).
Clarke, I.F., *Voices Prophesying War: Future Wars 1763–3749*, 2nd edn (1966; Oxford: Oxford University Press, 1992).
Clingman, Stephen, *The Novels of Nadine Gordimer: History from the Inside* (Johannesburg: Ravan, 1986).
Clowes, Edith W., *Russian Experimental Fiction: Resisting Ideology after Utopia* (Princeton: Princeton University Press, 1993).
Coker, Christopher, *The United States and South Africa, 1968–1985: Constructive Engagement and Its Critics* (Durham, NC: Duke University Press, 1986).
Condon, Richard, *The Manchurian Candidate*, new edn (1959; New York: New American Library, 1960).
——, *The Whisper of the Axe* (New York: Dial Press, 1976).
Conrad, Joseph, *Heart of Darkness*, new edn (1902; Harmondsworth: Penguin, 1973).
Conrad, Earl, *Rock Bottom* (Garden City, New York: Doubleday, 1952).
——, *Gulf Stream North*, new edn (1954; London: Gollancz, 1955).
Coover, Robert, *The Public Burning*, new edn (1977; New York: Grove, 1998).
Coquery-Vidrovitch, Catherine, *Africa: Endurance and Change South of the Sahara*, trans. David Maisel (1985; Berkeley: University of California Press, 1988).
Corn, David, 'Reagan's Bloody Legacy', *TomPaine.Common Sense*, http://www.tompaine.com (accessed 6 September 2004).
Cornis-Pope, Marcel, *Narrative Innovation and Cultural Rewriting in the Cold War and After* (New York and Basingstoke: Palgrave, 2001).
Cornis-Pope, Marcel and John Neubauer, eds, *History of the Literary Cultures of East-Central Europe*, Vol. 1 (Philadelphia and Amsterdam: John Benjamins Publishing, 2004).
Cortázar, Julio, *Hopscotch*, trans. G. Rabassa (1963; New York: Pantheon, 1966).
——, 'Apocalípsis en Solentiname', in Cortázar, *Alguien que anda por ahí* (Mexico: Hermes, 1977).
——, *Cartas 1969–1983*, ed. Aurora Bernárdez (Barcelona: Alfaguara, 2000).
COSAW, ed., *Buang Basadi / Khulumani Makhosikazi / Women Speak: Conference on Women and Writing* (Johannesburg: COSAW Publications, 1989).
Coupland, Douglas, *Life after God*, new edn (1994; London: Simon & Schuster, 1999).
Couto, Maria, *Graham Greene: On the Frontier – Politics and Religion in the Novels* (New York: St Martin's Press, 1988).
Cox, Michael, Ken Booth and Tim Dunne, eds, *The Interregnum: Controversies in World Politics 1989–1999* (Cambridge: Cambridge University Press, 1999).
Croft, Andy, *Red Letter Days: British Fiction in the 1930s* (London: Lawrence and Wishart, 1990).
Cronin, Jeremy, '"Even Under the Rine of Terror . . .": Insurgent South African Poetry', *Research in African Literatures*, 19 (1988), 12–23.
Cruse, Harold, *The Crisis of the Negro Intellectual*, new edn (1967; London: W.H. Allen, 1969).

Culture and Working Life Project, 'Albie Sachs Must Not Worry', in Ingrid de Kok and Karen Press, eds, *Spring Is Rebellious: Arguments about Cultural Freedom* (Cape Town: Buchu Books, 1990), 99–103.

Curry, Jane Leftwitch, ed., *The Black Book of Polish Censorship* (New York: Random House, 1984).

Da Cunha, Euclides, *Rebellion in the Backlands*, trans. Samuel Putnam (1902; London: Gollanz, 1944).

Davies, Catherine, *A Place in the Sun? Women Writers in Twentieth-Century Cuba* (London and New Jersey: Zed Books, 1997).

Davies, Norman, *Microcosm: A Portrait of a Central European City* (London: Jonathan Cape, 2002).

——, *Rising '44* (London: Macmillan, 2003).

Davis, Rocío G., 'Back to the Future: Mothers, Languages, and Homes in Cristina García's *Dreaming in Cuban*', *World Literature Today*, 74: 1 (2000), 60–8.

Davis, Robert Gorham, 'In Our Time No Man Is a Neutral', review of *The Quiet American*, the *New York Times* (11 March 1956), http://www.nytimes.com/books/00/02/20/specials/greene-quiet.html (accessed 4 May 2004).

Daymond, M.J. and Margaret Lenta, 'Workshop on Black Women's Writing and Reading', *Current Writing: Text and Reception in Southern Africa*, 2: 1 (1990), 71–89.

De Kock, Leon, 'South Africa in the Global Imaginary: An Introduction', *Poetics Today*, 22: 2 (2001), 263–98.

De Kok, Ingrid, 'Standing in the Doorway: A Preface', *World Literature Today*, 70: 1 (1996), 4–8.

De Kok, Ingrid and Karen Press, eds, *Spring Is Rebellious: Arguments about Cultural Freedom* (Cape Town: Buchu Books, 1990).

DeLillo, Don, *End Zone*, new edn (1972; London: Penguin, 1986).

——, *White Noise*, new edn (1984; London: Picador, 1986).

——, *Underworld*, new edn (1997; London: Picador, 1998).

Derrida, Jacques, 'Living On: Border Lines', trans. James Hulbert, in Harold Bloom, *et al.*, *Deconstruction and Criticism*, new edn (1979; New York: Continuum, 1986), 75–176.

DeShazer, Mary K., *A Poetics of Resistance: Women Writing in El Salvador, South Africa, and the United States* (Ann Arbor: University of Michigan Press, 1994).

De Vitis, A.A., *Graham Greene*, rev. edn (1964; Boston: Twayne, 1986).

Dewey, Joseph, *In a Dark Time: The Apocalyptic Temper in the American Novel of the Nuclear Age* (West Lafayette: Purdue University Press, 1990).

Diemert, Brian, *Graham Greene's Thrillers and the 1930s* (Montreal and Kingston: McGill-Queen's University Press, 1996).

Đilas, Milovan, *Članci; 1941–1947* (Zagreb: Kultura, 1947).

——, *Conversations with Stalin* (New York: Harcourt Brace Jovanovich, 1962).

Dirlik, Arif, 'The Postcolonial Aura: Third World Criticism in the Age of Global Capitalism', *Critical Inquiry*, 20 (Winter 1994), 328–56.

Dobrenko, Evgeny, 'The Disaster of Middlebrow Taste, or, Who "Invented" Socialist Realism', *South Atlantic Quarterly*, 94: 3 (1995), 773–806.

Doctorow, E.L., *The Book of Daniel*, new edn (1971; London: Picador, 1982).

Đông Hồ, 'War', *The Vietnam Review*, 4 (1998), 420.

Donoghue, Denis, 'Graham Greene, Autobiographer', *England, Their England: Commentaries on English Language and Literature* (New York: Alfred A. Knopf, 1988), 323–31.

Dooner, P.W., *Last Days of the Republic*, new edn (1880; New York: Arno Press, 1978).
Dorfman, Ariel and Armand Mattelart, *How to Read Donald Duck: Imperialist Ideology in the Disney Comic*, trans. David Kunzle (1975; New York: International General, 1975).
Dowling, David, *Fictions of Nuclear Disaster* (London: Macmillan, 1987).
Doyle, Dorothy, *Journey through Jess* (New York: Ten Star Press, 1989).
Drakulić, Slavenka, *How We Survived Communism and Even Laughed* (1988; London: Hutchinson, 1992).
Driver, Dorothy, 'Transformation through Art: Writing, Representation, and Subjectivity in Recent South African Fiction', *World Literature Today*, 70: 1 (1996), 45–52.
Du Bois, W.E.B., *The Ordeal of Mansart* (New York: Mainstream Publishers, 1957).
——, *Mansart Builds a School* (New York: Mainstream Publishers, 1959).
——, *Worlds of Colour* (New York: Mainstream Publishers, 1961).
Dugin, Aleksandr, *Misterii Evrazii* (Moscow: Arktogeia, 1996).
——, *Osnovy geopolitiki* (Moscow: Arktogeia, 1997).
Dumitriu, Petru, *Pasărea furtunii* (Bucharest: ESPLA, 1954).
——, *Incognito*, trans. Norman Denny (New York: Macmillan, 1964).
Dunn, Tony, 'The Real History Man: Howard Barker's Plays for Spring 1985', *Drama – The Quarterly Theatre Review (TQTR)*, 155 (Spring 1985), 9–11.
During, Simon, 'Literature – Nationalism's Other? The Case for Revision', in Homi Bhabha, ed., *Nation and Narration* (London and New York: Routledge, 1990), 138–53.
Dussel, Enrique, *The Invention of the Americas: Eclipse of 'the Other' and the Myth of Modernity*, trans. Michael D. Barber (New York: Continuum, 1995).
Dymshits, A., 'Protiv podzhigatelei voiny', *Zvezda*, 9 (1950), 180–2.
Edgar, David, *Plays: One* (London: Methuen, 1987).
——, *The Shape of the Table* (London: Nick Hern Books, 1990).
——, *Plays: Three* (London: Methuen, 1991).
——, *Pentecost* (London: Nick Hern Books, 1995).
——, *The Prisoner's Dilemma* (London: Nick Hern Books, 2001).
Edwards, Oliver, *The USA and the Cold War: 1945–63*, 2nd edn (1997; Oxon: Hodder and Stoughton, 2002).
Eisinger, Chester, *Fiction of the Forties* (Chicago and London: University of Chicago Press, 1963).
Eliot, T.S., *Selected Poems*, new edn (1954; London: Faber and Faber, 1961).
Elkin, A., 'Kuda idet pisatel' N. Shpanov?', *Komsomol'skaia Pravda*, 21 March 1959, 2.
Elliott, Emory, *et al.*, eds, *The Columbia Literary History of the United States* (New York and Guildford: Columbia University Press, 1988).
——, *The Columbia History of the American Novel* (New York: Columbia University Press, 1991).
Elsom, John, *Cold War Theatre* (London: Routledge, 1992).
Eltit, Diamela, *Por la patria* (Santiago: Las ediciones de Ornitorrinco, 1986).
Emecheta, Buchi, *Destination Biafra* (London: Allison and Busby, 1982).
Eschevarría, Roberto González, 'The Humanities and Cuban Studies, 1959–1989', in Damien Fernández, ed., *Cuban Studies since the Revolution* (Gainsville: University of Florida, 1992), 199–215.
Esterházy, Péter, *Bevezetés a szépirodalomba* (Budapest: Magvető, 1986).

250   Bibliography

——, *Fuvarosok* (Budapest: Magvető, 1983).
——, *Javított kiadás* (Budapest: Magvető, 2002).
Etkind, E., ed., *323 epigrammy* (Paris: Sintaksis, 1988).
Evill, Gill, ed., *Izinsingizi: Loudhailer Lives – South African Poetry from Natal* (Durban: Culture and Working Life Publications, 1988).
Evtushenko, E., *Vzmakh ruki* (Moscow: Molodaia gvardiia, 1962).
Fadeyev, Alexander, *The Rout*, trans. anon (1927; Moscow: Foreign Language Publishing House, 1956).
——, *The Young Guard*, trans. Volet Dutt (1945; Moscow: Progress Publishers, 1987).
Fanon, Frantz, *The Wretched of the Earth*, new edn, trans. Constance Farrington (1961; London: Penguin, 1967).
Farah, Nuruddin, *Sweet and Sour Milk* (London: Allison and Busby, 1979).
——, *Sardines* (London: Allison and Busby, 1981).
——, *Close Sesame* (London: Allison and Busby, 1983).
Fast, Howard, *Freedom Road*, new edn (1944; London: John Lane, 1946).
——, *My Glorious Brothers*, new edn (1948; London: Bodley Head, 1950).
——, *The Proud and the Free*, new edn (1950; London: Bodley Head, 1952).
——, *Spartacus*, new edn (1951; Hamilton and Co., 1959).
——, *Tony and the Wonderful Door* (New York: Blue Heron, 1952).
——, *The Passion of Sacco and Vanzetti: A New England Legend*, new edn (1953; London: Bodley Head, 1954).
——, *The Pledge* (Boston: Houghton Mifflin, 1988).
Faulkner, William, 'The Stockholm Address', in Frederick J. Hoffman and Olga Vickery, eds, *William Faulkner: Three Decades of Criticism* (New York: Harbinger, 1960, 347–8.
Foertsch, Jacqueline, 'Not Bombshells but Basketcases: Gendered Illness in Nuclear Texts', *Studies in the Novel*, 31: 4 (1999), 471–88.
Foley, Barbara, *Radical Representations: Politics and Form in U.S. Proletarian Fiction, 1929–1941* (Durham: Duke University Press, 1993).
Forrest, Katherine, *The Beverly Malibu*, new edn (1980; London: Grafton, 1993).
Forster, E.M., *Two Cheers for Democracy*, new edn (1951; London: Edward Arnold, 1972).
Fox, Pamela, *Class Fictions: Shame and Resistance in the British Working-Class Novel, 1890–1945* (Durham: Duke University Press, 1994).
Franco, Jean, *The Decline and Fall of the Lettered City: Latin America in the Cold War* (Cambridge, Mass. and London: Harvard University Press, 2002).
Frank, Pat, *Hold Back the Night* (London: Hamish Hamilton, 1952).
Freeborn, Richard, *The Russian Revolutionary Novel: Turgenev to Pasternak* (Cambridge: Cambridge University Press, 1982).
Freed, Richard M., *The Russians Are Coming! The Russians Are Coming!: Pageantry and Patriotism in Cold-War America* (Oxford: Oxford University Press, 1998).
Friedrich, Karl, and Zbigniew Brzezinski, *Totalitarian Dictatorship and Autocracy* (Cambridge, MA: Harvard University Press, 1965).
Fuentes, Carlos, *Don Quixote or the Critique of Reading* (Austin: University of Texas Press, 1976).
——, *Tiempo Mexicano* (Mexico: Joaquin Mortiz, 1971).
Fukuyama, Francis, *The End of History and the Last Man* (New York: Free Press, 1992).

Fulga, Laurenţiu, *Oameni fără glorie* (Bucharest: Editura tineretului, 1956).
——, *Steaua bunei speranţe* (Bucharest: Editura tineretului, 1963).
Funk, Nanette, and Magda Mueller, eds, *Gender Politics and Post-Communism: Reflections from Eastern Europe and the Former Soviet Union* (New York and London: Routledge, 1993).
Furmanov, Dmitry, *Chapayev*, trans. anon. (1923; London: Martin Lawrence, 1935).
Fussell, Paul, 'Can Graham Greene Write English?', in Fussell, *The Boy Scout Handbook and Other Observations* (Oxford and New York: Oxford University Press, 1982), 95–100.
Gaddis, John Lewis, *The Long Peace: Inquiries into the History of the Cold War* (New York and Oxford: Oxford University Press, 1987).
——, *We Now Know: Rethinking Cold War History* (Oxford: Oxford University Press, 1997).
García, Cristina, *Dreaming in Cuban* (New York: Ballantine Books, 1992).
García Márquez, Gabriel, *One Hundred Years of Solitude*, trans. Gregory Rabassa (1967; London: Pan, 1978).
——, *The Autumn of the Patriarch*, trans. Gregory Rabassa (1975; New York: Avon Books, 1977).
Gelman, Juan, *La Junta Luz: Oratorio a las Madres de Plaza de Mayo* (Buenos Aires: Libros de Tierra Firme, 1985).
——, *Pesar Todo: Antología* (Mexico: Fondo de Cultura Económica, 2001).
Gilbert, James, *Writers and Partisans: A History of Literary Radicalism in America* (New York: John Wiley and Sons, 1968).
Gilden, K.B., *Between the Hills and the Sea*, new edn (1971; Ithaca, NY: ILR Press, 1989).
Giles, Barbara, *The Gentle Bush* (New York: Harcourt, Brace and Co., 1947).
Gilfillan, Lynda, 'Black Women Poets in Exile: The Weapon of Words', *Tulsa Studies in Women's Literature*, 11: 1 (1992), 79–93.
Gilmore, Leigh, *The Limits of Autobiography: Trauma and Testimony* (Ithaca and London: Cornell University Press, 2001).
Glad, John, 'Vsevolod Kochetov: An Overview', *Russian Language Journal*, 32: 113 (1978), 95–102.
Gladkov, Feodor, *Cement*, trans. A.S. Arthur and C. Ashleigh (1925; London: Martin Lawrence, 1929).
Gordimer, Nadine, 'Writers in South Africa: The New Black Poets', in Rowland Smith, ed., *Exile and Tradition* (London: Longman and Dalhousie University Press, 1976), 130–5.
——, *Burger's Daughter* (London: Cape; New York: Viking, 1979).
——, *A Sport of Nature* (London: Cape; New York: Knopf, 1987).
Gorky, Maxim, *Mother*, trans. Margaret Wettlin (1907; Moscow: Raduga Publishers, 1949).
——, *The Life of Clim Samghin – Forty Years, A Tale*, trans. anon, 4 vols (1927–36; New York: Appleton-Century, 1930–8).
——, *My Universities*, new edn, trans. Ronald Wilks (1923; London: Penguin, 1979).
Goshal, Kumar, *People in the Colonies* (New York: Sheridan House, 1948).
Gray, John, *Post-liberalism: Studies in Political Thought* (London: Routledge, 1993).
——, *Enlightenment's Wake: Politics and Culture at the Close of the Modern Age* (London: Routledge, 1995).

Gray, Stephen, 'Some Problems of Writing Historiography in Southern Africa', *Literator*, 10: 2 (1989), 16–24.
Greene, Graham, *The Confidential Agent*, new edn (1939; Harmondsworth: Penguin, 1980).
——, *The Ministry of Fear*, new edn (1943; Harmondsworth: Penguin, 1982).
——, *The Heart of the Matter*, new edn (1948; London: Reprint Society, 1950).
——, *The Third Man and The Fallen Idol*, new edn (1950; Harmondsworth: Penguin, 1973).
——, *The End of the Affair* (London: Heinemann, 1951).
——, *The Quiet American*, new edn, ed. John Clark Pratt (1955; New York: Penguin, 1996).
——, 'The Man as Pure as Lucifer' (1955), in Greene, *Collected Essays*, new edn (1969; Harmondsworth: Penguin, 1981), 301–3.
——, *Our Man in Havana*, new edn (1958; Harmondsworth: Penguin, 1977).
——, *The Comedians*, new edn (1966; Harmondsworth: Penguin, 1976).
——, 'The Spy' (1968), in Greene, *Collected Essays*, new edn (1969; Harmondsworth: Penguin, 1981), 310–14.
——, *The Honorary Consul* (London: Bodley Head, 1973).
——, *The Human Factor* (London: Bodley Head, 1978).
——, *Ways of Escape*, new edn (1980; Harmondsworth: Penguin, 1981).
——, *Yours etc.: Letters to the Press 1945–1989*, selected by Christopher Hawtree (Toronto: Lester and Orpen Dennys, 1989).
——, *Reflections*, ed., Judith Adamson (Toronto: Lester and Orpen Dennys, 1990).
Greenwood, Sean, *Britain and the Cold War, 1945–91* (Basingstoke: Macmillan, 2000).
Grendel, Lajos, *Éleslövészet*, new edn (1981; Pozsony: Kalligram, 1998).
Guattari, Félix, *Molecular Revolution: Psychiatry and Politics*, trans. Rosemary Sheed (1977; London: Penguin, 1984).
Guevara, Ernesto Che, *Guerrilla Warfare* (New York: Monthy Review Press, 1961).
Gugelberger, Georg M., ed., *Marxism and African Literature* (London: James Currey, 1985).
Gunner, Elizabeth, 'Songs of Innocence and Experience: Women as Composers and Performers of *Izibongo*, Zulu Praise Poetry', in Cherry Clayton, ed., *Women and Writing in Southern Africa: A Critical Anthology* (London: Heinemann, 1989), 11–39.
Hallett, Vicky C., 'Red Square: A Scrutiny', *The Harvard Crimson Online*, http://www.thecrimson.com/fmarchives/fm_02_15_20001/article2A.html (accessed 7 July 2004).
Halmari, Helena, 'Dividing the World: The Dichotomous Rhetoric of Ronald Reagan', *Multilingua*, 12: 2 (1993), 143–76.
Hansberry, Lorraine, *A Raisin in the Sun*, new edn (1959; New York: Signet, 1986),
Haraszti, Miklós, *L'Artist d'Etat* (Paris: Librairie Arthème Fayarde, 1983).
——, *The Velvet Prison: Artists under State Socialism*, trans. Katalin and Stephen Landesmann (1987; New York: New Republic/Basic Books, 1987).
Harlow, Barbara, *Resistance Literature* (New York: Methuen, 1987).
Haut, Woody, *Pulp Culture: Hardboiled Fiction and the Cold War* (London: Serpent's Tail, 1995).
Havel, Václav, 'Na téma opozice', *Literární Listy*, 1: 4 (April 1968), 11–21.
——, 'Český úděl?', *Tvář*, 4: 2 (February 1969), 30–3.
——, *The Power of the Powerless: Citizen against the State in Central-Eastern Europe*, ed. J. Keane (London: Hutchinson, 1985).

——, *Selected Plays 1963–1983*, trans. Vera Blackwell, George Theiner and Jan Novak (London: Faber and Faber, 1992).
Heaney, Seamus, *The Government of the Tongue* (London: Faber and Faber, 1988).
Heinlein, Robert, *The Puppet Masters*, new edn (1951; London: Pan Books, 1969).
Heller, Joseph, *Catch-22*, new edn (1961; London: Corgi, 1993).
Hellman, Lillian, *Scoundrel Time* (Boston: Little, Brown, 1976).
Herbert, Zbigniew, *Report from the Besieged City and Other Poems*, trans. John and Bogdana Carpenter (1983; New York: The Ecco Press, 1985).
——, *Selected Poems*, trans. P.D. Scott and Czesław Miłosz (Manchester: Carcanet Press, 1985).
Hersey, John, *Hiroshima*, rev. edn (1946; London: Penguin, 1985).
Hewison, Robert, *In Anger: British Culture in the Cold War, 1945–1960* (Oxford: Oxford University Press, 1981).
Heyck, Denis Lynn Daly, *Surviving Globalization in Three Latin American Communities* (Ontario: Broadview Press, 2002).
Himes, Chester, *The Lonely Crusade*, new edn (1947; London: Falcon Press, 1950).
Hoban, Russell, *Riddley Walker* (London: Jonathan Cape, 1980).
Hobsbawm, Eric, *The Age of Extremes: A History of the World, 1914–1991* (New York: Pantheon, 1994).
Hodges, Donald C., *Argentina's 'Dirty War': An Intellectual Biography* (Austin: University of Texas Press, 1991).
Hoffman, Frederick J. and Olga Vickery, eds, *William Faulkner: Three Decades of Criticism* (New York: Harbinger, 1960).
Hofmeyr, Isabel, 'Not the Magic Talisman: Rethinking Oral Literature in South Africa', *World Literature Today*, 70: 1 (1996), 88–92.
Hogan, Michael J., ed., *The End of the Cold War, Its Meaning and Implications* (Cambridge: Cambridge University Press, 1992).
Holquist, Michael, *Dostoevsky and the Novel* (Princeton: Princeton University Press, 1977).
Holub, Miroslav, *The Fly*, trans. Ewald Osers, George Theiner and Ian and Jarmila Milner (Newcastle-Upon-Tyne: Bloodaxe Books, 1987).
Hove, Chinjerai, *Bones*, new edn (1988; London: Heinemann, 1990).
Hsiang-tung Chou, 'Let the Flames of Revolution Burn More Fiercely!', *Chinese Literature*, 12 (1967), 107–11.
Hu Wen, 'Militant Songs and Dances from Romania', *Chinese Literature*, 1 (1972), 89–92.
Huang Jisu, et al., *Qie Gewala*, in Liu Zhifeng, ed., *Qie Gewala: fanying yu zhengming* (Beijing: Zhangguo shehui kexue chubanshe, 2001), 13–69.
Huang Ti, *Gangtie yunshubing, Juben*, 10 (1953), 28–75.
Hue-Tam Ho Tai, ed., *The Country of Memory: Remaking the Past in Late Socialist Vietnam* (Berkeley and London: University of California Press, 2001).
Hughes, James Langston, *Simple Speaks His Mind*, new edn (1950; London: Victor Gollancz, 1951).
Hunter, Edward, *Brainwashing: The Story of the Men Who Defied It*, new edn (1956; New York: Pyramid Books, 1970).
——, *The Black Book on Red China* (New York: The Bookmailer, 1961).
Hutcheon, Linda, *The Politics of Postmodernism* (London: Routledge, 1989).
Huỳnh Sanh Thông, ed., *An Anthology of Vietnamese Poems*, trans. Huỳnh Sanh Thông (New Haven and London: Yale University Press, 1996).

Huyssen, Andreas, *After the Great Divide: Modernism, Mass Culture, Postmodernism* (Bloomington: Indiana University Press, 1986).
——, *Twilight Memories: Marking Time in the Culture of Amnesia* (New York: Routledge, 1994).
Inglis, Fred, *The Cruel Peace: Everyday Life in the Cold War* (London: Aurum Press, 1992).
Ionesco, Eugène, *Rhinoceros, The Chairs, The Lesson*, new edn, trans. Derek Prouse and Donald Watson (1954, 1959; Harmondsworth: Penguin, 1962).
Irele, Abiola, *The African Experience in Literature and Ideology* (Bloomington: Indiana University Press, 1990).
Isaacs, Jeremy, and Taylor Downing, *Cold War: For 45 Years the World Held Its Breath* (London: Bantam Press, 1998).
Isherwood, Julian, 'Obscure Polish Poetess Is Awarded Nobel Prize', *Daily Telegraph*, 4 October 1996, 18.
Ivanov, Anatoli, *The Eternal Call*, trans. anon. (1971–7; Moscow: Progress Publishers, 1979).
Iyayi, Festus, *Heroes* (Harlow: Longman, 1986).
Jameson, Fredric, 'Third-World Literature in the Era of Multinational Capitalism', *Social Text*, 15 (1986), 65–88.
Jamieson, Neil L., *Understanding Vietnam* (Berkeley and London: University of California Press, 1993).
Janion, Maria, *Do Europy – tak, ale razem z naszymi umarłymi* (Warsaw: SIC, 2000).
Janowska, Katarzyna, *Rozmowy na nowy wiek* (Krakow: Znak, 2001).
Jauss, Hans Robert, *Towards an Aesthetic of Literary Reception*, trans. T. Bahti (1977; Minneapolis: University of Minnesota Press, 1982).
Jebeleanu, Eugen, *Surâsul Hiroşimei* (Bucharest: Editura tineretului, 1958).
Jiménez, Mayra, ed., *Poesia campesina de Solentiname* (Managua: Ministerio de Cultura, 1983).
Juraga, Dubravka, 'Miloslav Krleža's *Zastave*: Socialism, Yugoslavia, and the Historical Novel', *South Atlantic Review*, 62: 4 (Fall 1997), 32–56.
Juraga, Dubravka, and M. Keith Booker, eds, *Socialist Cultures East and West: A Post-Cold War Reassessment* (Westport, CT, and London: Praeger, 2002).
——, *Rereading Global Socialist Cultures after the Cold War: The Reassessment of a Tradition* (Westport, CT, and London: Praeger, 2002).
Kadare, Ismail, *Gjenerali i ushtrisë së vdekur* (Tirana: Naim Frashëri, 1963).
——, *Shekulli im* (Tirana: Naim Frashëri, 1961).
Kaladjian, Walter, *American Culture between the Wars: Revisionary Modernism and Postmodern Critique* (New York: Columbia University Press, 1994).
Kaldor, Mary, *The Imaginary War: Understanding the East–West Conflict* (Oxford: Basil Blackwell, 1990).
Kapcia, Antoni, *Cuba: Island of Dreams* (Oxford and New York: Berg, 2000).
Kapuściński, Ryszard, *Busz po polsku*, new edn (1962; Warsaw: Czytelnik, 1990).
——, *Chrystus z karabinem na ramieniu* (Warsaw: Czytelnik, 1975).
Kemp, Amanda, Nozizwe Madlala, Asha Moodley and Elaine Salo, 'The Dawn of a New Day: Redefining South African Feminism', in Amrita Basu, ed., *The Challenge of Local Feminisms: Women's Movements in Global Perspective* (Boulder: Westview Press, 1995), 131–62.
Kennan, George F., 'The Sources of Soviet Conduct', in Kennan, *American Diplomacy 1900–1950* (Chicago: University of Chicago Press, 1951), 107–28.

Killens, John O., 'For National Freedom', *New Foundations* (Summer 1949), 245–58.
——, *Youngblood*, new edn (1954; London: Four Square Books, 1961).
Kimble, Judy and Elaine Unterhalter, '"We Opened the Road for You, You Must Go Forward": ANC Women's Struggles, 1912–1982', *Feminist Review*, 12 (1982), 11–35.
Kinkead, Eugene, *In Every War But One* (New York: Norton, 1959).
Kiparsky, Valentin, *English and American Characters in Russian Fiction* (Berlin: Otto Harrassowitz, 1964).
Kiš, Danilo, *Grobnica za Borisa Davidoviča*, new edn (1975; Belgrade: BIGZ, 1995).
Klaus, H. Gustav, ed., *The Socialist Novel in Britain: Towards the Recovery of a Tradition* (New York: St Martin's, 1982).
Klein, Marcus, *Foreigners: The Making of American Literature, 1900–1940* (Chicago and London: University of Chicago Press, 1981).
Kochetov, V., *Chego zhe ty khochesh'?* (Minsk: Belarus', 1970).
Konrád, György, *Kerti mulatság* (Budapest: Samizdat, 1985).
Korda, Michael, *Another Life: A Memoir of Other People* (New York: Random House, 1999).
Kramer, Bernard M., S. Michael Kalick and Michael A. Milburn, 'Attitudes toward Nuclear Weapons and Nuclear War: 1945–1982', *Journal of Social Issues*, 39: 1 (1983), 7–24.
Kraminov, D., *Pasynki Al'biona* (Moscow: Molodaia gvardiia, 1962).
Kranjec, Miško, *Rdeči gardist*, 3 Vols (Murska Sobota: Pomurska založba, 1964–7).
Krleža, Miroslav, *Zastave*, 5 Vols (Sarajevo: Oslobodjenje, 1976).
Krymov, Yuri, *Tanker Derbent*, trans. R. Dixon (1938; Moscow: Progress Publishers, n.d.).
Kuhiwczak, Piotr, 'Before and After *The Burning Forest*: Modern Polish Poetry in Britain', *The Polish Review*, 1 (1989), 57–71.
Kukorelly, Endre, *A valóság édessége* (Budapest: Magvető, 1984).
——, *A Memória-part* (Budapest: Magvető, 1990).
——, *Rom: A szovjetónió története* (Budapest: Jelenkor, 2000).
Kundera, Milan, *Žert* (Prague: Československý spisovatel, 1967).
——, *The Art of the Novel*, trans. Linda Asher (1986; London: Faber and Faber, 1988).
Kunene, Masizi, 'Some Aspects of South African Literature', *World Literature Today*, 70: 1 (1996), 13–16.
Kunkel, Francis L., *The Labyrinthian Ways of Graham Greene*, rev. edn (1960; Mamaroneck, NY: Paul P. Appel, 1973).
Lahusen, Thomas, and Evgeny Dobrenko, eds, *Socialist Realism without Borders*. Special number of *South Atlantic Quarterly*, 94: 3 (1995).
Lapin, Mark, *Pledge of Allegiance*, new edn (1991; London: E.P. Dutton, 1991).
Lauter, Paul, ed., *The Heath Anthology of American Literature*, Vol. 2 (Lexington, MA: D.C. Heath and Co., 1990).
Lazarus, Neil, *Resistance in Postcolonial African Fiction* (New Haven: Yale University Press, 1990).
——, *Nationalism and Cultural Practice in the Postcolonial World* (Cambridge: Cambridge University Press, 1999).
Lefter, Ion Bogdan, 'Poate fi considerat postcomunismul un post-colonialism?', in

Postcolonialism & Postcomunism: Caietele Echinox, Vol. 1 (Cluj-Napoca: Dacia, 2001), 117–19.

Le Minh Khue, *The Stars, the Earth, the River* (Williamtic: Curbstone Press, 1997).

Levering, Ralph B., *The Cold War, 1945–1987*, 2nd edn (1982; Arlington Heights, IL: H. Davidson, 1988).

Lewis, R.W.B., 'Graham Greene: The Religious Affair', in Lewis, *The Picaresque Saint: Representative Figures in Contemporary Fiction* (Philadelphia and New York: Lippincott, 1959), 220–74.

Li Huang, et al., *War Drums on the Equator*, trans, Gladys Yang, *Chinese Literature*, 7 (1965), 3–72.

Li Moran, et al., eds, *Zhongguo huaju wushi nian ju zuo xuan: 1949.10–1999.10*, 8 Vols (Beijing: Zhongguo xiju chubanshe, 2000).

Liebling, A.J., 'A Talkative Something-or-Other', in Greene, *Quiet American*, 347–55.

Lifton, Robert Jay and Richard Falk, *Indefensible Weapons: The Political and Psychological Case against Nuclearism* (New York: Basic Books, 1982).

Limonov, Eduard, *Eto ia, Edichka* (New York: Index Publishers, 1979).

Lipschutz, Ronnie D., *Cold War Fantasies: Film, Fiction, and Foreign Policy* (Lanham: Rowman and Littlefield, 2001).

Lockett, Cecily, 'Feminism(s) and Writing in English in South Africa', *Current Writing: Text
and Reception in Southern Africa*, 2: 1 (1990), 1–21.

Lomidze, Georgi, *National Soviet Literatures: Unity of Purpose*, trans. Nina Belenkaya (Moscow: Raduga, 1983).

London, Jack, 'The Yellow Peril', http://www.readbookonline.net/read/298/8662.html (accessed 27 September 2004).

Longinović, Tomislav Z., *Borderline Culture: The Politics of Identity in Four Twentieth Century Slavic Novels* (Fayetteville: University of Arkansas Press, 1993).

——, 'Postmodernity and the Technology of Power: Legacy of the *Vidici* Group in Serbia', *College Literature*, 21: 1 (1994), 120–30.

Loomba, Ania, *Colonialism/Postcolonialism* (London and New York: Routledge, 1990).

Luis, William, 'Reading the Master Codes of Cuban Culture in Cristina García's *Dreaming in Cuban*', *Cuban Studies*, 26 (1996), 201–23.

Lukács, Georg, *The Meaning of Contemporary Realism*, trans. John Mander and Necker Mander (1957; London: Merlin, 1963).

——, *The Historical Novel*, trans. Hannah Mitchell and Stanley Mitchell (1937; Lincoln: University of Nebraska Press, 1983).

Lukacs, John, *The End of the Twentieth Century and the End of the Modern Age* (New York: Ticknor and Fields, 1993).

McCauley, Martin, *The Origins of the Cold War, 1941–1949*, 2nd edn (1983; Harlow: Longman, 1995).

McDonad, Marianne, 'Poetry's Mozart is Nobel Winner', *Independent*, 4 October 1996, 7.

McHale, Brian, *Postmodernist Fiction* (New York: Methuen, 1987).

Mandelbaum, Michael, *The Nuclear Question: The United States and Nuclear Weapons 1946–1976* (Cambridge: Cambridge University Press, 1979).

——, *The Nuclear Revolution: International Politics before and after Hiroshima* (Cambridge: Cambridge University Press, 1981).

Mandelshtam, Nadezhda, *Hope against Hope*, trans. Max Hayward (1970; London: Penguin, 1976).
Mangua, Charles, *A Tail in the Mouth* (Nairobi: East African Publishing House, 1972).
Mannix, Patrick, *The Rhetoric of Antinuclear Fiction: Persuasive Strategies in Novels and Films* (Lewisburg: Bucknell University Press, 1992).
Mao Tsetung, *Quotations from Chairman Mao Tsetung* (Beijing: Foreign Languages Press, 1972).
Maqagi, Sisi, 'Who Theorizes?', *Current Writing: Text and Reception in Southern Africa*, 2: 1 (1990), 22–5.
March, Michael, ed., *Child of Europe* (London: Penguin, 1990).
Marchant, Fred, 'War Poets from Viet Nam', *Humanities*, 19: 2 (March–April 1998), http://neh.fed.us/news/humanities/1998-03/honey.html (accessed 24 November 2004).
Marchetti, Gina, *Romance and the 'Yellow Peril': Race, Sex and Discursive Strategies in Hollywood Fiction* (Berkeley, CA: University of California Press, 1993)
Marcus, Greil, *The Manchurian Candidate* (London: BFI, 2002).
Marinat, Alexei, *Eu și lumea: proză documentară*, new edn (1989; Chișinău: Uniunii Scriitorilor, 1999).
Markov, Dmitry, *Socialist Literatures: Problems of Development*, trans. Catherine Judelson (1975; Moscow: Raduga, 1984).
Marx, A., *Lessons of Struggle: South African Internal Operations, 1960–1990* (Oxford: Oxford University Press, 1992).
Masiello, Francine, *The Art of Transition: Latin American Culture and Neoliberal Crisis* (Durham: Duke University Press, 2001).
Mason, John, *The Cold War, 1945–1991* (London and New York: Routledge, 1996).
Maund, Alfred, *The Big Boxcar*, new edn (1956; London: Longmans, Green and Co., 1959).
May, Elaine Tyler, *Homeward Bound: American Families in the Cold War Era*, rev. edn (1988; New York: Basic Books, 1999).
Mayfield, Julian, *The Hit*, new edn (1957; London: Michael Joseph, 1959).
——, *The Long Night*, new edn (1958; London: New English Library, 1966).
Medhurst, Martin J., 'Rhetoric and Cold War: A Strategic Approach', in Martin J. Medhurst, Robert L. Ivie, Philip Wander and Robert L. Scott, eds, *Cold War Rhetoric: Strategy, Metaphor, and Ideology* (Westport, CT: Greenwood Press, 1990).
Medvedev, Zh. A., and R. A. Medvedev, *Kto sumasshedshii?* (London: Macmillan, 1971).
Meeks, Brian, *Caribbean Revolutions and Revolutionary Theory: An Assessment of Cuba, Nicaragua and Grenada* (London: Warwick/Macmillan, 1993).
Melley, Timothy, 'Agency Panic and the Culture of Conspiracy', in Peter Knight, ed., *Conspiracy Nation: The Politics of Paranoia in Postwar America* (New York: New York University Press, 2002).
Merril, Judith, *Shadow on the Hearth* (New York: Doubleday, 1950).
Meyers, Beth, *The Steady Flame* (New York: Bouregy, 1952).
——, *The Doctor Is a Lady*, new edn (1954; London: Transworld Publishers, 1961).
Miller, Chris, 'On Not Writing the East European Poem', *PN Review*, 30: 5 (2004), 69–72.
Miller, Christopher, *Blank Darkness: Africanist Discourse in French* (Chicago: University of Chicago Press, 1985).

Miller, Walter M., Jr, *A Canticle for Leibowitz*, new edn (1959; London: Corgi, 1963).
Miłosz, Czesław, *The Captive Mind*, trans. Jane Zielonko (London: Secker and Warburg, 1953).
——, *Witness of Poetry*, new edn (1983; Cambridge, MA: Harvard University Press, 1994).
Molefe, Sono, ed., *Malibongwe – ANC Women: Poetry Is Also Their Weapon* (Stockholm: ANC Publications, 1982).
Molloy, Sylvia, *At Face Value: Autobiographical Writing in Spanish America* (Cambridge: Cambridge University Press, 1991).
Montejo, Esteban, *The Autobiography of a Runaway Slave*, new edn, ed. Alistair Hennessy (1968; London: Warwick/Macmillan Caribbean, 1993).
Moreiras, Alberto, *The Exhaustion of Difference: The Politics of Latin American Cultural Studies* (Durham: Duke University Press, 2001).
Moses, Michael Valdez, *The Novel and the Globalization of Culture* (New York: Oxford University Press, 1995).
Mphahlele, Es'kia, 'The Tyranny of Place and Aesthetics: The South African Case', in Charles Malan, ed., *Race and Literature* (Pinetown, SA: Owen Burgess Publishers, 1987), 48–59.
Mthombothi, Barney, 'Introduction' to Fatima Meer, ed., *Resistance in the Townships* (Durban: Madiba Publications, 1989).
Mtshali, Oswald, 'Black Poetry in South Africa', in Christopher Heywood, ed., *Aspects of South African Literature* (London: Heinemann, 1976), 121–7.
Mudimbe, V.Y., *The Invention of Africa: Gnosis, Philosophy, and the Order of Knowledge* (Bloomington: Indiana University Press, 1988).
Mwangi, Meja, *Carcase for Hounds* (London: Heinemann, 1974).
——, *Taste of Death* (Nairobi: East African Publishing House, 1975).
Nadel, Alan, *Containment Culture: American Narratives, Postmodernism, and the Atomic Age* (Durham: Duke University Press, 1995).
Nash, June, *Mayan Visions: The Quest for Autonomy in an Age of Globalization* (New York: Routledge, 2001).
Ndebele, Njabulo, *South African Literature and Culture: Rediscovery of the Ordinary* (Manchester: Manchester University Press, 1994).
Nedelciu, Mircea, *Zmeura de cîmpie* (Bucharest: Cartea Românească, 1984).
Nelson, Cary, *Repression and Recovery: Modern American Poetry and the Politics of Cultural Memory, 1914–1945* (Madison: University of Wisconsin Press, 1989).
Nelson, Truman, *The Surveyor* (Garden City, NY: Doubleday, 1960).
Neumann, Victor, 'Perspective comparative asupra filozofiei multiculturale', in *Postcolonialism & Postcomunism: Caietele Echinox*, Vol. 1 (Cluj-Napoca: Dacia, 2001), 55–70.
Nevins, Jess, 'On Yellow Peril Thrillers', http://www.violetbooks.com/yellowperil.html (accessed 27 September 2004).
Ngara, Emmanuel, *Art and Ideology in the African Novel: A Study of the Influence of Marxism on African Writing* (London: Heinemann, 1985).
Ngugi wa Thiong'o, *The River Between* (London: Heinemann, 1965).
——, *A Grain of Wheat*, new edn (1967; London: Penguin, 2002).
——, *Devil on the Cross*, trans. Ngugi wa Thiong'o (1980; London: Heinemann, 1982).
——, *Matigari*, trans. Ngugi wa Thiong'o (1987; London: Heinemann, 1989).

——, *Decolonising the Mind: The Politics of Language in African Literature* (London: James Currey, 1992).
——, *Moving the Centre: The Struggle for Cultural Freedoms* (London: James Currey, 1993).
Nguyen Ba Chung, 'Imagining the Nation', *Boston Review*, 21: 1 (February/March 1996), http://www.bostonreview.net/BR21.1/chung.html (accessed 20 November 2004).
Nguyen Ba Chung, and Kevin Bowen, eds, *6 Vietnamese Poets*, trans. Martha Collins, Carolyn Forche, Linh Green, *et al.* (Williamtic: Curbstone Press, 2002).
Nguyễn Đình Hòa, *Vietnamese Literature: A Brief Survey* (San Diego: San Diego State University, 1994).
Nguyễn Duy, *Distant Road*, trans. Kevin Bowen and Nguyen Ba Chung (Williamtic: Curbstone Press, 1999).
Nguyen Khac Vien, and Huu Ngoc, eds, *Vietnamese Literature: An Anthology*, trans. Nguyen Khac Vien, Huu Ngoc, *et al.* (Hanoi: Red River, n.d.).
Nguyễn Minh Châu, 'Writing about War', *The Vietnam Review*, 3 (1997), 438–46.
Nietzsche, Friedrich, *Beyond Good and Evil*, new edn, trans. R.J. Hollingdale (1886; Harmondsworth: Penguin, 1975).
Ninh, Kim N.B., *A World Transformed: The Politics of Culture in Revolutionary Vietnam, 1945–1965* (Ann Arbor: University of Michigan Press, 2002).
Nkosi, Lewis, 'Fiction by Black South Africans', in G.D. Killam, ed., *African Writers on African Writing* (London: Heinemann, 1973), 109–17.
Northedge, F.S., and Audrey Wells, *Britain and Soviet Communism: The Impact of a Revolution* (London and Basingstoke: Macmillan, 1982).
Obiechina, Emmanuel, *Culture, Tradition and Society in the West African Novel* (Cambridge: Cambridge University Press, 1975).
O'Brien, Anthony, *Against Normalization: Writing Radical Democracy in South Africa* (Durham: Duke University Press, 2001).
O'Brien, Tim, *The Nuclear Age*, new edn (1984; London: Flamingo, 1987).
Okri, Ben, *The Famished Road* (London: Jonathan Cape, 1991).
On the Docks Group of the Peking Opera Troupe of Shanghai, *Haigang*, *Hongqi*, 2 (1972), 22–48.
Örkény, István, *Lágerek népe*, ed. Zsuzsa Radnóti, new edn (1947; Budapest: Szépirodalmi, 1984).
Orwell, George, *The Collected Essays, Journalism and Letters of George Orwell: Volume IV, In Front of Your Nose, 1945–1950*, ed. Sonia Orwell and Ian Angus (London: Secker and Warburg, 1968).
Osborne, John, *Look Back in Anger* (London: Faber and Faber, 1957).
Ostrovsky, Nikolai, *How the Steel Was Tempered*, trans. R. Prokofieva (1932–4; Moscow: Progress Publishers, n.d.).
Ouologuem, Yambo, *Bound to Violence*, trans. Ralph Manheim (1968; London: Heinemann, 1971).
Ovcharenko, A., *Socialist Realism and the Modern Literary Process*, trans. anon. (1968; Moscow: Progress Publishers, 1978).
Ovchinnikov, Vsevolod, *Korni duba: Vpechatleniia i razmyshleniia ob Anglii i anglichanakh* (Moscow: Mysl', 1980).
——, *Britain Observed: A Russian's View*, trans. Michael Basker (1980; Oxford: Pergamon, 1981).

Page, Bruce, David Leitch and Phillip Knightley, *The Philby Conspiracy* (New York: Ballantine, 1981).
Painter, David S., *The Cold War: An International History* (London and New York: Routledge, 1999).
Painter, Susan, *Edgar the Playwright* (London: Methuen Drama, 1996).
Páral, Vladimír, *Veletrh splněných přání* (Prague: Mladá fronta, 1964).
——, *Milenci & vrazi: Magazín ukájeni před rokem 2000* (Prague: Mladá fronta, 1969).
Parini, Jay, et al., eds, *The Columbia History of American Poetry* (New York and Chichester: Columbia University Press, 1993).
Parry, Benita, 'Signs of Our Times: Discussion of Homi Bhabha's *Location of Culture*', *Third Text*, 28/29 (1994), 5–24.
Parthé, Kathleen, *Russian Village Prose: The Radiant Past* (Princeton, NJ: Princeton University Press, 1992).
Pavić, Milorad, *Hazarski rečnik: roman leksikon u 100.000 reči* (Belgrade: Prosveta, 1984).
Peking Opera Troupe of Beijing, *Shajiabang*, *Hongqi*, 6 (1970), 8–39.
Pelly, Patricia, *Postcolonial Vietnam: New Histories of National Past* (Durham, NC: Duke University Press, 2002).
Pepetela, *Mayombe*, trans. Michael Wolfers (1984; London: Heinemann, 1996).
Petry, Ann, *The Street*, new edn (1946; London: Virago, 1986).
——, *The Narrows*, new edn (1953; London: Victor Gollancz, 1954).
Philby, Kim, *My Silent War: The Soviet Master Spy's Own Story* (New York: Grove, 1968).
Pietz, William, 'The "Post-Colonialism" of Cold War Discourse', *Social Text*, 19–20 (Fall 1988), 53–75.
Pirie, Donald, ed., *Young Poets of a New Poland*, trans. Donald Pirie (London: Forest Books, 1993).
Pochivalov, L., 'Chelovek na dne: Pokinuvshii rodinu – o sebe', *Literaturnaia Gazeta*, 10 September 1980, 14.
Polevoi, Boris, *Story of a Real Man*, trans. Joe Fineberg (1946; Moscow: Progress Publishers, 1977).
Polyson, James, Jodi Hillmar and Douglas Kriek, 'Levels of Public Interest in Nuclear War', *Journal of Social Behavior and Personality*, 1: 3 (1986), 397–401.
Poore, Charles, 'Books of the Times', *New York Times*, 15 June 1950, 29.
Popescu, Dumitru Radu, *The Royal Hunt*, trans. J.E. Cottrell and M. Bogdan (1973; Columbus: Ohio State University Press, 1985).
Pouchet-Paquet, Sandra, 'West Indian Autobiography', in William Andrews, ed., *African American Autobiography: A Collection of Critical Essays* (New Jersey: Prentice Hall, 1993), 196–211.
Pound, Ezra, *Selected Cantos of Ezra Pound* (London: Faber, 1967).
Pynchon, Thomas, *Gravity's Rainbow*, new edn (1973; London: Pan Books, 1975).
Quijano, Aníbal, *Modernidad, identidad y utopía en América Latina* (Quito: El Conejo, 1990).
Qosja, Rexhep, *Vdekja më vjen prej syve të tillë* (Prishtina: Rilindja, 1974).
Rabinowitz, Paula, *Labor and Desire: Women's Revolutionary Fiction in Depression America* (Chapel Hill, NC: University of North Carolina Press, 1991).
Rama, Angel, *La ciudad letrada* (Hanover: Ediciones del Norte, 1984).
——, *Las máscaras democráticas del Modernism* (Montevideo: Arca, 1994).

——, *Diario, 1974–1983* (Montevideo: Trilce, 2001).
Raudam, Toomas, and Edgar Rice Burroughs [Toomas Raudam], *Tarzani seiklused Tallinnas* (Tallinn: Fööniks, 1991).
Rawnsley, Gary D., ed., *Cold-War Propaganda in the 1950s* (Basingstoke and London: Macmillan, 1999).
Retamar, Roberto Fernández, *Fervor de la Argentina* (Buenos Aires: Ediciones del Sol, 1993).
Rhodes, Richard, *The Making of the Atomic Bomb*, rev. edn (1986; London: Penguin, 1988).
Richard, Nelly, *La Insubordinación de los Signos: Cambio político, transformaciones culturales y poéticas de la crisis* (Santiago: Cuarto Propio, 1994).
Rideout, Walter, *The Radical Novel in the United States, 1900–1954: Some Interrelations of Literature and Society* (Cambridge, MA: Harvard University Press, 1956).
Roa Bastos, Augusto, *I the Supreme*, trans Helen Lane (1974; New York: Knopf, 1986).
Robin, Régine, *Socialist Realism: An Impossible Aesthetic* (Stanford: Stanford University Press, 1992).
Robin, Ron, *The Making of the Cold War Enemy: Culture and Politics in the Military-Industrial Complex* (Princeton: Princeton University Press, 2001).
Rogin, Michael, *'Ronald Reagan,' the Movie and Other Episodes in Political Demonology* (Berkeley: University of California Press, 1987).
Rohmer, Sax, *The Mystery of Doctor Fu Manchu*, new edn (1913; London: Allan Wingate, 1977).
——, *President Fu Manchu*, new edn (1936; New York: Pyramid Books, 1963).
——, *The Shadow of Fu Manchu*, new edn (1948; New York: Pyramid Books, 1963).
——, *Emperor Fu Manchu* (Greenwich, Conn.: Fawcett, 1959).
Rose, Gillian, *Mourning Becomes the Law: Philosophy and Representation* (Cambridge: Cambridge University Press, 1997).
Rosenbaum, Jonathan, *Placing Movies: The Practice of Film Criticism* (Berkeley: University of California Press, 1995).
Rosenberg, Julius, and Ethel Rosenberg, *Death House Letters* (New York: Jero Publishing, 1952).
Ruthven, Ken, *Nuclear Criticism* (Victoria: Melbourne University Press, 1993).
Sachs, Albie, 'Preparing Ourselves for Freedom', in Ingrid de Kok and Karen Press, eds, *Spring Is Rebellious: Arguments about Cultural Freedom* (Cape Town: Buchu Books, 1990), 19–29.
Said, Edward, *Orientalism* (New York: Vintage-Random House, 1979).
Sakwa, Richard, *Postcommunism* (Buckingham and Philadelphia: Open University Press, 1999).
Sandoz, Mari, *Cheyenne Autumn* (New York: McGraw-Hill, 1953).
Sârbu, Ion D., *Jurnalul unui jurnalist fără jurnal*, 2 Vols (Craiova: Scrisul Românesc, 1991–3).
Sartre, Jean-Paul, *What Is Literature?* new edn, trans. Bernard Frechtman (1948; London: Methuen, 1981).
Saxton, Alexander, *The Great Midland*, new edn (1948; Berlin: Seven Seas Publishers, 1958).
Schaub, Thomas Hill, *American Fiction in the Cold War* (Madison and London: University of Wisconsin Press, 1991).
Schell, Jonathan, *The Fate of the Earth* (London: Pan, 1982).
Scriven, Michael and Dennis Tate, eds, *European Socialist Realism* (Oxford: Berg, 1988).

Seed, David, *American Science Fiction and the Cold War: Literature and Film* (Edinburgh: Edinburgh University Press, 1990).
——, *Brainwashing: The Fictions of Mind Control* (Kent, OH: Kent State University Press, 2004).
Selejan, Ana, *România în timpul primului război cultural 1944–1948: Vol. 2, Reeducare și prigoană* (Sibiu: Thausib, 1993).
Sembène, Ousmane, *God's Bits of Wood*, trans. Francis Price (1960; London: Heinemann, 1986).
Serafimovich, Alexander, *The Iron Flood*, trans. anon. (1924; Moscow: Progress Publishers, n.d.).
Shandong Provincial Peking Opera Troupe, *Qixi Baihutuan*, *Hongqi*, 11 (1972), 26–54.
Sharp, Joanne P., *Condensing the Cold War: Reader's Digest and American Identity* (Minneapolis: University of Minnesota Press, 2000).
Shava, Piniel Viriri, *A People's Voice: Black South African Writing in the Twentieth Century* (London: Zed Books, 1989).
Shaw, Tony, *British Cinema and the Cold War: The State, Propaganda and Consensus* (London: I.B. Tauris, 2001).
Sheehan, Neil, *A Bright Shining Lie: John Paul Vann and American Vietnam* (New York: Random House, 1989).
Sheldon, Michael, *Graham Greene: The Man Within* (London: Heinemann, 1995).
Sherry, Norman, *The Life of Graham Greene, Vol. 2: 1939–1955* (New York: Viking, 1995).
Shiel, M.P., *The Yellow Danger* (London: Richards, 1898).
Sholokhov, Mikhail, *Quiet Flows the Don*, trans. Robert Daglish (1928; Moscow: Raduga Publishers, 1988).
Shpanov, N., *Podzhigateli* (Moscow: Molodaia gvardiia, 1950).
——, *Zagovorshchiki* (Moscow: Molodaia gvardiia, 1951).
Shtemler, I., *Zvonok v pustuiu kvartiru* (St Petersburg: Russko-baltiiskii informatsionnyi tsentr BLITs, 1998).
Shute, Nevil, *On the Beach*, new edn (1957; Yorkshire: House of Stratus, 2000).
Siebers, Tobin, *Cold War Criticism and the Politics of Skepticism* (New York and Oxford: Oxford University Press, 1993).
Silko, Leslie Marmon, *Ceremony*, new edn (1977; London: Penguin, 1986).
Silverstein, Brett, 'Enemy Images: The Psychology of U.S. Attitudes and Cognitions Regarding the Soviet Union', *American Psychologist*, 44: 6 (1989), 903–13.
Simionescu, Mircea Horia, *Ingeniosul bine temperat*, 4 Vols (Bucharest: EPL / Eminescu / Cartea Românească, 1969–83).
Simonov, Konstantin, *Days and Nights*, trans. Joseph Barnes (1944; New York: Simon and Schuster, 1945).
Simpson, Christopher, *Science of Coercion: Communication Research and Psychological Warfare 1945–1960* (New York: Oxford University Press, 1994).
Sinfield, Alan, *Literature, Politics and Culture in Postwar Britain* (Oxford: Basil Blackwood, 1989).
Sitas, Ari, ed., *Black Mamba Rising: South African Worker Poets in Struggle* (Durban: Culture and Working Life Publications, 1986).
Skidelsky, Robert, *Oswald Mosley* (London: Macmillan, 1990).
Škvorecký, Josef, *Mirákl* (Toronto: Nakladatelství 68 / Sixty-Eight Publishers, 1972).
Slonim, Marc, *Modern Russian Literature from Chekhov to the Present* (New York: Oxford University Press, 1953).

Snel, Guido, 'Gardens of the Mind: Fictionalized Autobiography in East-Central Europe', in Marcel Cornis-Pope and John Neubauer, eds, *History of the Literary Cultures of East- Central Europe*, Vol. 1 (Philadelphia and Amsterdam: John Benjamins Publishing, 2004), 395–6.
Snow, C.P., *The New Men* (London: Macmillan, 1954).
Song of the Dragon River Group of Shanghai, *Longjiang song*, *Hongqi*, 3 (1972), 36–62.
Soyinka, Wole, *Season of Anomy*, new edn (1973; London: Rex Collins, 1980).
Spanos, William V., 'A Rumor of War: 9/11 and the Forgetting of the Vietnam War', *boundary 2*, 30: 3 (2003), 29–66.
Spender, Stephen, 'Introduction' to Anthony Graham, ed., *Witness out of Silence: Polish Poetry Fighting for Freedom* (London: Poets and Painters Press, 1980).
Sommer, Doris, *Proceed with Caution, When Engaged by Minority Writing in the Americas* (Cambridge, MA, and London: Harvard University Press, 1999).
Štajner, Karol, *7000 dana u Sibiru* (Zagreb: Globus, 1971).
Stanford, John, *A Walk in the Fire* (Santa Rosa: Black Sparrow Press, 1989).
Stanley, Liz, *The Auto/biographical I: The Theory and Practice of Feminist Auto/biography* (Manchester and New York: Manchester University Press, 1992).
Stent, Stacey, 'The Wrong Ripple', in Ingrid de Kok and Karen Press, eds, *Spring Is Rebellious: Arguments about Cultural Freedom* (Cape Town: Buchu Books, 1990), 74–9.
Stephanson, Anders, 'Fourteen Notes on the Very Concept of the Cold War', http://www.h-net.msu.edu/~diplo/stephanson.html (accessed 2 September 2003).
Stevenson, Philip, *Morning, Noon and Night* (New York: Putnam, 1954).
Strada, Vittorio, 'Introduzione' to Kočetov, V., *Ma, insomma, che cosa vuoi?*, trans. Massimo Picchianti and Chiara Spano (Rome: La nuova sinistra, 1970), 5–25.
Stratford, Philip, *Faith and Fiction: Creative Process in Greene and Mauriac*, new edn (1964; Notre Dame and London: University of Notre Dame Press, 1967).
Struve, Gleb, *Soviet Russian Literature 1917–50* (Norman: University of Oklahoma Press, 1951).
Sukhov, A.D., *Stoletniaia diskussiia: Zapadnichestvo i samobytnost' v russkoi filosofii* (Moscow: IFRAN, 1998).
Szulc, Tad, 'Fidelismo: The Unfulfilled Ideology', in Irvin Louis Horowitz and Jaime Suchlicki, eds, *Cuban Communism* (Brunswick and London: Transaction Publishers, 1998), 162–73.
Szymborska, Wisława, *View with a Grain of Sand: Selected Poems*, trans. Stanisław Barańczak and Clare Cavanagh (New York: Harcourt Brace and Company, 1995).
——, *Poeta i Świat* (Stockholm: The Nobel Foundation, 1996).
Taking Tiger Mountain by Strategy Group of the Shanghai Peking Opera Troupe, *Zhiqu Weihungshan*, in Anon, ed., *Geming yangbanxi juben huibian*, Vol. 1 (Beijing: Remin chubanshe, 1974), 7–73.
Temesi, Ferenc, *Por*, 2 Vols (Budapest: Magvető, 1986–7).
Thomas, Brian, *An Underground Fate: The Idiom of Romance in the Later Novels of Graham Greene* (Athens and London: University of Georgia Press, 1988).
Tian Han, *Hui chun zhi qu*, in Tian Han, *Tian Han quan ji*, 20 Vols, eds Dong Jian, et al. (Shijiazhuang: Huashan wenyi chubanshe, 2000), 109–51.
Tiffin, Helen, 'Rites of Resistance: Counter-Discourse and West Indian Biography', *Journal of West Indian Literature*, 3: 1 (1989), 28–46.
Tismaneanu, Vladimir, *Reinventing Politics: Eastern Europe from Stalin to Havel* (New York: The Free Press/Macmillan, 1992).

Tizard, Barbara, 'Old and New Paradigms: Research on Young People's Response to the Nuclear Threat', *Journal of Adolescence*, 12: 1 (March 1989), 1–10.

Todorov, Vladislav, 'Introduction to the Political Aesthetics of Communism', in Alexander Kiossev, ed., *Post-Theory, Games, and Discursive Resistance: The Bulgarian Case* (Albany: State University of New York Press, 1995), 65–94.

Todorova, Maria, *Imagining the Balkans* (New York: Oxford University Press, 1997).

Tolstoy, Alexei, *The Ordeal: A Trilogy*, trans. Ivy and Tatiana Litvinov (1919–41; Moscow: Progress Publishers, 1953).

——, *Peter the First*, trans. Alex Miller (1929–45; Moscow: Raduga, 1985).

Tomšič, Marjan, *Kažuni* (Ljubljana: Kmečki glas, 1990).

Tötössy, Beatrice, *Scrivere postmoderno in Ungheria* (Rome: ARLEM, 1995).

Truman, Harry S., '5th State of the Union Address', http://www.geocities.com/americanpresidencynet/1951.html (accessed 27 September 2004).

——, *Memoirs by Harry S. Truman, Vol. 2: Years of Trial and Hope, 1946–1952*, new edn (1956; New York: Signet, 1965).

Tsimbaev, N.I., *Slavianofil'stvo: Iz istorii russkoi obshchestvenno-politicheskoi mysli XIX veka* (Moscow: Izdatel'stvo Moskovskogo universiteta, 1986).

Turner, A. Festschrift, and Louis J. Budd, eds, *Toward a New American Literary History: Essays in Honor of Arlin Thomas* (Durham: Duke University Press, 1980).

Turton, Peter, *José Marti: Architect of Cuba's Freedom* (London: Zed Books, 1986).

Ugrešić, Dubravka, *The Culture of Lies*, trans. Celia Hawkesworth (1995; London: Weidenfeld and Nicolson, 1998).

——, *Štefica Cvek u raljama života*, new edn (1981; Belgrade: Free B92, 2002).

Unt, Mati, *Doonori meelespea* (Tallinn: Kupar, 1990).

Vaculík, Ludvík, *Sekyra* (Prague: Československý spisovatel, 1966).

Van Ash, Cay, and Elizabeth Sax Rohmer, *Master of Villainy: A Biography of Sax Rohmer* (London: Tom Stacey, 1972).

Vandalkovskaia, M.G., *Istoricheskaia nauka rossiiskoi emigratsii: "Evraziiskii soblazn"* (Moscow: Pamiatniki istoricheskoi mysli, 1997).

Vargas Llosa, Mario, *Contra viento y marea* (Barcelona: Seix Barral, 1983).

——, *The War of the End of the World*, trans. Helen Lane (1981; New York: Farrar, Straus and Giroux, 1985).

——, *The Perpetual Orgy: Flaubert and Madame Bovary*, trans. Helen Lane (1975; New York: Farrar, Straus and Giroux, 1987).

Vassanji, M.G., *The Gunny Sack* (Oxford: Heinemann, 1989).

Verdery, Katherine, *National Ideology under Socialism: Identity and Cultural Politics in Ceaușescu's Romania* (Berkeley: University of California Press, 1991).

Voitinskii, S., 'Bez znaniia dela', *Komsomol'skaia Pravda*, 3 October 1957, 4.

Von Laue, Theodore H., *The World Revolution of Westernization: The Twentieth Century in Global Perspective* (New York: Oxford University Press, 1987).

Vonnegut, Kurt, *Slaughterhouse-Five*, new edn (1969; London: Vintage, 1989).

Wagner, Richard, *Viena, Banat*, trans. Wolfgang Schaller (Bucharest: Univers, 1998).

Wagnleitner, Reinhold, and Elaine Tyler May, eds, *'Here, There and Everywhere': The Foreign Politics of American Popular Culture* (Hanover and London: University Press of New England, 2000).

Wald, Alan, *Writing from the Left: New Essays on Radical Culture and Politics* (London: Verso, 1994).

Walker, Martin, *The Cold War and the Making of the Modern World* (London: Fourth Estate, 1993).

Walsh, Rodolfo, 'Carta abierta de Rodolfo Walsh a la Junta Militar (1977)', *El latinoamericano*, http://www.ellatinamericano.cjb.net (accessed 27 November 2004).
Walsh, William, *A Manifold Voice: Studies in Commonwealth Literature* (New York: Barnes and Noble, 1970).
Wang Shuyuan, et al., *Dujuanshan, Hongqi*, 10 (1973), 46–83.
Watts, Jerry, *Heroism and the Black Intellectual: Ralph Ellison, Politics, and Afro-American Intellectual Life* (Chapel Hill: University of North Carolina Press, 1994).
Weart, Spencer R., *Nuclear Fear: A History of Images* (Cambridge, MA: Harvard University Press, 1988).
Weissbort, Daniel, ed., *The Poetry of Survival: Post-War Poets of Central and Eastern Europe* (London: Anvil Press, 1991).
Welton, Harry, *The Third World War: Trade and Industry – The New Battleground* (London: Pall Mall Press, 1959).
Wesker, Arnold, *The Wesker Trilogy*, new edn (1960; Harmondsworth: Penguin, 1987).
West, Nigel [Rupert Allason, MP], 'Cold War Tales', in Malcolm Bradbury, ed., *The Atlas of Literature*, new edn (1996; London: Prospero Books, 2001), 256–9.
West, W.J., *The Quest for Graham Greene* (London: Weidenfeld and Nicolson, 1997).
Westad, Odd Arne, ed., *Reviewing the Cold War: Approaches, Interpretations, Theory* (London: Frank Cass, 2000).
Whelan, Peter, *A Russian in the Woods* (London: Methuen, 2001).
Whitfield, Stephen J., *The Culture of the Cold War*, 2nd edn (1991; Baltimore and London: Johns Hopkins University Press, 1996).
Wicomb, Zoe, 'To Hear the Variety of Discourses', *Current Writing: Text and Reception in Southern Africa*, 2: 1 (1990), 35–40.
Williams, Raymond, *Marxism and Literature* (Oxford and New York: Oxford University Press, 1977).
Wixson, Douglas, *Worker-Writer in America: Jack Conroy and the Tradition of Midwestern Literary Radicalism, 1898–1990* (Urbana: University of Illinois Press, 1994).
Wolff, Larry, *Inventing Eastern Europe: The Map of Civilization and the Mind of the Enlightenment* (Stanford: Stanford University Press, 1994).
Worden, Nigel, *The Making of Modern South Africa: Conquest, Segregation, and Apartheid* (London: Blackwell, 1994).
Wright, Richard, *Uncle Tom's Children*, new edn (1940; New York: Signet Books, 1963).
Wu, William F., *The Yellow Peril: Chinese Americans in American Fiction, 1850–1940* (Hamden, Conn.: Archon, 1982).
You Have Struck a Rock: Women and Struggle in South Africa (Berkeley: South Africa Media Project, 1986).
Young, Robert J.C., *Postcolonialism: An Historical Introduction* (Oxford: Blackwell, 2001).
Zaostrovtsev, G., 'Synov'ia i pasynki', *Literaturnaia Zhizn'*, 18 July 1962, 3.
Zelinsky, K., *Soviet Literature: Problems and People*, trans. Olga Shartse (Moscow: Progress Publishers, 1970).
Zis, Avner, *Foundations of Marxist Aesthetics*, trans. Catherine Judelson (1976; Moscow: Progress Publishers, 1977).
Zur, Ofer, 'On Nuclear Attitudes and Psychic Numbing: Overview and Critique', *Contemporary Social Psychology*, 14: 2 (1990), 96–118.

Index

Achebe, Chinua 81, 85, 91, 92
Adameşteanu, Gabriela 169
Adorno, Theodor 199
Afghanistan 1, 41
Africa 84, 85–6, 90, 91, 132, 140, 141, 229; literature of 4, 8, 78–96, 176–91
African-American literature 8, 102, 104–8, 190
African National Congress 176, 178, 179, 180–1, 187, 188, 191
Aitmatov, Chingiz 96
Akhmatova, Anna 199
Aksenov, Vasilii 38–40, 41–2
Albania 56, 141, 164
Amadi, Elechi 83
Amado, Jorge 227
Amis, Martin 63, 64
Anderson, Benedict 146–7
Angola 1, 82, 155
Aptheker, Herbert 100
Argentina 237–8
Arguedas, José Maria 227, 231
Armah, Ayi Kwei 85, 89–90, 91
arms race, the *see* nuclearism
Asian literature 4, 7, 87, 114–28, 131–43
Atomic Energy Commission 2
Auezov, Mukhtar 96
Auster, Paul 66

Baldwin, James 102 106
Balzac, Honoré de 83, 84, 111
Bandung Conference of African and Asian States 11
Bănulescu, Ştefan 167–8

Barker, Howard 7, 46, 47, 51, 59; *The Power of the Dog* 47, 51–3
Baruch, Bernard 2
Batista, Fulgencio 147
Baudrillard, Jean 65
Bauer, Raymond A. 26
Bellamy, Edward 109
Berkoff, Steven 47
Berlin 64, 136
Berlin Blockade 2, 64
Berlin Wall 49, 197, 200–1, 208
Bhabha, Homi K. 146–7
Blandiana, Ana 164
Blish, James 26, 27
Bodor, Ádám 172
Borges, Jorge Luis 227
Botha, P.W. 177
Boullosa, Carmen 239
Bowen, Elizabeth 213
Bowert, Walter 24
brainwashing 16–17, 20, 24, 25, 26–8
Brecht, Bertolt 4, 90, 137
Brenton, Howard 47
Breytenbach, Breyten 190
Brezhnev, Leonid 163
Britain 31, 32, 33–6, 40–1, 67, 88, 213, 216; anti-Americanism in 11, 213–23
British Labour Party 47
Brown, Frank London 108–9
Bucher, Lloyd M. 18–19
Buckmaster, Henrietta 104, 109, 110
Bulgaria 31, 32–3, 162, 172
Burroughs, William 26, 27

Cambodia 1

Campaign for Nuclear Disarmament 64
canon formation 3–4, 8, 78, 85, 87, 96
Cardenal, Ernesto 234–5
Carpentier, Alejo 148
Castro, Fidel 9, 146–59, 216
Cavafy, C.P. 204–5
censorship 10, 170, 177, 198, 200–1, 208–9
Chaadaev, Pyotr 87
Childress, Alice 8, 105–7
Chile 176, 231, 236
China 5, 6, 15–18, 64, 94, 116, 131–43, 216; Cultural Revolution in 9, 132, 137, 139–40, 142; literature of 9, 131–43; Sino-Soviet split 5, 9, 132, 137; threat to United States 17–18, 19–28, 131
Chinodya, Shimmer 82
Churchill, Caryl 7, 47–8, 56–9; *Far Away* 47–8, 56–9
Churchill, Winston 2, 51–2, 64
Ciobanu, Ion C. 164
Civil Rights movements *see* protest movements
Cold War 1–3, 6, 32, 35–6, 41–2, 48–50, 63–5, 114–15, 117–18, 131–2, 160–62, 175, 195–6, 212–13, 218, 221; death toll during 1; discourse of 1–2, 2–3, 5–6, 15–16, 18, 25, 46, 49–50, 73, 131, 196, 208, 215, 226; end of 11–12, 46, 142–3, 161, 171–2, 195–6, 201, 208–9, 237, 239; first Cold War 6, 8; 'hot wars' 1–2, 9, 50, 131–2, 143; literature of 3, 4–5, 41–2, 46–7, 63, 65–6, 78–96, 102–4, 118–19, 127–8, 146–50, 162–3, 178, 191, 196–7, 199, 209, 213, 226; male power during 10, 123, 151–2, 177, 182, 185, 188; propaganda 5–6, 15, 16, 33, 41, 80, 119, 128, 162, 163, 200, 226–7; 'realist' interpretations of 48–50, 58, 59; representation during 3, 5–6, 7–8, 15–28, 31–42, 48, 55, 85–6, 126, 128, 131, 163, 197, 215; second Cold War 6; scepticism during 6, 11, 46–7, 53, 58–9, 66–7, 68, 71–2, 212–23; women's status during 10, 24, 68–9, 72–3, 105, 110, 123–4, 137–8, 152, 154–5, 163, 169–70, 177–91, 239; *see also* détente, postcommunism, Yellow Peril, postmodernism
Colombia 231, 234
Committee of 100 64
communism 31, 84–5, 100, 115–16, 131–43, 146–58, 160–73, 179–80, 212–23; literature of 4, 7, 31–42, 46–59, 83–5, 100–12, 114–28, 131–43, 151–2, 162–3, 179–80; loss of belief in 46–7, 163–73, 212; anti-communism 3–4, 5, 15–28, 36, 79, 80, 96, 100–12, 153, 195–209
Condon, Richard 6, 22, 27; *The Manchurian Candidate* 6, 16, 17, 20, 21–6, 28; *The Whisper of the Axe* 27–8
Congo 132
Conroy, Jack 103
conspiracy narratives 27, 41
consumerism 70, 142–3, 165, 216, 219
containment 163, 217, 221
Coover, Robert 66, 68–9; *The Public Burning* 66, 68–9
Cortázar, Julio 11, 227, 229, 235–6
Coupland, Douglas 73–4
Cruse, Harold 107
Cuba 9, 142, 146–58, 176, 180, 228–9; *see also* Fidel Castro; literature of 9–10, 146–58
Cuban Missile Crisis 35, 64, 66, 154, 155, 212
Czechoslovakia 32, 40, 165–7, 169, 170, 205

Davies, Norman 196
DeLillo, Don 7, 66, 67–8, 70; *End Zone* 66, 73, 74; *Underworld* 67, 70, 73; *White Noise* 66, 68
Derrida, Jacques 221
détente 3, 6, 38, 41
Đilas, Milovan 164
dissidents 42
Doctorow, E.L. 7, 66, 67–8, 70; *The Book of Daniel* 66, 67–8, 70, 74, 111
Dominica 1, 226, 233
Điện Biên Phủ 117

Đông Hồ 114
Dooner, P.W. 17
Dostoevsky, Fyodor 83, 86–7, 88
Du Bois, W.E.B. 101, 105, 108, 109
Dulles, John Foster 32
Dumitriu, Petru 163

Eastern Europe 7, 48, 51–3, 54, 64, 86, 141, 160–73, 195–209; anti-semitism in 37, 162; literature of 4, 7, 9, 10–11, 160–73, 195–209; see also Soviet Union and individual countries
ecological disaster 3, 50, 64, 69, 74
Edgar, David 7, 47, 53, 59; *Pentecost* 47, 53–5
Eliot, T.S. 215
Ellison, Ralph 101, 103
El Salvador 176, 236
Emecheta, Buchi 83
Esterházy, Péter 165, 167, 168, 172
Ethiopia 1
Evtushenko, Evgenii 35, 39, 42

Fadeyev, Alexander 82
Fanon, Frantz 88, 89, 90, 148
Farah, Nuruddin 85
Fast, Howard 100, 101, 104, 109–12
Faulkner, William 63, 64, 83
Fermi, Enrico 71
film 5, 15, 17, 26, 28, 69, 83, 101, 165, 220–1
First All-Union Congress of Soviet Writers 199–200
First, Ruth 177
Forster, E.M. 214
France 115, 117, 217
Fuentes, Carlos 227, 228
Fukuyama, Francis 93–4
Fulga, Laurenţiu 163
Furmanov, Dmitry 82

Gaddis, John Lewis 2, 46, 48–9, 50
Gallup Strike 109
García, Cristina 9, 150, 153; *Dreaming in Cuban* 9, 146, 148, 152–8
García Márquez, Gabriel 4, 11, 227, 229, 233
Gastonia Strike 109

Geneva Conference 118
Germany 31, 32, 36–7
Ghana 89
Giles, Barbara 100–1, 101, 104, 111–12
Gladkov, Feodor 84
globalisation 2, 4, 9, 12, 50, 143, 237
Gogol, Nikolai 83, 87, 88
Gordimer, Nadine 85, 92
Gorky, Maxim 4, 8, 80, 82–3, 84, 88, 90, 116, 200; *Klim Samgin* 84, 88
Graham, Greene, 11, 212–23; *The Third Man* 11, 214–15; *The Quiet American* 11, 214, 217–22
Graham, Shirley 8, 104, 105–7,
Greece 31
Grenada 226
Griffiths, Trevor 47
Guatemala 176, 226
Guattari, Félix 232
Guevara, Che 142–3, 229, 231–2
Guillén, Nicolás 148

Hammett, Dashiell 101
Haraszti, Miklós 198, 206
Hare, David 47
Harriman, Averell 32
Havel, Václav 169
Heaney, Seamus 209
Heinlein, Robert 16
Heller, Joseph 69
Herbert, Zbigniew 164, 202, 203–5, 209
Hersey, John 64, 69, 71
Himes, Chester 106, 109, 110
Hiroshima 64, 66, 69
Hô Chí Minh 114, 115, 117, 216, 218
Holub, Mirosław 205–6
Hoover, J. Edgar 15
House Un-American Activities Commission 69, 100; see also McCarthyism
Hove, Chinjerai 82
Huang Ti 136
Hughes, Langston 105
Hungary 136, 162, 164, 165, 167–8, 198
Hunter, Edward 16–17, 28
Hu Peng 131, 133–6

Huxley, Aldous 21
Huy Cận 119, 126

iron curtain 6, 10, 46, 64
Italy 31, 32, 36, 41, 167
Ivanov, Anatoli 82, 95–6
Iyayi, Festus 83, 90

Jameson, Fredric 78, 96
Japan 64
Jebeleanu, Eugen 162
Jerome, Alice 100
Jerome, V.J. 100, 101
Joseph, Helen 177

Kadare, Ismail 164, 165
Kataev, Valentin 80
Kennan, George F. 2; Long Telegram 2
Kennedy, John F. 28, 35, 64
Kenya 82, 84–6
Khrushchev, Nikita 35, 36, 111, 137
Killens, John O. 105–7, 109, 112
Kinkead, Eugene 17
Kiš, Danilo 165–6, 168, 170, 173
Kochetov, Vsevolod 36, 37, 38–40, 41; *Chego zhe ty khochesh'* 36–8, 39–40
Konrád, György 165, 168
Korda, Michael 212
Korea 1, 9, 16, 17, 19, 22, 28, 64, 95, 136, 138, 213
Kraminov, Daniil 33–6, 42; *Pasynki Al'biona* 33–5
Krymov, Yuri 82
Kundera, Milan 165, 167, 168, 170, 205

La Guma, Alex 90
Lamming, George 83
Lâm Thị Mỹ Dạ 119, 121–2, 123–4
Laos 1
Latin America 1, 4, 11, 137, 141, 147, 148–9, 167, 226–39; literature of 4, 7, 11, 87, 146–58, 226–39
Lebanon 176
Le Carré, John 221
Lewis, Sinclair 21
Lima, José Lezama 227
Liu Chuan 136–7
Lloyd George, David 34

London, Jack 17, 109
Lu Hsun 96
Lưu Trọng Lư' 119, 126

Mabuza, Lindiwe 180–1, 187, 190
Machado, Gerado 147
Machej, Zbigniew 208–9
Malange, Nise 178, 182–4, 186, 187, 188–9, 190
Mandela, Nelson 176, 177, 191
Mandela, Winnie 177
Mandelbaum, Michael 67
Mandelshtam, Osip 199
Mangua, Charles 82
Mao Zedong 5, 64, 131–2, 136, 139, 140–2
Marinet, Alexei 164
Marshall Plan 2
Marx, Karl 41, 89, 232
Marxism 42, 83–4, 94, 104, 107, 116–17, 119, 132, 147, 180, 208, 234
Mayfield, Julian 8, 105, 106, 107, 109
Mbeki, Govan 177
McCarthyism 8, 69, 100–12, 213, 215, 216
McGrath, John 47
Meer, Fatima 177
Merril, Judith 69, 73
Mexico 228, 236, 237
Miedzyrzecki, Artur 202–3
Miłosz, Czesław 196, 198, 201, 209
Mindszenty, Cardinal 17
Mofokeng, Boitumelo 185–6, 190
Morejón, Nancy 148
Morgenthau, Hans J. 49
Moscow Film School 83
Mosley, Oswald 33–4
Motley, Willard 106
Mozambique 176, 177
Mwangi, Meja 82

Naapo, Roseline 185–6, 189
Naidoo, Sana 178, 184, 187
nationalism 4, 9, 55, 94, 114–28, 131, 138, 146–58, 160–73, 176
NATO 64
Nedelciu, Mircea 169
neo-imperialism *see* globalisation

Neruda, Pablo 227, 230
Ngoyi, Lillian 177
Ngugi wa Thiong'o 4, 8, 82, 83–6, 90, 91
Nguyễn Đức Mậu 119, 125
Nguyễn Duy 119, 120–1, 123, 125–6
Nguyễn Khoa Điềm 119, 122, 126
Nguyễn Mỹ 120
Nicaragua 176, 231, 234–6
Nigeria 85, 92
Nigerian–Biafran Civil War 83, 92
Nixon, Richard 69
Nkrumah, Kwame 83
Non-Aligned Movement 11
Ntsongo, Alice 182, 187
nuclearism 2, 3, 7, 10, 26, 32, 50, 63–75; anti-nuclear protests 10, 64; literature and 7, 10, 63–75; nuclear anxiety 3, 7, 63–75; nuclear criticism 3, 64; nuclear family 24, 66, 68, 69–71; Nuclear Test Ban Treaty 212
Nyembe, Dorothy 177
Nyerere, Julius 83

O'Brien, Tim 66, 67–8, 69–70, 72; *The Nuclear Age* 66, 67–8, 69–70, 72, 73–4
Okri, Ben 85
orientalism 5, 80, 86, 219
Örkény, István 163
Orwell, George 2, 32
Ostrovsky, Nikolai 82, 84
Ouologuem, Yambo 85, 91
Ovchinnikov, Vsevolod 40–1, 42

Panama 1
Páral, Vladimír 165
Pavić, Milorad 167, 168
Pavlović, Živojin 165
Paz, Octavio 227
percentages deal 51–2
perestroika 127, 196
Peru 231
Petry, Ann 107, 109
Phạm Tiến Duật 119, 120–1, 123–5
Philby, Kim 215
Phổ Đức 122
Platonov, Andrei 80
Poland 52, 171, 196–8, 200–2, 205, 207, 215

Polevoi, Boris 82
Popescu, Dumitru Radu 166, 167
postcolonialism 3, 4, 8, 49, 78–96, 81, 83, 149, 172
postcommunism 9, 11–12, 48, 50, 53–4, 59, 79, 93–4, 171–3, 208–9
postmodernism 3, 6–9, 63–75, 163–73
protest movements 10, 64, 68, 105, 118, 176–91; *see also* resistance
Pynchon, Thomas 7, 26, 66, 68; *Gravity's Rainbow* 26–7, 66, 68

Qosja, Rexhap 165

Rama, Angel 11, 229–31
Ramgobin, Ela 177
Reagan, Ronald 191
resistance 4, 9, 11, 12, 81, 93, 107–10, 165, 176–91, 195–209, 212, 216–17, 226–39; *see also* protest movements
Roa Bastos, Augusto 227, 232–3
Robeson, Paul 105
Rockefeller, Nelson 227
Rohmer, Sax 6, 18–27
Romania 141, 161–3, 166–7, 170, 171, 173
Roosevelt, Franklin 32
Rosenberg, Julius and Ethel 3, 109
Russian Revolution 88, 94, 103, 132
Russell, Bertrand 64

Saldaña, Excilia 148
Salt, Waldo 100, 101
samizdat 168, 200
Sârbu, Ion D. 164
Sartre, Jean-Paul 32
science fiction 5, 15, 20, 64, 104
Scott, Walter 84, 89, 92
Scottsboro defence campaign 109
'Second World' 3, 31–42, 131–2, 141, 146–8, 160–3, 196–201; literature of 4, 5, 8, 11, 12, 31–42, 78–96, 114–28, 131–43, 146–58, 160–73, 195–209; *see also* nationalism *and* individual countries
Second World War 2, 32, 51, 64, 68, 82, 94, 160, 162–3, 198–9, 212, 226

Sembène, Ousmane 83, 85, 90, 96
Serafimovich, Alexander 82
Serbia 56
Sholokhov, Mikhail 4, 80, 82, 83–4, 88–9, 91–2
Shpanov, Nikolai 32, 38
Silko, Leslie Marmon 66, 74
Simionescu, Mircea Horia 169
Simonov, Konstantin 82, 96
Sisulu, Walter 177
Škvorecký, Josef 165–6, 169
slave narratives 147, 150
Slavophilia 31, 40, 88
space race, the 5, 70
Spanish Civil War 32, 103, 214
spy novels 5, 38, 213
Snow, C.P. 214
socialism *see* communism
socialist realism 7–8, 78–80, 83–4, 116–17, 127, 162, 200, 228
Solzhenitsyn, Aleksandr 165
Somalia 1, 85, 140–1
Somerset Maugham, W. 33
South Africa 10, 176–91
Soviet Union 6, 9, 20–1, 23, 31, 64, 83, 92–5, 116, 131, 136, 147, 162–3, 199; foreign involvement of 1, 9, 47, 83, 94–5, 116, 136–7, 160–1, 166, 172, 197, 198, 208, 215, 226–7; anti-Westernism in 6, 31–42; literature of 7, 8, 31–42, 78–96, 116, 162, 199–200; pro-Westernism in 31, 35, 38–9, 41–2; *see also* Stalin, Stalinism *and* Russian Revolution
Sovietology 80
Soviet Writers' Union 36
Soyinka, Wole 83
Spender, Stephen 11, 197
Štajner, Karol 168
Stalin 20, 22, 32, 37, 51–2, 95, 107, 136, 163, 164, 200
Stalinism 9, 11, 37–8, 79, 95, 161–2, 164, 199, 218, 212
Strada, Vittorio 37
Szymborska, Wisława 195, 196, 205, 206–9

Tambo, Oliver 177

Tanzania 85
Thatcherism 47
third way 11, 12, 59, 212, 222
'Third World' 1, 3, 8, 10, 11, 78–96, 132, 139–42, 163, 216, 229; crises in 1, 4, 8, 82–3, 85, 114–28, 231, 236–7; literature of 4, 5, 8, 12, 78–96, 114–15; *see also* nationalism *and* individual countries
Tian Han 132
Tito, Josip Broz 32
Tô Hũu 119, 126
Tolstoy, Alexei 4, 8, 82–3, 84, 88, 90–1
Tolstoy, Leo 83, 86
Tomšič, Marjan 167
Truman, Harry S. 15, 32, 64, 117; Truman Doctrine 2, 11, 49
Trường Chinh 116–17

'Un-American Renaissance' 8, 102–12
United Nations 15
United States 5, 17, 19, 26, 31–2, 35–6, 38–41, 64, 69, 114, 118, 120, 126, 136, 147, 151, 152, 155, 157, 163, 216; authoritarianism in 10, 21, 22, 24, 69, 212; foreign involvement of 1–2, 5, 10, 16, 114, 118, 120, 132, 162, 176, 191, 217–23, 226–7; literature of *see* individual authors; *see also* McCarthyism
Uruguay 236
US Communist Party 100, 106–107, 111
US Intelligence Council 28
USS Pueblo 18

Vaculík, Ludvík 165
Vargas Llosa, Mario 11, 227, 229, 232–3
Vassanji, M.G. 85
Vietnam 1, 8, 9, 64, 114–28, 132, 163, 213, 216, 217–22
Việt Minh 116–18, 218
Villaverde, Cirilo 148

Wager, Walter 27
Wagner, Richard 173
Walsh, Rodolfo 237–8

Waltz, Kenneth 49
Ward, Douglass Turner 106
Warsaw Pact 64
Wesker, Arnold 47
West Bank 176
Wright, Richard 105, 108

Xuân Diệu 115–16

Yalta Agreement 162, 199
'Yellow Peril' 5–6, 17–28
Yugoslavia 9, 161–2, 165, 166–7, 170, 195–6

Zhdanov, Andrei 7, 79, 162
Zimbabwe 82, 176
Zinberg, Len 110

eBooks – at www.eBookstore.tandf.co.uk

A library at your fingertips!

eBooks are electronic versions of printed books. You can store them on your PC/laptop or browse them online.

They have advantages for anyone needing rapid access to a wide variety of published, copyright information.

eBooks can help your research by enabling you to bookmark chapters, annotate text and use instant searches to find specific words or phrases. Several eBook files would fit on even a small laptop or PDA.

NEW: Save money by eSubscribing: cheap, online access to any eBook for as long as you need it.

Annual subscription packages

We now offer special low-cost bulk subscriptions to packages of eBooks in certain subject areas. These are available to libraries or to individuals.

For more information please contact webmaster.ebooks@tandf.co.uk

We're continually developing the eBook concept, so keep up to date by visiting the website.

www.eBookstore.tandf.co.uk